# A SHORT HISTORY OF
# WESTERN MUSIC

ARTHUR JACOBS

# A Short History of Western Music

## A LISTENER'S GUIDE

DRAKE PUBLISHERS NEW YORK

ISBN 0-87749-429-0

LCCCN 72-11453

Published in 1974 by
Drake Publishers Inc
381 Park Avenue South
New York, N.Y. 10016

Second Printing 1974

Printed in Great Britain

For discipline has no more open pathway to the mind than through the ear. When by this path rhythms and modes have reached the mind, it is evident that they also affect it and conform it to their nature. This may be seen in peoples. Ruder peoples delight in the harsher modes of the Thracians; civilized peoples, in the more restrained modes; though in these days this hardly ever occurs. Since humanity is now lascivious and effeminate, it is wholly captivated by scenic and theatrical modes. Music was chaste and modest so long as it was played on simpler instruments, but since it has come to be played in a variety of manners and confusedly, it has lost the mode of gravity and virtue and fallen almost to baseness, preserving only a remnant of its ancient beauty.

BOETHIUS (Roman philosopher, *c.* 475–*c.* 525)


'All the world's a performance. A monkey performs, lovers perform, Picasso's drawings are a marvel of performance, and the President of the United States performs his office. The word is growing old under my pen. Give me young words . . .'

'Like: situation, event, statement, variant, resultant, parameter?'

'These are "borrowed" words. One uses them and blushes a little.'

'I wonder why you neglected to mention "chance" in this essay?'

'Quite by chance, I assure you.'

LUKAS FOSS (American composer, b. 1922)

## TO MY STUDENTS

at the Royal Academy of Music,
Temple University, Philadelphia,
the University of Victoria, British Columbia
and the University of California, Santa Barbara

WHO OBLIGED ME TO THINK IT OUT

# Contents

The sub-headings mention, in order of their birth, some of the famous composers treated in each chapter. In a few cases a composer is treated in more than one chapter. The dates of the first 16 chapters are given to the nearest quarter-century, with some deliberate overlapping between chapters; the final four chapters split the twentieth century rather differently.

# Preface

'ONLY CONNECT': I have borrowed E. M. Forster's motto for my own in attempting to place a history of music within the comparatively small space of this book. Thanks to the gramophone record, the listener has a vaster historical span of music at his finger's command today than even 15 years ago, and infinitely greater than was enjoyed by the pre-gramophone music-lover (or amateur, which should mean the same thing). From a thirteenth-century song to an electronic composition of a year or two ago, the sound experience now lies to hand. I should like to offer a map connecting these experiences through some account of the process of composition as it has historically developed.

But not of composition only. The work of the composer has to be connected with the art of performance. Perhaps the most important new musical awareness of the last two decades has been the realization that the written note is not everything. In ancient music there may be no written note, in medieval music the written note may be imprecise or indecipherable, in Purcell or Vivaldi or Mozart the written note may have to be supplemented by others which are revealed only from a knowledge of contemporary customs of performance. Performance itself is linked to the historical evolution of instruments and of the musical occasion (a church service, an opera, a domestic party, a concert). A history of music which did not note the arrival of the upright piano would be like a history of the political process which failed to observe the invention of the railway and of television.

A broader, but no less essential, connection is that between the history of music and the history of political, literary and other events. The interaction is a complicated one, inadequately studied as yet. Political stability and economic prosperity allow the cultivation of music: the centres of power (whether residing in the Catholic Church in the Middle Ages, in the Paris of Louis XIV or in Victorian London) accumulate musical activity, and the demands of the dominant interests will determine in some degree what kind of musical activity that is. Yet the individual composer, the individual performer (two overlapping identities) has an influence that is unpredictable in creative scope and in its ability to change our social habits. Wagner, apart from the actual operas he wrote, altered Europe's whole conception of what going to the opera means.

In word-setting the composer works directly with the product of a contemporary writer, or an older writer, and the correspondence between literary and musical forms may be close. There are musical terms ('madrigal' is one) which make no sense unless they are regarded as poetic terms also. But, beyond such direct association, it is possible to observe similarities between the arts in general artistic aims – in matters such as clarity, scale, and dynamic range. Such similarities may be by a composer's deliberate choice: the musical movement called romanticism is largely a conscious effort to translate literary romanticism into musical terms, which accounts for the curious time-lag between them. But the similarity may simply arise from the common political, social and mental pressures and stimuli operating on artists of different kinds within a given social context. This is the justification of the attempt of some historians to establish labels which embrace the different arts and may extend to other modes of thought (philosophy, science) as well. Hence such words as 'baroque' – one of the style labels which was little more than scholars' jargon 25 years ago – are now as voguish as a record-sleeve design. The understanding of such terms, it is hoped, may be assisted by these present pages.

In the title the restriction to 'western music' is deliberate. In western-European lands arose both Gregorian chant and our earliest decipherable medieval courtly songs and dances; from these music has expanded in a way which, for all its variety, can still be considered a unit based on western Europe. As in political history, the outer boundary is not rigid; from the seventeenth century North America, and from the eighteenth century Russia began to be included. From across the boundary the Arab world exercised great influence in medieval times; and today we seem to have begun a fruitful interaction with the musical cultures of the Far East and the Indian subcontinent. But it is an interaction, not an assimilation, and the word 'western' is thus still meaningful.

The book is written deliberately as a listener's history. The reader of this book, whether his interest be general or that of a student, lives in the gramophone age. Most previous histories of music, though they may condescend to add a list of records, are based on the reproduction of music type and the reference to available printed scores. The works discussed in this present volume are all, or all except a handful out of hundreds, available on record: that is, they were available in the British or U.S. record catalogue in late 1971 and are likely to remain so in present or future recordings or in reissues – or, even if they temporarily disappear from sale, will remain in record libraries. There have been many times in the writing of this book when I have deliberately changed my choice of musical example from a textbook favourite to one which, were the reader at my elbow, I could illustrate immediately from my record shelves.

As in my first Penguin publication, *A New Dictionary of Music*, I have preferred wherever possible to use English rather than foreign titles for works: thus *Orpheus*, rather than *Orfeo* or *Orphée* (Gluck); *Cycle*, not *Zyklus* (Stockhausen). But I have provided the original names as well where any doubt of identification can occur, and have retained a composer's deliberate use of foreign-language (including ecclesiastical Latin) titles.

Dates of works are, unless otherwise stated, the dates (when known) of completion of composition, except that stage works (operas, ballets, etc.) are given the date of first stage production. Spellings have been modernized, not only in English but in foreign languages: thus *Kapellmeister*, not *Capellmeister*, and *prattica*, not Monteverdi's *pratica*. Russian spellings follow those of *A New Dictionary of Music*.

In editing the volume *Choral Music* for Penguin Books I resolved one of the difficulties of catering for both British and transatlantic music-lovers by choosing the American denominations of time values: that is, in preferring wholenotes, half-notes and quarter-notes to semibreves, minims, crotchets, etc. The self-explanatory nature of the American system seems to me to establish its superiority beyond doubt. I have here adopted it again (though with an explanation to British readers in the first one or two places where it is used), not without a hope that British educationists will feel inclined to do the same. Given a few years of leadership by our Royal Schools of Music, such terminological monstrosities as the hemidemisemiquaver could be banished to the museum.

I owe much to the specialized advice of my friends and colleagues Denis Arnold, Margaret Bent and Peter Dickinson. Such shortcomings as survive are, of course, my own.

Arthur Jacobs

*London, 1971*

# Acknowledgements

Translations of texts have been taken from the following books:

pp. 34–5 Alec Harman, *Medieval and Early Renaissance Music*, Rockliff, 1958

p. 71 and pp. 141–2 *Grove's Dictionary of Music*, 5th edition, Macmillan, 1954, articles 'Madrigal', 'Vivaldi'

p. 7 (top) and p. 100 Oliver Strunk, *Source Readings in Music History*, Faber, 1952

p. 167 Alfred Einstein, *Gluck*, Dent, 1936

pp. 174–5 Karl Geiringer, *Haydn: A Creative Life in Music*, Allen & Unwin, 1947

p. 197 and p. 198 A. W. Thayer, *Life of Beethoven*, rev. E. Forbes, Princeton, 1964

p. 302 Howard Hartog (ed.), *European Music in the Twentieth Century*, Routledge & Kegan Paul, 1957

p. 304 Nicolas Slonimsky, *Music since 1900*, Coleman-Ross (N.Y.), 1949; new edition, Scribner (N.Y.), 1971.

p. 334 (bottom) *Perspectives of New Music* (New York), issue of autumn 1962 and spring 1963

# I

## Clergy and Troubadours

ABOUT the year 1250 – that is, 35 years after Magna Carta
was signed at Runnymede – *Sumer is icumen in* was written in a
manuscript at Reading Abbey in Berkshire. It is a round for
four voices with additional parts for two lower voices who
interchange phrases with one another. For the English-
speaking world it has become the most famous piece of
medieval music – a fate it owes to its cheerful words, its
melodic appeal and its rhythmic swing. It happens also to be
an astonishing historical curiosity, the only known piece
earlier than the fifteenth century to be written in six distinct
vocal parts.

Why should this secular song appear in a monastic manuscript, in the hand of John of Fornsete, the monk who kept the
abbey's records? We might at first be tempted to say that
perhaps it is not a secular song at all, for the manuscript also
gives an ecclesiastical Latin verse for the music, *Perspice
christicola* (*Look, O worshipper of Christ*). But the way in
which 'Sing cuccu' is set so exactly to the two notes of the
cuckoo's cry may persuade us that the English words are the
original.

If we accept the above dating for *Sumer is icumen in* (a
minority of historians have placed it later) then the song
originated within the lifetime of Thomas Aquinas, the most
famous of medieval theologians, and of Roger Bacon, the chief
medieval forerunner of the scientific method of observation
and experiment. Aquinas was a Dominican monk, Bacon a
Franciscan friar; and here we have the clue to the apparently
strange preponderance of 'ecclesiastical' music and musical
documents in the Middle Ages. The clergy, monastic and
otherwise, constituted the learned profession of the period.
An educated, literate person not of noble rank was a clerk:
and 'clerk', 'cleric', and 'clergy' all relate to the same idea.
Latin, the Catholic Church's language, was the language of

official documents. From clergymen the feudal lord re-cruited his administrative officers ánd the king his 'civil service'. Thomas à Becket (1118–70) was an archdeacon before Henry II appointed him Chancellor of England – and, later, Archbishop of Canterbury. The clergy were similarly the custodians of music as a 'learned' art; and *Sumer is icumen in* is a product of such art.

At a time when the beautifully proportioned structures of Salisbury and Wells Cathedrals were rising (the Gothic style in architecture having originated in France in the 1140s), it need not surprise us that the Church also brought a highly cultivated musical accomplishment to its service. But we need some imagination to realize how much the Church's dominant cultural role colours our knowledge (or ignorance) of medieval musical activity in general. Formal teaching of music was confined to the Church's song-schools, where boys were trained to take part in church services – mass and the offices (services such as matins and vespers, obligatory for the clergy at fixed hours of each day).

Manuscript compilations of music for these services survive to give us considerable knowledge of western church music from the era when Gregorian chant was codified, some time after the year 600. Christian chant, ultimately deriving from the synagogue, had assumed varying forms, among which the Gregorian gradually superseded the others in western Europe. It was named after Pope Gregory I ('the Great', reigned 590–604), the defender of Rome's claims against Constantinople and the invading Lombards of the north, and the organizer of a new, tightly organized papal admin-istration: whether he actually participated in musical de-liberations is unknown. It is this chant, a collection of unharmonized and unbarred melodies, which until the late 1960s formed the international basis of Roman Catholic worship; 'plainsong' or 'plainchant' is its commonly accepted synonym.

But we can form no such idea of secular music till about 1150, for almost no decipherable examples survive. The first medieval Latin treatises on music (such as the famous

*Musica enchiriadis* or *Musical Handbook*, dating from the ninth century or earlier and formerly attributed to the Flemish Benedictine monk Hucbald) make no mention of secular music. Nor should we expect them to, for they are didactic works dedicated to the Church's purpose. But such music must have flourished. The vehemence with which medieval ecclesiastical writers denounced dancing as lascivious and ungodly shows the persistence of what they detested. To what kind of music the peasants danced at harvest time, Christmas and other celebrations we do not know. What songs did the sailors sing who in the eleventh century had reopened the Mediterranean to western navigation after its domination by Islam? Or what the Viking warriors, who had not only ravaged England and Spain but had pushed through the Continent as far as Kiev and Novgorod, and almost to Constantinople? What music was commanded for weddings and other celebrations by the wealthy burgesses, living in towns where the newly won charters freed the inhabitants from feudal obligations?

We are not told. As to the music of the goliards, those wandering scholars of the eleventh and twelfth centuries, knowledge is almost entirely withheld by the difficulties of deciphering such of their written music as exists – though a good deal of their verse, in praise of sensual delights, has survived, and has received a famous twentieth-century musical setting in Carl Orff's *Carmina burana* (see p. 301). We are similarly ignorant of the music – probably very simple and repetitive – to which the travelling minstrels of the tenth century and later sang their epic chronicles of valour, the *chansons de geste* (songs of deeds). It is only with what is broadly called troubadour song, from some time after 1100, that secular music is accessible in written, understandable form (though some problems in decipherment remain).

It took written form because it was a musical (and poetic) art cultivated among the highest ranks of a newly stabilized feudal society. The earliest written rule of knighthood dates from 1128, and the twelfth century witnessed a growing cultivation of chivalrous ideals (often with a link between an idealistic love and the cult of the Virgin Mary). The new poet-composers celebrated such ideals, writing not in Latin but in the vernacular tongue – first of all in Provençal, at that time spoken over a large region which now lies in southern France, but which was not yet subject to the French crown. Among the first exponents was Guillaume IX (1071–1127), the reigning duke of Aquitaine in this region.

The duke's grandson, Richard I of England, was also a patron, if not a practitioner, of the art. Familiar legend tells how, when he fell into captivity, his minstrel Blondel sought him out by singing a song known to both, and waiting for the king's answer. Though historians do not substantiate the story, Blondel de Nesle himself (c. 1150–1200) is no fictitious figure. Like some others of this later period, he wrote in French; but the distinction between the Provençal *trouba-dours* and the northern French *trouvères* seems mainly a linguistic, not a musical one.

Though some of these poet-composers were of noble rank, Blondel was himself a commoner. So, among his gifted compeers, were Bernart de Ventadorn or Ventadour (1145–95) and Adam de la Halle (c. 1230–c. 1288), who is famous as the author-composer of *The Play of Robin and Marion (Li gieus de Robin et Marion)*, a pastoral dialogue with songs inserted.

The music to more than 1,400 songs by these courtly poet-composers survives, each song notated as a single line of melody. Their art influenced that of their German counter-parts, the Minnesinger (the word is both singular and plural, from *Minne*, love). Celebrated among these was Walther von der Vogelweide, who died about 1230 and who is named as the hero's teacher in Wagner's *The Mastersingers* (see p. 244). Tannhäuser and Wolfram von Eschenbach, both named in Wagner's *Tannhäuser*, were also historic figures among the Minnesinger; Wolfram was himself the author of the epic poem which inspired Wagner's *Parsifal*.

Heard today, these Provençal and French courtly melodies have an air of freshness and simplicity. They are, as we have noted, unharmonized: accompanying them on his small harp, the minstrel perhaps played an outlined version of the sung melody. Or they may have been used for dancing, with percussion accompaniment: a form which became standard is one called the *ballade*, which implies the dance – from late Latin *ballare*. (The French word is used to denote both the verse form and its corresponding music.)

Musically the ballade has a first section which is repeated with a different ending, and which is then followed by a new section – a form which is conventionally represented as AA'B. In another type, the *virelai*, a refrain is heard at both the beginning and end (form ABBAA), giving a musical unity not unlike that of a modern song with its emphasis on the refrain or chorus. If we may rely on modern reconstructions, which are not without a certain speculative element, rhythms of these minstrel songs are strong and regular; their up and down movement follows what seems to us a normal contour. More surprisingly, many of them convey a strong major-key feeling instead of conforming to one of the modes (see below) which alone were recognized by theorists and which did not include the major key. Despite this, the influence of church melodies is also found in some of these secular songs.

The same feeling of regular rhythm and 'normal' melodic contour is given by the music of the thirteenth- and fourteenth-century dance called the *estampie*. This is the first type of purely instrumental dance music that has come down to us in written form – another sign of the cultivation of a secular music under high social patronage after 1200. We learn something of it from Johannes de Grocheo, who, writing in Paris apparently about 1300, is the earliest surviving medieval theorist who deals in some practical detail with secular music. The estampie, he tells us, is constructed of several sections in each of which a musical sentence is stated twice, the second statement varied to suggest an answer to the first. Like troubadour song, it is monophonic (consisting of one melody line only, without harmony). In practice, a drum was probably used for rhythmical accompaniment, if available.

Whereas courtly song and secular dance were newly acquiring high social standing and a written form in the twelfth and thirteenth centuries, church music continued to develop on two lines which had been initiated some time before the year 900. Both methods were treatments of the fundamental material, the received melodies of Gregorian chant, which already contained two strongly expressive devices – the alternation between soloist and choir, and the contrast between *syllabic* chanting (one note to one syllable) and *melismatic* chanting (one syllable stretched rhapsodically over several notes, particularly at expressive words like 'Alleluia'). The two lines of development were the *extension* of the chant and the *harmonization* of it by an added, simultaneous melody (the technique called *polyphony*).

In whatever form ('basic' chant, extended chant, polyphonic setting) this music was couched not in our major or minor scales but in one of four *modes*, corresponding to the white notes of the piano keyboard from D to D (Dorian mode), from E to E (Phrygian), from F to F (Lydian), or from G to G (Mixolydian). Such a modal melody comes to its end on D if Dorian, on E if Phrygian, etc., D or E being then the *final* (the home note, corresponding to a modern keynote).

The above names apply only if the actual melody falls within the octave mentioned (D to D, etc.); if the melody falls so that the final comes in the middle of the range of notes, not at the extreme, the names Hypodorian, Hypophrygian, Hypolydian, Hypomixolydian were used (from the Greek for 'under'). Only such modal scales (and not the major and minor) were recognized in musical theory until the sixteenth century – though, as we have seen, certain earlier music, including that of many troubadour melodies, sounds major to our ears.

The extension of the chant seems to have started not with the music but with the words. New words, amplifying the devotional text, were inserted in a given melody of the plainsong: for instance, the words '*Kyrie, eleison*' (Lord, have mercy) were expanded into '*Kyrie, Deus Sempiterne, eleison*'

(Lord, eternal God, have mercy). The melody remained the same, the extra words being fitted to a chain of notes that had previously been more spaciously taken up by the final vowel of '*Kyrie*'. Later extra music was also interpolated – sometimes a free variation on the melody of the chant, sometimes apparently an independent addition to it. Such an interpolation, whether of words or music, is called a *trope*. (This, at any rate, is the interpretation of trope accepted by most historians, though it has recently been challenged.)

One type of trope is the *sequence* – which became divorced from its parent chant and achieved independent use as a type of hymn, with some repetition of the melody to accommodate parallel verses of the text. The element of *repetitive* song, or *strophic* song, may be called a popular element, whether showing popular influence or catering for popular circulation or both. Hundreds of such sequences were composed from the eleventh to the thirteenth centuries and even later, winning a popularity which later seemed to menace the supremacy of the basic chant – or so we may deduce from the fact that all but four of these sequences were banned much later for liturgical reasons by the papal Council of Trent (1545–64).

One of the four excepted from the ban was the thirteenth-century *Dies irae* (Day of wrath), the text of which is associated by most modern music-lovers with Verdi's *Requiem* (though it is not strictly a part of the Requiem Mass). Another sequence was later readmitted, the *Stabat Mater* (on the vigil of Mary at the Cross), with words uncertainly attributed to Jacopone da Todi (1230–1306). Mention of this text may recall to the modern listener the later musical settings in the smooth polyphony of Palestrina or the sweetened rococo style of Pergolesi. But its poetic imagery is that of the bleeding heart: we may link it, in substance as well as in date, with those Italian penitents who about the year 1260 mortified their flesh by flagellation and sang hymns of the kind called *laudi spirituali* (spiritual praises). These are not in Latin, like the *Stabat Mater*, but in Italian. Such hymn-singing in the vernacular had already been encouraged by Francis of Assisi (1182–1226).

But as a creative form of new composition, such extensions of plainsong had by now taken second place to polyphony – that is, the combination of the plainsong with simultaneous, newly composed melodies. Polyphony as a principle seems to contain the germ of almost all the future development of western music, and it would seem extraordinary to find it simply as the spontaneous invention of early medieval monks. Recent scholarship, however, has pointed to the existence of polyphony in various European and non-European folk cultures; and there is a famous, though not altogether clear, description by the Welsh writer Giraldus Cambrensis (*c.* 1147–1220) of his untutored countrymen singing 'as many melodies as there are people, and a distinct variety of parts'. Polyphony may indeed have secular, folk origins in western Europe. But as a learned art it developed in the service of the Church, as an added melody set above or below a chant and proceeding (at first) rhythmically in step with it, note by note.

The first type of notated western polyphonic composition was called *organum* – a term which may (or may not) have come from the organ. In its early stages (to about 1100) two types were recognized. In *strict* or *parallel organum*, an added voice moved at a fourth or fifth below the prescribed plainsong tune – and the two voices could themselves be doubled at the octave above, no doubt in recognition of the compasses of men's and boys' voices in worship. In *free organum* the composer varied the intervals. Music of this kind favours the intervals of a bare fifth (C to G)* and bare fourth (C to F), and regards the third (C to E) as dissonant, not (as it seems to us) an agreeable concord. In both these procedures the principal and the added voice moved together, that is, note against note.

Tropes themselves (extended chants) had early been subjected to the addition of an extra part in organum style. The

* As in common musical usage, all such intervals (differences of pitch) are measured from the lower note to the higher unless otherwise specified.

famous English document from Winchester Cathedral, dating from about 980 and known as the Winchester Troper, consists principally of two-part organa of this kind. It is written in a system of notation not as sophisticated as the stave (see below, p. 28) and the exact pitch of the notes cannot be ascertained, though general characteristics can. Later examples can be deciphered more exactly.

Taking a considerable step forward, early twelfth-century composers began to move the two melodies at different pace, instead of confining the added chant to a note-against-note movement with the given plainsong. The plainsong was delivered very slowly, as a lower voice, while the organal (added) voice went faster, having several notes in succession against each note in the plainsong part. The organal part was delivered in free rhythm, not with a regular pulse; and since the Greek word *melisma* is used for a chain of notes in free, rhapsodic style, the type of composition itself is known as melismatic organum. Manuscripts from two centres give us the chief evidence of this form of composition – from the Abbey of St Martial at Limoges, a principal city of Aquitaine, and from the monastery of Santiago de Compostela in Spain, which drew importance as a place of pilgrimage in honour of St James.

But the rise of Paris, 'this walled and partially paved town, the most important in transalpine Europe',* site of a new and famous university, led to the emergence of new musical developments there. In the second half of the twelfth century arose the 'school of Notre Dame' in Paris – the principal composers being Léonin (active *c.* 1160–80) and Pérotin (from about 1200). Organum was now extended to the provision of two or three upper parts, not just one, so that, while the slowed-down plainsong part proceeded below, a polyphony of up to four independent parts could be created. Moreover the added parts, instead of being melismatic (in free, unmeasured rhythm), now obeyed a regular rhythmic pulse. The plainsong melody so used was called the *tenor* (from the

* Michael Grant, *The Civilizations of Europe*, Weidenfeld & Nicolson, 1965.

Latin verb 'to hold'), since it formed the given element; the next voice above it was called the *duplum*, and the next above, the *triplum* (from which the English word *treble* is derived). So slowly moved the plainsong part that it can hardly have been thought suitable for voices, at any rate exclusively: a primitive organ was perhaps used.

The regular rhythms of the added parts were not at the arbitrary disposition of the composer: they had to conform to one of five or six recognized patterns or *rhythmic modes*. Composers then began to put the plainsong tenor into this rhythmic shape as well. This was the basis of the important form known as the motet. The composer took as his basis a melodic fragment of plainsong and put it into one of the rhythmic modes, establishing a regular rhythmic pattern. Once the chosen fragment of plainsong had reached the end, it was begun again (maintaining the same pattern of rhythmic repetition). This transformed plainsong was probably allotted in performance to an instrument, not to a voice.

Above this the composer set one or (usually) more melodies, each generally having its own set of words. (The French '*mot*', word, is considered the origin of *motet*.) Sometimes these upper words were devotional and in Latin, sometimes secular and in the vernacular. This use of simultaneous, different texts (so odd from our later point of view, which expects a single conceptual meaning for each musical work) leads to the necessity of identifying motets and other similar words by compound title. Thus in the anonymous Notre Dame motet *En non Diu! Quant voi; Eius in oriente*, from the twelfth century, 'En non Diu!' and 'Quant voi' are the opening words of the amorous French verses sung as the added upper parts, and 'Eius in oriente' identifies the original Latin plainsong from which the tenor (lowest part) is taken, though these words would not have been sung as part of the motet. Transcribed into modern notation, the piece displays a tripping 6/8 rhythm, typical of its period – as is the division of the eighth-note (quaver)* now into two, now into three.

*See Preface, p. 14.

The word 'motet' always indicates polyphony; the word 'conductus' not always. As the name suggests, the word originally signified music for escorting, and often the music is repeated for successive stanzas of the text. In this sense conductus (the plural in medieval usage was either *conductus*, as in classical Latin, or *conducti*) was used for the monophonic chant which accompanied processional movement in church services or in the medieval religious drama (see below).

Since this was a freely composed form, not based on plainsong, the term 'conductus' was also appropriated for the type of twelfth and thirteenth-century polyphony which is similarly not based on plainsong (unlike the motet). Here the composer invents his own tenor (lowest part) and builds on that. The polyphonic conductus further differs from the motet in using one text, not several simultaneously. The tenor, moreover, is rhythmically similar to the upper parts (and, like these parts, it was probably sung instead of being allocated to an instrument, as with the motet). Thus conductus is a simpler kind of music than motet, more direct and less likely to demand that the listener respond on several planes at once.

Medieval religious drama to Latin texts, performed in church (and sometimes known as liturgical drama, though the drama was really an interpolation into the liturgy, not part of it), used music as an essential means of expression. It is thought that instruments were employed as well as voices: and *The Play of Daniel* (a twelfth-century French work, surviving in a thirteenth-century copy) has proved successful in modern revivals with ancient instruments played *monophonically* – that is, united in following only one melodic line, with ornamentations and with percussion.

There are earlier examples: a play for performance at Easter matins, dealing with the discovery of the empty tomb of Jesus, is to be found in the Winchester Troper. A nearly contemporary English source gives an account of an actual performance of the play. Here we have 'our earliest surviving music-drama, with costumes, properties, and careful directions as to action and gesture'.* From the previous reference to the Winchester Troper it will be recalled that the music cannot be interpreted with certainty: not because of a failure of scholarship to break the code of the notation, but because the notation indicated pitch only approximately, not exactly.

The problem of notation was one that exercised medieval writers, particularly in relation to teaching in the Church's song-schools. To an Italian monk called Guido of Arezzo (he died in 1050) are ascribed two vital innovations: the 'stave' of parallel horizontal lines on which the note symbols are placed, and of the use of name symbols (*ut, re, mi, fa, sol, la*) for the first six notes of what is now our major scale. (The 'Guidonian hand', also ascribed to him, is a classroom diagram for teaching different notes by pointing to different joints of the fingers.) By *position* on the stave pitch was fixed; by the *shape* of the note, time value was indicated. At first this indication of time value retained a certain ambiguity, leading to doubt in present-day interpretation of the rhythms of such music; but by 1300 an unambiguous system of duration, the ancestor of our own, had become established.

Even medieval music that we can read with accuracy (such as that in Johannes de Grocheo's treatise of 1300, already referred to) does not tell us everything a modern score would tell, nor does it allow us to know exactly how the music sounded to its original hearers. Medieval composers do not specify which instruments, if any, are to be used. Nor can we do more than conjecture to what extent a written melody was varied, ornamented or supplemented in performance. It is only much later in musical history, approximately in Beethoven's day, that a composer's written score begins to contain *all* indications of the notes to be performed, with no exercise of initiative or discretion by the performer: and medieval music, as written, particularly requires such decision-making by editor or performer.

Contemporary illustrated manuscripts, however, are

* W. L. Smoldon in the *New Oxford History of Music*, Oxford University Press, 1954, vol. 2.

informative about what instruments were available and how they were played. Large, loud-toned organs of crude mechanical action were used in large churches: the depression of a key called for a blow with the clenched fist! Smaller organs, capable of more nimble playing, were made in two kinds, *portative* (portable, one hand playing the keyboard and one blowing the bellows) and *positive*, resting on the floor or table. A scientific device, rather than an instrument for performance, was the *monochord*, used in the church's song-schools for demonstrating the mathematical basis of musical intervals, and consisting of a string stretched over a sound-box and equipped with a movable bridge (enabling a greater or lesser length of string to be vibrated). A real musical instrument developed from this was the *organistrum* or *hurdy-gurdy* (in the strict sense of that English word) in which the stretched string (or more strings than one) was sounded by being rubbed by a rotating wheel; the pitch was determined by mechanical stopping of the strings in response to the pressure of keys played with the fingers.

A twelfth-century illustration from the Hunterian Psalter (Glasgow University Library)* shows, as well as the organistrum, a small harp resting on the knee; tuned bells suspended on a frame and played with hammers; a four-stringed specimen of the *lira*, a bowed instrument with a pear-shaped body; a three-stringed fiddle held downwards to rest on the knee; a psaltery (many-stringed instrument of the zither family) hand-plucked by two plectrums of quill; a triple pipe, and a bone flute (blown downwards like a recorder).

The tabor or finger-drum was also known: generally the player held a three-holed pipe in his other hand. But the development of bigger drums seems to have waited for the stimulus of contact with the Arab civilization – a contact which also gave the West the shawm (a loud, double reed instrument, ancestor of the oboe) and the lute, whose very name (like *sugar*, *cotton*, and other imports of the period) is

*Reproduced in *European Musical Instruments* by Frank Harrison and Joan Rimmer, Studio Vista, 1964.

Arabic. The lute came into western usage via Spain, the southern half of which was still Moorish (and Moslem) up to about 1100. Although the Moors were expelled from almost all Spain during the next century, in an aggressive drive contemporaneous with the three Crusades (1095, 1147, and 1187), Arab civilization left its mark on Spanish music as on Spanish architecture.

Music which already sounds to modern ears definitely Spanish is to be found in the thirteenth-century collection of troubadour-like songs made by the Spanish King Alfonso X ('the Wise'), who may himself have been the composer of some of them. Reigning from 1252 to 1284, Alfonso established at his court in Toledo a tolerant climate for the meeting of Christian, Arabic and Jewish cultures. Palermo in Sicily – with half a million inhabitants, twice as many as Paris – was another place of fruitful contact: there the immensely powerful, twice-excommunicated Emperor Frederick II patronized Provençal troubadours, wrote the first modern textbook of ornithology, and introduced Christian scholars to Arabic numerals and algebra.

Of the many Arabic treatises on music, two at least were translated into Latin and stimulated the development of European musical theory. Music, already studied as part of mathematical science in the Islamic East, entered at the newly regulated universities of the West. It was classed as one of the seven liberal *artes* (the Latin word signifying in this case branches of knowledge rather than arts) and placed in the group of four mathematical subjects, the *quadrivium* – along with geometry, arithmetic (Arabic word) and astronomy. Naturally music was also interpreted by means of Christian symbolism. Triple meter (three or six beats to a bar, as we should say) being preferred in practice to duple meter, it was called *perfect* time with the reminder that three symbolized the Trinity: duple was called *imperfect*.

In this Europe England was militarily, dynastically and culturally involved – through the Norman conquest, and through the marriage of Henry II to Eleanor of Aquitaine (1152). The beginnings of Oxford University, modelled on that of Paris, date from about 1167. English composers are believed to have participated along with Pérotin in the Notre Dame school. But at home they were to develop in their own special way.

# 2

# A New Art

O UR brief general consideration of western European music in the early Middle Ages (up to about 1300) now enables us to place *Sumer is icumen in* more fully in context. Music surviving from this period is relatively scarce, and historians of medieval music cannot survey their field like those recounting the age of Bach or the age of Beethoven.

For instance, among composers of the fourteenth century – the period we are about to consider – by far the best known is the French priest, poet and musician, Guillaume de Machaut (*c.* 1300–1377), who served the kings of Bohemia, Navarre, and France, and spent his later years as a canon of Rheims, where the French monarchs were customarily crowned. The reason for Machaut's reputation is not that scholars have given long and weighty consideration to a great quantity of other composers' work and have decided that Machaut's is the best. It is because, of all the music that survives from this time, Machaut wrote more than half. But this survival itself is probably no accident: when copies of one composer's work are relatively abundant, the indication is that he was more highly valued than others in his time. In Machaut's own case royal and princely patronage encouraged the making of special manuscript copies for conservation in the patron's library.

*Sumer is icumen in* is the only piece of such complexity to survive from the mid thirteenth century. But if York Minster were the only known example of what is called the Early English architectural style, common sense would suggest that there must have been other examples of comparable or equal merit. So with this music, which is that architecture's contemporary. There are indeed other thirteenth-century pieces displaying that exchange of alternate phrases between voices (*rondellus*) which is how the two lower parts of *Sumer is icumen in* proceed. What is more, as Frank Harrison has pointed out in discussing this work,* one of these swapped phrases is identical with the first notes of a piece of plainsong associated with Easter – suggesting that the composer deliberately borrowed it, as French composers used a borrowed plainsong theme for their motets.

Those French motets, however, we have noted as favouring the intervals of the fifth and the fourth: that is, these intervals (C–G, C–F, etc.) were felt by listeners as satisfying points of repose. To modern ears they seem bare and stark; the intervals of a third and a sixth (C–E, C–A) seem mellower and in that sense preferable. The attraction of *Sumer is icumen in* is partly that it employs thirds and sixths in this modern way. It seems to have been a specially English fashion. In some late thirteenth-century examples of English ecclesiastical two-voiced conductus (that is, music all newly composed, without a plainsong basis), the harmonic effect is almost entirely of parallel thirds and sixths.

Not long afterwards developed the style which historians call English discant or English descant – to be understood as an English variety of the general style called discant, which applies only to music having a plainsong basis. It is in fact a development of organum, Pérotin himself (p. 25) having been known as 'optimus discantor' (an excellent composer of discant). In the earlier organum the plainsong was delivered in an unrhythmical succession of very slow notes; in discant it is speeded up into a simple and consistent rhythm. English discant, with added voice lines above and below the plainsong, emphasizes the sonorous effect of the interval of a fifth or sixth with a third between (C-E-G or C-E-A).

Flowering from about the middle of the fourteenth century, English discant was still in evidence in much of the music of the so-called Old Hall manuscript of about 1410. Although this music is conservative in style, its emphasis on the interval of the third is shared by the emphatically new music which burst forth in both France and Italy in the fourteenth century. Politically, it will be recalled, England continued to be deeply involved in French soil. The battle

* Arthur Jacobs, *Choral Music*, Penguin Books, 1963.

T–B

of Crecy (1346) led to a considerable extension of English dominion there; later, after Agincourt (1415), Henry V of England was even able to secure for himself the crown of France.

New music: the term is naturally a recurrent one in history. Today's modernists give a filial veneration to Webern and consider the writing of tonal music old-fashioned. In the nineteenth century the new ideals of Liszt and Wagner stood opposed to the practices of Brahms and other continuations of the classical sonata and symphony. After 1600 new ideals of monody and opera made the older polyphonic forms (represented by the sixteenth-century madrigal, both Italian and English) old-fashioned. There was no less a decisive division in the fourteenth century, when the new music was above all a freer music – free, that is, of rhythmic restrictions, and also distinguished by new forms and harmonies.

The initial document of the new style is *Ars nova musicae* (*The New Art of Music*), a Latin treatise written about 1325 by Philippe de Vitry (1291–1361), a French composer, poet, diplomat (in the service of the French court) and, from 1350, bishop. It is from de Vitry's title that the term *ars nova* has been borrowed for general historical use. Strictly its precepts were applied to French music only, and the term might somewhat pedantically be confined to that. But new, and to some extent similar, ideas were evolved in Italy too, making it convenient to extend the term. In visual art this is the period of Giotto (1266–1336), who moved towards a more natural, less symbolized type of representation; in literature, the period not only of Chaucer (1340–1400) but of Dante (1265–1321) and Petrarch (1304–74), the first great figures of Italian literature. De Vitry was himself a friend of Petrarch. The two men met at the court of Avignon – the southern French city under papal jurisdiction, to which the seat of the papacy was removed between 1305 and 1378.

A decree promulgated in 1324 by one of the Avignon popes, John XXII, includes the following denunciation:

Certain disciples of the new school, much occupying themselves with the measured dividing of time, display their methods in notes which are new to us, preferring to devise ways of their own rather than to continue singing in the old manner; the music, therefore, of the divine offices is now performed with semibreves and minims, and with these notes of small value every composition is pestered. Moreover, they truncate the melodies with hockets [see below], they deprave them with discantus [improvisation], sometimes even they stuff them with upper part made out of secular song. . . . Their voices are incessantly running to and fro, intoxicating the ear, not soothing it . . .

Wherefore . . . we straitly command that no one henceforth shall think himself at liberty to attempt these methods, or methods like them, in the aforesaid offices, and especially the canonical Hours or in the celebration of the Mass. Yet for all this, it is not our intention to forbid, occasionally, the use of some consonances, for example the octave, fifth, and fourth, which heighten the beauty of the melody . . .

It will be observed that what is denounced is the embellishing of the chant with matter which is held to divert the attention towards the embellishment or the performer, and away from the service. The reference to the 'new school' with their 'measured dividing of time' makes it clear that the direct attack is on de Vitry or his fellows. The explicit purpose of the *Ars nova* treatise had been to set forth not a new method of composing, but a new system of notation: it presumably codified and rationalized a type of music which had already arrived in practice. New rhythms (the 'measured dividing of time') required new notation, and de Vitry provided it.

Already in the thirteenth century musicians had developed a gradation of time values for notes under the name of the *long*, the *breve*, and the *semibreve*; but under the five or six rhythmic modes (see p. 26) these were grouped only to make the beat divide into 3 (1 + 1 + 1, 1 + 2, 2 + 1) not into two equal sub-beats (1 + 1). Thus *Sumer is icumen in* could be notated (starting 2 + 1, 2 + 1, making a bar of modern 6/8) but not *Baa, baa, black sheep*. De Vitry evolved a practical nottiaon for rhythmic groups un-notatable before, including the march tread of what today we call 2/4.

He also brought into his system two smaller note values, the recently invented minim (to which he gave the value of one third or one half the semibreve, according to rules laid down) and the semiminim, one half the minim. Moreover he established time signatures, indicating at the beginning of a piece what rhythmic grouping is to be used. (There were as yet no bar-lines.) Our modern C, for four quarter-notes (crotchets) in a bar, does not derive from C for 'common time' but from de Vitry's use of an imperfect circle to denote duple meter. Triple meter had its symbol in a perfect circle, by that association with the Christian 'perfection' of the Trinity which we have already noted.

The new rhythmic shapes are evident if we listen to, say, the Agnus Dei from the only surviving mass by Machaut, known as the Notre Dame Mass. The composition of a mass in this sense means the composition of the Ordinary (that is, the unvarying portion of the liturgical text) – a type of setting familiar in such works as Bach's *Mass in B minor* and Beethoven's *Mass in D*. In church use the texts set by Machaut would be interspersed with plainsong settings of the Proper, that is, the texts allotted to the particular occasion in the church year. Machaut's is perhaps the first known specimen of a polyphonic setting of the entire Ordinary by a single composer : an apparently earlier anonymous setting known as the *Tournai Mass* (from its Belgian, at that time French, city of origin) may not be the work of a single composer.

Machaut's mass is for four voices.* The division of the beat into two (rather than three), characteristic of the ars nova, prevails. The Agnus Dei ('O lamb of God' – the final section of the Ordinary) begins by moving the two upper voices faster than the two lower. Transcribed into modern notation, the piece is in 3/2 time, each of the upper voices freely using a mixture of time values from dotted whole-notes down to eighth-notes. As in the thirteenth-century style, the piece is based on a borrowed plainsong, which has become the tenor.

---

* 'For four voices', in this conventional use, indicates 'for four vocal lines', not necessarily four single voices; by extension, contrapuntal music is described as being for two, three voices, etc., even when instrumental and not vocal lines are meant.

But now the tenor is treated not as the lowest line of melody, as the second lowest; another strand, the contra-tenor, goes below the tenor or intertwines with it. Since words are not provided for this contra-tenor line (as they are for the upper lines) we may assume that it was either sung to a vowel or played on an instrument.

In this type of composition, as in the thirteenth-century motet, the borrowed tune in the tenor could be repeated as often as needed for the length of the work. But by a subtle musical device Machaut and his French contemporaries generally laid out the tenor line in such a way that not only the notes of the melody were repeated, but a constant rhythmic pattern was repeated as well. Moreover the rhythmic pattern differed in length from the melody – so that the notes of the melody, on the second and later repetitions, bore a different rhythmic stress. This principle of construction is called *isorhythm* (Greek *isos*, equal). Graphically this overlapping of repetitions of melodic pattern (M) and rhythmic pattern (R) might begin like this:

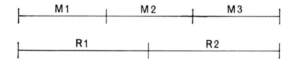

The contemporary name for the melodic unit was *color* and for the rhythmic unit, *talea* (a cutting). In this Agnus Dei, however, the full complexity of such overlapping is not experienced because there is no exact melodic repetition. But there is partial repetition of rhythms, and this extends not only to the tenor but to all three other voices as well. Rhythm is thus an element unifying the piece, a unity which is perhaps needed because the several voices have independent melodies which do not seem to imitate (or follow) each other.

Isorhythm is also characteristic of Machaut's (and other fourteenth-century) motets, most of them to secular rather than religious words. *Motet* still indicated, as previously, a polyphonic setting with two or more texts sung simultaneously, and with a tenor part which repeated a fragment

of plainsong. Isorhythm (recurrent rhythmic patterns) unified the plainsong tenor part. What is more, the rhythmic
period was often telescoped towards the end of a composition,
audibly producing an acceleration which one might compare
to the final, faster section in an operatic finale by Mozart or
Rossini.

A similarly audible, sensual effect was produced by the use
of *hocket* (the word is said to be cognate with 'hiccups'), a
kind of staggered melody on the off-beats of another melody.
Machaut himself is on record as declaring himself pleased
with certain of his works, 'having heard them several times' –
supposedly the first western example of a composer's referring to the test of actual performance. But it is not wrong to
regard this music as artificial, at least in the sense of 'full of
craft' (like a Bach fugue). Artificiality, including great complexity of rhythm and strange clashes of simultaneous notes,
was carried even further by Machaut's successors working at
the papal court of Avignon, and elsewhere. Indeed it has been
said that in the exercise of conscious artifice, joined with an
extreme freedom of aural effect, there is nothing to parallel
this late development of fourteenth-century ars nova until
we come to Schoenberg and the modernists of the present
century.

Turning back to Machaut's Agnus Dei, we note that the
final cadence has a peculiar musical flavour, one indeed that
stamps the music as medieval to modern ears in the same way
that pentatonic music (corresponding to the black notes of the
piano) sounds Chinese. In this cadence the four voices move
from a close-spaced chord of E minor (E, G, B, E) to the final
chord of F, C, F. Thus not only does the top E rise to F (which
is the progression of leading-note to keynote – a universal
convention of finality in later music), but B rises to C, which
sounds like another leading-note-to-keynote progression, one
fourth down. This is the so-called double leading-note
cadence so characteristic of the period. It will also be noted
that the final chord, as given above, is of keynote and fifth
only: the third (which would have made the chord F, *A*, C,
F) is omitted, since the composer's primary concern at such a

cadence is not with harmonic effect but with the contrapuntal relationship of the tenor to each of the other lines. But in the piece itself thirds abound.

Such thirds, as we have seen, had their special place in English music from the thirteenth century; but in France they are characteristic of the fourteenth and ars nova. Indeed it will be recalled that they were by implication condemned in the papal attack (pp. 34–5), which specifically permitted 'the octave, the fifth, and the fourth'. The interval of a third is – to even greater extent – a feature of Machaut's secular works (which exceed his ecclesiastical ones in number). He wrote ballades which maintain the traditional AA'B form (see p. 21) but which, unlike the older ones, are polyphonic instead of consisting of a single melodic line.

What is more, these new ballades have their main tune on the top line, and it appears that this top line was the only one given to a voice (the others being played on instruments). Though the idea of a tune on top seems natural and obvious to modern ears, it turned upside-down what we have seen to be the old principle of composing additional parts on top of a basic melody in the tenor. This distinctive practice is named by modern historians the treble-dominated style or the ballade style.

Similar, though not precisely the same, developments are to be seen in Italian music (also associated with new, and complicated, methods of notation). Italian composers of this time preferred wholly original music to music based on a plainsong tenor. They made no use of isorhythm but did use hocket (a more sensual device) and, to a remarkable extent, canon. It is plausible to suggest that this preference for sensual rather than intellectual qualities in art is typically Italian as opposed to French – southern as opposed to northern. (The learned, intricate art which was to conquer Italy in the fifteenth century was, as we shall see, a northern import.)

Canon, in which a musical theme is chased from one voice to another, was found picturesquely appropriate to the type of composition known as *caccia* (chase) in which the poetic text dealt with hunting – often as a symbol for amorous pursuit. As hunter follows quarry, so one voice imitates, at short distance, the melodic curves of the other voice: usually the caccia has only two such voices, over an instrumental bass line (called, in conformity with the usage we have already observed, the tenor). Such works characterize two Italian composers of the first half of the fourteenth century, both known by their places of origin, Jacopo da Bologna and Giovanni da Firenze (i.e., Florence).

These composers also wrote madrigals. The origin of the Italian term is uncertain, and the fourteenth-century madrigal has in any case no direct connection with the more familiar Italian and English type of the sixteenth century. Fourteenth-century examples for two or three voices correspond to a special poetic form. Two or three stanzas set to identical music are followed by a *ritornello* or refrain to different music. This type of madrigal was also cultivated by the most acclaimed Italian composer of the next generation, Francesco Landini (1325–97). Though blind from birth, he was also widely famed as a virtuoso of the organ, lute, and flute (i.e., the transverse flute, which existed alongside its cousin, the end-blown recorder). He worked in Florence – a city torn by strife and ravaged by plague, but still one of Europe's main textile and banking centres, where Petrarch and Boccaccio wrote and Giotto had painted. In the church of San Lorenzo in Florence, Landini's tomb shows the celebrated musician seated at his portative organ.

Though he cultivated the madrigal and caccia, Landini left more works in the form of ballata. By this time Italian music was evidently experiencing French influence, because the ballata (although etymologically it corresponds with the French ballade, being derived from a word for dancing) corresponds musically not to the ballade but to the French virelai (see p. 21). The most important characteristic of the ballata, distinguishing it from the madrigal and caccia, is that it ends as it begins: that is, the tune of the first section also serves as conclusion. To this form Landini brings his characteristically smooth melodies (mostly proceeding by

step, that is, to the adjacent note, upwards or downwards),
with an impression of sensuality and vivacity in the flowing,
varied rhythm.

More of his music happens to be preserved than that of any
other composer of his time (as with Machaut earlier) and so
he has given his name to the so-called Landini sixth – in
general use in Italy at that period. The form 'sixth' is mis-
leading: this is not the interval of a sixth, but refers to the
progression of a melody at a conclusion or intermediate
cadence. Instead of moving direct from leading-note to tonic
(e.g. B–C, or from the seventh to the eighth note of the supposed key of C), it drops intermediately to the sixth, i.e.,
B–A–C. Such a cadence closes, for example, Landini's
*Questa fanciull', Amor* (Cupid, make this girl tender . . .) – a
ballata which is in three parts of which only the top line seems
intended for voice, the lower two for instruments.

It should be noted that such music, though full of movement of a well-contrasted kind, is not expressive – that is, not
apparently designed to strike an emotion similar to that of its
text. (Here we see the difference from what I shall call a
Renaissance composer's attitude.) Even when his text tells of
bitter grief in love, there is no sense of pathos in the melody
set to particular words or phrases, nor in the harmony
resulting from the combinations of the parts.

Modern editions of medieval music, incidentally (and
indeed of music right up to the seventeenth century),
customarily have what may seem to be extra flat, sharp, or
natural signs printed *above* certain notes, or in brackets before
them. This indicates an editor's conjecture as to how this
music was actually performed. For ease of singing and
naturalness of the melodic line, certain unwritten 'accidentals' were observed. A singer faced on paper with the
downward then upward melodic shape of B–F–G would sing
the F as an F sharp (a note for which in medieval times there
was no written symbol). The principle of this type of alteration
is covered by the term '*musica ficta*' (fictitious or feigned
music). Medieval theorists are not consistent in their accounts of it, and a modern editor's task of deciding what extra

'accidentals' should be inserted is only part of the wider task of appreciating how much has to be supplied not from the written (or, later, printed) copy but from knowledge of current practice.

Such background knowledge (and not any indication on the written music) must also be drawn on to conjecture what instruments were employed. Instruments were used even to perform music that looks all sung, most of them of types already described (p. 29). Along with the lute, now beginning its long period of courtly and domestic popularity in the West, the triangle and the flat cymbals were borrowed from Arab civilization. Pageantry and dancing were the two functions which naturally gave the greatest stimulus to the development of instrumental music. Instruments, other than the organ, stand for frivolous diversion in Chaucer's depiction of his 'clerk of Oxenford' and his bedside 'companions':

> For hym was lever have* at his beddes heed
> Twenty bookes clad in blak or reed
> Of Aristotle and his philosophye
> Than robes riche, or fithele, or gay sautrye.

The 'fithele' is the fiddle, in medieval times sometimes played on the shoulder, sometimes rested downwards on the knee; a popular large kind had five strings. The fourteenth-century psaltery was shaped something like a modern zither (strings stretched across a soundboard) and played with the fingers or with quill plectrums.

About this time, too, and probably in Britain, were made the first members of the harpsichord family – that is, of instruments in which the plucking of strings is effected from a keyboard. The clavichord, in which the keyboard triggers a mechanism that does not pluck the string but hits it, seems also to have originated in the fourteenth century. Keyboard music is the only kind which in this period we can safely say was intended for one instrumental medium alone, since it is written down as polyphonic music to be played by a single performer (and only organ, harpsichord, or clavichord

* 'For he would sooner have . . .'

would permit this). The technical advances of the organ, which permitted the virtuosity of a Landini, must also have encouraged the composition of those organ paraphrases of the chants of the Mass which we find from the fourteenth century: the choir's chanting of the given tune would alternate with such a paraphrase of the tune (a sort of extended variation of it) played as an organ solo.

But few examples of such art survive. Even out of the meagre store of surviving keyboard music of the fourteenth century, the choir's chanting of the given tune would alternate transcriptions of secular vocal pieces by Machaut, Jacopo da Bologna, Landini and others). And of *all* music surviving, the majority is again secular. This is the period in which 'learned' western European music first devotes itself primarily to social entertainment.

# 3

## 'The English Countenance'

Our king went forth to Normandy
With grace and might of chivalry.
There God for him wrought marvellously,
Wherefore England may call and cry:
*Deo gratias.*

THESE words (here given in modern spelling) come from what is now called the Agincourt Song, celebrating Henry V's victory of 1415 and probably composed soon after. Possessing such a link with national history, and so direct a musical appeal, it may be regarded a landmark in English music comparable with *Sumer is icumen in* of nearly two centuries before. It is not more complicated than the latter: it is simpler. The evolution of music is to be regarded as the multiple ebb and flow of tides rather than an upward advance; and here we see music resting on no contrapuntal ingenuity but on a plain melody straightforwardly harmonized.

The Agincourt Song has a two-voiced *burden* or recurring section, repeated by a three-voiced chorus. Then comes a succession of verses (two-part), each ending with the same words (*refrain*); after each verse the burden recurs. This somewhat detailed exposition is necessary because the terms 'burden', 'refrain', and 'chorus', often confused in other usages, are here quite distinct. 'Chorus' is not a formal term: it literally implies the use of more than one person to a part, and this seems to be one of the first indications of solo and choral alternation in polyphonic music.

The recurrence of the burden, which comes both first and last, gives us a link with Continental polyphonic song such as the French virelai and the Italian ballata. The English type has its own special name – the *carol* (deriving, like ballade and ballata, from a term signifying the dance). The carol was not yet confined to music linked with Christmas or other church festivals. Its distinguishing feature is its verse-and-burden form; and, as in the above example, the mingling of English and Latin words was characteristic.

Who composed, who performed the Agincourt Song? Although far more composers are known by name from the fifteenth than the fourteenth century, this song bears no name on either of the two slightly differing manuscript versions in which it has come down to us. Modern authorities no longer accept earlier suggestions that the broad tune of the verse has a popular origin. But the popular *nature* of the carols is indisputable: most are in the major key, frowned on in ecclesiastical theory. As to the harmonization, the three-part writing carries on what we have already recognized as a favoured practice of English composers.

About this period the Chapel Royal assumes musical importance in England. This was the name given to the staff of musicians attached to the sovereign's household: 'chapel' refers not to a building but to a corporate body, moving whither the court moved. Apparently instituted as far back as the twelfth century in imitation of the papal court, the Chapel Royal included many leading English composers (also in their capacities as singers and, later, organists) between about 1400 and about 1700. The institution is paralleled in the royal musical establishments of other countries. Philip the Good, reigning duke of Burgundy from 1419 to 1467, supported such an establishment on a particularly munificent scale – fostering an art which becomes the subject of the next chapter.

A collection of music which was in use by the English Chapel Royal in the early fifteenth century has been preserved and is now known as the Old Hall Manuscript (from the hall near Ware, Herts, which has been its home since 1893). It contains nearly 150 pieces, most of them settings of parts of the Latin Mass. A *Gloria* and *Sanctus* are the work of a composer named as Roy Henry: authorities differ on whether this alludes to Henry IV (reigned 1399–1413) or Henry V (reigned 1413–22). Among other composers represented in the collection we may name two: a certain Pycard (nothing else about him is known), who shows himself an ingenious practitioner of canon in its various devices, and Lionel (or Leonel) Power, who died in 1445 as a lay member of the community of Canterbury Cathedral.

Power composed what seems (as far as surviving manuscripts can tell us) to have been the first mass in a new musical fashion, soon widely copied. When originally sung in plainsong, the five sections of the Ordinary of the Mass (Kyrie, Gloria, Credo, Sanctus, Agnus Dei) had been five separate pieces of music without interconnection, and the same applies to most of the polyphonic settings hitherto. The sections were set as quite separate compositions, and a choirmaster would feel free to select for a service a Gloria by one composer and a Credo by another. Machaut's mass (see p. 36) was an exception in being conceived as one complete work but even this seems to show few consciously conceived connections between its sections. That was Power's innovation: the use of one single theme in the tenor of all sections. Power's unifying theme was itself borrowed from plainsong – by obvious analogy with the practice of borrowing which for more than a century had been the basis of the motet.

The medieval Latin term for such a given theme was *cantus firmus* or fixed song. (It is a term that survives in modern academic usage, when a student may be asked to write a counterpoint to a cantus firmus, that is, to a melody stipulated by the teacher: *canto fermo* is the Italian equivalent.) Accordingly, a mass where such a theme is stated in each section is called a cantus firmus mass. The name given to Power's composition, the *Alma redemptoris* mass (or where the wholly Latin use is preferred, *Missa alma redemptoris*), indicates that the plainsong fragment he uses is one that originally bore the words 'Alma redemptoris mater' (Gracious mother of the redeemer) though these words are not of course heard in Power's mass itself. This unifying device commended itself to subsequent composers right up to the seventeenth century – and the unifying theme was, as we shall see, sometimes borrowed not from the plainsong of the Church but from the alien domain of secular song, just as it had occasionally been in the motet.

That some of Power's compositions have come to light in Continental manuscript collections suggests that Power himself visited the Continent. The suggestion approaches certainty in the case of Power's more celebrated contemporary, John Dunstable, more of whose work survives in French and Italian than in English collections. In the Old Hall Manuscript there is one work which the collector left anonymous but is now known to be his, the motet *Veni, Sancte Spiritus* (Come, holy spirit). Dunstable was a musician not of the Chapel Royal (as far as is known) but in service to King Henry V's brother, the Duke of Bedford. In that capacity he probably worked for a number of years in France, since the duke became regent of France in 1422 (it was under his regency that Joan of Arc was burned at the stake in 1431). Dunstable was buried in London in 1453 – in his sixties, it may be guessed.

On the Continent Dunstable was not merely known, but regarded as a leader. It was mainly through him that the suavity which stamped English musical composition passed to the Franco-Flemish composers, Dufay and Binchois, who worked at the court of Burgundy (see next chapter). The capital of Burgundy (a country stretching over much of the southern and central part of modern France as well as over much of the Netherlands) was Dijon; while Paris remained the seat of the Duke of Bedford as regent of France. Since the Duke of Bedford married a sister of Duke Philip of Burgundy, there was doubtless musical contact between the two courts. At any rate, a contemporary French poet, seeking to complement Dufay and Binchois, wrote that they had learned to make their music attractive by following '*la contenance anglaise*' and Dunstable in particular.

This 'English countenance' or English quality, as displayed by Dunstable, partly showed itself in a more evident feeling for chords – that is, for the harmonic effect of notes sounded together, rather than for the contrapuntal flow of melodies producing those chords. Moreover some of his melodic phrases themselves follow the notes of a chord (a feature that leads to the suavity referred to above). He permitted himself a technical freedom: when basing a work on a borrowed plainchant, he ornamented the chant freely and transposed it in pitch – a freedom in which he was followed by Continental composers. Dunstable brought his individuality to bear on the old, conservative form of the isorhythmic motet (of which *Veni, Sancte Spiritus* is an example) as well as on the newer types of composition in which the voices mainly move together, as in his three-part setting from the Song of Solomon, *Quam pulchra es* (How fair art thou).

If the isorhythmic motet represents a peak of musical achievement by the medieval mind, with its treatment of music as a discipline related to mathematics, then such a piece as *Quam pulchra es* seems to herald a new attitude of responsiveness to the literary text. At 'Veni, dilecte mi' (Come, my beloved) the music stops its onward movement for a poised, intense expression. This is an attitude which represents the composers of the succeeding Renaissance era, in so far as we may borrow that term from the visual and literary arts. Dunstable seems to represent a bridge between the medieval and the newer ideal. By 1500 (the approximate date of the next considerable source of English music – the collection known as the Eton Choirbook) the new feeling for harmonic progression has become normal even among composers who are not pioneers nor of the first rank.

Apart from harmony, one new feature found in the Eton Choirbook (a minority of pieces only) may be called significant: the use of the device known as *imitation*. The beginning of a theme, heard at first in one voice, is echoed a moment later by another voice (and perhaps by others in their turn). Exceptional indeed in the medieval period, the use of imitation is perhaps *the* characteristic of the newer style, such imitation attaining remarkable complexity and subtlety and indicating an equality of voices in such a composition. In this style (already more highly developed by the Franco-Flemish composers, as we shall note in the next chapter), the predominance of one vocal line is now obliterated; instead every voice, from the highest to lowest, plays an equally important (and indeed similar) part in the web of sound.

Among the music of the Eton Choirbook (so called because it was made for use in Eton College, founded by Henry VI in 1440) is the first musical *Passion* by a named composer – Richard Davy (*c.* 1467–*c.* 1515). Such a Passion (that is, a dramatic exposition of the story of the Crucifixion) was quite separate from the older traditions of medieval religious drama or liturgical drama (see p. 27) – literary compositions set to music and performed in church as an interpolation in the prescribed liturgy, but not forming part of it. Many such dramas had dealt with the events of Easter (that is, the Resurrection) but none with the preceding events (the Passion) commemorated in Holy Week. In any case, such dramas seem to have fallen largely into disuse after 1400.

The source of the Passion as a form of musical composition is to be found in the Church's liturgy itself. From as early as the fifth century the ritual for Holy Week included the chanted narration of the events leading to the Crucifixion. In its original plainsong form the narration was at first not dramatized by the allocation of different voices to the different characters. But such dramatization began to be used from about the twelfth century – Jesus being sung by a low voice, the Evangelist-Narrator by a middle voice, and the crowd by a high voice. The next step was to set the crowd in chorus, that is, in polyphony; two anonymous English examples of about 1450 are the first known such settings.

Davy's, surviving in incomplete form, is their successor; and, being liturgical, it is in Latin. The gospel on which it is based is that of Matthew. The new device of imitation, one voice seeming to echo its predecessor, is aptly put to use in the shocked reaction, 'Truly this was the son of God' – a type of expression to be paralleled in Bach's *St Matthew Passion* nearly two and a half centuries later.

Among the other composers represented in the Eton Choirbook (of which nearly half the leaves were lost at an early date, leaving our knowledge incomplete) is John Browne, whose biography remains a matter of conjecture, but who is considered by some authorities the greatest English composer of his time. Others represented include Robert Fayrfax (1464–1521) and William Cornysh (c. 1465–1524) – both of whom, as members of the Chapel Royal, accompanied Henry VIII to his celebrated meeting with Francis I of France near Calais on the 'Field of the Cloth of Gold' in 1520 (peace between the two countries having been signed six years previously). Both composers wrote masses of lofty style in complex counterpoint, but among Cornysh's surviving works are some three-voiced secular songs of unaffected simplicity – which may well have catered for a vogue at court. Henry VIII himself composed such songs, but only flattery would accord him more than amateur status.

The Eton Choirbook measures $23\frac{1}{2} \times 17$ inches: it was thus big enough to be placed on a lectern and read (at a pinch) by the whole choir standing round. Eton College's choral establishment for the conduct of the daily services in chapel was 10 men and 16 boys. Conforming to the custom of the time, this music was not written in the fashion of a modern score, where the parts for different performers are ranged vertically, with a bar by bar correspondence. Here each part (first treble, second treble and so on) is written separately, high or low on either the left-hand or the facing right-hand page. No overall, bar-by-bar view of the music is possible, and it is no wonder that errors crept into manuscripts to set problems for future scholars.

This layout was maintained in the early days of music-printing, an invention which, begun at this time (see p. 59), was to transform the propagation of musical culture. A fine specimen of English music-printing is known from as early as 1530 (not, as was formerly thought, the work of the famous Wynkyn de Worde), but the printing of music in Britain did not attain major commercial importance until after Elizabeth came to the throne in 1558.

Music conceived for voices, at this period and later, was often performed by instruments instead. It could readily be taken over by the family of viols, the different sizes corresponding to the different ranges of the human voice. It seems to have been Henry VIII who introduced the instrument (flat-backed and fretted, with a soft, rather reedy, nasal tone) to England by inviting players from Venice and Flanders. Less suited to literal borrowing, and therefore needing to develop its own repertory, was the harpsichord or virginals. (The latter term was used chiefly, but not solely, to indicate a small instrument.) From the pen of Hugh Aston (*c.* 1480–1522) there survives a piece for virginals in an idiom remarkably apt and resourceful for the keyboard. It is a hornpipe – a dance which then (and until the mid eighteenth century) was in triple, not 4/4 time, and carried no association with sailors.

Aston's piece is an approach to variation form, forecasting what was to be a popular type of keyboard piece throughout the Elizabethan age. It is also – to use a word which sums up an important new feature of both vocal and instrumental music of this time – florid. The melodic line seems to flower into clusters of relatively rapid notes placed between, or adorning, the principal notes. In singing it seems to represent an exuberance, in harpsichord music a dexterity of the fingers which serves to keep the music going and prevents it dying away with the sound of the plucked string. But it is found associated with other tone qualities too.

Aston's best-known contemporary among English musicians was John Taverner (1495–1545), organist of Wolsey's Cardinal College (now Christ Church, Oxford) – an appointment which he gave up in 1538 to become an agent for Thomas Cromwell in the suppression of the monasteries under Henry VIII. Most of his eight masses are based on plainsong, but one is based on the popular song *The western wind*, and is therefore known by that name. Two other English composers of the time, Christopher Tye (*c.* 1500–1573) and John Shepherd (*c.* 1520–*c.* 1563), based masses on this tune too.

Taverner was not merely the most accomplished English composer of his generation but also the begetter of a special, and peculiarly English, form which persisted for about a century and a half – the *In nomine*. One of Taverner's masses bears the title *Gloria tibi Trinitas* (Glory to thee, Trinity), being based on a plainsong melody of that name. In setting one of the sections of the mass, the Benedictus, and in coming to the words 'in nomine domini' (in the name of the Lord), Taverner incorporated the original melody of the *Gloria tibi Trinitas* as long, stretched-out notes in the alto part, with partial imitation of that melody in faster-moving parts in the other free notes. When later transcribed for keyboard use, the whole section was simply entitled *In nomine*; and later composers, exercising their contrapuntal facility by writing fantasias (usually for viols or virginals, less often for lute) on this plainsong theme, continued to use the *In nomine* title and sometimes began by actually quoting not merely the plain-song but Taverner's own contrapuntal treatment of it.

Though applied in the *In nomine* to a specifically English form, this type of contrapuntal, imitative instrumental writing was a Continental technique, transferred from a type of vocal writing which was itself imitative and based on equality of importance between the voices. This technique ripened in Italy, but did not originate there. It was brought by musicians from a small (but economically and politically important) area of northern Europe. This art, and its transplantation throughout the fifteenth century and the first half of the sixteenth, occupy our attention in the next chapter.

# 4

## From Burgundy to Italy

HENRY VIII, whose reign (1509–47) was mentioned in the previous chapter, is the first English king who appears to us fully rounded, human, comprehensible – thanks largely to Holbein's famous portrait. This is a new and northern kind of portraiture traceable to Jan van Eyck (*c.* 1386–1441), a Fleming who worked at the court of Burgundy. The effective centre of this rich dukedom moved from Dijon north to the mercantile cities of Flanders – Lille, Bruges, Antwerp. It is from this region that the Franco-Flemish or Netherlandish school of composers flowered, the composers who were to take their art to the more fertile soil of Italy.

Until the Burgundian state crashed in military defeat in 1477 (its Flemish parts then going to the Hapsburg dynasty, its 'French' region to France) the court gave employment to such musicians as Guillaume Dufay (*c.* 1400–1474) and Gilles Binchois (*c.* 1400–1460). Moreover the court 'chapel' included musicians from Italy, Germany and Portugal as well. Conversely, Franco-Flemish musicians had gone afield: they had been employed at Avignon in southern France during the exile of the papacy there (1300–1378) and during the succeeding period when rival papacies operated from Avignon and Rome (the Great Schism, 1378–1417). Afterwards, with Rome's supremacy re-established, Franco-Flemish musicians continued to find employment in the papal chapel. Dufay himself went to Rome, became a choirman in 1428, and stayed (with some interruption) for about ten years. He wrote works to Italian and French, as well as Latin texts.

The attraction was not merely spiritual and not merely to Rome. This was the era of rising, powerfully led city states. New dynasties arose, such as the Sforza in Milan and the Medici in Florence, for whom Botticelli painted his sensuous pagan allegories. In Florence, too, that fundamental textbook of government, Machiavelli's *The Prince*, was published in 1513; Castiglione's *The Courtier*, similarly a textbook for a gentleman's accomplishment (music included!), was published in 1528, to win international celebrity.

This is the society which nourished the Renaissance in the visual arts. (The special term 'High Renaissance' is used for the period beginning about 1500: Leonardo da Vinci's *The Last Supper*, a chief manifestation of the new visual intensity, dates from 1495–7.) The music of this period is itself known as Renaissance music, but this makes sense mainly as a time equation. The concept of a rebirth, or a rediscovery of the antique, so evident in both the visual arts and literature, is applicable in the music of the period to a much smaller extent; and the most notable rediscovery – the attempt to recreate Greek drama as Italian opera – belongs to the later (baroque) age and will be described in chapter 7.

Yet there is something distinctively new in this music. It is enshrined in three related ideas: a polyphony of similar, rather than contrasting, melodies; the chorus as a body for performing polyphony; and a sense of harmony determined by the bass line and propelled by the need for discord to move to concord. We use these terms in the musician's sense: a *discord* or *dissonance* means not an objectionable sound but one which seems unstable, requiring to move to the stability of a *concord* or *consonance*. In Machaut's period the composer wrote down his tenor line and then fitted other lines each in counterpoint to the tenor; what we feel to be occasional dissonances *between* the other lines were then not part of the composer's logic. Now they become so.

What is more, the dissonances must have been felt as more purposeful, more conspicuous in the new music, because its texture was more homogeneous. In the older music the different melodies were undertaken mainly by soloists or very small groups with a resulting emphasis on a variety of simultaneous tone colours. The new style was choral: the word 'chorus', which we noted in the last chapter, now occurs more frequently in manuscripts. In a larger and therefore more homogeneous and less individualized vocal ensemble, the progress from discord to concord must have been more sharply defined to the ear.

Some writers label the older polyphony Gothic and the newer one Renaissance, though we may decide to treat the latter word with reserve. The striking thing about this new polyphony, practised in Italy, is that it was the work of foreigners – the Franco-Flemish. They are to be found still in command a century after Dufay, when Adrian Willaert was appointed to St Mark's, Venice, in 1527 and Jacques Arcadelt as singing-master to the boys of St Peter's, Rome, in 1539.

An illustration in a contemporary manuscript shows Dufay with an organ, Binchois with a minstrel's harp. The implication is that one was particularly inclined to church music, the other to secular diversion. In fact, though both were clerics, they were equally adept at both functions. Their *chansons* (at this period the French word means a polyphonic setting of a secular song) are for three parts, with the chief melody on top and with some imitation of its phrases in the other voices. Moreover, this style of writing now came to be adopted also in the mass and in the motet – a word which now begins to take on its modern meaning of any polyphonic piece on an ecclesiastical text other than that of the Ordinary of the Mass. Here too the tune is on top, the composition may be free (not based on a plainsong), and there is a sense of harmony which includes successions of chords of the sixth.

Not only are chords felt strongly as chords, but they begin to show what modern theorists call *harmonic rhythm*: that is, the succession of different intervals, and the sense of discord resolving on to concord, suggests its own distribution of strong and weak accents in performance. New expressive possibilities arose in the interaction of this accent with verbal accent. Composers gradually showed a greater sensitivity in their music to the expressive and pictorial connotations of words. At first favouring a polyphony of three voices, Dufay later sometimes raised the number of his voices in polyphony from three to four – a distribution which led to the developed cultivation of higher and lower vocal notes, and which has remained standard up to today – when our terms are soprano, alto (or contralto), tenor, and bass.

The original meaning of 'tenor' we have already encountered, a line which held (Latin *tenere*) the fundamental melody; 'soprano' (upper) is the Italian translation of the Latin *superius*, already current in medieval usage. An additional line slightly above or below tenor pitch was called *contratenor*; and when Dufay and his contemporaries now required *two* such additional lines, they designated the higher and lower respectively as contratenor *altus* and *bassus* (our modern alto and bass).

With Dufay, whose fame was international, the mass becomes firmly recognized as a unified composition, the biggest and most varied single musical task within a composer's scope. (An earlier example by Power was noted on p. 46.) The unification is commonly accomplished by the use throughout the work of a given melody (*cantus firmus*) in the tenor. The choice of this cantus firmus was left to the composer, and sometimes the choice fell not on an ecclesiastical but a secular melody. Dufay based one such mass on the tune of his own three-part chanson entitled *Se la face ay pale* (If my face is pale) and another on a tune of unknown authorship, *L'homme armé* (The armed man). Both are for four voices, but in both there are certain sections where the tenor, or the tenor and one other voice, drop out and leave the lighter texture of a duet or trio.

Comparisons of, say, Machaut's mass with Dufay's mass *L'homme armé* will show the difference between the old and the new polyphony. Machaut sometimes proceeds (as in the Gloria) *homophonically* (all voices moving together, in the same rhythm), sometimes (as in the opening of the Agnus Dei) in a rather abrupt and angular counterpoint; in *both* styles the sections are short-breathed, coming to frequent stops. Dufay's contrapuntal lines are altogether smoother and longer – and overlapping to make a seamless, non-stopping texture where no metrical phrase is exactly repeated. It is above all a predominantly smooth melodic style, and the harmony is smoother too.

As in fourteenth-century music, instruments participated to reinforce the voices (doubling their lines) or to replace them. But, again as for the previous era, we do not know the exact details of this instrumental performance: it is one of the many matters where custom and practicability dictated usage. Morevoer, manuscripts give only general indications of what words are to be fitted to the music, and how: here too the performers were evidently expected to attend to details.

Within this new, seamless polyphony, the device of *imitation* between the different vocal parts was later to be exploited both as an aural delight and as a structural principle of composition. But this is not yet so habitual with the two chief composers of the generation following Dufay's: Okeghem and Obrecht. Jan (latinized as Johannes) Okeghem (*c.* 1420–*c.* 1495) served three kings of France as court composer. Jacob Obrecht was born in 1450 in Bergen-op-Zoom – now in Holland, then within the territories of the duke of Burgundy; he died in 1505 as a musician of the culturally important Italian ducal court of Ferrara, where the reigning Este family patronized (from about 1530) the first permanent theatre in post-Roman Europe.

Okeghem, like Dufay, wrote a mass on *L'homme armé,* and several others based on secular song tunes. In some (apparently late) works he abandoned this use of a given tune (cantus firmus) altogether, seeking to unify the work by other means. His mass '*Mi-Mi*' has no reference to the girl whose tiny hand was frozen. Two bass notes a fifth apart (each called *mi* in the contemporary nomenclature of *hexachords*, or six-note groups) serve to open all the five movements; and all the movements end on a *mi*, giving the mass a particular atmosphere – that of the Phrygian mode, corresponding to the scale found on the white notes of the piano from E to E. It seems to be the first mass written with this special effect, which other composers were to copy. Sometimes Okeghem makes consistent use of exceptionally low bass notes, down to C below the modern stave. (But there is no evidence enabling us to compare absolutely, in vibrations per second, the pitch of a written note today with any century before the seventeenth.)

Obrecht writes music of what seems to modern taste a more accessible kind than Okeghem's, that is, with rhythms more corresponding to bodily energy, and with expressive harmony which itself contributes (especially at cadences) to this rhythmic force. Yet he was also attracted by hidden symbolism, not detectable to the ear. His mass *Sub tuum praesidium* (founded on a plainsong fragment of that title, but with other chants also quoted) has been shown to bear subtle mathematical proportions disclosing the 'magic' number 888.

Such occult symbolism apart, Obrecht is able to exhibit a good deal of sheer musical ingenuity. Yet such musical ingenuity – for instance the presenting of a thematic element upside-down or in reversed order of notes – is not to be thought of as exclusively medieval. It is in fact paralleled in certain procedures of Bach, of Beethoven, and of the 12-note composers of our own century: among the last-named, Webern was knowledgeable in medieval and Renaissance music and had chosen to write his doctoral thesis on the composer Isaac (see below). Similarly Stravinsky, in re-working a motet by Gesualdo, revived the musical technique called parody, a practice much favoured in the fifteenth century by Obrecht and other composers.

In such contexts as the present, *parody* has no sense of mockery: it consists of borrowing the whole or nearly the whole texture of a previously composed work (whether by the composer himself or someone else) and incorporating this, with additions or variations, in a new work. Thus the four-part mass by Josquin Després, *Missa Mater Patris*, printed in 1514, is a *parody mass* (probably the first of its kind) because its several movements are united by the parodying (taking-over) of a motet for three voices, *Mater Patris* (Mother of the Father) by a contemporary, Antoine Brumel (c. 1475– c. 1520).

To mention Josquin Després (c. 1440–1521) is to introduce the composer generally considered, both in his day and ours, as the supreme master of the style of the period. (He is often referred to simply as Josquin, a name which is itself a diminutive; compare the English 'manikin', which uses this Flemish–Dutch diminutive ending.) Després is the contemporary of Raphael and Leonardo da Vinci, and was born only about 40 years before Luther, who said of him: 'Other composers do what they can with the notes, but Josquin does what he wishes.'

He was well served by that new medium, the printing-press: Ottaviano Petrucci, who worked in Venice and is regarded as the father of the printing of music from movable type, published 17 of Després's 19 masses and included several of his chansons in the *Odhecaton A* (the word is from the Greek for hundred songs) of 1501, the earliest printed collection of part-music. Of his motets (using the word to mean, at this period, any polyphonic music to devotional words other than those of the Ordinary of the Mass), about 100 appeared in printed collections issued during and shortly after his lifetime either at Venice or (with the significant growth of music-printing in Germany) at Nuremberg and Augsburg, a city to be further mentioned below.

These Latin motets show a regard for the special tone colours of voices (for instance, in contrasting duet passages for high and for low voices) and for musical word painting. The expressiveness lends itself to such chosen texts as David's Lament for Saul and Jonathan (*Planxit autem David*), or the Psalmist's *Miserere* (Psalm 51, or 50 in the Vulgate: 'Be gracious to me, O God, in thy true love'). Characteristically the composer divides his texts into short phrases, and each phrase is set to music in which the voices follow one another in overlapping imitation. The next phrase of the text follows (still overlapping) to a new musical phrase, and this in turn is similarly imitated. Sometimes, for contrast, there are passages in solid chords. This division into sections, with overlapping, is known as *motet style* – though it occurs in the masses too, and was later to provide the expressive and structural idiom of the Italian madrigal.

Després's secular French polyphonic songs, or chansons,

favour this same motet style and are in a free form (not tied to the prescribed old-established patterns such as the virelai). One such song, in four parts, *Adieu mes amours*, is held to be Després's reminder to his employer, Louis XII of France, that his salary was overdue! Before entering into his service, Després had worked for princely Italian patrons at Milan and Ferrara and had spent about eight years as a musician in the papal establishment at Rome. The light-hearted four-part song *El grillo è buon cantore* (The cricket is a good singer) is one of his few Italian-language settings: it is a *frottola*, a type of song in a formal pattern with certain repetitions of sections. The melody-line, on top, was accompanied either by other voices in a purely supporting role (often, as in this case, without polyphonic complexity) or by the lute.

A Spanish song form which forms a counterpart to the frottola is the *villancico*. One of its leading practitioners, Juan del Encina (1468–1529), is also notable as a poet and playwright at a time when Spain began (with Columbus's expedition in 1492) its century of exploration and mercantile war.

Among the most noted of Després's contemporaries was Heinrich Isaac, another north-European musician who found fortune in Italy: he died in Florence, where he had previously served the Medici family, in 1517. It is conjectured that he was born about 1450, but nothing is known of his early life and he is variously described as Flemish and as German. The latter term may simply mean that he was a subject of the Empire (the 'Holy Roman Empire') which was shedding its (already purely formal) connection with Rome and emerging as the chief German-speaking power in Europe. Among its chief cities was Augsburg, seat of the Fugger family of bankers, the richest private citizens in Europe; and it was in Augsburg that Isaac took employment to the Hapsburg Emperor Maximilian I in 1497. The emperor's musical establishment (chapel) was then in the process of being transferred to its new centre, Vienna. Isaac is thus the first of the great composers to be associated with the Austrian capital and its imperial musical activity – a line stretching up to Mahler.

The most famous composition to which Isaac's name is attached is *Innsbruck, ich muss dich lassen* (Innsbruck, I must leave thee). Just before 1600, this tune was adapted to devotional words ('O Welt, ich muss dich lassen' – 'O world, I must leave thee') and is familiar as one of the chorales of Bach's *St Matthew Passion*. It seems possible, if not probable, that Isaac did not actually write the tune but merely composed the four-part vocal arrangement of it which made it so widely known. He also used the melody in his *Missa carminum* (*Song Mass*) which incorporates various songs, all treated with the canonic ingenuity typical of the period.

Besides songs in German, Isaac wrote others in French and in Italian (each in its different national style). Among the latter are some, now lost, which were sung in the streets of Florence at carnival-time – or were these also mere arrangements by Isaac of already popular ditties? Isaac's monumental contribution to church music was a collection of 58 four-part settings of the Proper of the Mass (that is, of those texts which vary in use according to the ecclesiastical calendar) covering the whole of the church year. This compilation, called the *Choralis Constantinus*, is based on the plainsong of ritual in use at Constance in Switzerland: typically of the new era the plainsong is more often heard in the treble than in the traditional tenor part. It was completed by Isaac's pupil, Ludwig Senfl (*c.* 1499–1543).

Isaac's attachment to the Empire was exceptional: as we have seen, Italy was the region to which the leading composers of the Franco-Flemish region gravitated. Their special, local art was fertilized to new, luxuriant growths on the warmer soil. Among others of this group we must name Jean Mouton (*c.* 1470–1522): although no written records survive to disclose his presence in Italy, Petrucci in Venice printed a book of his masses about 1508. Mouton was certainly the teacher of Adrian Willaert (*c.* 1490–1562), whose appointment as musical director of St Mark's in 1527 began the era of Venice's musical glory – some decades after

Venetian painting reached its glory in Giovanni Bellini and Giorgione (died 1510).

As yet, up to about 1500, no Italian composers whatsoever won eminence in the imported northern forms. But some Italians of the late fifteenth century cultivated the modest form of the frottola. Among them Bartolomeo Tromboncino (his dates are uncertain) may be remembered if only for his delightful name – that is, 'little trombone', '*trombone*' itself being the Italian for big trumpet. The surname of a professional musical family, surely! Enlarged trumpets, we may note, had been the precursors of the trombone, which had reached its present-day shape by 1500: when the Emperor Charles V was crowned by the pope at Bologna in 1519 as successor to Maximilian I, trombones took part with other wind instruments in the ceremonial procession. So did crumhorns, double-reed instruments (of varying sizes) with a bent tube: their buzzing sound, much favoured in the sixteenth century, has been heard again in a mid-twentieth-century revival.

Likewise heard in that procession, and likewise destined to be cultivated again in our own historically minded age, was the cornett. ('Cornet' is the more accurate form, but the other spelling is used to distinguish it from the modern, brass-valved instrument.) In origin an animal horn (Italian *corno*) bored for finger-holes, it was now made of wood and blown through a trumpet-like mouthpiece. Capable of agile solos, or blending sonorously in ensemble with trombones, the cornett is an essential of sixteenth- and seventeenth-century sound.

# 5
## 'Mistress Music'

'Is it not singular and admirable that one may sing a simple tune or tenor (as the *musici* call it), while three, four, or five other voices, singing along, envelop this simple tune with exultation – playing and leaping around, and embellishing it wonderfully through craftsmanship, as though they were leading a celestial dance, meeting and embracing each other amiably and cordially?' In those lines speaks a sixteenth-century enthusiast for polyphonic music, an art traditionally built from one basic line of melody to which the skilled composer added other lines of his own.

The enthusiast was the great Reformer, Martin Luther (1483–1546), whose tribute to the musical skill of Josquin Després we have already quoted (p. 59). The Italian word *musico* in the above quotation indicates, at this period, simply a professional musician. Late in life Luther wrote a poem called *Mistress music* (*Frau Musica*) and a treatise, *In Praise of Music*, from which the above lines are quoted.* Married to a former nun, he settled into domestic felicity. Skilled as a singer, lutenist, and flutist, he used to join with his children and friends in evenings of domestic music-making. Personal taste must have reinforced the evangelical zeal with which Luther made congregational hymn-singing a vital element in the new church services. 'I wish,' he wrote to a friend in 1524, seven years after he had nailed his famous ninety-five theses on the church door at Wittenberg, 'after the example of the Prophets and the ancient fathers of the Church, to make German psalms for the people, that is to say, sacred hymns, so that the word of God may dwell among the people by means of song also.'

These theses – challenging the established doctrines of the Church, especially on the sale of indulgences – mark the

---

*Luther's verses are set in Hindemith's cantata, *Frau Musica*, 1928; revised, with the English title *In Praise of Music*, 1943.

beginning of the Reformation, a movement hardly less important in the history of music than in religious and political history. Luther's translation of the Bible (completed in 1534) marks the beginning of the modern German language; the Lutheran hymn-tune stands at the root of a new musical growth which we now identify as Protestant church music, and which was later to be cultivated by two of the greatest European masters, Heinrich Schütz and Johann Sebastian Bach.

Meanwhile, within the Catholic Church, the intensified activity known as the Counter-Reformation found its musical counterpart in the lofty art of such late-sixteenth-century composers as Palestrina and Lassus. As we shall see, there is by no means an absolute gap between Protestant and Catholic composition of this kind. Moreover, although Luther encouraged the use of the vernacular tongue in church in place of Latin, yet Latin masses and motets continued to be sung in some Lutheran congregations even into the eighteenth century: the music of Bach (see p. 156) yields examples.

Thanks to Bach's harmonizations, certain Lutheran hymn-tunes have remained well known – for instance, *Ein' feste Burg*, known in English as *A stronghold sure*, of which the words and possibly the tune are by Luther himself. It needs an effort to realize that Bach's and similar versions do not represent the original form of the hymn-tunes. Originally they appeared unharmonized and unbarred – perhaps to be delivered in free rhythm, like plainsong. Nor are they the only type of monophonic (single-line) composition surviving from this time. The mastersingers (*Meistersinger*), *bourgeois* inheritors of the old tradition of the *Minnesinger* (see p. 20), likewise set their German texts to unharmonized and unbarred melody – music subjected to a prescribed formal pattern and having many florid decorations. The celebrated Hans Sachs of Nuremberg (1494–1576), later to become the hero of Wagner's *The Mastersingers*, was a keen propagator of Lutheran hymnody.

Uncomplicated, easy-to-sing hymns in the vernacular

tongue are the natural expression of a popular religious movement. We have already noted the Italian 'songs of praise'
(*laudi spirituali*), and the encouragement given to popular
hymn-singing by Francis of Assisi in the early thirteenth
century. Among predecessors of Luther's reforming zeal, the
followers of Jan Hus (burned as a heretic in 1415) had evolved
their own hymns in the Czech language – one of which the
patriotic Dvořák was to quote in his *Hussite Overture*. But no
type of hymn has had such a powerful influence on music as
the Lutheran, to which the name of *chorale* is usually given in
English musical use. (It is a synthetic, mock-foreign substitute for the German noun, *Choral*, but useful in avoiding
confusion with the English adjective, *choral*.)

Some Lutheran chorales were newly composed tunes, but a
greater number seem to have been adaptations of Gregorian
tunes with the original Latin words translated into German,
or else adaptations of secular songs newly fitted with
devotional words. Thus the Gregorian hymn *Veni, creator
spiritus* ('hymn' in this sense referring primarily to a musical
and poetic form in stanzas, not to congregational use) became *Komm, Gott Schöpfer, heiliger Geist* (Come, God the
Creator, holy spirit) – the German words being a translation
of the Latin. So too, later, a lovesong by Hans Leo Hassler
(1564–1612), altered in metre and fitted to a new text,
became the chorale *O, sacred head*, familiar in Bach's *St
Matthew Passion*.

Not only were the chorales soon harmonized in simple
congregational style, with the tune either in the tenor or in
the treble; they were also made the basis of polyphonic compositions suitable only for performance by a trained choir.
Luther's musical adviser, Johann Walter (1496–1570) published such settings as early as 1524 in Wittenberg. In their
use of 'imitation' between voices, and in the way that the
voices 'play around' the melody (to use the phrase quoted
from Luther at the beginning of this chapter), these settings
apply to the new German hymn-tunes a treatment similar to
that accorded to plainsong by contemporary Italian composers
working with the material of the Roman Catholic Church.

Lutheranism soon became a princely, and therefore official, religion in certain German states, particularly in the north (including Saxony and Brunswick); but in Brandenburg-Prussia and in some other German states it was Calvinism which became the new state religion. It should be remembered that, despite the usual association of Luther's name with the Reformation, it is the Calvinist (and not the Lutheran) churches of Europe which are called Reformed. The teachings of John Calvin (1509–64) demanded the suppression of all instrumental church music, and of formal choirs, on puritanical grounds. When Bach in 1717 entered the service of a Calvinist prince, Leopold of Anhalt-Köthen, no church music was required of him: only the psalms were chanted, unaccompanied.

Calvinism's centre was Geneva – 'the Protestant Rome' – where John Calvin himself, French-born, had become head of the State. Successive editions of what was called the Genevan (i.e. Calvinist) Psalter were published from 1542 – the texts being a selection of the Psalms, paraphrased (some of them by Calvin himself) into rhymed metrical French verse. By 1562 all the psalms in the Bible had been so treated, many of them set to tunes selected or composed by the Frenchman, Loys (Louis) Bourgeois (c. 1510–c. 1561). Psalms, being directly biblical, are not in a strict sense hymns (original literary compositions); but those of the Genevan Psalter, being metrical and intended for congregational singing, may perhaps be regarded as the Calvinist counterpart of the Lutheran chorale. Indeed some of their tunes were adopted by the Lutherans (and, at a further remove, were treated by Bach).

The Genevan Psalter inspired the similar psalters designed for Protestant use elsewhere. Geneva itself became the refuge for a body of English Protestants during Mary's reign, and an English psalter edited by Thomas Sternhold was published there in 1556 – the forerunner of the famous *Whole Book of Psalms* edited by Sternhold and Hopkins and published in London in 1562 (Elizabeth having come to the throne four years previously). The familiar setting of *All people that on earth do dwell* (Psalm 100, the tune now being known as the *Old hundredth*, or, in America, the *Old hundred*) is taken from the Genevan Psalter.

The first prayer-book of John Knox's Calvinist Church of Scotland (1564) included the complete book of Psalms in metrical form, the Geneva Psalter having been raided for 42 of the tunes. (This prayer-book constitutes, incidentally, the first example of music-printing in Scotland.) In Holland, similarly, a psalter based on Calvin's replaced an earlier one of 1540. The psalter brought to America by the Pilgrim Fathers in 1620 was one that had been published in Amsterdam eight years previously for an English congregation, combining English, French and Dutch sources. (There is further reference to English psalters in the next chapter.)

In Geneva itself Calvin's church prescribed strictly sober psalm-settings in chordal style. But some polyphonic elaboration (Luther's 'playing around') was allowed in psalm-settings intended for private edification within the home. The two types of setting, which we might also call strict and free, or hymn style and motet style, are to be found in the work of the chief French Protestant (Huguenot) composer of the time, Claude Goudimel (*c.* 1505–72). It should be noted that French Protestantism, on which was to fall the Massacre of St Bartholomew (1572), was Calvinist, not Lutheran (as an incautious acquaintance with Meyerbeer's opera, *The Huguenots*, might suggest).

Goudimel sometimes treated the same psalm-tune in these two different ways – as indeed with the tune and words of Psalm 23, *The Lord is my shepherd*. Apart from his church music, Goudimel also wrote chansons of the new and livelier kind then coming into vogue, with strongly marked rhythms and clear division on the lines of a poetic stanza, without much overlapping – *not* a seamless texture, but one which was probably influenced by the Italian frottola, noted in the last chapter. Other composers of such chansons, a term now used for all secular French polyphonic songs, include Claudin de Sermisy (*c.* 1490–1562) and Clément Janequin (*c.* 1485–*c.* 1560). Janequin is famed particularly for his long descriptive and imitative chansons entitled *The Song of the Birds* (*Le Chant des oiseaux*) and *War*, later known as *The Battle* (*La Bataille*).

In Italy that renewal within the Roman Catholic Church which is called the Counter-Reformation is marked by the papal approval given in 1540 to Ignatius Loyola's newly founded Society of Jesus, with its military-like discipline. From 1545 to 1564, at intervals, the papal Council of Trent carried out its deliberations on questions of church organization and church doctrine, strengthening the pope's rule and bringing it into line with the new stature of monarchs in other lands. The council's resolutions on music (1562) were admonitory but in many respects imprecise. They called for the exclusion of any music 'in which anything impious or lascivious finds a part', meaning any works based on the tunes of chansons and madrigals, the original words of which might linger too closely in the listener's memory. They also encouraged composers to seek out verbal audibility, thus promoting homophonic textures (the voices moving together) and syllabic melody, so that the words of prayer might be distinctively heard. According to a story which has now been exposed as nineteenth-century romantic fiction, the council might have banned polyphonic music altogether (as an impure, secular accretion) had they not been dissuaded by the genius of Palestrina in composing a special mass dedicated to the new pope, Marcellus II.

In fact, if any composer helped to save polyphonic music within the church, it was presumably Jacobus de Kerle (*c.* 1531–91), who dedicated to the cardinal-legates of the council a musical setting of specially written prayers – and, in a preface, justified the use of music in worship by means of a biblical reference to David, exactly as Luther did in his *Mistress Music*!

The juxtaposition of the Flemish name of de Kerle with that of the native Italian, Giovanni Pierluigi da Palestrina (*c.* 1525–94), is significant. This period sees the end of the Franco-Flemish leadership of music in Italy and the rise of great Italian composers; the rise too of a powerful Spanish school of church composers, active both in Rome and in their own country, and celebrated beyond it. The most famous are Cristobal Morales (*c.* 1500–1553) and Tomás Luis de Victoria (1540-1611), who even received a gift from distant Lima in Peru, the recently founded (1535) city of the conquistadors.

To the Franco-Flemish composers, before their dominance came to an end, we chiefly owe the birth of an important new form – the madrigal, in its new, sixteenth-century sense. (The earlier usage is referred to on p. 40.) The form was born suddenly, in a printed book of 'the new madrigals by divers most excellent musicians' published in Rome in 1533; it grew prodigiously, the number of published collections (including reprints) rising to about 2,000 by the year 1600. Thereafter, although the term 'madrigal' continued in use, its essential polyphonic character is lost. In essence the madrigal is a polyphonic song in a free form (not having a prescribed pattern of musical repetitions, like the frottola) in which the voices use a counterpoint of short, imitative phrases to express the text – that is, both to suggest the general emotion and to paint certain important poetic phrases. It is a 'serious' kind of music treating a 'serious' kind of verse. Its predecessors – the motet, frottola, and French polyphonic chanson – all contribute to it.

The madrigal was one of the two great gardens of music (the mass and motet constituting the other) which flowered so impressively in sixteenth-century Italy. The church music naturally adhered to the traditional Latin texts; but the madrigal was set to Italian verse, often of high literary quality. The poet most often set by the madrigalists is Petrarch, of two centuries back (see p. 34), but there are also numerous settings of the two most important sixteenth-century Italian poets, Ariosto and Tasso, each famous for their chivalric epics of the Crusades. Tasso, living until 1595, wrote lyrical poems expressly for madrigal-setting. The madrigal is the music of aristocratic recreation and festivity, whether performed by professionals or amateurs: it is music which aims to describe, to delight, to move to passion. The various voice parts (usually four or five) each keep their own springing rhythms, and answer each other's phrases; or they join together by two, three, or more for special effect. As compared with contemporary church music, the idiom is generally bolder, the effect deliberately more striking, more personal, and more pictorial.

The four major early practitioners of the madrigal are Arcadelt and Willaert, holders of important posts as church musicians in Rome and Venice respectively (see p. 55); their Franco-Flemish compatriot, Philippe de Verdelot (*c.* 1480–*c.* 1540); and one Italian, Costanzo da Festa (*c.* 1490–1545) of Rome. Festa's madrigal *Quando ritrova* (still showing a top line predominance which belongs to the frottola) is well known in English as *Down in a flowery vale*. Arcadelt's madrigal *Il bianco e dolce cigno*, also well known, is a setting of a poem which breathes the typical atmosphere of the madrigal. Here, as often, the word *morire*, to die, carries an added, erotic meaning.

> The white and gentle swan
> Dies singing, and I
> In weeping come to my life's end.
> Strange, contrasted fate,
> That he dies disconsolate
> And I die of bliss . . .

So the text begins – after which the composer altered the original poem in order to provide a rhyming couplet at the end, a poetic device which composers often valued as a spur to a clinching finality in the music. By the rise and fall of the interlocking melodies and the varying tensions of the harmony, the madrigal composers provided a musical interpretation of emotionally suggestive words such as 'dies', 'strange', 'disconsolate' in the lines quoted above. Willaert's compatriot and pupil, Ciprien de Rore (1516–65), seems to have established the precedent by which most later Italian madrialgs are in five or more voices, rather than in three or four as before.

If we mention here a lesser composer, the Italian Francesco

Corteccia (1504–71), it is because a 'programme' of madrigals he wrote for the marriage of Duke Cosimo I de' Medici at Florence in 1539 gives us an extraordinarily vivid picture of the festive and theatrical role of such music. The entrance of the bride was to be followed by the performance of a comedy with mythological characters and incidental music. The list of items ran as follows:

*Ingredere* [entrance music] in eight parts, sung over the archway of the great door of the Porta al Prato with 24 voices on the one side and, on the other, four trombones and four cornetts, for the entry of the most illustrious Duchess;

*Sacro e santo himeneo* [Blessed and holy Hymen], in nine parts;

*Vattene almo riposo* [Begone, gentle repose], in four parts, sung by Aurora and played by harpsichord and little organs with various stops, at the beginning of the comedy;

*Guardane almo pastore* [See, gentle shepherd], in six parts, sung at the end of the first act by six shepherds and then repeated by them and played as well by six other shepherds with crumhorns;

*Chi me l'a tolt' oimè!* [Who has taken him from me, alas?], in six parts, sung at the end of the second act by three sirens and three sea-nymphs with three lutes all together;

*O begl' anni dell'oro* [O beautiful, golden years], in four parts, played at the end of the third act by Silenus with a violone, playing all the parts and singing the soprano [the meaning of 'playing all the parts' is uncertain];

*Hor chi mai canterà?* [Now who will ever sing?], in four parts, sung at the end of the fourth act by eight huntress nymphs;

*Vientene almo riposo* [Come, gentle repose], in five parts, sung at the end of the fifth act, at nightfall, and played by four trombones;

*Bacco, Bacco evoè* [Bacchus, Bacchus, hail], in four parts, sung and danced by four votaries of Bacchus and four satyrs with various instruments all at once – which, at nightfall, was the end of the comedy.

The use of instruments in performing madrigals, which may come as a surprise to those used only to the un-accompanied vocal performance of such music, is well authenticated not only in this but in many other instances. But it is to be noted that the instruments play the vocal parts (either with the voices or as an alternative to them): there are not special instrumental parts, such as Monteverdi was later to provide. It is to be noted too that there is only one voice or a few voices to each part.

Various examples of cycles of madrigals are to be found – by Palestrina and Rore, for instance – and it is to that tradition that a famous work belongs which was published in Venice in 1597 and is often confusingly stated to be a forerunner of opera. This is *The Amphiparnassus* (*L'amfiparnasso*, the 'lower slopes of Parnassus', the mountain of the muses) by Orazio Vecchi (1550–1605). It is a set of madrigals which encompasses a miniature three-act comedy based on the traditional comic figures of the popular Italian theatre of the day, *commedia dell'arte* (literally, comedy of art; the exact meaning is disputed). But *The Amphiparnassus* is a work only to be heard, not staged, and no doubt the Florentine innovators of opera about 1600 (see chapter 7) would have considered it totally removed from their way of thinking both about drama and about music.

The madrigal was not always festive in intent or amatory in tone. A special class, to devotional texts (but for social use, not for the church), had the name of spiritual madrigals. Rore composed a cycle of eleven madrigals on stanzas by Petrarch invoking the Virgin; another Franco-Flemish composer among the Italian madrigalists, Philippe de Monte (1521–1603), numbered eight books of spiritual madrigals among his extraordinarily large total of madrigals (about 1,200). Palestrina wrote 56 such works – and in later life, as a composer consecrated to the musical service of the Church, appears to have 'blushed and grieved' at having written music for profane love-poems among his 83 other madrigal settings.

Palestrina, who took that surname from the small town where he was born, is a composer who has given his name to a style and a period. 'Prince of Music' was the inscription on his coffin, buried in the old church of St Peter's, Rome, where he had been choirmaster from 1550 to 1555 (a position formerly held by Arcadelt and then by Festa) and again from 1571 till his death. In the nineteenth century the loftiness and suavity of his style won rapturous praise from such composers as Wagner and Gounod. Romantic tribute was completed in 1917 with the opera *Palestrina* by the German composer Hans Pfitzner (1869–1949) which not only enshrines the legend that Palestrina prevented the Council of Trent from banning polyphony in church (see above, p. 68), but adds a scene in which the composer is shown writing down his *'Pope Marcellus' Mass* at the direct dictation of angels.

Mid-twentieth-century scholars, however, tend to see Palestrina's art as a highly finished yet somewhat narrow one, and to choose the more versatile Lassus (see below) as a better epitome of his age. Palestrina's music is in some ways conservative, in particular rejecting the tendency towards greater expressiveness through chromaticism which his contemporaries were developing. Sometimes, for instance in his *Missa ad fugam* (*Mass in Fugal Style*), written throughout in double canon, he exhibits what seems to be a medieval, backward-looking addiction to mathematical construction. Yet in some of his other masses (he wrote 105, with about 450 motets and other liturgical compositions, including a famous setting of the *Stabat Mater*, referred to on p. 23) we can hear clearly enough the beauty of line, the expressiveness within a deliberately restricted style, the balance of sound, the close control of the whole, all unified. The regularity of flow in Palestrina's music, and the consistency with which he treated progression of discord to concord, led later theorists to adopt him as a model for an academic 'Palestrina style'.

It remains to be added that the *'Pope Marcellus' Mass*, though perhaps the best known of Palestrina's masses, is not typical, because it is entirely an original composition, making no use of given material. Some of his others are based on given melodies, whether plainsong or secular (two on *L'homme armé*); but the largest group of his masses (52 of them) are *parodied*, that is, re-worked from a previously existing musical composition (his own or someone else's). One of these parody masses is the *Mass 'Veni, sponsa Christi'*, based on Palestrina's own motet *Veni, sponsa Christi* (Come, bride of Christ), itself based on a plainsong antiphon (sung liturgically before or after a psalm or canticle). Palestrina was himself concerned, by papal direction, in the preparation of what was considered an authentic printed edition of plainsong; and it should not be forgotten that a service using Palestrina's (or anyone else's) polyphonic settings consisted of a mixture of these with the unadorned plainsong itself.

The grammar of music up to this time still expected melodies to fall into one of the four church modes (see p. 22), none of which correspond exactly to our major or minor scales. But the modes originally classified only melody. Although a composer in adding melodies polyphonically to a modal tune was supposed to keep to that mode, harmony had evolved in practice towards the polarization of music as major or minor: thus, listening to the splendid six-part polyphony of the *Osanna* in Palestrina's '*Pope Marcellus*' *Mass*, we feel as firmly as possible in C major. Adapting grammar to practice, therefore, theorists now came additionally to recognize the Ionian (C to C) and Aeolian (A to A) modes, forecasting our modern major and minor scales.

Palestrina was a native-born Italian; Roland de Lassus (1532–94) was a Franco-Flemish composer, though known also under the italianized name of Orlando di Lasso. Said to have been thrice kidnapped as a boy because of his beautiful voice, he was certainly taken in boyhood to Italy and became choirmaster at the important Roman church of St John Lateran at the age of about 20. He spent the last 34 years of his life as musical director of the Bavarian ducal chapel at Munich, but retained his contact with Italy, and in 1574 received the Knighthood of the Golden Spur from Pope Gregory XIII, to whom he had dedicated a volume of five five-part masses. But it is not so much the masses as the motets of Lassus which are particularly admired – using the term 'motet' to include, as usual, any polyphonic settings of ecclesiastical Latin texts apart from those of the Ordinary of the Mass. Among these motets (750 or more) are Lassus's celebrated *Seven Penitential Psalms of David*, published in 1584, but composed up to 20 years before.

His church music is of a more intense and passionate style than Palestrina's; his secular music shows him not as a Roman (as Palestrina was) but as a cosmopolitan, equally adept in the Italian madrigal, the French chanson, and in German polyphonic song-settings. These German settings were described in their publication as *Lieder* (songs) or *Liedlein* (little songs): among them it is somewhat surprising to find, especially in a volume dedicated to a Catholic nobleman, some settings of Lutheran hymn-tunes. It seems clear that the popularity of these hymn-tunes in German must have transcended the division between Protestant and Catholic; clear, too, that this was an age when devotional texts, whether as German hymn-tune or Italian spiritual madrigal, were welcome on social occasions.

Like Lassus, Giaches de Wert (1535–96) was a Fleming who came to Italy at an early age. Unlike Lassus, he never worked elsewhere, serving the ducal court at Mantua for 25 years – rewarded when the freedom of the city of Mantua was eventually conferred on him and his heirs for ever. Important as a composer of madrigals and as an influence on Monteverdi, Wert was succeeded at the Mantuan ducal chapel by Giovan Giacomo Gastoldi (*c.* 1555–1622), famous as a composer of polyphonic songs which are in a rather lighter vein than true madrigals – more inclined to chordal movement, and less to contrasting rhythms between the parts. Again unlike the normal madrigal, these works of Gastoldi tend either to be *strophic* (the music repeated entire for each stanza) or at least to have whole sections repeated – these two types being called the *balletto* and *canzonetta* respectively. The former, as its name suggests, was intended for dancing, and had a fa-la refrain. These are the direct ancestors of Morley's *balletts* and *canzonets* in England, discussed in the next chapter.

Another composer of direct influence on English taste was Luca Marenzio (1553–99), who perhaps brought the Italian polyphonic madrigal to its greatest expressiveness in response to the text and in resourceful handling of the new, chromatically expanded harmony: in addition to a fully modern sense of major and minor, modulation to nearly related keys now becomes a structural principle. (Such modulation, in what we shall now call *tonal* as distinct from *modal* music, serves to establish the basic key of a work or section by making it the centre of excursions to and through various other keys.)

Marenzio shows a directness of expression which may be thought of as typically Italian, fused with the Franco-Flemish contrapuntal genius which originally launched the madrigal. 'If I leave, I die' (*S'io parto, i, moro*), proclaims the text of one of his most celebrated examples. The music to these opening words displays the tension between successive major and minor chords, the interplay of different simultaneous rhythms, the anxiety suggested by 'suspended' notes, and the subtle feeling of one note which is sounded by one voice and taken over by another. Marenzio's career took him as far as the Polish court at Cracow. He furnishes the possibly unique example of an Italian composer of this period who never held a church appointment – though, through personal influence, he had rooms in the Vatican and taught John Dowland (see p. 92) there in 1595.

In the Italian music of this period Venice (a mercantile republic with an elected doge, not a princely city) has a special place for two reasons. Firstly, it continued as the chief Italian centre of music-printing: of works mentioned in this chapter more were printed at Venice than anywhere else. Secondly, the formation of a definite Venetian school of composition was prompted by the peculiar architectural and civic character of St Mark's Church – the clergy of which was responsible directly to the doge. The church, with its two organs facing each other in opposing apses, allowed Willaert to develop the use of two choirs answering each other, or joining massively together. This use of double choirs, though not unknown before, became a Venetian speciality, and was developed by Willaert's pupil Andrea Gabrieli (*c.* 1520–86), uncle of Giovanni Gabrieli (see p. 119). It may have been the Venetian example which led Palestrina to cast his *Stabat Mater* in an eight-part, double-choir texture.

Venice was also an important nursery of new forms of instrumental music. Andrea Gabrieli and other composers not only transcribed polyphonic vocal music for keyboard (harpsichord or organ) but also wrote original keyboard pieces. The French chanson, for which the Italians used their own word *canzona* as an equivalent, was a popular basis for such keyboard transcriptions. Hence canzona now also becomes a term for an original keyboard piece in song-like style. Keyboard works in a more serious style were given the name of *ricercare* – from the Italian word for seeking out. Both forms were contrapuntal – that is, they give the impression of a piece for several voices, with imitation, arranged for a keyboard player. The canzona, as it developed, began to be divided into a number of sections; ricercare normally implies the continuous, non-sectional exploitation of a theme or set of themes. Both ricercares and canzonas were also written as pieces for instrumental ensemble (an ensemble of cornetts and trombones being particularly favoured). In this form the canzona with its often lively rhythms may be reckoned the ancestor of the *church sonata* of the seventeenth century.

Another notable keyboard form is the *toccata* (from *toccare*, to *touch* the keys), showing off the organist's or harpsichordist's technique in scales and ornamented passages: the Venetian, Claudio Merulo (1533–1604), introduced a sustained, ricercare-like section as a middle section of a toccata. Keyboard instruments and the lute were both favoured for dance pieces, often found in pairs, a slow dance in 2/4 time being followed by a quick in 3/4. Such sequences are the *pavan* and *galliard* (to give these names their English forms), and the *passamezzo* and *salterello* – this last-named surviving, surprisingly, in the finale of Mendelssohn's *Italian Symphony*, where the composer spelt it *saltarello*.

Ballet in the French sense (the word is itself an adaptation of the Italian) was established at the French court with *The Queen's Dramatic Ballet* in 1581, with music by the Italian-born Baltazarini di Belgioioso (died *c.* 1585). In 1589 appeared Thoinot Arbeau's important French publication *Orchésographie*, subtitled 'Treatise in the form of a dialogue through which all persons may easily learn and practise the honest exercise of dancing', and containing nearly 50 dance-tunes. Capriol, an imaginary character in this book, lent his name, nearly 350 years later, to Peter Warlock's suite of dances taken from this collection.

# 6

## *Elizabethan England: A Golden Age?*

THE long reign of Elizabeth I (1558–1603), with its fury of mercantile and intellectual activity, and its crushing defeat of the Spanish Armada in 1588, may be taken by political historians as a self-sufficient period. For present purposes, however, it is convenient to extend the period at each end – to begin with the break between England and the papacy in 1534, during the reign of Henry VIII, and to continue until, say, the death of Shakespeare (1564–1616). His plays furnish, as we shall see, the clearest and most accessible evidence of the extent to which English culture of that age was a musical one.

Yet Shakespeare reflects only the latter part of the age. The world of Thomas Tallis – commonly and rightly regarded as a great Elizabethan, though he died in 1585, about five years before Shakespeare began his career as a dramatist – was a different one. He was probably born about 1505. In Elizabeth's reign he held the appointment of organist of the Chapel Royal jointly with William Byrd, who was about 40 years his junior. (The two men also secured from Elizabeth a legal monopoly of music-printing and music paper: it turned out less profitable than they hoped.) Before Byrd was born, Tallis already held a post, presumably musical, at Waltham Abbey in Essex – and was one of those who received financial compensation when in 1540 this abbey fell under the seizure of monastic lands by Henry VIII. Tallis was therefore a youthful contemporary of Taverner and Tye (see chapter 3) and was among the first to follow Taverner in composing instrumental fantasias of the *In nomine* type: he left two for viols, one for lute.

Pieces for virginals and for organ (a relatively small instrument at this time, without pedals) also came from Tallis's pen. But his greatness rests on his vocal music for use in church, to texts both in Latin and (for the newly reformed

Church of England) in English. The change in the Church from one language to the other was not sudden, but gradual. Even when English had been well established, compositions which would have previously found a place in the Roman service continued to be published. A collection of 17 motets by Tallis and 17 by Byrd was issued in 1575 under the non-liturgical (or, at least, neutral) title of *Cantiones sacrae* or sacred songs. So they are called for short, but the actual description on their title-page is even more cautious: *Cantiones quae ab argumento sacrae vocantur* (Songs called sacred because of their text).

The most audacious of Tallis's motets, *Spem in alium nunquam habui* (I have hoped in none other), is, unprecedentedly, in 40 parts (eight five-part choirs). It seems likely to have been written as an exhibition of mastery more than with a hope of practical use – unless, as has been rather boldly conjectured, it was actually used not in a service but in a pageant-like choral spectacle on the story of the Book of Judith (with which the text is associated). Here and elsewhere Tallis's writing for voices seems to both singer and listener to have a marvellously natural flow. In his famous Latin setting of the *Lamentations of Jeremiah* (in five parts) he combines gravity of tone with that flexibility of vocal expression characteristic of the English Elizabethans.

The substitution of English for Latin in worship called forth those specifically English musical forms, the *service* and the *anthem*. The former comprises music for the obligatory texts of morning and evening prayer and for those of Holy Communion, which corresponds to the Latin Mass. A *great service* denotes an elaborate polyphonic setting, a *short service* a more concise, chiefly chordal style: Tallis's 'in D minor' (or, as Tallis himself would have more correctly described it, 'in the Dorian mode') is a short service in four parts. It is perhaps the earliest service regularly used in Anglican cathedral worship today, giving some substance to Tallis's title 'father of English cathedral music'. Tallis also wrote at least 17 anthems – the anthem being a counterpart to a Latin motet, with an English text chosen from the Bible but not forming an obligatory part of the liturgy. Sometimes he transferred to the new ritual the characteristic, imitative, overlapping counterpoint of the contemporary Latin motet; sometimes (as in the anthem *If ye love me*) he sticks to a plainer syllabic setting, presumably for general use. The Chapel Royal cultivated a more elaborate style.

We speak of *cathedral music*, alluding to those few and special churches – principally cathedrals, but also including the Chapel Royal and the chapels of Oxford and Cambridge colleges – which maintained a professional choral establishment. For these the great store of Anglican services and anthems were written. It was in cathedral use, too, that the new form of Anglican chant took root for the choral chanting of prayers when no formally composed service was used. Anglican chant was essentially an adaptation of Latin plainsong to the new English texts, and was established in *The Book of Common Prayer Noted* (i.e., supplied with musical notes) of 1550, the work of John Marbeck or Merbecke (*c.* 1510–*c.* 1585). In parish churches the new prayers were not chanted but were read in alternation by the minister and the parish clerk; the one form of regular music-making in parish-church worship was the singing of psalms in their metrically paraphrased, hymn-like form. The metrical psalter of Sternhold and Hopkins (already mentioned in the previous chapter, p. 66) became a standard work in the 1562 edition.

In this period a number of other psalters were compiled for which leading composers were commissioned either to furnish original settings of the metrical psalms or to supply harmonizations of previously accepted tunes. One of these, Archbishop Parker's Psalter, of which a few copies appear to have been printed (1567 or 1568) but never put on public sale, includes nine settings by Tallis. One of these is the source of the famous *Tallis's canon* (associated only since 1732 with the words 'Glory to thee, my God, this night'), and another is the source of Vaughan Williams's *Fantasia on a Theme of Tallis* (1910) for double string orchestra.

Tallis may be considered as almost exclusively a church

musician; even more so his contemporary, Robert Whyte or
White (*c.* 1530–74), who wrote similarly for Latin and
English worship. His *Lamentations of Jeremiah* (in Latin) have
been ranked with Tallis's. Such a preoccupation with church
duties is not to be found with the composers who were born
in the 1540s and after, whose creative activity falls within the
time of Shakespeare's. The greatest of these, in their range of
compositions as well as in their height of achievement, are
William Byrd (1543–1623), Thomas Morley (1557–1603) and
Orlando Gibbons (1583–1625). All held church appoint-
ments and all wrote church music of first importance: yet
they shared also in the flowering of secular music and contributed notably to it in dances, in other instrumental music
(for lute, for virginals and for ensembles) and in that new
English form, the madrigal. John Dowland (1563–1623), in a
much-travelled career, never took a church post, supporting
himself as a lutenist and as a composer principally of lute
solos and of songs with lute accompaniment.

Such composers catered for the leisure of a class (court,
nobility, rich merchants) who followed the ideals of learning,
the arts, and elegance. The taste was set by Italy – just as in
literature Edmund Spenser (*c.* 1552–99) used the Italian
title *Amoretti* for his cycle of English love sonnets.
Castiglione's treatise of behaviour, *The Courtier*, whose
original appearance in 1528 we have already noted, was
translated into English in 1561. 'My lords,' (says one of the
'instructors'),

you must not think I am pleased with the Courtier if he be not
also a musician, and, besides his understanding and cunning upon
the book, have skill in like manner with sundry instruments. . . .
And principally in courts, where (beside the refreshing of vexations
that music bringeth unto each man) many things are taken in hand
to please women withal, whose tender and soft breasts are soon
pierced with melody and filled with sweetness.

Italian terms of music and dancing were adopted and
anglicized. The Italian words '*la volta*' (the leap) form the
energetic dance called the lavolta – which Queen Elizabeth

can be seen dancing with the Earl of Leicester in a celebrated contemporary painting. 'The gentleman' (I quote from a modern authority's description of the dance) 'throws his left arm round the lady's back, clasping her about the waist; with his right hand placed firmly beneath her bust, and his left thigh pushing her forward, he helps her with a powerful thrust to rise into the air.' There is a lively modern musical reincarnation of this dance and its music in Benjamin Britten's opera *Gloriana* (1953).

Such new, imported customs and terms at the top of society met and fused with older, more popularly distributed elements of music and dance. It is partly as an illustration of this fusion that Shakespeare's plays prove so illuminating. (It is worth recalling that ordinary citizens were among his audiences: the references in his texts to music, as to other technical matters, were not designed to be understood only by an élite.) Music becomes material for metaphor and pun. So 'division' in its special musical sense of 'variation' is used by Juliet in the moments before her agonized parting from Romeo:

> Some say the lark makes sweet division:
> This doth not so, for she divideth us.

In the same play Peter, Capulet's servant, bandies musical terms with professional musicians whom he contemptuously names 'Simon Catling' (from cat-gut), 'James Soundpost' (the soundpost is an internal part of the body of a stringed instrument) and 'Hugh Rebeck'. The rebec (an ancestor of the violin, principally used for dance music) was still played, although the viols were the newly fashionable family of instruments. Hamlet, at the entry of the players, seizes on a musical point to make one of his savage jokes:

'O the recorder . . .'

'. . . Will you play upon this pipe?'

'I have no touch of it, my Lord.'

''Tis as easy as lying: govern these ventages with your fingers and thumb, give it breath with your mouth, and it will discourse most eloquent music.'

Just as the stage directions of the plays require music (instrumental and vocal) to provide incident, diversion, and atmosphere, so references to music in the spoken text help to define the moods, disposition, and social status of the characters. Cassius, an evil man, 'hears no music'; Brutus, his opposite, loves it. Indeed, how should a right-minded man *not* respond to music, since music was held philosophically to be the expression of cosmic nature herself? Lorenzo in *The Merchant of Venice* is allowed to put the point with poetic inspiration:

> There's not the smallest orb which thou behold'st
> But in his motion like an angel sings,
> Still quiring to the young-eyed cherubims:
> Such harmony is in immortal souls;
>       . . . . .
> The man that hath no music in himself,
> Nor is not moved with concord of sweet sounds,
> Is fit for treasons, stratagems, and spoils;
> The motions of his spirit are dull as night
> And his affections dark as Erebus:
> Let no such man be trusted.*

Yet a member of the upper classes, for all his knowledge of music and practical skill in it, was not expected to perform in public. That would be not only to demean himself socially to the level of a 'fiddler' (a term already denoting a shabby professionalism) but also to indicate social over-indulgence instead of proper moderation. 'Much music marreth man's manners,' wrote Roger Ascham (1515–68), who had been tutor to the young Elizabeth. Desdemona may sing the *Willow song* in the private company of her maid; but that Ophelia should sing uninvited before a court assembly is a sign of her mental derangement. When Malvolio comes to rebuke Sir Toby Belch and Sir Andrew Aguecheek for their

---

*Lines included in Vaughan Williams's *Serenade to Music*, Oxford University Press, 1938.

noisy merry-making, he does so in terms of social distinction:
'Do ye make an ale-house of my lady's house, that ye squeak
out your coziers' catches without any mitigation or remorse
of voice?' ('Coziers' are cobblers; a catch is a round, often
with bawdy double meanings.)

In an earlier scene Sir Toby thinks to recommend Sir
Andrew by saying that he 'plays o' the viol de gamboys', but
Maria takes this as no recommendation at all. Nor, apparently, would the audience have done. An addiction to
playing solo on the bass viol (which is the instrument meant)
is, in the literature of the period, the sign of a nincompoop, if
John Manifold's entertaining study of the matter is correct.*

Shakespeare's contemporaries are equally free with
musical allusions. In *The Knight of the Burning Pestle*, dating
from about 1610 (usually ascribed to Beaumont and
Fletcher, but possibly the unaided work of Francis Beaumont), a citizen and his wife are listening to some 'act music'
(i.e., a musical interlude between the acts of a play):

'The fiddlers go again, husband.'
'Ay, Nell, but this is scurvy music! I gave the whoreson-gallows
money, and I think he has *not* got me the waits of Southwark. If I
hear them not anon, I'll twinge him by the ears. You musicians,
play *Baloo*!'
'Nay, good George, let's ha' *Lachrymae*.'

The references here deserve comment. The waits,
whose original function of giving warning by means of
musical signals had by then been superseded, were town
musicians whose services could be hired. The citizen apparently complains that deputy musicians of lesser quality
had taken their place! The reference to *Lachrymae* as evidently
a popular tune is illuminating. This (Latin for tears) was an
alternative name for the song *Flow, my tears* by John Dowland,
which seemed to have been first printed (pirated, without the
composer's consent) in 1596.

In Shakespeare's own works, similarly, there are many
references to types of songs and dances and to actual titles of

* *The Music in English Drama from Shakespeare to Purcell*, Rockliff, 1956.

songs – including the most famous 'Elizabethan' song of all. 'I would have sworn', says Mistress Ford of Falstaff in *The Merry Wives of Windsor*, 'his disposition would have gone to the truth of his words; but they do no more adhere and keep place together than the Hundredth Psalm to the tune of *Green Sleeves*.' In fact *Greensleeves* (as it is now usually spelt) may be older than Elizabeth's reign. The well-known words admittedly date only from 1580, but they were evidently set to the already existing tune which had circulated orally – and continued to do so. As to the tune itself, a private manuscript copy of an arrangement for lute dates from 1594, though it seems never to have reached print until nearly a century later – in 1686, in the seventh edition of *The Dancing Master*, one of John Playford's popular collections (see p. 134).

Other popular airs of Elizabeth's time are likewise known to us from arrangements, or variations, designed for the lute or the virginals. *Go from my window*, *The Carman's Whistle*, *Fortune my foe* (mentioned in *The Merry Wives of Windsor*), *Sellinger's round*,* and *Walsingham* are all examples of such songs varied for the virginals by William Byrd (1543–1623); *Go from my window* and *Walsingham* are also among the works chosen for variations by John Bull (1563–1628). Most such pieces for virginals remained in manuscript, the most famous manuscript collection being the Fitzwilliam Virginal Book (297 pieces by various composers) named after Viscount Fitzwilliam, 1745–1816, into whose hands it came, and not published till 1899. Also notable, and also available in modern editions, are *My Lady Nevill's Book* (42 pieces by Byrd) and the *Mulliner Book*, consisting of 123 keyboard pieces by Tallis and various other composers and 11 further pieces for cittern and gittern – two different types of plucked-string instrument, the former flat-backed, the latter an early form of guitar.

---

*Not a round in the sense of a perpetual canon for voices, but a round dance. In 1953 six English composers, at Benjamin Britten's invitation, wrote chamber-orchestral variations on this tune in Byrd's harmonizations. In the following year Michael Tippett extended his composition into a *Divertimento: Sellinger's Round* for chamber orchestra.

When the first *printed* collection of such music came out, its novelty was attested by its title: *Parthenia, or the Maidenhead of the first music that was ever printed for the virginals* (1612 or 1613). The pun on 'maidenhead' ('Parthenia' in Greek) and 'virginals' was doubtless intentional, though the name 'virginals' apparently comes from the Latin *virga*, a rod or jack – and certainly does not refer to the Virgin Queen, since it pre-dated her reign.

The 21 pieces contained in *Parthenia* are by Byrd, Bull and Gibbons, and form a miscellany of dances, fantasias (contrapuntal pieces, sometimes foreshadowing fugal style) and preludes (pieces usually devoted to brilliant, ostentatious scale passages). Bull's keyboard pieces, often very difficult to play and with some modern-seeming touches in the harmony, constitute his chief fame. Rapid scale passages (often, it must be admitted, giving an impression of busyness and dexterity rather than of anything more deeply musical) are frequent. Also characteristic not only of Bull, but of this period of English music in general, is the use of *cross-relations* between the parts: for example, F sharp in one part is heard against F natural in another. On one pavan and galliard by Bull is the title or motto, *St Thomas Wake*, apparently an exhortation to Thomas à Becket! It is this pavan which is the basis of Peter Maxwell Davies's *St Thomas Wake* (1969), a 'foxtrot for orchestra'.

It should be added that this John Bull is *not* the original of the archetypal figure of the original Englishman (18th century) – though, in this patriotic connection, it is amusing that a piece of his has been alleged (inconclusively, since the manuscript is lost) to be an early minor-key forerunner of the tune of *God save the Queen*.

Byrd is as important a composer for the virginals as Bull. His *Pavan: the Earl of Salisbury*, found in *Parthenia*, has a grave eloquence of melody which has made it the best known of all Elizabethan keyboard pieces. Yet Byrd is altogether a greater figure, touching almost every available type of music and touching it with genius. He wrote many rounds and canons to exercise his ingenuity and delight the sociable performer:

the well-known *Hey ho, to the greenwood* is certainly his, *Non nobis domine* less certainly ascribed. For the virginals he wrote dances, variations (the frequent title *A ground* indicates variations on what we now call a ground bass, i.e., a repeated tune in the bass), fantasies (including some of the *In nomine* type) and even a curious early specimen of illustrative music, 15 movements collectively called *The Battle*, including 'The burying of the dead' and 'Galliard for the victory'. He wrote fantasias and other works for a consort of viols.

Himself a Catholic when the throne was Protestant, he nevertheless held the position of organist, jointly with Tallis, at the Chapel Royal from 1572, serving Elizabeth and then James I. He wrote for both Roman and Anglican worship. His Latin church music includes three masses (one each in three, four and five parts) and over 200 motets. Some of these are in the volume of *Cantiones sacrae* which he shared with Tallis (see above); others are in two further volumes of *Cantiones sacrae* (by Byrd alone, and this time actually so entitled) and two entitled *Gradualia*; still others remained in manuscript in his lifetime. His Anglican church music includes a 'great' service and over 60 anthems, of the two kinds then evolving – the *full anthem*, for choir throughout, the organ being used (if at all) only to double the voices; and the *verse anthem*, in which solo voices alternate with chorus, and in which the organ (or sometimes stringed instruments) has an independent part.

In 1588 he brought out his collection of *Psalms, Sonnets, and Songs of Sadness and Piety*, all for five voices. They are not madrigals: they are, as Byrd's own preface says, solo songs originally conceived for a voice with viols and now with the words fitted also to what had been the original viol parts. Many of the pieces in Byrd's late sets (*Songs of Sundry Natures*, 1589; *Psalms, Sonnets and Songs*, 1611) are also of the nature of solo and accompaniment. Some others, while genuinely polyphonic (voices of equal importance), are of a style deriving from conservative English tradition and do not belong to that newly fashionable, Italian-derived form, the madrigal.

Italian madrigals seem to have been known in England well before the publication of the two famous volumes which anglicized them: *Musica transalpina* (1588) edited by Nicholas Yonge (Young) and *Italian Madrigals Englished* (1590) edited by Thomas Watson. Each of those volumes, in addition to 'transalpine' (Italian) madrigals with English words, had room for two works by Byrd. His contributions to the 1588 collection go at least part of the way to the Italian style and those in the 1590 collection are, exceptionally for Byrd, real madrigals – a six-part setting of *This sweet and merry month of May* and another four-part setting of the same text.\*

What, then, is a real madrigal in English music? It is a work composed in the characteristic tone-painting manner of the Italian madrigalists, set to English verse which was itself indebted to Italian example. The extent to which Italy furnished general models for Elizabethan culture has already been noted. Not only Spenser but such other poets as Sir Philip Sidney, Samuel Danyel and Michael Drayton wrote sonnets and other love poetry in a style emulating the Italians (generally known as the Petrarchan style). English composers, it is true, generally neglected these major writers, but they set their madrigals to lesser poetry of the same type, some of it directly translated or imitated from the Italian. The music follows the sense of the poem, in emotional terms or by direct illustration (a high note for such a word as 'heaven', a duet section when 'two' is mentioned); the voices are balanced in contrapuntal equality, and a given musical phrase will recur from one part to another. Moreover 'you must not make a close (especially a full close) till the full sense of the words be perfect'.

The quotation in the last few lines comes from *A Plain and Easy Introduction to Practical Music* (1597), the most famous treatise of its time, written by Morley himself, the 'founder of

---

\*The four-part setting is included in *The Penguin Book of English Madrigals, for four voices*, ed. Denis Stevens, 1967. A sequel, *The Second Penguin Book of English Madrigals, for five voices*, 1970, includes Morley's *Now is the month of maying*, referred to on the next page.

the English madrigal'.* Morley's two chief Italian models were Alfonso Ferrabosco (1543–88) who had three periods of residence in England, and Marenzio (see p. 75), the two composers mainly represented in *Musica transalpina*. Morley adapted Italian terminology to English use. In his treatise he makes it clear that the madrigal is essentially amorous in content ('for as you scholars say that love is full of hopes and fears, so is the madrigal or lovers' music full of diversity of passions or airs') and that it is essentially a *serious* kind of music. To a lighter kind of music of the same kind he gave the name of *canzonet* (after the Italian *canzonetta*, literally little song): unlike the madrigal proper, the canzonet may repeat sections of the music, even though this lessens its close observance of the meaning of the text. Generally still lighter in tone was the *ballet* or *ballett* (to avoid ambiguity, the second form is now preferred), which was strophic in form (the music completely repeated for each verse), often with a *fa-la* refrain. Although the original Italian term, *balletto*, indicates that the music was to be danced to, the practice seems not to have been known in England.

It is true that between the terms 'madrigal' and 'canzonet', and between 'canzonet' and 'ballett', distinction is not always rigid. But it will be clear that Morley's celebrated *Now is the month of maying*, for instance, is purely a ballett, not a madrigal at all. Morley's own taste was predominantly for lighter vocal style, a fact which in some degree accounts for the relative popularity of his work, both then and now. His work in other musical fields should not be overlooked. He was enrolled in 1592 as a Gentleman (i.e., an adult singer) of the Chapel Royal, perhaps combining this with the post he already held as organist of St Paul's Cathedral, and his church music includes a famous setting of the Anglican burial service; but his chief lustre lies in his madrigals and similar pieces.

Moreover, he inspired others. It was he who shepherded

*Joseph Kerman, *The Elizabethan Madrigal*, Oxford University Press, 1967 – the American book which has made everything previously written on this subject out of date.

together 23 other composers to contribute pieces to the anthology which stands as a monument of the English madrigal school, *The Triumphs of Oriana* (1601). It was modelled on a famous Italian madrigal anthology of the previous decade, *The Triumph of Doris*: as each madrigal of that anthology had ended 'Viva la bella Dori!' so those of Morley's compilation ended 'Long live fair Oriana!'. Oriana was Queen Elizabeth,* the anthology being a tribute to her, with a dedication to one of her court favourites, Lord Howard of Effingham (the admiral who defeated the Spanish Armada; later created Earl of Nottingham). It has been conjectured that *The Triumphs of Oriana* may have been intended for public performance at a tournament or similar ceremony. Of Morley's own two contributions, one (*Hard by a crystal fountain* in six parts) is simply a re-working of an Italian madrigal by the Venetian composer Giovanni Croce (*c.* 1560–1609) – whose authorship Morley does not acknowledge, an attitude which was not necessarily considered reprehensible at the time.

Like other madrigals and similar works achieving published form, *The Triumphs of Oriana* was not printed in score (i.e., with the voice parts printed one below the other) but in part-books, each singer having his own book, which did not include the others' music. Some of Morley's *Canzonets for Five and Six Voices* (1597) had a novel feature: with the *cantus* (soprano) part was included a lute part which could replace all the other sung parts. This lute part was rather crudely prepared but it heralded a new type of vocal music soon to shine and flourish: solo songs with lute accompaniment (or, as it was then put, 'airs to the lute'). Shortly afterwards, in 1600, Morley himself brought out one of the earliest English collections in this form, *The First Book of Ayres or Little Short Songs, to sing and play to the lute with the bass viol.* (The spelling *ayre*, used here by Morley, has been adopted in modern times

---

* The ingenious attempt by Elizabeth Cole (in *Choral Music*, ed. Arthur Jacobs, Penguin Books, 1963) to identify Oriana not with Elizabeth but with Anne of Denmark, Queen to James I, cannot now be sustained.

to specify this form, though it was not a consistent use of the period.) This volume includes *It was a lover and his lass* – presumably a setting written for the original production of *As You Like It*, probably about 1600.

We have already seen that it was no new thing for a viol to take the place of a voice in concerted music or (see the case of Byrd, p. 88) vice versa. Compositions were often described as 'apt for voices or viols'. But the participation of the lute marked a new relationship between soloist (voice) to accompaniment (lute). The accompaniment, in a single player's hands (whether that player was also the singer or not), was capable of a new responsiveness to the soloist's flexible style. The great practitioner of this new art – and he was a practitioner not only as a composer, but as one of the great lutenists of Europe – was John Dowland (1563–1626).

Dowland's *First Book of Songs or Ayres of Four Parts, with tablature for the lute* was published in 1597. The songs were 'of four parts' – conceived, that is, as four melodic lines, which could therefore be sung by the appropriate voices. Unlike the separate part books of the madrigal, lute songs were printed with all parts in a single book – not like a modern score, however, but in such a way that an open double page would present the parts facing different ways for four singers round a table. Under the uppermost part was printed the lute accompaniment, in tablature. (This term indicates the special way, different from staff notation, of writing and printing music for lute; the word also alludes to various systems of notation for other instruments, using letters, numbers, or graphical illustration as in modern guitar notation.) Dowland's publisher, anxious evidently to secure the widest appeal for the work, also specified two possible alternatives for the lute – the orpharian (a kind of cittern, see above) and the viola da gamba (meaning in this case the bass viol, playing from the lute tablature and encompassing the harmonies as well as the bass line).

To have a solo voice singing to an independent instrumental accompaniment – this was the distinctive new idea. At first it was as an alternative to part-singing, but in his

*Second Book of Songs or Ayres* (1599) Dowland included some which are set only for solo singer and lute (without further vocal parts). His *Third and Last Book of Songs or Ayres* came out in 1603, but a fourth book is in effect constituted by *A Pilgrim's Solace, wherein is contained musical harmony of three, four, and five parts to be sung and played with the lute and viols* (1612). His mastery lies in the appeal of his tunes, the expressiveness of the lute accompaniments and, often, the aptness of the music to the words – though the music which admirably fits a first stanza may be repeated for a second stanza not quite the same in mood or verbal accent.

It happens that in *Lachrymae* or *Flow, my tears* the words of the second stanza so agree with those of the first, and Dowland's musical skill illumines such phrases as 'Flow my tears, fall from your springs' (verse 1) and 'Down, vain lights, shine you no more' (verse 2). Starting with the two stanzas mentioned (AA), the complete form is AABBC, but Dowland's forms vary from pure stanza repetition (AAA . . .), as in *I saw my lady weep*, to a song with no repetitions at all save a kind of motto at the end: *In darkness let me dwell*. An analysis of smaller detail would probably reveal his songs as no less varied than Schubert's.

His professional success was immediate. The early fame of *Lachrymae* we have already noted (p. 85) and many composers paid it the tribute of variations. He travelled in Italy and Germany and secured an engagement with King Christian IV of Denmark at an exceptionally high salary. Pieces composed by him for viols and for lute appear in French and German collections of the period. In England the sonnet by Richard Barnfield beginning 'If music and sweet poetry agree' compares him with Spenser. Dowland was one of the composers who contributed to the collection of hymns and metrical psalms brought out by an amateur composer, Sir William Leighton, in 1614 under the title *The Tears or Lamentations of a Sorrowful Soul*. Among the other 18 contributors were Bull, Byrd and Orlando Gibbons.

Like Byrd and Morley, Gibbons was an all-rounder; but he seems to have been inclined to what his contemporaries would have called 'the graver sort of music' as naturally as Morley was to the lighter. For 19 years he was organist of the Chapel Royal, then for the remaining two years of his life organist of Westminster Abbey. His impressive production of music for the Anglican rite includes, among his full anthems, the eight-part *O clap your hands together* (re-used for the coronation in Westminster Abbey of Queen Elizabeth II in 1953) and the jubilant six-part *Hosanna to the son of David.* Of his verse anthems some are with string (instead of organ) accompaniment, including *This is the record of John.* The use of verse technique in this sense (that is, of solo passages) is also found in the second of Gibbons's two services.

The new vogue for what were effectually solo songs, which we have seen pioneered by Morley and Dowland, apparently did not attract Gibbons. His only set of *Madrigals and Motets* (1612) was styled as 'apt for viols and voices', after the old manner. All its contents are five-part and include the famous *The silver swan,* as well as *What is our life* and *Dainty fine bird.* They are hardly madrigals (in the Italian sense used above) or motets as the word is usually understood, but dignified part songs of the earlier tradition practised by Byrd. *The silver swan* follows the musical form ABB, common in the lute song. Gibbons's skill in keyboard music, exemplified in *Parthenia* (see above), is paralleled in his fantasies and other works for consort of viols. He is also one of the composers who wrote curious, amusing vocal fantasies weaving together the *Cries of London* – the words, the the vocal inflexions, of street-traders and beggars.

Apart from joining with voices, the family of viols had become the recognized medium for what we should now call chamber music. The phrase 'consort of viols' indicates a chamber-music combination usually of treble, tenor and bass viols (roughly corresponding in pitch to the modern violin, viola and cello). Consorts were also made of different-sized recorders, and even of transverse flutes. But these occupy a lesser place: at any rate a smaller quantity of original music was written for them. The term 'broken consort' indicates a mixture of, for instance, viols and wind instruments.

Another composer who set the *Cries of London* was Thomas Weelkes (*c.* 1575–1623), a composer especially celebrated for his madrigals, the best-known of which, the six-part *As Vesta was from Latmos Hill descending*, formed his contribution to *The Triumphs of Oriana*. His contemporary, John Wilbye (1574–1638), was almost exclusively a madrigalist – and, some authorities would say, the greatest of them all. *Sweet honey-sucking bees* (five-part) is his most famous. Among other composers represented in *The Triumphs of Oriana* are John Bennet (dates uncertain), whose contribution was the sprightly and delightful *All creatures now are merry-minded*; Michael Cavendish (*c.* 1565–1628), Robert Jones (?–1617), and Francis Pilkington (*c.* 1562–1638). The last three also wrote ayres of distinction, as did Thomas Campion (1562–1620, also notable as a poet), John Danyel (*c.* 1565–*c.* 1630, brother of the poet Samuel Danyel), and Philip Rosseter (1568–1623).

Giles Farnaby (*c.* 1560–1600) brought a highly individual gift to both vocal and instrumental music. His canzonets (light madrigals) sometimes overstep contemporary rules of harmony; his virginal pieces sometimes show a quaintness in their titles (*A Toye; Giles Farnaby's Dream*) and in the music itself. Characteristic of the time are his florid, yet neat and steady-rhythmed, variations for the virginals on the folksong *Loth to depart*. More than 50 of Farnaby's pieces are in the Fitzwilliam Virginal Book – a sufficient sign of his stature. It is to be noted that, although such composers continued to write for the virginals as a solo instrument, this period has left us only one English example of a composer recommending a keyboard accompaniment to songs: Martin Peerson (*c.* 1580–*c.* 1650) in his *Private Music* of 1620. Generally the consort of viols, and later the lute, were judged appropriate.

Perhaps only half of the works discussed in this chapter were printed at the time, yet the spate of printing alone (plus the references to music in general works) suggests a sudden and substantial permeation of English society by new, diversely composed secular music. A famous passage in Morley's *Plain and Easy Introduction to Practical Music* exposes the supposed plight of any gentleman cut off by ignorance from fashion:

> But supper being ended, and music-books (according to the custom) being brought to the tables, the mistress of the house presented me with a part, earnestly requesting me to sing. But when, after many excuses, I protested unfeignedly that I could not, everyone began to wonder. Yea, some whispered to others, demanding how I was brought up . . .

As this is part of the author's attempt to sell his wares, so to speak, modern authorities are disposed to see in it a little of the advertiser's exaggeration. Yet its general relevance to some conditions is clear: we know too that it was not unusual in barbers' shops to find a cittern (the flat-backed instrument mentioned above, p. 86) hung on the wall so as to be available for impromptu music-making by waiting customers.

Not merely the spate of composition, but the welcome which such composition met in society, has led to the labelling of Elizabethan (and post-Elizabethan) England as a golden age. Discounting mythological parallel, let us merely record again that then, but never again till our own day, English musicians were internationally recognized as equal in skill and leadership with composers anywhere. It is a judgement which still stands among non-British historians, who regard it as part of a larger social phenomenon: 'The same accumulation of intellectual and artistic force that produced Sidney, Shakespeare, Bacon, Donne and Inigo Jones also produced Morley, Weelkes, Dowland, and Orlando Gibbons.'[*]

[*] Gustav Reese, *Music in the Renaissance*, Dent, 1954.

# 7
## The Coming of Opera

THE English diarist John Evelyn (1620–1706), being in Venice in 1645, found it necessary to provide his fellow-countrymen with a definition of a new art form:

> Comedies and other plays represented in recitative music by the most excellent musicians vocal and instrumental, together with variety of scenes painted and contrived with no less art of perspective, and machines for flying in the air, and other wonderful notions. So, taken together, it is doubtless one of the most magnificent and expenseful diversions the wit of man can invent.

This was *opera*, a word now to pass from Italian into world usage. At first, however, 'opera' was not the normal Italian term: it means, properly, a *work*, not necessarily in the musical sense. The classical Italian term for the new art form is *melodramma*, i.e., a drama to melody, and certain of the first works bear the equally expressive description of *favola in musica*, a story in music. The full title of Monteverdi's *Orpheus* of 1607, the first opera by the first great composer of opera, is given in the printed version of the libretto as *La favola d'Orfeo rappresentata in musica* (the story of Orpheus represented in music).

Representation and recitative: Evelyn picked on two essentials here. The representational aspect of the music was much the concern of the composers themselves. As for 'recitative', the word is not French, despite its current bogus-French pronunciation in English: it is an English word on the analogy of *narrative* and translates the Italian *recitativo*, from *recitare*, to act. Recitative music enables the singer to declaim expressively (as an actor does) the lines of a drama: at any rate in its Italian origins, it derives its rhythms from the words and is not tied to strict musical metre. It forms a single-line melody and is supported by harmonies considered simply as chords, not as the combination of other simultaneous melodies.

That musical expression should be concentrated on the power of a single line of melody to express feelings indicated by words, instead of on the combinations of many melodies together (in which the expression of the words must compromise with the needs of counterpoint) – this clearly parallels the transition from the madrigal to the lute song, described in the last chapter. Giulio Caccini (*c.* 1545–1618), as one of the earliest composers of opera, was also well known in his day for his songs of this kind, two of which were introduced to England in 1610 in the cosmopolitan collection *A Musical Banquet*, edited by Robert Dowland (*c.* 1586–1641; son of John Dowland and likewise a composer and lutenist). Single-line melody of this kind (whether in recitative or in the more regular form of aria or lute song), accompanied by chords, bears the technical name of *monody* – from the Greek words for single and singing.

Caccini was a singer and composer in service to the court at Florence (where the Medici family had by this time become hereditary grand-dukes). He was one of a circle of connoisseurs who discussed the possibility of creating a musical drama in the spirit of ancient Greek tragedy. From the deliberations of this circle (known as the Camerata, and meeting at the palace of Giovanni De' Bardi, Count of Vernio) opera as we know it began. It was not without ancestry. Some short dramatic scenes of the 'nymphs and shepherds' variety (belonging, that is, to the favoured category of poetry called *pastoral*) – had already been set to music for performance as interludes (*intermezzi*) in plays presented at court festivities and the like. Music for such festivity has already been described (p. 71).

We have already stated (p. 72) why Vecchi's *The Amphiparnassus*, published at Venice at about this time, is not to be regarded as a forerunner of opera. Opera was conceived in Florence alone – though one of its first manifestations took place in Rome. There, in 1600, a drama on a religious allegorical subject, in which formal solos, choruses, dances and instrumental numbers were linked by recitative, was staged under the auspices of a religious society. This was *The*

*Representation of Soul and Body* by Emilio De' Cavalieri (*c.* 1550–1602), himself a member of the Camerata. It is to be considered the first example of Roman opera, often to be influenced in subject or treatment by the dominant presence of the papacy. The allegorical subject, derived from the old mystery plays, was an acknowledgement of Rome's spiritual rule. But in general the subject of opera was classical, not Christian.

Thus the myths of Daphne (pursued by Apollo, and metamorphosed into a laurel) and of Eurydice (to recover whom, Orpheus descended into Hades) were pressed into service by the Camerata to provide the plots of the earliest Florentine operas. They were given private performances in noble society, with some noblemen participating among the singers and instrumentalists. *Daphne* (*Dafne* is the Italian spelling), composed by Jacopo Peri (1561–1633) was performed in 1597: only the literary text, not the music, survives. Peri's *Eurydice* (1600), the first opera of which the music has come down to us, includes certain numbers composed by Caccini; Caccini also set the whole of the same libretto himself, his work receiving a performance two years later.

Though choral and purely instrumental sections had their place, the dramatic and musical essence of early Florentine operas was expressed in an almost endless recitative. Dull as it tends to look on paper today, such music moved its original hearers and must have been performed with an intense expression of individual words and phrases. The ends of such phrases (in both the musical and literary sense) were written in longer notes than the rest; a singer could dwell on such a point and create a special emotional intensity.

This style of musical composition, in which the rise and fall of the melody and the qualities of musical expression serve only to *represent* the feeling conveyed by the words, is called the representational style (*stile rappresentativo*). The accompaniment, being now considered subsidiary, and formed not out of melodies but only of chords, was now written down in a new way. In the part provided for a keyboard player or lutenist, only the bass note was written on the stave, the upper notes being worked out by the player. Caccini wrote in the preface to his *Eurydice*, dedicated to De' Bardi:

After composing the fable of Eurydice to music in *stile rappresentativo*, I felt it part of my duty to dedicate it to your illustrious lordship, whose especial servant I have always been and to whom I find myself under innumerable obligations. In this work your lordship will recognize that style which, as your lordship knows, I used on other occasions many years ago. ... [Here Caccini names a pastoral intermezzo and other pieces.] The harmony for the reciting parts in the present *Eurydice* is supported above a *basso continuato*. I have indicated the most necessary fourths, fifths, sixths and sevenths, and major and minor thirds, for the rest leaving it to the judgement and art of the player to adapt the inner parts in their places. The notes of the bass I have sometimes tied, in order that the note may not be struck again during the many passing dissonances, with offence to the ear.

What Caccini here calls *basso continuato* (continued bass) is now called *basso continuo* or just *continuo*. Caccini's harmony is indicated by reference to the bass, the figure 3 in conjunction with the bass note C (for instance) indicating the interval of a third above (E) and 10 indicating the tenth above (the E an octave higher). But soon a simplified convention was established by which 3 indicated an E in *any* octave above (a third, a tenth, etc.) at the player's choice. This is the convention that henceforth obtained right through the music of the next 250 years and is still used for scholastic purposes today, a bass line bearing figures being known as a *figured bass*.

In such a type of writing the bass line itself acquires a special importance, greater than that of any inner parts. Although a single harpsichord or lute *could* suffice to fill the functions of such a continuo, a combination of instruments was often preferred. At the first performance of Peri's *Eurydice* two kinds of lute and a *lira grande* (a bowed instrument) combined with the harpsichord to interpret the continuo part, and there were no independent instruments.

Monody, representational style, continuo – all these

aspects of the new way of composing music contrast with the strictly contrapuntal style of the Italian madrigal as we considered it in chapter 5. Yet the greatest of the composers in the new style still retained the term 'madrigal' for a concerted vocal piece, even with the addition of independent instrumental parts (that is, different from the vocal lines and a continuo bass). He was Claudio Monteverdi (1567–1643) who explicitly labelled the old and new style as first practice and second practice (*prima prattica* and *seconda prattica*). In the first practice the music is mistress of the poetic word; in the second, the poetic word is mistress of the music.

Composing a great diversity of music (see also next chapter, p. 118) Monteverdi did not give up using the first practice where he considered it appropriate, for instance in some of his masses. But he let the second practice progressively invade his madrigals. The first four of his books of madrigals (he published nine such books, besides other collections) are without a continuo part. The fifth book (1605) is set 'for voices with *basso continuo* for harpsichord, chitarrone [a large, lute-like bass instrument] or other similar instrument': and whereas most of the 19 madrigals in this book require the instrumental bass only to double the vocal bass, the last six give the bass line to the instrument only. In the remaining books Monteverdi went further in writing independent instrumental parts (not only as a continuo) to join with the voices or sometimes to perform as an ensemble on their own.

The word 'madrigal' was by now obviously being used as an envelope for whatever vocal-instrumental forms Monteverdi produced. In his seventh book he took the opportunity of publishing a ballet (danced, to both vocal and instrumental music) on the pastoral theme of *Thyrsis and Cloris* (*Tirsi e Clori*). In the sixth book occurs a madrigal-setting (for four vocal parts plus continuo) of the famous *Lament of Ariadne*. In its original form, occurring in Monteverdi's opera *Ariadne* (in Italian, *Arianna*) of 1608, the same music is cast in the form of a solo song with continuo. The link between new opera and new-old madrigal is clear.

The music of *Ariadne* is nearly all lost, except for this

lament. *Orpheus* not only survives but has, in our historically conscious twentieth century, re-entered the living opera house. Produced in Mantua, where Monteverdi served the reigning ducal family, it not only employs the expressive flexibility of recitative but also the architectural strength of formal arias, choruses, orchestral *ritornelli* (intermediate or recurring passages) and dances. It is typical of the classical vogue of the time, to be seen also in contemporary literature and painting, that the rise of the curtain is followed by a prologue sung by the Spirit of Music, and that the opera ends with an apotheosis in which Orpheus ascends to heaven in company with Apollo – their short, florid duet being followed by chorus, *ritornello*, and dance.

In certain respects even Monteverdi's printed score cannot tell us exactly what the original audiences heard. The parts for the continuo instruments are, of course, not written out in full and must be newly realized (worked out) for a modern performance. Marks of expression are generally lacking. We are not sure how far the singers would have ornamented their parts at their own discretion or at the composer's personal direction. We have an actual example of the extent of such possible alteration – for the composer himself wrote out an alternative and specially embellished version of the aria in which Orpheus (tenor) challenges the resistance offered by Charon (bass), the ferryman of the Styx.

The printed score valuably lists the instruments used at the first performance – and a striking array it makes, especially in contrast to the mere continuo of the earlier Florentine operas. Recall that at this period there was no such thing as a regular orchestra – an orchestra of standard size and proportions playing a standard repertory. Assemblies of instruments had to depend on local resources, local finance and the imagination and demands of composers (usually directing performances of their own works). For *Orpheus* Monteverdi assembled two harpsichords, two pipe-organs, two *chitarroni*, one regal (reed-organ), and two double-bass viols (all the foregoing being continuo instruments, used in various combinations), ten violins and two higher-pitched, small violins, three bass viols, a recorder, two cornetts, four trombones, and four trumpets (playing ceremonious, fanfare-like music, and accompanied by a kettledrummer – though, as is customary, no part appears for him in the written score).

For Mantua too Monteverdi wrote that short dramatic work which partakes of the characteristics of both opera and ballet, *Il Ballo dell'ingrate* – the dance of those ladies who are ungrateful or unkind in refusing the delights of love. As a punishment they have been consigned to Pluto's kingdom, and the work depicts Cupid's arrival to discover how they are faring there.

But it was after his move to Venice, where he was appointed musical director of St Mark's Cathedral in 1613, that Monteverdi's dramatic gifts rose to their greatest height. Though declining as a political power, Venice knew no decline in the lavishness of its festivities public and private, for which money was furnished by Venetian notables and rich foreign visitors. Later in the century public entertainments were even offered in convents. Musical performance was an essential expression of such pomp and festivity, and Monteverdi's position at St Mark's (something of a state church, as we noted in reference to Willaert on p. 76) made him the city's chief musician.

In 1624, at a Venetian nobleman's palace, Monteverdi produced his *Combat of Tancred and Clorinda*. Tasso's epic of the Crusades, *Jerusalem Delivered*, is the source of the text. Hero and heroine (Christian Crusader, Saracen girl-warrior) are both armed, the former on a horse, and the only other character is a narrator. In this short dramatic work, contributing further to that expressive use of music which we have recognized as being at the root of opera, Monteverdi introduced what he described as an innovation – the 'excited style' (*stile concitato*), marked by quick repetitions of a note. History preserves Monteverdi's own recollection of the performers' hostility: 'At first the musicians, especially those who had to play the basso continuo, thought the playing of a note 16 times to the bar was more ridiculous than praiseworthy.'

In 1637 in Venice, for the first time anywhere, opera ceased to be entirely a private diversion and acquired a public, paying audience. Or, to be more exact, for the first time a noble family founded a theatre and admitted the public to parts of it, still reserving the boxes for the nobility. More and more such theatres were founded, Venice boasting 16 by the end of the century. With broader audiences the more showy qualities of Italian opera were destined to become more prominent: in particular, more emphasis was laid on aria (a regular tune), less on recitative. The beginnings of this are already evident in the two surviving operas composed by Monteverdi for the new type of theatre: *The Return Home of Ulysses* and *The Coronation of Poppaea*, from 1641 and 1642 respectively.

A minority of scholars have questioned whether the former score is Monteverdi's at all; and it can in any case hardly rank with *Poppaea*. The heroine of the latter (Poppaea in correct Latin, Poppea in Italian) is the mistress of the Emperor Nero, exalted above the legitimate empress against the advice of the philosopher Seneca, who kills himself. Deities (Mercury, Cupid) and allegorical characters (Fortune, Virtue) participate, but their presence only emphasizes by contrast the naturalness and indeed sensuality of the human characters. The recitative maintains continuous yet contrasted dramatic flow, and the solos and duets are straightforwardly melodious and regular. Especially notable are Seneca's farewell to his disciples, Nero's rejoicing on the death of Seneca, and the final love-duet. A further contrast of musical styles is prompted by the insertion of comic material for servant characters. The chorus now becomes less important – and indeed in Italian operas of later in the century is usually dropped altogether, except for an occasional battle-cry and the like.

Italy being still at this period a multiplicity of states, operatic history is itself multiple, proceeding along different social and musical lines. In Rome two operatic composers of some importance at this period were Stefano Landi (*c.* 1590–*c.* 1655) and Luigi Rossi (1597–1653), who also wrote an

*Orpheus.* But papal authority did not always smile on opera, and its chief centre remained Venice. A particularly prolific and successful composer of operas there was Monteverdi's pupil, Pier Francesco Cavalli (1602–76). In his own time the most celebrated of his 41 works was *Jason* (*Giasone*) of 1649; but the two works chosen for modern revival at Glyndebourne (1967, 1970, in somewhat altered editions by Raymond Leppard) were *Ormindo* (this hero, rather exceptionally, boasts no mythological or classical origins) and *Callisto* (the title-role is that of a nymph and the story is from Ovid). In the cheeky page of the former work, with his comments in song on the corruptions of the society round him, we recognize a typical 'comic opera' element of the future. Cavalli typifies a tendency for Italian opera in the seventeenth century to become more attached to *musical* regularity, less to a detailed dramatic expression of the words. The contrast between the mainly recitative operas of the early 1600s and the total victory of the aria in Alessandro Scarlatti (see p. 119) about 1700 is striking.

The spread of opera outside Italy has two aspects: the exporting of Italian works, usually sung in Italian by Italians, and the attempted founding of other national types of musical drama. Not surprisingly, since the Austrian Empire bordered on the Republic of Venice, the Venetian example spread quickly to Vienna: Monteverdi's *Ulysses* and Cavalli's *Aegistheus* (*Egisto*) were performed there as early as the 1640s, and Italian opera was particularly encouraged by four successive Austrian emperors between 1637 and 1740 who all composed such operas (or parts of them). Heinrich Schütz, who had left his native Saxony to study in Venice under Giovanni Gabrieli, and paid a second visit to Venice while Monteverdi was working there, not only brought back the new Italian concerted manner of music (see next chapter, p. 117) but himself composed the first German opera, *Daphne* (1627), of which the music is lost. The text is a German adaptation of the libretto originally written in Italian for Peri's Florentine setting, 30 years before.

While in England:

Think this your passage, and the narrow way,
To our Elysian field, the Opera –
Tow'rds which, some say, we have gone far about
Because it seems so long since we set out.

These lines were uttered (can 'opera' really have been pronounced 'operay'?) at a kind of public lecture-recital in costume in London in 1656. The author, Sir William Davenant (appointed poet laureate in succession to Ben Jonson in 1637), was alluding not only to the awkward surroundings of that particular performance but to the fact that he had tried to establish opera some years before. The essential element of recitative was not new in England: it had been composed to English words as early as 1617 by Nicholas Lanier (1588–1666) in Jonson's *Lovers Made Men* – which, as a masque, combined the pleasures of music, acting, dance and scenery. But only now was it harnessed to a full-length and fully dramatic work, *The Siege of Rhodes*, produced in 1656 and generally reckoned the first English opera.

The story was 'sung in recitative music', according to the title-page of the printed libretto – meaning that recitative, instead of spoken dialogue, connected the various songs and choruses. The score, now lost, was jointly written by Henry Lawes (1596–1662), Matthew Locke (*c.* 1630–77), Henry Cooke (*c.* 1615–72), Edward Coleman (?–1669) and George Hudson (dates unknown).

The words were by Davenant himself, and it has been plausibly suggested that he had not originally conceived the work as an opera at all. Under Cromwell, who had constituted himself lord protector in 1653, the public theatres had been closed on puritanical grounds. Davenant wished to have them reopened, and found a musical version of his text more acceptable to authority than the spoken one he had originally planned. His piece succeeded, but it was significant that when it was revived in 1661 (by which time it was not necessary to include music as a gesture of theatrical respectability) a second part was added with hardly any music in it. It seems that the English were to prefer their operas diluted.

Such dilution – that is, the text not all sung, but partly in spoken verse – was duly provided by Locke in his *Psyche* of 1675, with some additional music by an Italian, Giovanni Battista Draghi (1640–1710). Ten years later no less a figure than Dryden failed with an attempt at all-sung opera, *Albion and Albanius* – a failure mainly ascribed to inferior music, insensitive to English words, by the French composer Louis Grabu. More success attended Dryden in a 'diluted' opera – or, to use the term which has now become accepted for this type of work, a semi-opera – *King Arthur* (1691). The composer was Henry Purcell (1659–95), who had already written *Dioclesian* (1690) in this semi-opera category and was to follow with *The Fairy Queen* (1692), *The Indian Queen* (1695) and *The Tempest* (?1695). (The last of the five acts of *The Indian Queen* is by Purcell's not untalented brother, Daniel, *c.* 1663–1717; and it appears possible that *The Tempest* is not by Henry Purcell either – perhaps by John Weldon, 1676–1736.)

In *King Arthur*, Arthur only speaks and does not sing. In such semi-operas song is the utterance of supernatural characters, or purely subservient ones, while choruses, dances and orchestral interludes are employed to heighten the impressiveness of a spectacle or to provide pleasant diversion. Purcell's individual numbers in *King Arthur* are of a masterly quality. Among them are the solo and chorus 'How happy the lover' (the descending ground-bass in a minor key, even to 'happy' words, is typical), and the famous *Fairest Isle*; and amid the refined taste of the whole we may be pleasantly shocked by the rollicking jollity of the *Harvest home*. Because of the loose structure (*King Arthur* does little credit to Dryden as dramatist or as poet) this music goes largely to waste in the present-day musical world - unless we accept Colin Graham's ingenious remodelling of the work (for the English Opera Group in 1970) in more conventionally operatic form. A similar barrier of taste surrounds *The Fairy Queen*, which is based on *A Midsummer Night's Dream* yet sets none of Shakespeare's words to music.

Useless to conjecture whether Purcell, had he not died at

36, would have imposed his musical personality more strongly on the English theatre. On the stage today he lives only in *Dido and Aeneas* – his only all-sung opera (less than an hour in duration) and untypical because it was destined not for the public theatre but for a girls' school in Chelsea (1689). The librettist was Nahum Tate. Here too a descending ground-bass in a minor key provides the technical structure of the famous lament, *When I am laid in earth*. In that aria of Dido's, no less than in the jollity of *Come away, fellow-sailors*, and in the vigorous expressiveness of the recitative, *Dido and Aeneas* marvellously weds melody to the English tongue. It detracts nothing from this work to indicate its indebtedness to a court masque, *Venus and Adonis*, composed by Purcell's teacher, John Blow (1649–1708), and performed about 1684.

By this time England was undergoing operatic influence from a nearer quarter than Italy. Charles II, restored to the throne in 1660, after spending some years of his exile in France, had formed his musical taste on French models. Directly emulating Louis XIV, he established a band, the Twenty-four Violins (that is, violins and lower-pitched members of the violin family), to play at the Chapel Royal. Louis Grabu, later to be the composer of Dryden's ill-fated *Albion and Albanius*, became director of music at the English court. The king sent his favourite young English composer, Pelham Humfrey (1647–74) to study in Paris (as well as in Italy). No wonder that French dance rhythms show clearly in the music of Humfrey's great pupil, Purcell. Of Charles II the great eighteenth-century musical historian, Charles Burney, was to write: 'The passion of this prince for French music changed the national taste.'

Locke's *Psyche* of 1673, already referred to, was prompted by a work of the same name presented at the French court two years before. The composer of this 'tragedy-ballet' was Lully; the words were the combined work of Molière, Corneille, and Lully's favoured operatic librettist, Quinault. Such names are enough to remind us of the quality of the French theatre, both spoken and musical, in the era when Louis, the 'Sun-King', drew all the most radiant talents into his orbit. He was the direct patron and benefactor of Molière's company and the godfather of one of Molière's children. He gave a pension to Corneille and made Racine his historiographer royal. Louis had been only five years old when he mounted the throne of France in 1643; he was apparently still in his teens when he took a fancy to the young, Italian-born Lully. He made him a member of the Twenty-four Violins (the court orchestra, soon to inspire Charles II's imitation) and then founded for him a special string orchestra at court (Les Petits Violons, the little violins) which soon overtook the fame of the senior body.

By origin Lully was a Florentine, born Giovanni Battista Lulli in 1632. He was taken to France in boyhood and placed in service (at first as a scullion, so we are told) to Mlle de Montpensier – 'La grande Mademoiselle', cousin of Louis XIV. An excellent violinist, he also seems to have acquired uncommon skill in the subtle art of court intrigue. He composed music for the court ballets, and danced in them – as did the king himself. He collaborated many times with Molière: in fact, the latter's famous *Le Bourgeois gentilhomme* (The Would-Be Gentleman) of 1670 was originally styled not a play but a comedy-ballet. In 1672, ousting the previous holders, he contrived to acquire even a royal monopoly of operatic performance. Then began the astonishing process by which this Italian upstart (for so his French fellow-artists must often have called him) did more than anyone else to lay the foundations of French opera. A contemporary whom he displaced, Robert Cambert (*c.* 1628–77), had to retire to London.

Lully's 14 all-sung serious operas were called by him sung tragedies (*tragédies-lyriques*) – suggesting a parallel to the spoken tragedies on lofty dynastic subjects, with which Racine succeeded (and Molière failed). Though the operas customarily began with a prologue glorifying Louis XIV himself, they were not court operas but were performed to the paying public of Paris.

Lully won, and kept, his public. From frequent performances, audiences were sometimes able even to join in singing some of the tunes, as we know from first-hand accounts. So firm was Lully's achievement that France was to remain the only western country with a strong indigenous operatic tradition, capable of withstanding the otherwise all-conquering Italian opera of the early eighteenth century. In place of the *recitativo secco* or *dry recitative* of the Italians (in which the voice is partnered only by the continuo instruments) Lully standardized the *accompanied recitative* – accompanied, that is, by full orchestra. Both here and in his arias (more closely interwoven with recitative than in Italian opera) he took pains to achieve a properly accented, dramatic declamation of the French language at a time when that language was receiving (from Molière, Corneille, and Racine) its classic dramatic expression in the theatre. He retained chorus and ballet as important elements of opera. He established the *French overture*, consisting of a slow movement with dotted rhythm, followed by a quick movement in fugal style (sometimes with a slower-paced ending). Purcell, Bach and Handel all took up the model.

The resultant type of opera was a serious, monumental type of entertainment. Comic elements were excluded in the later examples. Though he owed a debt to such Italians as Cavalli, he left French opera bearing his own, strongly characteristic imprint. He exerted his royally appointed monopoly to make sure that he would have no competition: in 1673 other theatres were forbidden to employ more than 'two voices and six violins' in any performances. Yet his mastery was musical, not merely legal. Under him French opera took over from ballet the character of spectacular entertainment (a stage performance in French is *un spectacle*) but acquired a devotion in its vocal part to dramatic truth rather than musical dazzle. It is an emphasis which was to be carried on by Rameau, Gluck, Cherubini, and Berlioz.

The last of his operatic collaborations with Quinault (1686) was *Armide*. This opera is based on the same Italian epic of the Crusades (Tasso's *Jerusalem Delivered*) which had provided the text for Monteverdi's *Combat of Tancred and Clorinda*. In 1687 Lully died of an abscess, caused by accidentally striking himself on the foot with a long staff used for beating time. It is ironic that this dictator of music at one of the most splendid courts known to history survives in the experience of most music-lovers as the composer of one song, *Bois épais* ('Dense wood, redouble thy shade . . .', from the opera *Amadis of Gaul*, 1684) and of one simple little ditty which has achieved the supreme immortality of being generally shorn of its composer's name: *Au clair de la lune*.

Whether at the court of Louis XIV or before the dignitaries of republican Venice or in the Restoration theatre, opera had one constant concomitant: visual astonishment, in splendid perspective, clever machinery and other prodigies of stage-craft. This was an age of great engineering (Vauban, the 'genius of fortification', was also in service to Louis XIV) and the operatic stage presented a kind of instant engineering obedient to the canons of art.

John Evelyn on his Italian trip wrote of 'Cavaliere Bernini, a Florentine sculptor, architect, painter and poet, who . . . gave a public opera (for so they call those shows of that kind) wherein he painted the scenes, cut the statues, invented the engines, composed the music, wrote the comedy and built the theatre all himself.' This was the Bernini (not really a Florentine, but born in Naples) who designed the baldachino of the new St Peter's, Rome – a work which commands the adjective often given not merely to opera in its first emergence but to the whole period 1600–1750 in music: *baroque*.

# 8

## Baroque: The Italian Roots

'BAROQUE', says the guide in St Peter's, Rome, as he points to Bernini's pillars, twisted as though groaning under their weight. In painting and architecture the term denotes a certain flamboyance and extra energy of style, which in its grander manifestations seems to stun the spectator's senses by sheer pomp and splendour. In some cities – for instance in Prague, to which the style was brought by Italian architects as a deliberate manifestation of the Counter-Reformation – the confident exhilaration of the new style hits the spectator with the force of a fanfare.

Borrowed from the art historians, the word 'baroque' has been attached to music of approximately 1600–1750 – that is, from Monteverdi's day to that of Bach and Handel. It does not denote one style of composition (in the sense that we talk of Bach's style or Wagner's style); nor could we expect such a unity to spread across a period that embraces both Shakespeare's plays and Gray's *Elegy in a Country Churchyard* (1751). Yet certain ideas on the philosophy and the construction and the performance of music were widely shared over this period.

Baroque became international, but its origins were Italian. At this time, in music, instruments were elevated to an importance previously almost monopolized by the voice; and of the instruments special favour was given to the violin, the possessor of a strength, range, and flexibility of articulation which the voice might envy. The baroque violin is not our modern violin in all details; strung with gut (at a lower tension than today's), played with only occasional vibrato and with a bow of different shape, its sound must have been in several respects different. But it was a violin, not a viol; it had the violin's capacity for both soulful and brilliant music. The great centres of violin-making from the mid sixteenth century had been Brescia and Cremona in north Italy, and now the latter city was to bring forth the work of Nicola Amati (1596–1684), the long-lived Antonio Stradivari (?1648–1737) and Giuseppe Guarneri (known as Guarneri del Gesù, 1698–1744) – the most famous members of their respective families of makers.

In this era the orchestra emerges, its positive loudness or massiveness of tone being achieved by multiplicity of instruments, often several to a part. The orchestra performs with voices (but not just doubling the vocal parts) or on its own: it is heard in the opera house, sometimes in churches, in special institutions like the orphanage-conservatories of Venice (see p. 142), or as an element of diversion or festivity at a royal, noble or similar establishment. String tone, in particular that of the violin family, becomes recognized as the basis of the orchestra, with woodwind, brass and percussion variously added. It is this constitution which distinguishes the orchestra from certain previous combinations – military or processional wind-and-percussion bands, or the instrumental groups disposed at opposite ends of St Mark's, Venice, to play the music of Giovanni Gabrieli (see below, p. 118). The orchestra, string-centred, achieved its greatest discipline and its chief fame at the Paris Opera under the command of Lully.

As to individual instruments, there were a few notable improvements during 1600–1750 – particularly the improvement of the transverse flute and the virtual invention of a new instrument, the oboe; but in general the composer's stock of instrumental and vocal resources remained broadly similar, and likewise the relation of composer, performer, and listener. Although print was now the common medium of diffusion in music (pieces were printed even if only for presentation to a patron), the print did not confer on a composer an absolute, detailed authority: marks of expression were only partially adequate, performers might select or omit movements at choice, and performers were indeed *expected* to add ornamentation and cadenzas in appropriate style at the recognized points.

As in earlier times composers were always performers too.

Some became specially famous as performers – among them the organist Girolamo Frescobaldi (1583–1643) and the violinist Arcangelo Corelli (1653–1713), as later Bach and Handel. Increased virtuosity of performers matched the baroque urge to an ever more expressive and stunning music. Composers wrote to fulfil a specific commission or a general demand, or to provide instructional material for their pupils. They were in some sense servants, craftsmen or entertainers, certainly not oracles possessed of a divine message. They wrote for their present audiences – but not always the same one. In addition to the still-dominating musical demands of princely and clerical establishments, those of a new public were beginning to be felt.

There were the audiences at the new public opera houses; there were private associations of middle-class music-lovers (often called an academy or collegium musicum); there were city councils requiring music for civic ceremony. Short pieces in the nature of lessons or exercises (words often used for the actual titles of such pieces) could serve the amateur in an age when 'lover of music' and 'performer for the love of it' were virtually synonymous. The public concert properly so called (open to all on payment at the door) also made its first appearance in this period, though only to a modest extent. The first such concerts seem to have been those organized in London by the violinist John Banister in 1672; Germany did not follow until some 50 years later (Hamburg, 1722); nor Paris till 1725. Churches, however, served in many cities as auditoriums of music for a general and numerous public. Frescobaldi is claimed by a chronicler to have drawn 30,000 people to hear him play the organ in St Peter's, Rome.

Technically, the baroque period is also the period of the *continuo*. As we have seen (p. 100) the continuo is a continuous bass line which governs the harmony of the music. In an ensemble the harpsichordist, organist, or lutenist would perform the written bass line and supply the harmony to it which he worked out from known rules, with or without the help of a figured bass. Where a cello or bass viol, a bassoon, or choral bass voices participated in the ensemble, they were generally put to reinforcing the continuo bass line.

Yet the continuo is not (as some accounts seem to suggest) what *makes* baroque; it is a sign or manifestation of it. It is not even a universal sign, since it does not apply to solo music (for keyboard or lute or violin) when a single texture incorporates melody, bass, and harmonization. Moreover there are such works as Corelli's duos for a violin and a bass instrument which do not specify that the filling-in of harmonies by a keyboard instrument is a necessity: the bass line is allocated to a keyboard instrument *or* a violone (a double-bass rather smaller than the present-day one), and the latter must have played only the bass line, without any supporting harmonies. What makes such music essentially of the baroque is its antithesis between treble and bass (usually the treble is florid, the bass more slow-moving) and this in turn is an example of the baroque delight in contrasting planes within one piece of music, whether between treble and bass, between voices and instruments, between spatially separated groups of performers, or between successive movements in different rhythm and tempo (the suite of dances; the toccata and fugue).

Compare two apparently quite dissimilar pieces of music from the beginning and end of our baroque century-and-a-half: the prelude to Monteverdi's *Orpheus* of 1607 and the Sanctus of Bach's *Mass in B minor* from the late 1740s. The one begins an opera, the other is ecclesiastical; the one is instrumental only, the other sets to music the words of a prescribed religious text. Monteverdi writes an extended fanfare: there is no real harmonic progression, the one major chord being maintained throughout. Bach's harmony begins to move immediately. But both pieces, being exultant (the one to give a festive opening to an operatic occasion, the other to express 'Holy, holy, holy is the Lord God of Hosts'), convey the mood by employing the same characteristic dotted rhythm, repeated over and over again.

In both cases three trumpets convey (both in their actual melodies and in the ceremonial and symbolic associations of the instruments) the same exaltation – and, because of the availability of notes determined by the construction of the instrument, both pieces are sounded in the same key, D major. The rest of the orchestral space is occupied mainly by the homogeneous sound of the strings–or to be more precise, of the violin family, which by Monteverdi's time had almost (not quite) ousted the earlier, less powerful viols. Rhythmically both pieces convey a single, firm and regular beat, avoiding the simultaneous cross-rhythm of the preceding madrigal age. Both pieces evoke splendour and power: Monteverdi bids us take sensual pleasure in the major chord and the trumpets' decoration of it; Bach invites us to feel awe in the broad octave-tread of the bass line.

Thus rhythm, melody and instrumental tone colours all help to represent an emotion or mood. Monteverdi's claim actually to have originated a musical symbol for the mood of excitement has already been noted (p. 103). By Bach's time theorists had attempted to codify the proper musical devices for expressing the different passions or *Affekten*, as the German philosophical term has it. (The English word *affection* is sometimes used to translate this, in such a case having the sense simply of a feeling.) In such ways musicians and theorists of other countries took over the baroque from Italy. We deal in the next chapter with this phenomenon, and reserve for a later chapter a consideration of five major figures of the late or high baroque – Bach, Handel, Domenico Scarlatti (all born in 1685), Vivaldi, and Rameau – devoting the rest of the present chapter to Italy in the seventeenth century.

That century saw the establishment not only of opera but of its kindred form, oratorio, and of sonata, cantata, symphony, overture, concerto, toccata, prelude, fugue. All these terms (or their foreign-language equivalents) were in current use by 1700. Though the meanings were not in all cases the same as those of today (especially the sense of 'symphony'), they lead naturally to our present usage. The musical language and concepts of the baroque are still with us: to most listeners baroque music sounds more modern (that is, more readily appreciable, and emotionally more powerful) than the music of before 1600. The Benny Goodman band of the

1930s (with Alec Templeton's *Bach Goes to Town*), the Swingle Singers and the Moog Synthesizer in the 1960s all attached themselves to Bach, not Byrd.

One reason is that it is the first music to establish tonality as the basic element of musical structure. True enough that well before 1600 most music begins to present itself as being in one of our major or minor keys. But only after 1600 do we find, as the chief and most frequently encountered structural scheme, a progress from one key to another and back, sometimes with diversions of key on the way. Thus the various structural features of the piece (its emotional climaxes, its division into sections, its repetitions and quasi-repetitions) are made to depend on the hierarchy of keys in relation to the home key (that in which the piece begins and ends).

Some of the music written even before 1600 has this strong sense of key structure: we have already noticed it in Marenzio's madrigals, for instance (p. 75). But, conversely, some music composed after 1600 still lacks it. If we ask why, for instance, a keyboard piece by Frescobaldi seems to wander in comparison with one by Bach or Domenico Scarlatti, the reason is perhaps that Frescobaldi's journeying from one key to another does not seem driven by the kind of purposive motion by which the later composers progress strongly towards a final key. Frescobaldi's toccata No. 11 (from his first book of toccatas, partitas [variations] and other pieces, 1637) is such a wandering piece. Or, considering the overall shape of a piece in several movements, we may contrast a Corelli sonata, having all movements in the same key, with a Bach or Handel sonata, where the later composer engages our emotions with a shift to a different key in the middle movement, and then a return.

The term '*concerto*' had not yet achieved its somewhat exclusive nineteenth-century and present-day meaning. Like its adjective '*concertato*' (the two words corresponding, like our English 'concert' and 'concerted'), it indicated an ensemble of instruments playing independent parts in the new style. The *concerto grosso* (literally, large concert) and the *trio-sonata*, both to be discussed below, are works of this kind.

But a work for instruments *and voices* may also be described as 'in *concertato* style', and may even be called a concerto, provided that the instrumental parts are independent and do not, as in the pre-baroque style, double the voices. In this sense the concertato style invaded the church. True, composers sometimes wished to write in the older style, without independent instrumental parts, but in such a case they did so with the consciousness that it was an older style – the first practice rather than the second practice, to use Monteverdi's terms.

Had Monteverdi composed no opera, he would still be notable for his infusion of the new concertato style into the madrigal (the last five of his nine books of madrigals require independent instrumental accompaniment); for his church music in the same, deliberately new style; and for his innovations in harmony, with a freer use of discord and of chromatic harmony (the use of notes outside the key) for the purpose of a more passionate expression. A similarly adventurous treatment of harmony (perhaps indeed still more audacious, though less skilled) is shown in the madrigals of the famous 'musician and murderer', Carlo Gesualdo, Prince of Venosa (*c.* 1560–1615), though these have no independent instrumental parts.

The most famous of Monteverdi's church compositions is his *Vespers*, published in 1610, in which solo voices, chorus and orchestra are combined to give precisely that effect of decorated splendour which seems most typical of the baroque in music. Cornetts and trombones are required, and recorders and flutes, as well as strings and at least one organ; and bassoons would normally have been brought to strengthen the bass line, though Monteverdi did not write special parts for them. Although Monteverdi was at this time still employed at the ducal court of Mantua (his appointment to the musical directorship of St Mark's, Venice, was not to come till 1613), the *Vespers* employ the characteristically Venetian twofold choir, one body of singers and instrumentalists answering the other, or both joining forces.

This Venetian style had found a distinguished exponent

in Giovanni Gabrieli (1557–1612), who worked at St Mark's in the lesser role of second organist. The famous *Sonata pian e forte*, from a set of works dated 1597, is not only one of the first compositions to specify soft and loud (*piano, forte*) but one of the first to specify mixed instrumental groups with exactitude: a group of cornett and three trombones contrasting with another of viola and three trombones. (Incidentally, Gabrieli dedicated this and other works to members of the international Fugger banking family, a sign of the new patronage by mercantile wealth rather than nobility.) Thomas Coryat, an English visitor, reported from Venice in 1608 on the delightful and unfamiliar sounds of St Mark's including 'ten sackbuts [trombones], four cornetts, and two *viole da gamba* of an extraordinary greatness'.

If it be wondered why Monteverdi, the first great composer of opera, did not touch its near relative, oratorio, the prosaic answer is perhaps that he did not work in Rome. Oratorio takes its name from the oratory in which Filippo De' Neri (St Philip Neri), the 'Apostle of Rome', conducted religious exercises with prayers and hymns in the vernacular tongue (instead of Latin). Neri died in 1595, but his Congregation of the Oratory, a community of priests, continued. It was for this organization that De' Cavalieri's *Representation of Soul and Body* was staged in Rome in 1600 (see p. 99). Only in the middle of the seventeenth century was oratorio, as we know it, established; that is, action was dispensed with and a narrator (*historicus*) employed instead. Such a work, composed about 1650, was *Jephtha*, by Giacomo Carissimi (1605–74). Fifteen other oratorios of his survive, mainly on Old Testament subjects, and all with texts in Latin; but De' Cavalieri had employed the vernacular, i.e. Italian, and it was again preferred by later composers such as Alessandro Stradella (*c.* 1645–82) and Alessandro Scarlatti (1660–1725).

Alessandro Scarlatti's son, Domenico (p. 143) was to be a virtuoso harpsichordist and chiefly a composer for that instrument. But Alessandro himself is chiefly famous as the composer of about 115 operas (some 50 are still extant, however rarely performed) and the establisher of Italian serious opera (*opera seria*) in what became its dominant eighteenth-century form – with lofty plots unbroken by comedy, with *castrato* (eunuch) singers for the leading male roles, and with *da capo* arias (first strain, contrasting strain, first strain again) as the main song pattern. Operas of this type, which was also to be Handel's chosen form, gave immense opportunities for vocal display – the singers freely indulging in variation and decoration of their melody, especially on the repeated section ending in a da-capo aria. Such works also managed to complement the composer's kingly and noble patrons by displaying monarchical virtue on the stage: Scarlatti's *Statira* (the heroine is the beloved of Alexander the Great) is an example from 1690.

At this time Scarlatti was musical director to the court of Naples, a region still held under viceregal rule by the declining empire of Spain. But he was apparently active in papal Rome too, for *Statira* seems to have been written for the festivities arranged on the occasion of two marriages in the family of Cardinal Pietro Ottoboni, one of the most wealthy and influential Roman patrons of the arts. In fact, Ottoboni was himself the librettist. In works like this Scarlatti helped to establish not merely a style of opera, but a style of melody and harmony called Neapolitan: much of what we think of as Handelian style really stems from here.

Scarlatti, and Stradella and Carissimi too, also contributed notably to opera's other near-relative, the Italian cantata. Strictly '*cantata*' in Italian means nothing more than a piece that is sung (as '*sonata*' means a piece that is sounded or played): but the term '*cantata*' in Italian usage at this period meant an extended work on a dramatic subject for a solo voice (or occasionally for two or more soloists) with accompaniment of continuo (occasionally for a small instrumental ensemble in addition).

Like the opera, the cantata proceeded by recitative, aria, and *arioso* (a section sung in regular metre, but without the regular form of an aria); and the subject was also operatic (the singer taking the character of a historical or mythical personage, or a nymph or shepherd). But cantatas were always works for concert performance, never for the stage: they were happily classified by Charles Burney, the eighteenth-century English musical historian, as 'narrative chamber music'. An important early practitioner of the form was the Roman composer Luigi Rossi (see p. 104). Alessandro Scarlatti standardized the form into two recitatives and two arias, and himself wrote about 600 such cantatas.

A prolific and skilled composer of opera, oratorio and cantatas (one of which, for two female voices, describes a card-game), was the Venetian, Antonio Caldara (1670–1736), who became vice-conductor of the Austrian emperor's musical establishment in Vienna. Absorbing the Venetian love of rich texture, the new Neapolitan harmonic style of Scarlatti, and the fluent string technique of Corelli (see below), he was among the first to write masses in what we may call operatic style, as a succession of solos, duets and choruses with full orchestral accompaniment. This is indeed the Viennese style of church music such as we encounter in the *Nelson Mass* and similar works by Haydn (see p. 184).

Like the cantata (sung piece), the sonata (sounded or instrumental piece) now took on a more precise meaning. Previous usage had been loose: Giovanni Gabrieli's *Sonata pian e forte* had been published as part of a set of 'sacred symphonies' (he used the Latin term, *Symphoniae sacrae*). Often 'sonata' or 'sinfonia' had indicated an instrumental prelude or interlude in a predominantly vocal work. Later in the seventeenth century, however, the *sonata* was usually an independent instrumental piece, commonly for two, three, or four instruments. Unlike the old canzona (see p. 77), it was not even theoretically designed as a contrapuntal piece: it was for melody instruments (top) plus continuo (bass).

The sonata for a single melody instrument plus continuo is found as early as 1617 in a Venetian publication by Biagio Marini (*c.* 1595–1665) which bore the general title of *Affetti musicali* (musical passions). But this form was less frequently cultivated in the seventeenth century than the trio-sonata – so-called because, although there were usually four performers, there were three lines of music.* The two upper, equally weighted voices were usually given to violins, and the bass line was performed both by a melody instrument (usually bass viol or cello) and a keyboard instrument (which filled in the harmonies too on the regular continuo principle). Possibly the first practitioner of the form was Monteverdi's contemporary at Mantua, Salomone Rossi (c. 1570–c. 1630; not to be confused with Luigi Rossi, above) – a Jew, exempted through his art from the stigma of the yellow badge imposed on Jews in Italy at this time. Rossi also wrote madrigal-like settings of Jewish liturgical texts in Hebrew.

The duchy of Mantua was devastated by a war of succession in 1628–31; the great musical patronage extended by the reigning Gonzaga family was finished. Bologna, by contrast, was a university city in the papal dominions: here the church of San Petronio acquired an exceptional reputation for its instrumental accompaniments, based on the newly fashionable violin family. Here Corelli went as a boy to study the violin.

In a series of publications from 1681 Corelli proved himself one of the great figures of musical baroque. He wrote both trio sonatas and 'solo' sonatas; he also pioneered the concerto-grosso form, later so widely cultivated. All these forms feature a contrast of fast and slow movements. All are to be classified, according to the custom of the time, as either 'for the chamber' (da camera) or 'for the church' (da chiesa). 'Chamber' works include movements with dance titles, such as saraband, jig and gavotte. In the 'church' works (written to enhance the occasion of a service – not, of course, as a setting of the ritual words) the movements bear no such titles, though the rhythm and style of dances can sometimes be heard. In the solo sonatas a highly developed technique of violin playing is demanded: Corelli, requiring great agility in rapid passages and a soulful utterance in slow tempo,

*On this analogy the sonata for single melody instrument and continuo ought to be called a duo sonata. It is customarily, and confusingly, called a solo sonata.

seems to have transferred to the violin the style of Italy's own instrument, the human voice. His solo sonatas include a famous set of variations on a favourite theme, of apparently Portuguese origin, known in Italian as the *Follia* (also employed by various other composers – though the tune to which Frescobaldi applies the name *Follia* is, exceptionally, a different one).

The *concerto grosso* is the first specifically orchestral form. (Handel's English examples were published as 'grand concertos' which is perhaps a good English equivalent.) The term implies an orchestra, and, in social terms, this in turn implies an establishment where an orchestra is maintained. The concerto grosso, if of da-chiesa type, would mark the status of the prince's chapel: if da camera, would entertain his guests. The *Christmas Concerto* by Corelli (1712) includes a movement in that gently rocking 6/8 time which had already come to be a symbol of pastoral repose. (There are examples also in Alessandro Scarlatti, and even earlier in Frescobaldi.) This is the rhythm and melodic style which Handel was to reproduce in the 'Pastoral Symphony' in *Messiah*, Beethoven in the last movement of his symphony No. 6 (the *Pastoral Symphony*), and Berlioz in the 'Shepherds' Chorus' of *The Childhood of Christ*.

The concerto-grosso form normally implies the division of the musical material between a small group of instrumentalists (*concertino*, little consort) and a larger group (*ripieno* or *concerto grosso*: this latter term is sometimes applied to the large instrumental group, sometimes to the piece itself). In Corelli's examples ripieno and concertino divide the music between them, but the instruments of the concertino do not behave like soloists (as we should say), playing more difficult music. That differentiation is evident, however, in the music of Giuseppe Torelli (1658–1709), who not only wrote concerti grossi but also concertos for solo violin and orchestra. As against Corelli's favoured scheme of four movements, Torelli preferred three (fast-slow-fast) and moreover based many of his movements on the ritornello principle – the use of an identifiable recurring section. In the next chapter we shall note a widespread adoption of this formal plan.

However, Corelli's is the famous, Torelli's the obscure name – both to their own time and to posterity. Pirated editions of Corelli's music (there being in those days no assured legal copyright, national or international) appeared in Amsterdam and London, testifying to its popularity. In Rome, where most of his music was originally published, Corelli was a leading performer at the palace of Cardinal Ottoboni (see p. 120). The young Handel, more than 30 years Corelli's junior, also won the protection of Ottoboni when he visited Rome; he absorbed Corelli's influence and may be assumed to have met Corelli himself.

By such visits, as well as by the journeys abroad of Italians themselves (the transformation of the Florentine Lulli into the Parisian Lully has already been noted) and the publication of music, the baroque style was exported from Italy to become an international musical favourite.

# 9

## Baroque Exported

IN German-speaking countries, from the independent
merchant city of Hamburg in the north to imperial Vienna;
in England under the Stuart kings and the Commonwealth;
in France under the Sun-King, Louis XIV – in all these countries, and elsewhere, the new baroque taste in music spread
from Italy. In France the new ideas were absorbed and
developed into a characteristically new national style, so
strong that French baroque (dominated first by Lully, then
by Rameau) itself became an article of export. As German
princes and princelings based their palaces and manners on
the emulation of Versailles, so they required the elegance of
French dance music and the special style of the French
overture (see p. 110).

The new style, in its international developments as well as
in its origin, may be said to be rooted in three things: the
violin, the orchestra (by itself, or with independent parts as
an accompaniment to voices) and the opera (also, especially
in France, the ballet). As experts in all three, Italian
musicians continued to voyage abroad and to take posts
there. A fascinating map in Paul Henry Lang's *Music in
Western Civilization** reveals the penetration of these Italians
as far west as New Orleans in Louisiana, as far east as St
Petersburg (which by then had taken Moscow's place as
capital of Russia). Under the Empress Anna (reigned
1731–40), Russia was to gain its first permanent court
orchestra and to see its first visiting Italian opera company.

Nearer conquests naturally came first, cemented not
merely by the travels of the Italians but by the visits of
foreign musicians to Italy. The Thirty Years War (1618–48),
though it brought massacre and impoverishment to individual cities and particular regions of Germany, was by no
means a total war in the modern sense and did not halt the

* Dent, revised edition, 1965.

new artistic developments. Thereafter the new centres of power became the chief nurseries of musical activity, as also of science, philosophy, literature and painting. The most important city of north Germany was (and still is) Hamburg, where the first German stock exchange had been founded in 1558 and which had replaced Antwerp as the leading North Sea port; somewhat to the east, Lübeck was beginning to suffer from the competitive rise of Denmark and Sweden as military and commercial powers, but at least escaped the ravages of the Thirty Years War and continued prosperous.

In middle Germany the dominant state was traditionally Saxony, with Dresden as its capital and Leipzig as its leading industrial and university city. Saxony's rival (and ultimate destroyer) was Brandenburg–Prussia – its capital being Berlin, where Italian opera and French ballet were first presented at court during the reign of Frederick I (reigned 1688–1713, father of Frederick the Great). The Austrian emperor maintained his splendid court in Vienna, and his victory over the Czechs at the Battle of the White Mountain (1620) extended his direct rule to Bohemia: all Czech (Bohemian) cultural, as well as political, independence was crushed, and German remained the only official language at Prague until 1860. Bohemian musicians, stifled for expression at home, later underwent a dispersal almost as remarkable as the Italian, fulfilling decisive, individual roles in European music: Gluck (p. 165) and the Stamic family are the most famous examples.

We turn now to the early influence of Italian baroque on German composers. At Leipzig in 1618 and 1626 the German composer Johann Hermann Schein (1586–1630) published collections of concerted settings of Lutheran texts with the Latin title *Opella nova* (little new works) and a German subtitle which we may translate: 'Sacred concertos in the Italian manner customary nowadays'. The same composer, publishing a suite of dance pieces for viols, gave it the Italian title of *Banchetto musicale* (*Musical Banquet*: compare Robert Dowland, p. 98). Heinrich Schütz (1585–1672), the greatest German composer of the period, went to Venice, studied there with Giovanni Gabrieli, and brought out a collection of five-part Italian madrigals as his first published work. On the model of the double chorus used at St Mark's, Venice, he set the *Psalms of David* (1619) in German for multiple choruses, solo singers, and instrumentalists playing independent (concertato) parts. To Schütz's German opera, *Daphne*, I have already referred (p. 105); he also used the form of a dramatic scene for some of those concerted works he called by Gabrieli's title, *Sacred Symphonies* (*Symphoniae sacrae*) – comprising an early volume to Latin texts, and two later volumes in German.

Although Schütz published no purely instrumental works, he rivals Bach in emotional power and exceeds him in variety of vocal forms – from madrigal and opera to oratorio and passion (one setting of each of the four Gospel versions, in German). Alongside the *Christmas Oratorio* (*The Story of the Joyful and Merciful Birth of God's and Mary's Son, Jesus Christ*) and the Easter oratorio (*The Story of the Joyful and Victorious Resurrection of our only Redeemer and Saviour, Jesus Christ*), may be placed *The Seven Words of our Dear Saviour and Redeemer Jesus Christ, Spoken by Him on the Cross*, an oratorio-like setting with narrator. In contrast to the magnificently complex psalm-settings of 1619 already referred to, there are the calvinistically plain psalm-settings of 1628.

Schütz lived to the age of 87 (a revealing portrait of him in old age survives) and his long working life spanned the Thirty Years War (1618–48) with its Catholic–Protestant enmity. He was a Protestant who took part in the germanizing of the liturgy: his *Musical Exequies* (*Musikalische Exequien*) are explained as a 'concert in the form of a German funeral mass'. Yet he was nevertheless able to compose for a Catholic prince a collection of 41 four-part Latin motets (some of them to words of St Augustine) under the title of *Sacred Songs* (*Cantiones sacrae*): these stand with assured poise between the severity of the old church style and the emotional expressiveness which Schütz had brought home from Monteverdi's Italy.

Schütz's music lacks one feature which, thanks to our acquaintance with Bach, we now regard as characteristic of German Protestant church music: the incorporation of *chorales* (Lutheran hymn-tunes) into the musical texture. Such employment of chorales was, however, practised by some of Schütz's contemporaries including Schein, Franz Tunder (1614–77) and Tunder's son-in-law Dietrich Buxtehude (*c*. 1637–1707), who succeeded Tunder as organist at Lübeck, becoming his son-in-law in the process. The evening musical performances (*Abendmusiken*) held by Buxtehude in his church on the Sundays preceding Christmas were famous, and Bach as a youth of 20 is said to have walked more than 200 miles to hear them. Buxtehude's *The Last Judgement*, written to be spread over five *Abendmusiken* in 1683 (22 years before Bach's arrival!), is in effect an oratorio which makes use of chorales, and contrives to preach a Christian message by an operatic personification of Avarice, Pride, Lust and so on.

If Italy gave German composers an unchallenged inspiration for vocal music, France was beginning to provide instrumental models. Such German composers as Georg Muffat (*c*. 1645–1704) borrowed the French name of '*ouverture*' for their orchestral dance suites, where the dances proper were preceded by a movement in the style of the French overture established by Lully – not only in his operas. Four such ouvertures (today more usually called orchestral suites) were later to be written by J. S. Bach, in whom the absorption of both Italian and French models is apparent.

Music for woodwind and brass consorts, forming the municipal bands of some German cities, also survives from this period. Among the composers of such music, Johann Christoph Petzold or Pezel (1639–94) was both a violinist and a trumpeter, for some time in municipal employment at Leipzig. Saxony was Lutheran, and it was chiefly in the great churches of Lutheran cities such as Leipzig that the organ now acquired a new potential and the organist new importance – half virtuoso, half musician-of-all-work.

The German (and Dutch and Scandinavian) organ of

1650–1750 was a highly developed instrument of bright-toned, admirably balanced sound, with a pedal keyboard and two or sometimes three manuals: there was no *swell* (i.e. no crescendo, only a choice of louder or softer levels of tone) and little chance of swift changes of registration. It is this type of instrument, not a few examples of which survive in reasonably authentic condition, which is commonly thought of today as the baroque organ, so different from the nineteenth-century French or English types.

Cultivating the organ as a solo as well as a continuo instrument, the German composers continued to attend also to the harpsichord and the more intimate-sounding clavichord, suitable only for domestic use. These composers were almost invariably keyboard players themselves: the approximate identification of a German composer as an organist and the Italian as a violinist becomes understandable in the context of this time – though we shall note various exceptions. A composer particularly attracted to the clavichord's atmosphere was Johann Jacob Froberger (1616–67), who had been a pupil of Frescobaldi in Italy and who took the brilliant, 'improvisatory' form of the keyboard toccata and interlarded it with more solid contrapuntal passages – the model for the later (e.g. Bach's) toccata and fugue pattern. He was also among those Germans who (here following French rather than Italian models) wrote suites of dances for the harpsichord: the word '*partita*' is sometimes used by such composers to mean suite in this sense.

The first composer to apply the term 'sonata' to a solo keyboard piece seems to have been Johann Kuhnau (1660–1722). In this sense the sonata differs from the suite by not being in dance forms. Kuhnau's *Biblical Stories with a Construction in Six Sonatas* (1700) represent such Old Testament episodes as the combat of David and Goliath, and do so in a serious and not merely whimsical musical form. Heinrich Ignaz Franz Biber (1644–1704), a violinist-composer and the director of music at Salzburg Cathedral, similarly wrote sonatas for violin and keyboard instrument depicting episodes from the lives of Jesus and Mary.

In the fugue, usually for keyboard, German composers found a form which could combine old-fashioned contrapuntal intricacy (a theme chased by imitations of itself according to regular procedures) with the new structure based on key relationships. Among the industrious practitioners before Bach was Johann Pachelbel (1653–1706) with 94 short fugues, each to precede the singing of the Magnificat in church. He likewise wrote chorale-preludes – a type of work which in origin is exactly what its names implies, a *prelude* in which the organist introduced the hymn-tune (*chorale*), giving it a rather free musical treatment before the congregation sang it. In this form the hymn-tune is presented in its entirety only once, though often with the lines of the hymn separated by other musical matter.

Thus the *chorale prelude* is to be distinguished from the *chorale partita* in which the hymn-tune is treated simply as the theme of a set of variations – a form initiated earlier by such composers as Jan Pieterszoon Sweelinck (1562–1621) and Samuel Scheidt (1587–1684). Though Dutch, Sweelinck is in some sense the founder of the north- and middle-German organ school which reaches a culmination in J. S. Bach; and it should be likewise noted that Buxtehude, a master of both the chorale prelude and the chorale partita, was by origin a Dane.

In England Dowland had already (p. 92) composed melody-and-accompaniment music in true post-1600 (baroque) style rather than in the earlier, contrapuntal style. Yet some survival of the older musical traditions may be seen in the work of Byrd's pupil, Thomas Tomkins (1572–1656), who continued to write what are in effect madrigals and balletts – though in his publication of 1622 he simply called them songs. We may contrast these with the *Madrigals and Ayres* (published in 1632) by Walter Porter, furnished with instrumental 'toccatos [sic], sinfonias and ritornellos to them'. Porter (*c.* 1595–1659) is said to have been an English pupil of Monteverdi, and certainly here is Monteverdi's instrumental transformation of the old vocal forms.

In instrumental music the English tradition of fantasias for consort of viols was prolonged – for example, in the work of John Jenkins (1592–1678), William Lawes (1602–49) and Matthew Locke (*c.* 1630–77), formerly famous for music to *Macbeth* which is apparently not by him. William Lawes also wrote songs, some in the new declamatory style (called by English contemporaries recitative music – the word 're-citative' correctly used as an adjective). So did his elder brother Henry Lawes (1596–1662), celebrated in a sonnet by Milton.

The long-lived Jenkins in his later years cultivated the newer type of string music – trio sonatas for two violins and bass viol. It should be noted that in England as elsewhere, even after the brighter-toned violin had ousted the treble viol, the bass viol (viola da gamba) remained in use – both in consort and as a solo instrument, where it was frequently used for performance of elaborate variations or 'divisions'. Christopher Simpson (?–1669), a celebrated player and composer for the instrument, wrote a classic treatise called *The Division-Violist* in 1659. Another continuing English tradition was that of convivial rounds and catches, some-times (not always) to comic or improper words: John Hilton (1599–1657) was the compiler of the collection *Catch that Catch Can* (1652) which includes his own *Come, follow, follow me* . . .

Henry Purcell, the greatest English composer of the baroque, shows now the liveliest appreciation of new modes of expression, now the influence of the older, pre-baroque, equal-voiced contrapuntal style. His teachers were John Blow (see p. 108) and the short-lived, but greatly gifted Pel-ham Humfrey, composer of a fine solo setting of John Donne's *Hymn to God the Father*; from them and such contem-poraries as Locke and William Lawes, Purcell absorbed the declamatory or recitative style of vocal utterance which is found not only in his operas (see earlier chapter, p. 107) but in anthems, songs, and those short concert-dramatic pieces to which the Italian word '*scena*' is appropriately applied. *Saul and the Witch of Endor*, for soprano, alto and bass voices with continuo, is the best known. 'Alto' in this period of English music (and later) indicates the male alto voice, today still part of English cathedral establishments and known in other contexts as counter-tenor.

The aptness with which Purcell found a musical counterpart to the natural, spoken English tongue is famous: out of a thousand choices, we may instance his setting of the words 'Each dart his mistress shoots, he dies' at the end of the song *Anacreon's defeat*, or any of the conversational passages in *Dido and Aeneas*. But the music itself does not imitate speech in syllable-for-syllable setting (as, for instance, Mussorgsky, a great realist, liked to do). It expands into florid, expressive and even descriptive musical phrases: we may recall the setting in *Dido and Aeneas* of '*Darkness* shades me' in Dido's final lament and the Sorceress's 'to *storm* her lover on the ocean'. The latter occurs in a regular song, the former in an 'irregular' recitative, but the expressive language is the same, and the dotted rhythm of both is eminently baroque.

So is the *passacaglia* or ground-bass which is so characteristic of Purcell – not only in the operas, but elsewhere, for instance in *Now that the sun* (one of the hymns for solo voice and continuo, apparently included for private devotional use) and in the famous four-part *Chacony* for viols. The term 'chacony' is an English variant of *chaconne*, and one which composers seem to have used almost (but not quite) interchangeably with *passacaglia*. It is a musical form originally derived from a dance, in fairly slow triple time, and is musically based on the constant repetition of a single phrase in the bass covering several bars. It is thus a variation form – but different from the variations on a complete, given tune such as those written by Byrd (see p. 88). This *Chacony* of Purcell's, being written for viols, is apparently an early work and is to be linked with the fantasias and works entitled *In nomine* in which he continued the earlier (Elizabethan) tradition of contrapuntal string-writing – using a consort of viols without continuo.

Later he struck out in the new Italian manner with two series of trio sonatas, for two violins with continuo. The first series was entitled *Sonatas of Three Parts*, the second, *Sonatas of*

*Four Parts*, but the requirement for performance is the same: the first set considers the continuo as one part, whereas the second set recognizes that two instruments were employed to interpret the continuo – keyboard and cello (or bass viol). One of the trio sonatas (No. 6 in the second set) consists solely of a *passacaglia* which in its very key, G minor, recalls the earlier *Chacony*. Another of this set (No. 9 in F) is the so-called *Golden Sonata*: scholars know no reason for the name and give it no special preference over the other sonatas. For the 24-strong string orchestra which Charles II founded (on the example of Louis XIV) to play in the court chapel as well as in secular surroundings, Purcell wrote 21 anthems for solo voices, chorus, strings and continuo (organ). These, with their virtuoso solos and long, purely orchestral interludes, are likely to be considered decorative rather than devotional. John Evelyn in his diary considered the violins inappropriate, 'better suiting a tavern or playhouse than a church'.

Purcell's other anthems are not written in this new orchestral style but in an older style, mostly having only organ accompaniment; most have *verse* passages (that is, where one or more solo voices take over from the chorus). The funeral anthem *Thou knowest, Lord, the secrets of our hearts* (now part of the actual burial service of English cathedral usage) has no verse and its solemnity is emphasized by the participation of trombones as well as organ. A special category of Purcell's music is occupied by his ceremonial works (odes and welcome-songs): these were mostly written for the feast of St Cecilia (which began to be formally commemorated in London at this time) or for royal birthdays and other such occasions, and are a kind of secular counterpart to the anthems with strings. Like some others *Hail, bright Cecilia* (1692) requires what was then a large orchestra: oboes, recorders, trumpets, kettledrums as well as strings and continuo (harpsichord or organ).

Purcell also wrote eight suites (called *lessons*) for the harpsichord and a number of individual pieces or movements, one of which is *A New Irish Tune* (doubtless Purcell's arrangement, not his composition), better known today as *Lilli-*

*burlero*. Though he had been organist of Westminster Abbey, he left no important organ works: the English organ (lacking pedals) was little cultivated as a solo instrument and the English organist was not accorded the status of his German contemporary.

Ironically the best-known tune to which Purcell's name has been attached is not by him: the so-called *Trumpet Voluntary*, actually *The Prince of Denmark's March* by Jeremiah Clarke, written for harpsichord. Clarke (*c.* 1659–1707) was, like Purcell, a pupil of John Blow (1649–1708), whose own chief distinction – in what we should now, rather unfairly, call a Purcellian style – lay in church music, in some two-part motets to Latin words (which cannot have been intended, at this period of English history, for actual church use), and in his *Venus and Adonis*, already referred to (p. 108). Among other composers of English songs (both for the stage and otherwise) at this period should be mentioned John Eccles (1656–1735).

The chief London music publisher of this time was John Playford, in whose third book of *Ayres and Dialogues* by various composers (1676) a significant line appears which was not in the preceding book of seven years before. The music was described as 'being most of the newest ayres and songs, sung at court and in the public theatres'. The dominance of the court and the theatres over public taste could not be more precisely indicated.

In France the role of the court in musical patronage and in the setting of taste was no less decisive. Of Lully's employment by Louis XIV, and of his development of ballet and opera and his collaboration with Molière, I have already spoken in chapter 7. To celebrate the birth of the dauphin, or crown prince, in 1662, the king commanded a ballet in the square before the Tuileries Palace in Paris, attended by 15,000 people. When the dauphin became a young man with his own establishment, the musician appointed to his chapel was Marc-Antoine Charpentier (1634–1704), who also became the theatrical collaborator of Molière when the latter broke off his partnership with Lully. Having previously studied in Rome with Carissimi, celebrated for his oratorios, Charpentier himself composed a succession of oratorios (in Latin), using either chorus or a solo voice as narrator, and other soloists as characters: typical titles are *The Judgement of Solomon, Cecilia Virgin and Martyr* (compare the previous reference to Cecilia, p. 133), and *The Denial of St Peter*, in which Peter's denying of Jesus is followed by the chorus's observation, 'And immediately the cock crew'.

Performances of such works were in the nature of sacred concerts. For the actual service of the church, Charpentier wrote masses, motets and other works in a vein characteristically gentler and less pomp-laden than Lully's: for instance a mass intended for Christmas Eve, in which the Latin words of the rite are set to traditional carol tunes. Strings and flutes, as well as organ, accompany the voices. Michel Richard Delalande or Lalande (1657–1726), whose posts included that of music master to the royal princesses, was another composer of such instrumentally accompanied church music, as well as of ballets and operas.

The French court also maintained an official harpsichordist. Jacques de Chambonnières (1602–c. 1672) succeeded his father in this post during the reign of Louis XIII and survived into that of Louis XIV. For his instrument he wrote suites of dances, some of them with the type of picturesque titles familiar from Couperin (see below). This type of harpsichord-writing, with ornamentation of a distinctively French kind, descends from the characteristic style of the lute – an instrument still cultivated, among others by the celebrated lutenist-composer Denis Gaultier (c. 1603–72). Gaultier is one of the composers who use the word 'tombeau' (tomb) as the title of a musical memorial piece, a usage revived by Ravel (p. 282). Lute technique even shows an influence on French organ music of the period – despite the contrary natures of the lute, whose sounds fade immediately, and the organ, with its sound sustained as long as the player wishes. But the lute was soon succeeded in fashionable taste by the guitar, less exacting in its technique. Robert de Visée (c. 1650–1725) published a *Book of the Guitar*, dedicated to the

King, in 1682 and entered the royal service as guitarist about this time.

It was Chambonnières who brought the Couperin family (who came from his part of France) to Paris and to court. Louis Couperin (*c.* 1626–61) was a violinist-composer who, despite his short life, achieved mastery of the new style of harpsichord music based on dance measures. No less than ten other members of the family – singers, instrumentalists, and composers – are to be found listed in dictionaries of music, but the title of Couperin the Great (le Grand) belongs to Louis's nephew, François Couperin (1668–1733). He became one of the four court organists of Louis XIV and taught most of the royal children. Deliberately adopting the Italian manner, he began in 1692 to compose trio sonatas. His church music, much of it for one, two or three solo voices with continuo, is also in a graceful Italian style rather than in the monumental style established by Lully. But his most famous works are for harpsichord: his 27 suites (he used the French term '*ordres*') of short pieces. Nine further pieces are contained in his treatise on *The Art of Playing the Harpsichord* (1717).

Couperin's suites comprise as few as four or as many as 22 pieces, usually all in one key in its major and minor forms: thus the suite No. 14, beginning with the piece picturesquely entitled *The nightingale in love*, is all in D major or D minor. Couperin takes his rhythms from dances, though for the titles of his movements he chooses a picturesque phrase more often than a type of dance. His form is chiefly that of the *baroque sonata*: the movement comes to a halt about halfway through in the dominant key (or, if it began in the minor, then it halts in the relative major), and the second half takes the music back to the opening key. Or sometimes Couperin adopts the form of the *rondeau* (a French word more familiar in its italianized form, *rondò*), in which one strain constantly recurs in the same key with episodes between the recurrances. More rarely he writes variations or a chaconne. The picturesque titles, sometimes romantic and sometimes humorous (for example, *Little Pinch-Without-Laughing*), give only general indications of mood: they do not offer a programme to be followed through the progress of the pieces. In mood as well as in their titles, these pieces of Couperin's have often suggested a parallel to the paintings of Watteau (1684–1721), with their romantically imagined pastoral scenes, in which the present delights of court are blended with those of classical mythology. Such a style in visual art, intimate and charming rather than grand, is called *rococo*; and Couperin's harpsichord pieces may similarly be said to show the baroque (a grand style) changing to rococo. It is significant that Couperin attaches much importance to the full and correct use of ornaments to grace the melody; his is an art of delicate detail above all. Couperin also requires the application of the convention of inequalities: that is, notes written as if of equal value (for instance, two eighth-notes) were sometimes played unequally – the first note longer, the second shorter, or vice versa. It is disputed how far this convention should be applied to non-French music and to slightly later periods: but there appears no doubt that, for instance, Rameau's music (see next chapter) requires it.

One of Couperin's contemporaries, and a member of the court orchestra, was Marin Marais (1656–1728): he too was one of the first Frenchmen to compose in the new, Italian-inspired form of trio sonatas, and he is also remembered as one of the last virtuosi of the bass viol (viola da gamba). A boy born in 1694 played the harpsichord before Louis XIV at the age of six: he was Louis Daquin, who lived till as late as 1772. His famous harpsichord piece, *The Cuckoo*, shows a combination of brisk technique and tender fancy that may be said to stem from Couperin's example. The French harpsichord style was well known to such German composers as Bach, whose use of French dance names acknowledges the fact.

# 10

# A Climax of Style

WHEN Johann Sebastian Bach died in 1750 no wave of grief swept across musical Europe. No commemorative concerts were held. His employers, the city council of Leipzig, met next day and settled the appointment of his successor, but they passed no motion of regret at Bach's death nor any message of condolence to his widow. The man in charge of their church music, a rather stubborn character, had died: that was all.

The exalted rank which is customarily accorded to Bach today originated not in his own time, but in the nineteenth century – in the first biography of him (by J. N. Forkel, 1802) and in the zeal of such composers as Mendelssohn and Schumann, and (before them in England) the elder Samuel Wesley (1766–1837). How different was the life and posthumous fate of Handel! – born, like Bach, in 1685 in Germany, dying in England in 1759. A cosmopolitan, Handel had come to London as a purveyor of that fashionable musical entertainment, Italian opera, and remained as the inventor of English oratorio. A laudatory biography by John Mainwaring followed within a year of his death (it was the first book ever devoted to one composer's life and works) and his fame has since known no interruption.

The year 1685 was also that in which Domenico Scarlatti was born – an Italian composer whose concentration on one form, the single-movement harpsichord sonata, contrasts strikingly with the variety of Bach's and Handel's output. He died in Spain in 1747. With these three composers we consider in this chapter two more. The genius of Scarlatti's fellow-countryman, Antonio Vivaldi (c. 1678–1741), was mainly poured into that rather new form, the concerto for solo instrument and orchestra; while Jean-Philippe Rameau (1683–1774) not only continued the specifically French styles of opera and harpsichord music but also, in a famous treatise on harmony (1722), made himself the founder of the theory of harmony, in the modern sense of the term. All five are masters in the period of late baroque, in which, particularly in Bach, a close-packed counterpoint may be found in combination with the essentially harmonic structure of baroque style. Yet in these very composers we shall see in varying degrees a new, simpler style coming to favour: a style which has little use for counterpoint and which is described as *rococo* or *galant* (i.e. courtly, elegant).

These terms are, in origin, French: we have already applied the term 'rococo' to the harpsichord music of Couperin and compared that music with the painting of Watteau. In emotional terms we may say that the baroque in music is grandiose, the rococo is more delicately fanciful. The baroque enlarges and dramatizes the passions; the rococo presents them intimately. The firm balance of opposites between treble line and bass line tends to disappear in rococo music – as is shown by the adoption of the Alberti bass (named after the otherwise obscure composer, Domenico Alberti, *c.* 1710–40). This is a device in keyboard music by which the left hand keeps up a busy rhythm by simply breaking up a chord into its constituent notes; the effect is to diffuse the bass line. Destined to become a commonplace with Haydn and Mozart, this device is to be found half a century earlier in such a piece as *The Cyclops* by Rameau – from a set of harpsichord pieces dated 1724, some of which continue Couperin's practice of fanciful titles.

Rameau's chamber music also shows the stirrings of a new style: his trios for harpsichord with violin (or flute) and viola (or second violin) are not trio sonatas in the old sense, with the keyboard as continuo instrument: on the contrary, the keyboard is the virtuoso leader of the group. As orchestrator, Rameau also exploited a new expressiveness of instruments: in his scores the clarinet (invented by J. C. Denner, 1655–1707) makes some of its earliest orchestral appearances, and oboes and bassoons sometimes assume a solo, pathetic character. But Rameau's chief fame is as an opera composer, a continuator of the French operatic style established by

Lully – though characteristically modifying Lully's style in the direction of a more ornamented melody and a richer harmony.

French opera does not enthrone the standard musical unit of contemporary Italian opera – the da-capo aria in strict ABA form, preceded by (and distinct from) its recitative. It *may* employ such a form, but otherwise may more flexibly mingle song and recitative. Dance and spectacle call forth purely orchestral numbers with a considerable amount of instrumental tone painting. From *Hippolytus and Aricia*, a 'lyric tragedy' of 1735, in five acts with a prologue, let us take as an example the opening of Act 2, where King Theseus (bass) has descended to hell to rescue a friend. Forty-seven quick bars of urgent orchestral music are followed by three bars of recitative (accompanied by harpsichord) as Theseus remonstrates with Tisiphone (tenor), one of the Furies; then a defiant song (38 bars) for Tisiphone, a conversation in recitative for both (with harpsichord) and a longer, imitative duo which continues the defiance – beginning fast, ending slowly. Then 'the back of the stage opens, discovering Pluto on his throne and the three Fates at his feet' – to a bold passage in bare octaves from the orchestra.

All the above sections except the recitative gain their own unity from repetition or partical repetition of the music, but in ways much less rigid than the da-capo form. The words are fitted one syllable to one note, almost without exception, and there is no coloratura. It is all over quickly and concisely. Speed, as well as flexibility, distinguish such passages from the formal disposition of recitative and aria in Italian usage. Along with this opera of Rameau's should be mentioned three of his others on classical or mythological subjects: *Castor and Pollux* (1733), *Dardanus* (1739) and *Zoroaster* (1749), all likewise in five acts. In his flexibility of expression, in his use of the chorus, in his storms and other atmospheric effects in the orchestra, Rameau points forward to Gluck. And in *Zoroaster* he also anticipates Gluck in relating the overture (previously a self-contained formal introduction, as in Lully) to the music sung in the opera itself.

French opera was for French consumption: Italian opera
conquered Europe. (A famous clash of French and Italian
taste, in Paris itself, is described later on p. 163.) The close
relationship with the French language perhaps restricted the
export of French opera; Italian opera, even though performed by Italians in Italian to non-Italian audiences, was
(and is) much more easily appreciable on musical terms
alone. Italian opera thus becomes a pan-European
eighteenth-century musical language, and history affords us
the spectacle of Handel, a German, learning this language in
Hamburg, perfecting himself in it in Italy, and becoming the
pre-eminent professor of it in London.

In Italy itself, almost all composers of importance naturally
took to opera: a rare exception is Francesco Durante (1684–
1755), eminent in Naples as church musician and teacher.
As a son of Alessandro Scarlatti, Domenico Scarlatti
naturally wrote operas; so did Vivaldi (about 50). Yet they
found their chief celebrity in other works. Both passed their
last years outside Italy, Scarlatti in Madrid and Vivaldi in
Vienna. As a Neapolitan, Scarlatti was subject to Spanish
Bourbon rule and had taken post in Spain to the Infanta
Maria Barbara. Venice, where Vivaldi was born and worked,
had leagued itself with Austria in war; and though the precise
reason for Vivaldi's coming to Vienna is uncertain, the
attraction of the Austrian capital and court for north Italian
musicians was potent, and Italian opera was well established
there.

It is not only in the activity of his last years that Vivaldi's
life is uncertainly documented: we do not know the exact
year of his birth nor the extent of his travels. We know that he
was called the red priest (from the colour of his hair) but for
good or bad reason did not celebrate mass. He was in charge
of the music at one of the famous orphanages or hostels for
girls in Venice. There were four such institutions in the city:

... all for illegitimate or orphaned girls or whose parents cannot
support them. These are brought up at the State's expense and
trained exclusively in music. Indeed they sing like angels, play
the violin, flute, oboe, cello, bassoon – in short no instrument is

large enough to frighten them. They are cloistered like nuns. The performances are entirely their own and each concert is composed of about forty girls. I swear nothing is more charming than to see a young and pretty nun, dressed in white, a sprig of pomegranate blossom behind one ear, leading the orchestra and beating time with all the grace and precision imaginable.

The quotation is from the pen of a French traveller, de Brosses: the word 'conservatory' in its musical sense derives from these orphanages. It was apparently for the girls of such an institution (from 1704 to 1740, with intervals of leave) that Vivaldi mainly destined his famous and extraordinarily numerous concertos. Over 450 are known, nearly three quarters of them using stringed instruments (and continuo) only, without wind. A virtuoso of the violin himself, he employed the violin as his most common solo instrument in concertos; but he also wrote concertos for cello, mandolin (and two mandolins!), the little sopranino recorder (imitating birdsong in the concerto called *The Goldfinch*) and other instruments. More rarely he writes in what appears to be the older concerto-grosso form, in which the contrast with the full orchestra is supplied not by a soloist but by a small group of instruments (concertino). But even in these works he frequently uses the individual instruments of the concertino in a very solo-like way, giving distinctive and difficult music to the performer.

He gave the fanciful title of *The Inspiration of Harmony* (*L'Estro armonico*) to his first published set of concertos, composed about 1712: in only three does he preserve the old four-movement form (slow-fast-slow-fast). The rest are in the pattern which henceforth he nearly always observed: two outer fast movements, the first in general somewhat grand and the last somewhat lively, with a soulful second movement coming between and being couched in a different key. His set of four concertos called *The Four Seasons* (part of a collection dating about 1725, entitled *The Rivalry of Harmony and Invention*) for solo violin, are of this kind – and include certain picturesque details, for instance the barking of a dog and the reeling of a drunken man, which can hardly be appreciated musically without a knowledge of the accompanying poems.

Vivaldi's soulful middle movements are instrumental evocations of a human song. His outer movements, with their lively rhythms, their bold and assertive themes, their sequences (the same phrase repeated, sometimes over and over, at different degrees of the scale) form one of the clearest manifestations of baroque harmonic architecture. Sometimes the texture, instead of being simply of melody and bass line with harmonic filling between, takes on a more elaborate counterpoint; sometimes, at the opposite extreme, it becomes a passage in unison or octaves. In these outer movements the opening material invariably reappears later in another key or keys and then returns finally in the opening key again. This recurring material is called the *ritornello*.

The same key-scheme (home–away–home) is even more readily appreciable in the construction used by composers of this period for dance-movements and the like. We have already encountered it in referring to Couperin (p. 136). The form is binary (twofold): the music halts about midway with a cadence in the dominant key (or the relative major, if we began in the minor). Then, continuing the same type of melodic figures and the same rhythms, the composer leads the music back to the opening key. It was this form which was fashioned and polished with such skill by the composer whose music breathes the genius of the harpsichord as Chopin's does that of the piano: Domenico Scarlatti (1685–1757). As we should expect, he was himself a harpsichordist of celebrity. He wrote more than 550 short keyboard pieces, now usually called sonatas (a contemporary published title was *Essercizi*, exercises). The later sonatas, written when Scarlatti was in Spain, were mostly grouped in pairs.

Some of these later sonatas show, in their percussive style and the chords used, the influence of Spain's own instrument, the guitar. But the absorption of such an influence is only one aspect of Scarlatti's freedom in writing for harpsichord. Rapid scale passages, contrast of high and low registers, the use of crossed hands, an instant variation in texture from thick chords to bare two-part harmony – all these are characteristic, and formed a direct inspiration to later composers when the piano had displaced the harpsichord.

Often Scarlatti's sonatas show an anticipation of *sonata form* in a more modern sense (see below, p. 176). That is, within the first half of the work, the arrival of the new key will coincide with a new melodic idea; and then, as the second half approaches its close, this new idea will recur in the tonic (home) key. Thus the sonata in G (L.335, K.55, to quote the old Longo and new Kirkpatrick numbering) begins in G; the arrival of D major is marked by a new galloping figuration, which duly recurs at the return of G major near the end of the piece.

As this example shows, Scarlatti makes typical baroque use of strong rhythms, sequences, and emphatic cadences. He often allows a momentary imitation of one voice by another but rarely pursues fugal style proper. An exception is the well-known *Cat's Fugue* in G minor (L.409, K.30): the nickname springs from the very odd intervals of the theme, thought to have been suggested by the steps of the composer's cat up the keyboard. (The late Edward J. Dent, having failed to induce a cat to confirm this hypothesis experimentally, suggested an alternative origin in the cat's nocturnal cry.)

Like Domenico Scarlatti, Handel was famous as a harpsichordist. The two men met when Handel arrived in Italy as a young man, and it is said by Mainwaring, Handel's early biographer, that Cardinal Ottoboni (see p. 120) was host at a contest in Rome between the two – at which neither musician could establish superiority at the harpsichord, though Scarlatti himself was the first to admit Handel's superiority at the organ. In Italy Handel won his spurs as a composer too – particularly with the opera *Agrippina* (on an episode in the youth of Nero), successfully produced in Venice in 1709. He was 25.

Even before this he had already absorbed the Italian opera tradition – in its exported form. Hamburg, the chief mercantile city of North Germany, had a public opera house where operas had been produced fairly regularly since 1678.

Thither Handel came from his native city of Halle, playing the violin (and later the harpsichord) in the opera orchestra, and teaching private pupils too. He was befriended by Johann Mattheson (1681–1764), composer, theorist and critic: Hamburg at this time was the seat of the first important musical journalism in Germany. Handel's first opera, *Almira*, successfully produced in Hamburg in 1704, was sung mainly in German, but the source of the libretto was Italian and some of the arias were left in Italian. Presumably the audience, having followed the story in the German recitatives, was willing for the soloists to abandon themselves to the more singable language in their arias. In works by Reinhard Keiser (1674–1739), director of the Hamburg Opera and the first important German operatic composer, we find the same practice – for instance in his most famous work, the title of which is literally translated *Croesus Overbearing, Overthrown and Again Exalted* (1710, revised 1730).

Handel's success in Italy enhanced his status when he returned to Germany. He became the Elector of Hanover's *Kapellmeister* (a term which, like the Italian *maestro di cappella*, means the director of music for a regular establishment, not necessarily a chapel). What prompted him to make his first visit to England in 1710–11 we do not know. But he liked it, apparently found Hanover dull on his return, came back to London in 1712 and settled there for good. In 1713 he won a royal pension of £200 annually from Queen Anne. On the succession of George I, first of the Hanoverians, in 1714, the pension seems to have been confirmed and later doubled; and Princess Caroline (the future Queen of George II) added another £200 in recompense for teaching her daughters. Handel enjoyed financial security. It is significant of that free-enterprise age (the South Sea Bubble exploded in 1720) that Handel not merely secured further income as performer, opera manager, and teacher, but also directly involved himself in speculative risk by leasing theatres for a series of performances (in 1730 in partnership; in 1740 alone). The result was acute financial embarrassment, twice (1735, 1745–6), though not bankruptcy in a legal sense.

Handel acquired something of royal, or official, status. Although research has punctured the old story that the *Water Music* healed a rift between the composer and George I, yet this music seems to have its origin in one or more royal boating parties in 1715–17. (It really consists of three long suites; the Handel–Harty suite beloved of certain conductors is a very small selection from the whole, re-edited and re-orchestrated.) The *Music for the Royal Fireworks* was part of the official celebration (1749) of the Treaty of Aix-la-Chapelle (Aachen) which ended the War of the Austrian Succession. In 1727, when George II was crowned, Handel was commissioned to write four coronation anthems, of which *Zadok the Priest* has been performed at every Coronation since. The oratorios also have their secular, patriotic, flag-waving side: audiences recognized that 'See, the conquering hero comes', in *Judas Maccabaeus* (1747), alluded to the vanquisher of the Scots at Culloden, the Duke of Cumberland.

In the longer term oratorio was the means by which Handel became not merely England's royal but her national British composer. Even his Italian operas penetrated beyond their aristocratic patrons. The florid arias could hardly be converted to popular use, but the march from Handel's first London opera, *Rinaldo* (1711), turns up with highwaymen's words in that popular pastiche, *The Beggar's Opera* (1728); and the minuet tunes from the opera overtures – such as that from *Berenice* (1737) – were heard both instrumentally and sometimes with words set to them. With variable success Handel persisted with Italian opera until *Deidamia* (1741): the artistic resources afforded by its performers, headed by famous castrati, obviously meant much to him. With force and wit Addison in the *Spectator* attacked the scenic extravagances and the 'forced thoughts, cold conceits, and unnatural expressions' of Italian opera, 'the reigning entertainments of the politer part of Great Britain'; but Handel's operas have nevertheless proved capable of revival in the twentieth century.

In essence a Handel opera is a succession of imposing solo

arias, most (but not all) in da-capo form (ABA), of which the singer would normally ornament the final section so that it acquired the character of a variation of the first. The number of arias allotted to the various characters reflected the importance of the singers for whom they were originally intended. The arias displayed a refined vocal art (with rapid runs, trills, sustained swelling and diminishing of the voice, and so on) to display a fixed passion. In an aria the character of a lost and lovesick heroine, or of a vengeful tyrant, or of an ardent young hero is frozen into music. Between the arias stands recitative (solo or conversational) to move the plot onwards or establish the situation. Usually it is supported only by continuo (dry recitative), though at a few moments of emotional climax other instruments may be required (accompanied recitative). Duets are rare, and ensembles in the later operatic sense almost unknown (though all soloists customarily come together in a brief, simple finale). Handel occasionally made bold sorties into the irregular and unconventional – the depiction of the hero's madness in *Orlando* (1733), with a brief passage in 5/8 time, is famous – but the operas are dominated by regularity and balance rather than by dramatic urgency. Among the most celebrated of Handel's London operas are *Julius Caesar* (*Guilio Cesare*, 1724); *Alcina* (1735), which exceptionally uses a ballet and chorus; and *Xerxes* (*Serse*, 1738) from which comes the aria in praise of a plane tree's shade, later known as 'Handel's Largo' (though the composer's tempo-marking was *larghetto!*).

But why not a dramatic work in English? Handel composed such a work in *Acis and Galatea* – historically classified as a masque, but advertised in an unauthorized performance of 1732 as 'a pastoral opera'. The work had originally been performed 14 years before as a private entertainment for the Duke of Chandos, an ennobled war-profiteer who had become Handel's patron. (For the chapel of lordly establishment, at Cannons, Edgware, near London, Handel also wrote the imposing Chandos anthems.) Then, replacing a classical source by a biblical one, Handel wrote a further dramatic work under the name of *Haman and Mordecai*, which was presumably also staged for the Duke, in 1720.

Twelve years later Handel revived the work with a new title, *Esther*, when it was acted in private performances at Cannons. Later in the same year (May 1732) Handel extended the work considerably and gave it without action – i.e., as a concert work – in public at the King's Theatre, Haymarket. Thus English oratorio was born. The story that the Bishop of London had intervened to prevent the representation of biblical characters on the public stage is based on shaky, second-hand testimony and should be treated with suspicion. There were better reasons for Handel's adoption of a policy of presenting such works 'in still life' (the delightful expression of the eighteenth-century musical historian, Charles Burney) rather than with action. It was economical for the management, and later allowed Handel to perform oratorios during Lent, when the presentation of plays and operas was restricted. But the oratorios were none the less given as concerts *in theatres*; they were not devotional but dramatic exercises, and Grassineau's musical dictionary of 1740 defined oratorio as 'a sort of spiritual opera'. Handel never gave his oratorios in church – except for some later performances of *Messiah* in the Foundling Hospital, London.

*Messiah* (1742), though so much the best known, is by no means a typical Handel oratorio. It is not merely that it has a Christian subject, and all Handel's other oratorios save *Theodora* (1750) have subjects drawn from the Old Testament or later Jewish history. A more important point is that Handel's general pattern in oratorio (but not in *Messiah*) was to present a kind of drama with each soloist impersonating one or more named characters. The chorus sometimes participates in character (as 'the people'), sometimes propounds a moral lesson, sometimes describes a happening. The use of the chorus, no less than the use of the English tongue and smaller reliance on the da-capo aria, distinguishes Handel's oratorios from his operas. The heroic roles were tenors, not castrati. The choruses were not amateurs but professionals, the soprano line being sung by boys, the alto by men (both being borrowed from the principal churches). The contemporary commentator who applauded *Deborah* (1733) as 'very magnificent, near a hundred performers, of whom twenty-five singers' gives us a vivid clue on the proportions considered appropriate.

The other dramatic oratorios on biblical or apocryphal subjects, or on Jewish history, are *Athalia* (after Racine's play), 1733; *Saul*, 1739; *Joseph and his Brethren*, 1744; *Belshazzar*, 1745; *Judas Maccabaeus*, 1747; *Joshua*, 1748; *Alexander Balus*, 1746; *Susanna*, 1749 and *Jephtha*, 1752. Nondramatic is *Israel in Egypt* (1739) which is like some vastly extended anthem, and the *Occasional Oratorio* (1746), a patriotic medley. *The Triumph of Time and Truth* (1757) is an allegorical work adapted from two of Handel's earlier works with Italian texts. *Semele* (1744), on a classical myth, was based (with alterations) on a text by Congreve which had been *intended* for the opera stage. But it was performed under Handel's direction 'after the manner of an oratorio' (that is, in concert form). But the expression 'after the manner of' indicates that it is not itself to be called oratorio, a term better reserved for religious (or at any rate loftily ethical) works. *Hercules* (1745) is a work of similar type. Both make considerable use of the chorus. *The Choice of Hercules* (1751) is a different, one-act work, of less importance.

In the intervals of the oratorios a concerto by Handel was customarily given – it might be one of the organ concertos, with the composer as soloist, supplying improvisations and decorations of his own; or one of his grand concertos (this being the anglicized form under which his concerti grossi were published) for strings, with a solo group of two violins, cello and harpsichord. The twelve concertos published as his opus 6 (1740), each in four or five movements, display rich invention and show Handel as an inheritor of Corelli's design (rather than, as Bach was, an inheritor of Vivaldi's).

Like Bach, Handel frequently used material in more than one place, with or without alteration. It is a surprise for a modern listener to hear his *Concerto a due cori* (literally, concerto for two choirs; actually for a double orchestra) and to find a perky, wind-band version of 'Lift up your heads' from *Messiah*. Moreover, Handel's borrowing of passages and themes from other composers was somewhat excessive, even for that age, so that a kind of back-handed immortality has been awarded to such a composer as Johann Caspar von Kerll (1627–93) because Handel inserted an organ canzona of his into *Israel in Egypt* (to the words 'Egypt was glad when they departed').

Even in his lifetime Handel had achieved veneration. A statue of the still-living composer was erected in Vauxhall Gardens, one of the leading public pleasure-grounds of London. After his death he was musically canonized. A festival in commemoration of the centenary of his birth (held one year too early, in 1784) was on a scale unprecedented in Britain: 525 performers gave *Messiah* in Westminster Abbey. Approximately half were singers, half instrumentalists; and if the scale was greater than Handel had known, the proportions were still those of Handel's age – 26 oboes, 26 bassoons, as against 26 violas and 21 cellos.

By this time a Bach too had died in London: not Johann Sebastian but his eighteenth child, Johann Christian (1735–82), who like Handel had gone to Italy for study before settling in England. It is tempting to say that Handel and J. C. Bach accepted Italian supremacy where J. S. Bach remained German. Tempting, but untrue. J. S. Bach never left Germany, yet, like Buxtehude and other German predecessors, he took what he wanted from Italian forms and terms. 'Aria' in such a work as the *St Matthew Passion* means the florid song in da-capo form (ABA) as in Italian opera. Bach embraced the concerto in both current Italian forms (concerto grosso and solo concerto) and paid the best possible homage to Vivaldi by transcribing his concerto for four violins into a concerto for harpsichords. From France he borrowed dance forms, orchestral technique, the stately dotted rhythms of Lully's overture (the 'French overture'), the facility and the free style of Couperin's harpsichord-writing. (But no English influence can be claimed; the naming of Bach's *English Suites*, for harpsichord, remains a puzzle.)

Though Bach was in general a conservative (and, as we shall see, met some hostile criticism on that account), his are the first known concertos for harpsichord and orchestra. In seven of these, a single harpsichord is the solo instrument; in three, two harpsichords are used; in two, three harpsichords; and in the Vivaldi transcription four. At least four of the other concertos are transcriptions from works by Bach himself in other forms. The harpsichord transcriptions evidently represent Bach's liking for a thicker, heavier texture than that of Vivaldi's favourite violin sound.

This preference we may legitimately call German; and likewise the complexity of both counterpoint and form which we find in Bach's *Brandenburg Concertos* as compared with the concertos of Vivaldi. The six *Brandenburg Concertos* (dedicated in 1721 to the Margrave or ruler of Brandenburg) are all for different combinations of instruments. To the standard three movements, the first concerto tacks on a dance movement containing interludes called trios, scored for woodwind in three parts only: thus the trio which is a middle section in a Mozart or Beethoven minuet or scherzo is in origin a genuine (threesome) trio. The third Brandenburg concerto, for nine-part string orchestra (plus keyboard continuo) consists of two movements only, so obviously corresponding to the first and third of conventional concerto form that modern scholars think it appropriate to perform some slow movement (or, at least, an extended keyboard cadenza) between the two. The sixth concerto is also for strings and continuo only – but a different selection of instruments, including two gambas* and, amazingly, excluding violins. In the fourth concerto Bach uses as his solo instrument one violin and two recorders (inadequately replaced by flutes in most present-day performances); in the fifth he uses a flute (not recorder), a violin and a harpsichord, which is given the climax of the first movement as a solo; the second is for trumpet, flute, oboe and violin with the usual string orchestra.

* 'Gamba' is used colloquially in English for the bass size of the viol (viola da gamba) family, which alone survived in customary use up to this period. See p. 131.

The attention of Bach at this time seems to have been concentrated by force of circumstances. on instrumental music. He had accepted a post at Köthen (then spelt Cöthen), seat of the reigning German prince of Anhalt–Köthen, where worship was Calvinist and psalms were the only music sung in chapel. Bach's job was to direct the court orchestra, in which his princely patron himself liked to join. (He played the gamba.) As well as the *Brandenburg Concertos*, Bach, when at Köthen, wrote violin concertos and orchestral suites (he used the French-derived name, ouvertures). He also wrote the French and English suites for harpsichord (suites of movements derived from dances – the 'French' set without preludes, the 'English' with) and the first book of the most celebrated of all keyboard works of the baroque period, the *Well-tempered Clavier* or *Forty-eight Preludes and Fugues*.

Strictly the *Well-tempered Clavier* is the title only of Bach's first book of 24 preludes and fugues; a second book of 24 'new preludes and fugues' followed more than 20 years later, in 1744. The later set seems to have been destined partly for the instruction of the young Johann Christian Bach; the earlier, for the instruction of two children by Bach's earlier marriage – two children later to become famous in their own right, Wilhelm Friedemann Bach (1710–84) and Carl Philipp Emanuel Bach (1714–88). Indeed the whole scheme bears an instructional character. The word 'well-tempered' shows one object of demonstration. For technical reasons* it is now the universal practice to tune keyboard instruments with a slight degree of divergence from true tuning, so that they sound equally well in all major and minor keys. In Bach's time this system of tempering had only recently asserted its superiority, but Bach's pieces formally *required* the equal-tempered keyboard. It should be further noted that 'clavier' means only keyboard and could be applied equally to the harpsichord, the clavichord, the pianoforte (Bach tried an early, unsatisfactory model and disliked it) or the organ.

*See the article 'Temperament' in my *A New Dictionary of Music*, Penguin Books, 1958.

The *Forty-eight* is bewildering in its richness. The fugues – one of them lithely scampering in only two parts, the remainder in three, four, or five parts – are replete with intricate technical devices, applied to pieces of every mood. The preludes vary even more. On the one hand, a prelude might be a simple expansion of a sequence of chords (the famous No. 1 of Book 1, on which Gounod felt impelled to add a violin melody to which a third party later set the words of the *Ave Maria*); on the other, a prelude might actually include a complete and particularly complex fugue (Book 1, No. 7). But the contrapuntal texture should not distract us from the essential form, which (typically of the baroque) is one of harmonic progression – from the home key to another (normally the dominant of a major key, and the relative major of a minor key) and back again. This applies to preludes and fugues alike. Exactly the same applies to Bach's simpler instructional works, the two-part and three-part *Inventions* (his own name for the three-part works was *symphonies*). Bach's dance movements, though in free style (the number of parts not constant, as in strict contrapuntal style), obey a similar formal plan of departure from a key and a return to it.

From Bach's years at Köthen spring also the six sonatas (otherwise called partitas) for unaccompanied violin, and the six suites (otherwise called sonatas) for unaccompanied cello – No. 5 of these being written for a five-stringed instrument smaller than the standard one. From the violin sonata in D minor comes the famous *chaconne*: like other movements in these sonatas (especially the fugal movements) it is a test of a violinist's ability to suggest the impossible – continuous contrapuntal lines all supposedly realized by a single player's bow. (There is a parallel in the way that French lutenists similarly suggested contrapuntal lines.) The bow then used, with outward-curving stick and hairs less taut than on our modern bows, probably made it easier for the bow to sound more than one string at once; but modern scholarship has overruled the idea, put forward by Albert Schweitzer and other Bach experts of a former generation, that the earlier bow could execute three-string and four-string chords without jumping.    .

Bach's final post (from 1723 until his death) was as cantor of St Thomas's School in Leipzig, a post from which he superintended the music at St Thomas's and three other city churches. The principal service at St Thomas's and St Nicholas's on Sundays and certain festivals lasted about five hours (from 7 a.m.); in the course of it a cantata was performed (except in most of Advent and Lent) for which soloists, choir, and orchestra were available. Passion music was given at the afternoon service (Vespers) on Good Friday. It was for his Leipzig duties that Bach composed the greater number of his church cantatas, each on a literary text alluding to the gospel reading for that particular day in the Church's year. Recent research has shown that the composition of these works in Leipzig was concentrated in the first few years – showing, incidentally, an enormous pressure of work, an average of perhaps three new cantatas per month in the first year!

'The influence of the opera aria is never far away in Bach's cantatas.'* From the Italian operatic manner he borrowed the aria, the duet, the recitative; from German tradition he retained the chorale, both in straightforward form (when presumably the congregation might join in) and as a basis for elaborate choral and orchestral counterpoint. He borrowed freely from his own secular works: the well-known opening to the so-called *Christmas Oratorio* (really six separate cantatas for successive services from Christmas to Epiphany) illustrates the point. The work opens uniquely for Bach – with a kettledrum solo. This bold and festive start seems appropriate enough for a work celebrating the birth of a Saviour, but it was even more appropriate in the guise in which it first appeared – in a secular cantata to celebrate the birthday of the Queen of Poland, which begins with the words 'Sound, ye drums! blow, ye trumpets!'

*J. A. Westrup, *Bach Cantatas*, B.B.C., 1966. Because of the advances of recent research in dating Bach's works, all commentaries published before 1960 should be treated with due reserve.

Like other composers, Bach tried in each movement to find a type of musical expression which would express the basic sentiment ('affection' in the language of the time) of the words, and like them he sometimes employed a pictorial touch. Thus in a secular cantata about Hercules the serpents that attacked the hero in his cradle are alluded to by a snake-like, curling figure in the bass. Yet when Bach adapted this movement for another part of the *Christmas Oratorio* ('Prepare thyself, Zion') he retained the bass though no serpents are present or required! It does not do therefore to seek a *constant* use of symbolism in Bach, nor to find in his church works a particularly religious form of expression. Even the recitatives in the *St John* and *St Matthew Passions* (1724 and 1729 respectively, both revised later), vivid though their expression is, will not be taken as unique by an audience familiar with the recitative in Bach's secular cantatas (written for princely celebrations and the like), or indeed with the recitative of contemporary Italian opera.

The *Passions* are works of huge dimensions: though designed as part of a church service, they cannot be accommodated into the normal length of a modern concert without substantial cuts. Mingling biblical text with comments by individuals (arias) and by the people (chorales) they achieve an extremely striking and, in a real sense, dramatic effect. (Busoni and Gordon Craig separately considered staging the *St Matthew*.) Following tradition, Bach gave to both Passions a tenor narrator and a bass Jesus: in the *St Matthew* the utterances of Jesus, except the last two, are haloed by a sustained string accompaniment. The *St Matthew* is generally considered the superior of the two: just consider, as showing extremes of its musical expression, the terse choral exclamation 'Barabbas!' (on the diminished-seventh chord for harsh effect) and the very long, powerfully climaxed opening chorus in which, through the web of polyphonic movement (two four-part choruses, each with its own supporting orchestra), the slow-moving notes of a traditional chorale penetrate in the sound of an additional, unison choir of treble voices.

Lutheran worship as practised in Leipzig did not exclude Latin altogether. Bach's Latin *Magnificat* (1723) was designed for use at Vespers on one of the Church's chief feasts (Christmas, Easter, Whitsun). The Sanctus in Latin (Holy, holy, holy) was also occasionally included. One of Bach's six settings of this text became part of that famous but problematic work, the *Mass in B minor*. Problematic, because in Lutheran usage only the first two sections of the mass (Kyrie and Gloria) were admitted and given the name 'missa' or 'mass'. Bach not only set these two parts (the Lutheran missa) but the remainder of the traditional Roman Catholic text as well, incorporating his already-composed Sanctus. Yet the whole work, even if he had intended it for performance in Catholic worship elsewhere, would have been declared unsuitably long for the purpose (two hours: half as long again as Beethoven's *Mass in D*), and unsuitable also because of small alterations in the text. Its function or purpose, in the sense that we can usually postulate such a thing for a musical work of this period, remains uncertain.

In Leipzig Bach's official duties did not include that of organist: but he continued to compose for the instrument on lines he had already begun at Weimar. Nearly half of Bach's work for organ is founded on chorales. In the *Little Book for the Organ* (*Orgelbüchlein*) of 1717 he treated each chorale straight through, quite briefly, but with harmonic and contrapuntal touches which cannot be appreciated without a knowledge of the original words of the chorale: thus the text 'Through the fall of Adam, all was lost' prompts Bach not only to write falling figures but to a suggestion of the writhings of the serpent that tempted Eve. With these may be contrasted the longer, but less pictorial, treatment of the *Eighteen Chorales*, collected and revised by Bach between 1747 and 1749 (but written earlier). Some of these chorales were submitted to variations, and others to fugue. In others again, the chorale theme appears only intermittently in a work of free, concerto-like style. Still others are arrangements of cantata movements themselves based on chorales.

The celebrated prelude and fugue for organ in E flat

(nicknamed the 'St Anne' fugue, because its opening coin-
cides with a well-known hymn of that name by the English
composer William Croft, 1678–1727) comes from Part III of
the collection which Bach called *Keyboard Practice* or
*Clavierübung* (Parts I, II and IV are for harpsichord or clavichord). The even better-known toccata and fugue in D
minor, however, comes from Bach's earlier days at Weimar.
(There is *another* toccata and fugue in this key, from the same
period.) Bach also wrote trio sonatas for the organ – that is,
he reduced for one instrument the texture which we have
previously met in chamber music. A suggestion that these
works of Bach were written for a harpsichord with pedals,
not for the organ, is now discounted.

As cantor of St Thomas's, Bach was also director of music
to the university. In 1736 he acquired a more high-sounding
honour, that of Royal Polish and Electoral Saxon Composer
(that is, composer to the king-elector of Saxony, whose court
was in Dresden). It was as such, *and* as 'musical director in
Leipzig', that Bach described himself on the title page of the
*Goldberg Variations* for harpsichord, 1742 (part of the *Keyboard Practice*). Though nicknamed after Goldberg, a harpsichordist who was required to play to his insomniac patron, it
was called by Bach simply 'Aria with diverse variations'.
Bach was received too by a mightier sovereign, Frederick
(not yet styled the Great) of Prussia in Berlin in 1747. After
acquitting himself with distinction in improvising on the spot
in contrapuntal style, Bach followed up the visit by dedicating
to him his *Musical Offering*, a number of pieces all based on a
theme proposed to him by the king himself.

*The Art of Fugue* – 13 fugues and four counterpoints, all on
one and the same theme – is a sequel to *The Musical Offering*.
It is a work of astonishing ingenuity: fugue No. 13 presents
two simultaneous three-part fugues, each the exact and complete inversion of the other – inversion, that is, as though the
written music were reflected in a mirror and then read in its
new form. Bach left the final fugue unfinished at his death: it
was triumphantly completed by Donald Tovey (1875–1940).
Although *The Art of Fugue* is a scholastic exercise, and

although in consequence Bach left no directions for its mode of performance, comparative analysis makes it clear that it is a work for harpsichord. Twentieth-century orchestrations of it are as irrelevant as orchestrations of the organ works.

In 1729 Bach began to direct the performances of the Leipzig Musical Society (Collegium Musicum) and seems to have found the task very congenial. This society's concerts were of the type of private subscription concerts or 'academies' general at the period, and the society itself had been founded a quarter of a century previously by a composer whose music was more modern and more immediately fashionable than Bach's: Georg Philipp Telemann (1681–1767). Telemann's music is predominantly light, airy, and averse from complicated counterpoint. There were those who felt that Bach's music, by contrast, was overloaded and bombastic – among them a composer and music critic younger than Bach, Johan Adolph Scheibe (1708–76) who launched a famous attack on Bach in 1737 in the pages of a weekly journal of music published in Hamburg.

A new taste was showing itself for the Telemann style rather than the Bach style – a taste consonant with the inclination of the new philosophy towards 'nature' and 'reason', and with the desire of the rising middle class to be diverted rather than faced with stupendous grandeur. Baroque was dying. And, such is the overlap of musical styles and periods, a composer whose brief life was over long before Bach's was a key figure in the new style and the favoured new forms. He was an Italian: Pergolesi. The 'philosopher' of that style was a philosopher in the true dignity of that word, and a Frenchman: Rousseau.

# 11

# Clarity and Sentiment

'TO SING two melodies at once is like making two speeches at once in order to be more forceful.' Thus Rousseau expresses the case for clarity, and against complexity, in music. In doing so he implicitly suggests that singing and speech are comparable, rational modes of discourse – a view appropriate to a period often called the age of reason. Jean-Jacques Rousseau (1712–98), the author of *The Social Contract*, the most famous political treatise of its time ('Man is born free, but is everywhere in chains') was also the author of an important *Dictionary of Music* (1767) and an influential amateur composer, specifically of comic opera. Such opera, as we shall see, takes on a special importance in the middle and late eighteenth century as a more naturalistic art than the serious opera of Handel and Rameau. Its naturalness assisted its appeal to the new, less sophisticated middle-class audience whose power and patronage was beginning to vie with that of the nobility and courts.

It was at this time that philosophers referred to an imaginary 'state of nature' to test present laws and institutions. The 'noble savage' was contrasted with corrupt modern man. Novelists exalted purity of feeling, devotion, kindness rather than heroism. Before Goethe and Lessing in Germany came the English 'novel of sentiment' – Samuel Richardson's *Pamela**\** (1740), Fielding's *Tom Jones* (1749). Verse celebrated the supposed delights of nature and the simple life: Gray in his *Elegy* averted his eyes from heroes and statecraft towards the 'rude forefathers of the hamlet' and Cowper evoked the domestic bliss of 'the bubbling and loud-

---

**\*** The alert opera-goer catches a reference to Richardson and to the international vogue for this type of English novel in the opening scene of Tchaikovsky's *Eugene Onegin*. The period is the 1820s, but Mme Larina is thinking back to her impressionable girlhood of perhaps 40 years before.

hissing urn' and 'the cups that cheer but not inebriate'. Music too grew simpler in texture and more modest in feeling. It was on grounds of reason and naturalness in music that Scheibe, in 1737, attacked J. S. Bach; it was to 'good sense and reason' that, as we shall see, Gluck appealed in the preface to his opera *Alkestis*.

In instrumental as in vocal music, the baroque taste was similarly succeeded by a liking for the 'naturally' graceful, for tunes which are charmingly expressive without pomp or complication. The tone colours of the orchestral instruments (especially those of oboe, flute, and the newly invented clarinet) were newly explored to yield emotional pathos. In so far as this music suggests grace and prettiness of a fragile, Dresden-shepherdess kind as distinct from the older pomp, its style is often called by the French word '*galant*', taken into other languages too as an approximate equivalent for 'decorous', 'graceful', 'well mannered'. The term '*rococo*' (already mentioned on p. 139) suggests something similar.

But, as we shall see, the new musical taste, especially in Germany, is not merely for the 'well-mannered' but for the expression of feeling in a rather special, intense way – such as might be musically suggested by sudden pauses or a sudden change from major to minor. The label 'expressive style' (as a translation of the German *empfindsamer Stil*) denotes music of this kind. Inevitably these new tastes, which were to displace baroque ideals, were formed while some of the last and finest manifestations of baroque were still in course of creation. The leading exponent of the 'expressive style' was Johann Sebastian Bach's second son, Carl Philipp Emanuel Bach (1714–88), who served Frederick the Great of Prussia. When Emanuel brought his father to court in 1747, Johann Sebastian offered the king those ingenious baroque complexities (p. 157) of a type which Emanuel's own art had quite discarded.

In London a striking clash of ideals had already occurred nearly 20 years before. In 1728, while Handel was still engaged in flattering the aristocratic taste with the baroque edifices of Italian 'serious opera', the event took place which 'made Gay rich and Rich gay' – the production of *The Beggar's Opera*. The poet John Gay (1685–1732) wrote the words to tunes already in common currency, and a harmonization and overture were provided by the German-born musician resident in London, Johann Christoph Pepusch (1667–1752). To the fortune of the theatre proprietor, John Rich, *The Beggar's Opera* played for 62 nights – not, as is sometimes said, uninterruptedly, but still making an unprecedented London run.

It spread to other cities, and grew so popular that ladies' fans and other objects were decorated with its songs. It was recognized as being spiced with topicality. The fight between Polly and Lucy was taken to refer to the scandalous brawl which had broken out on stage between Francesca Cuzzoni and Faustina Bordoni, two jealous opera stars, in *Astianatte*, an opera by Handel's now barely remembered rival, Giovanni Bononcini (1670–1747).

Yet *The Beggar's Opera* was not musically a parody of Italian opera. Most of its songs were taken from a collection of popular ballads, Durfey's *Pills to Purge Melancholy*, and few were operatic in origin: the only adaptation from Handel was, as we have seen (p. 146), a march from the opera *Rinaldo* (1711). The tunes, simple in themselves, were not treated in any elaborate or operatic fashion,* there was spoken dialogue in place of recitative, and the roles required actors capable of song, not operatic performers. What diverted the public was the familiarity of the tunes, wedded to the cleverness of the verse and to a spectacle of low people (highwaymen, whores, a corrupt jailer, a receiver of stolen goods) behaving with the same avowals of lofty principle as were commonly heard from high-born heroes of operas and plays.

The piece was also considered to have its reference to current political corruption. Were not the principles of Peachum, the receiver of stolen goods, those of the Prime Minister, Sir Robert Walpole (to whom was ascribed the

*Benjamin Britten's re-working (1948) of *The Beggar's Opera* is much more operatic than the original.

dictum 'Every man has his price')? Gay's sequel to *The Beggar's Opera*, entitled *Polly*, was refused the obligatory licence for performance, apparently for political reasons, and was never staged until 1777, long after the author's death. Such works, being based on popular tunes, are called ballad operas. Over a hundred were composed during the decade that followed the success of *The Beggar's Opera*, among them *The Gentle Shepherd* (Edinburgh, 1729) with words by the poet Allan Ramsay (1686–1758).

Evidently British operatic taste still favoured a succession of simple tunes within a spoken drama – a taste which had swayed the theatrical course of Purcell (p. 107) and was to do likewise for Thomas Arne (1710–78), the leading English composer of the century. Arne's *Love in a Village* (1760) was a work of such a kind, though it was not a ballad opera (compiled from traditional tunes) but a *pasticcio* (Italian for pie) – compiled from various known composers, with additions by Arne himself, unfettered in those days by either copyright or moral disapprobation.

Arne also essayed serious opera, turning to its much-set poet, Pietro Metastasio: he composed an *Artaxerxes* in English and an *Olimpiade* in Italian (1762, 1764). But it was in a not fully operatic work, *Alfred*, that Arne gave his countrymen 'Rule, Britannia'. *Alfred* (1738) was in fact an attempt to revive the old mixed genre (speech, music, spectacle, dance) of the masque; so was *Comus* (1739), to an adaptation of Milton's verse, which displays Arne's gift at its richest. His Shakespearean songs, written for stage productions of the plays, are also well known, and his symphonies are referred to below (p. 170).

A ballad opera called *The Devil to Pay* (words by Charles Coffey), originally produced in London in 1731, crossed the seas to Germany in 1743 and seems to have sparked off the type of German comic opera which was similarly natural and of the people. The German type, however, had music which was expressly composed and did not use pre-existing popular songs. Rather the other way round: some of the simple, straightforwardly appealing melodies invented by the first important German composer of such works, Johann Adam Hiller (1728–1804) became everyday popular songs. The name given to this type of German comic opera, using spoken dialogue as a link between the music, is *Singspiel* (literally, a play with songs). Though never attaining the official patronage and status won by Italian and French opera, the singspiel was cultivated both in North Germany, by Hiller and others, and in Vienna, particularly by Karl Ditters von Dittersdorf (1739–99), a friend of Mozart and Haydn. Mozart's juvenile piece for three characters, *Bastien and Bastienne* (1768), belongs to this type.

Many singspiel entertainments borrowed their plots from France – from the type of light comic opera now becoming prominent in Paris. *Bastien and Bastienne* itself takes its plot from the most famous of such operas, *The Village Soothsayer* (*Le Devin du village*), composed by Jean-Jacques Rousseau himself and first given in 1752. Shortly afterwards came the comic operas of François-André Philidor (1726–95), and the Italian-born Egidio Romoaldo Duni (1709–75); one of Philidor's is *Tom Jones* (1764), based on Fielding's novel. Such works were a development of the *vaudeville*, a type of French play incorporating songs with new words set to pre-existing tunes. Being thus descended from spoken plays, French comic opera as a type retained the use of speech between songs: right through the nineteenth century the distinction between the Paris theatres called the Opéra and the Opéra-Comique was precisely that the latter employed spoken dialogue, the former recitative.

Exceptionally, however, Rousseau's *The Village Soothsayer* links its numbers by recitative. Such a deliberate homage by Rousseau to the Italian manner was consistent with Rousseau's passionate championing of Italian against French music. In 1752–4 the performances in Paris by a visiting troupe of Italians of several Italian comic operas – notably Pergolesi's *The Maid as Mistress* (*La serva padrona*) – aroused the literary quarrel known as the War of the Comedians (*guerre des bouffons*). To a Rousseau the serious and stately French operas of Rameau, and the characteristic French way of declaiming them, seemed unnaturally stiff and contrived when compared to the music and the manner of the new Italian comic operas.

New indeed: these comic operas had but recently come into fashion at those two operatic centres, Naples and Venice. Comic elements having been purged from serious opera by this time (as they had not been in the period of Monteverdi and Cavalli), it became the custom to present a separate comic work as relief between the acts of a serious opera. Such a comic work may carry the plural label of *intermezzi* (intermissions), since its two short acts were to be played in the two intervals of a three-act serious opera.

Of this type of work *The Maid as Mistress* is characteristic. Produced in Naples in 1733, it has a comic domestic plot, only two singing characters (soprano and bass – a third character is mute), an orchestra of only strings and continuo, and melodies of mainly short but regular phrases. Words are much repeated, allowing the skilled actor much opportunity for varied, humorous expression. Much of the music ascribed to Pergolesi is spurious, including another comic opera, *The Music Master* (*Il maestro di musica*), but the authenticity of *The Maid as Mistress* is not in doubt. It displays Pergolesi's graceful but lightweight style as clearly as does his *Stabat Mater* – a devotional work for two solo singers and orchestra, sometimes mistakenly performed today as a choral work.

A work very similar in plot and style to *The Maid as Mistress*, and antedating it by eight years, is *Pimpinone* (partly in Italian, partly in German), by the German composer Telemann, produced in Hamburg in 1725 between the acts of a serious opera. The resemblance between the two is neither coincidental nor a sign of plagiarism, because the clever maidservant and the bumbling old rich man are stock characters of Italian comedy: Telemann had adapted his libretto from an earlier *Pimpinone* (1708) by the Italian, Tomaso Albinoni (1671–1750). After their initial popularity as filling-in pieces, Italian comic operas grew to independence and greater length. *Opera buffa*, the Italian for comic opera, is an internationally recognized term for such works, in which the comic bass or *basso buffo* is a stock ingredient – the inevitable heavy father or obtuse guardian or long-suffering husband.

In the comic operas of such composers as Nicola Logroscino (1706–85) are to be found some of the first examples of the big operatic finale – that is, the final number of an act covering a considerable amount of action and including several musical structures without intervening recitative. This type of finale, which was to prove a means of such musical excitement in Mozart and Rossini, is also found in an opera based on Richardson's *Pamela*. This was *The Good Girl* (*La buona figliuola*), by Nicola Piccini (1728–1800), produced in Rome in 1760. The libretto had been fashioned by the famous Italian playwright, Carlo Goldoni (1707–93). Two further great successes in this field were *The Barber of Seville* (*Il barbiere di Siviglia*), by Giovanni Paisiello (1740–1816), produced in St Petersburg in 1782 (28 years before Rossini's version), and *The Secret Marriage* (*Il matrimonio segreto*) by Domenico Cimarosa (1749–1801), produced in Vienna in 1792 – when it is said that the Emperor Leopold II commanded an encore of the whole work.

French having become an international polite language, it is not too surprising to find court circles in Vienna receptive also to French comic opera. Christoph Willibald Gluck (1714–87), holding the position of musical director at the Viennese court theatre, seized on the vogue and composed some French operas of his own, among them *The Drunkard Reformed* (*L'Ivrogne corrigé*) of 1760. French-styled though these works are, it is not surprising if a Czech dance flavour peeps in occasionally, since by family origin Gluck was one of those Czech (Bohemian) musicians who emerge as a new European force in this period. Others include Jiři Antonín Benda (1722–95), composer of *melodramas*, i.e., spoken plays with carefully integrated musical accompaniment; Josef Mysliveček (1737–81), a highly successful composer of Italian operas; Jan Křtitel Vaňhal (1739–1813), symphonist and friend of Mozart; and the Stamic family associated with music at the ducal court of Mannheim (see below, p. 170).

Though French and German comic operas were welcome as light amusement, serious opera in Vienna right up to the end of the eighteenth century meant Italian opera. This type of opera Gluck decisively and deliberately reformed. He gave to the music a more flexible, less formal role in the drama. With him, vocal expression becomes more supple, more intense, more dynamic. Even when an aria represents, in the older fashion, a static response to a situation, Gluck favours a new simplicity of melodic line, demanding in the singer an emotional intensity instead of a capacity for florid art. The famous lament for Eurydice ('Che farò senza Euridice?') in *Orpheus* (1762) is the pre-eminent example. Such an art seemed to its advocates more natural, more true to life than the flights of baroque; and a taste for such naturalness in serious opera was as characteristic of the age as the taste for the light unpretentiousness of comic opera, or for the clarified texture of the new orchestral music. (The symphony, as we shall see, grew out of the operatic overture.)

Besides *Orpheus* Gluck's two great reformed Italian operas are *Alkestis* (1767) and *Paris and Helen* (1770), all three having texts by Ranieri di Calzabigi (1714–95), a gifted writer as firmly dedicated to reform as his composer. Before this, Gluck had similarly reformed the ballet, bringing to that art a hitherto unknown urgency of orchestral passion in *Don Juan* (Vienna, 1761); though this is now never performed, one of its movements is familiar from the composer's re-use of it in his later (French) version of *Orpheus*–and its echo is decisively heard in Mozart's *Don Giovanni*, just as the echo of *Alkestis* is heard in Mozart's *Idomeneus*.

With Gluck the orchestra acquires a new forcefulness of expression, the chorus a new dramatic importance. When Orpheus with his lyre appears at the entrance to Hades, the menace of the dog Cerberus is represented in high howls of the double-basses (one of many points quoted admiringly from Gluck by Berlioz in his *Treatise on Orchestration*). The chorus, representing the Furies, resists, threatens, then weakens and finally yields to the power of song. By eliminating dry recitative (accompanied by harpsichord) and using an orchestral texture throughout, Gluck presented the drama in more continuous, flexible form. With Gluck the formerly predominant da-capo aria becomes exceptional and an aria may be freely – that is, dramatically – interrupted: so in *Paris and Helen* the outraged Helen interrupts the impetuous Paris in the middle of a stanza when he turns a song of formal compliments into a passionate avowal of illicit love. In *Alkestis* the overture ceases to be a formal piece inviting the audience to a festive evening, and instead foreshadows the drama and leads into the opening chorus.

There are hints of Gluck's procedures in two Italian predecessors, Niccolo Jommelli (1714–74) and Tommaso Traetta (1727–79), some of whose operas were designed for productions in Germany and Austria. But Gluck's name shines out principally because of his longer-lasting success, but also because his ideas are expressed in cogent literary form in the preface to *Alkestis*, which was presumably written by Calzabigi, the librettist, although signed by Gluck. It begins:

> When I undertook to write the music for *Alkestis*, I resolved to divest it entirely of all those abuses, introduced into it either by the mistaken vanity of singers or by the too great complaisance of composers, which have so long disfigured Italian opera and made of the most splendid and most beautiful of spectacles the most ridiculous and wearisome. I have striven to restrict music to its true office of serving poetry by means of expression and by following the situations of the story, without interrupting the action or stifling it with a useless superfluity of ornaments; and I believe that it should do this in the same way as telling colours affect a correct and well-ordered drawing, by a well-assorted contrast of light and shade, which serves to animate the figures without altering their contours.

Proclaiming that he had 'sought to abolish all the abuses against which good sense and reason have long cried out in vain', Gluck defined as his chief object 'a beautiful simplicity'. In practice the composer fell a little short of principle: *Orpheus* has a purely formal overture, and both *Orpheus* and *Alkestis* are marred for modern audiences by the avoidance of true tragedy and the mechanical intervention of deities to provide a happy ending. (A deity also intervenes in *Paris and Helen*, but not so disturbingly.)

The title-role of *Orpheus* was written for a male alto (castrato), setting a problem for posterity. The most common practice today, inaugurated not by Gluck but by his admirer, Berlioz, is to assign it to a (female) contralto. Gluck himself, when he brought the opera to Paris (with a French text; produced 1774), re-wrote the title-role for a tenor and made several other important revisions and additions; the *Dance of the blessed spirits* is one of them. He similarly revised *Alkestis* for Paris (1776); and also, seeking to bring the same concept of dramatic truth to works with original French texts, gave Paris an *Iphigenia in Aulis* (1774), and an *Iphigenia in Tauris* (1779), both operas of major importance. At this time French connoisseurs of opera engaged in furious debate between the merits of Gluck and of another visiting operatic composer, Piccini (see above, p. 165); but it was an unreal rivalry, into which the composers themselves refused to be drawn.

Such was the inferior standing of German opera (which had to wait for Mozart to establish it) that Gluck wrote no stage works in that language. But he did write individual songs in German, songs which do not belong to the class of the operatic aria but which seek a more intimate expression and were intended for domestic use with simple keyboard accompaniment. The nineteenth-century German song, as illuminated by Schubert, is foreshadowed in these works of Gluck and of Johann Friedrich Reichardt (1752–1814) and the long-lived Carl Friedrich Zelter (1758–1832) who survived to become Mendelssohn's teacher and collaborator in reviving Bach's *St Matthew Passion* (see p. 226).

As a young man, Gluck had worked in Milan as a chamber musician to a princely patron, and had there become a pupil and friend of Giovanni Battista Sammartini (1701–75) – one of the first composers to write symphonies as concert works. One of the meanings of the Italian *sinfonia* is simply overture, in the operatic sense, and the symphony in our usual sense of the term came to birth as the Italian operatic overture (in three movements, fast-slow-fast), now detached from the theatre and made to serve as a concert piece. The early symphony belongs to the galant as distinct from the baroque style. The keyboard continuo becomes superfluous (that is, it is not necessary for completion of harmony); the musical texture is continuous (not broken into the contrasted small and large groups of the concerto grosso); the phrases are short and regular, and answer each other.

Moreover, while a baroque orchestral movement commonly pursued a single musical mood and idea, these early symphonies often have movements in a dual construction (with a second subject which is at first in a contrasting key, then finally is brought into the home key). This is the sonata-form scheme already noted in Domenico Scarlatti; we now note it, too, in the work of J. S. Bach's two most celebrated sons, Carl Philipp Emanuel Bach (1714–88) and Johann Christian Bach (Mozart's future mentor). The former was an important composer of keyboard music in what his contemporaries recognized as the new expressive style, with expectant pauses, swift changes between major and minor, sudden accents, and so on; and his *Essay on the True Art of Playing Keyboard Instruments* (1753–62) is a prime document of the new musical approach.

C. P. E. Bach favoured not the harpsichord but the clavichord, which (because the metal striker which hits the string remains in contact with it so long as it sounds) allows the player a more expressive control. But both instruments were being superseded in practical use by the piano, for which C. P. E. Bach's late keyboard works were written.

Chamber music at this period is not yet fully separated from orchestral. Many works written for four string parts were evidently conceived as suitable either for quartet or (with double-basses reinforcing the lowest line) for string orchestra. But at least such music has shed its baroque shapes and textures: the string quartet is self-sufficient, distinguishing itself from the older trio sonata in requiring no keyboard continuo. To write for continuo was still the habit of two of the last great masters of the Italian baroque violin tradition,

Francesco Geminiani (1687–1762) and Giuseppe Tartini (1692–1770), composer of the famous *Devil's Trill* sonata (for violin and continuo), a posthumous discovery. But the newer taste is evident in a later generation: Luigi Boccherini (1743–1805) wrote about 90 string quartets and 125 string quintets, mostly using an extra cello. Boccherini's cello concerto in B flat (he was himself a cellist) is only now beginning to establish its true self after defacement by a nineteenth-century editor, Grützmacher. What is called the Boccherini minuet is from the quintet in E, opus 13, No. 5.

The symphony, in its new sense as an independent concert work (with oboes, bassoons and horns often required as well as strings), was cultivated widely from the mid eighteenth century. The name '*ouverture*' in French, '*overture*' in English, was still sometimes encountered as a synonym. Arne's eight 'overtures' published in 1743, are rather old-fashioned, with fugal writing which looks back to Lully; so are the eight symphonies (1750) by William Boyce (1710–79) remembered as the composer of the song *Heart of oak*. The newest symphonic ideas were being hatched elsewhere: by such composers as Sammartini in Milan, by C. P. E. Bach in Berlin, by Boccherini (who worked mainly in Spain but also in Prussia) and by François-Joseph Gossec (1734–1829) in Paris.

Another important nursery of the symphony proved to be the German city of Mannheim, at that time (till 1778) the seat of one of the most important German princes, the Elector Palatine. Musically minded visitors reported on the exceptional virtuosity of the court orchestra there, particularly its violinists, and on the capacity of this orchestra for attack, gradations of tone, and expression. The successive directors of this orchestra were among the pioneers of what we now think of as the Haydn–Mozart type of symphony. Of these Jan Václav Stamic (1717–57), a Bohemian known by the germanized name of Johann Wenzel Stamitz, was one of the first composers regularly to use a contrasting second subject in his fast sonata-form movements for orchestra, and one of the first to expand the number of movements in a symphony from three to four by adding a fast finale after the minuet. His successor as director of music at Mannheim was Christian Cannabich (1731–98). We know from reports that the Mannheim orchestra in 1756 was exceptionally large for its time, with 20 violins, four each of violas, cellos and double-basses, a pair each of flutes, oboes, and bassoons, four horns, a trumpet and a pair of kettledrums.

The horns form an exceptionally important element in the new, symphonic orchestra: their long-sustained notes bind the whole texture together (replacing, in a way, the old keyboard continuo). In the new way of writing orchestral music, the keyboard instrument (harpsichord or piano) ceased to be a normal harmonic necessity. Yet it was still often present in practice, not least because – in those pre-baton days – it was the usual place for the 'conductor' to sit, unless he happened to be a violinist (in which case he led with his own instrument). Haydn on his visits to London in the 1790s was to direct his symphonies from the keyboard, contributing occasional solo interpolations of his own as well as (presumably) keeping the orchestra in time with rhythmic figures or chords. Mozart in his piano concertos makes it clear that the soloist is expected to carry on the old continuo function in the *orchestral passages as well*.

To mention these composers is to turn our attention to Vienna, still the great meeting-place of Italian, Bohemian, German and other musicians under imperial patronage. Here too the symphony was developed by Georg Christoph Wagenseil (1715–77), Georg Matthias Monn (1717–50) and others. A lighter and more loosely constructed Viennese type of work was the serenade – usually in five movements, and by origin intended for out-of-doors. The terms 'cassation' and 'divertimento' signify much the same as 'serenade' in this sense. A Viennese composer who numbered both symphonies and divertimenti among his works was Karl Dittersdorf, whose name we have already encountered as an operatic composer (p. 163). Michael Kelly, the Irish tenor who sang in the first performance of *The Marriage of Figaro* (1786), tells us that Haydn, Dittersdorf, Mozart and Vaňhal used at this time to play string quartets together for their pleasure. The 'golden age of Vienna', the establishment of what was to become music's classical style, had begun.

# Vienna and the Classic Style

NOT all the composers usually labelled as Viennese could properly claim that origin. Not, certainly, the three who are usually grouped as the Vienna classics: Haydn was born on Austria's Hungarian border, Mozart in Salzburg, Beethoven at Bonn in the German Rhineland. But Vienna called them. Haydn came when he was eight to be a choirboy at St Stephen's Cathedral; Mozart, a prodigy harpsichordist, played in Vienna at the age of six, and later settled there when he had shaken off Salzburg (and his employer, the prince-archbishop, had shaken *him* off). Beethoven came to Vienna at 21 to study with Haydn, for the presence of every successive great musician increased the magnetism already exerted by the Austrian capital with its court, its theatres, its prosperity and its aristocratic patrons of music – often themselves amateur performers.

Haydn, Mozart and Beethoven were not, as we might too easily assume from today's concert programmes, lone and dominating figures. Only towards the end of his lifetime was Haydn recognized as the greatest musical figure of his generation; Mozart never in his lifetime. In the eyes of the Viennese public, the opera *A Rare Thing* (*Una cosa rara*) by Vincente Martín y Soler quite eclipsed *The Marriage of Figaro*, which had been produced earlier in the same year (1786). Martín (1754–1806), a Spaniard who had previously lived in Naples, was only one of many composers who gravitated naturally northward from Italy to what was still the greatest Catholic capital. Another was Antonio Salieri (1750–1825), composer to the court and conductor of the Italian opera in Vienna: he seems to have personally intrigued against Mozart, though the story that he poisoned Mozart is mere fiction – a fiction which itself took operatic form in Rimsky-Korsakov's *Mozart and Salieri* (1898, on a text by Pushkin). Prominent also in Vienna's musical life were composers from Bohemia, among them Vaňhal (see last chapter) and Leopold Koželuh (germanized as Kozeluch, 1752–1818). Of native Austrian composers Dittersdorf was a friend of both Haydn and Mozart and a successful and honourably ranked composer. But Haydn himself in the year 1785 had no doubt of where genius lay: 'I tell you before God, and as an honest man, that your son is the greatest composer I know, either personally or by name; he has taste, and apart from that the greatest science in composition.' Franz Josef Haydn (1732–1809) paid that tribute to Wolfgang Amadeus Mozart (1756–91) in conversation with the younger composer's father, Leopold Mozart (1719–87) – himself a composer, now known to be the originator of the 'Toy Symphony' long ascribed to Haydn.

The younger Mozart reciprocated, in a more filial way, Haydn's admiration. The first six of Mozart's ten celebrated string quartets form a set dedicated to Haydn. Sheer seniority enabled Haydn to pioneer the paths which Mozart was to follow in the field of the string quartet and the symphony (Haydn's title to be the father of these forms is acceptable only if we allow numerous grandfathers and uncles) and also in the sonatas for harpsichord or its conquering successor, the piano. In concertos and operas, however, Mozart's mighty achievement sprang from different roots; while Haydn's *The Creation* and *The Seasons* – late works, written after Mozart's death – belong to a new, prophetic choral vein which no circumstances in Mozart's life prompted him to try.

'Circumstances' . . . the pressure of outside events, of private patrons and particular occasions, necessarily regulated the composer's world. Security came with service to a rich and sympathetic prince or nobleman, or with service in an important church post. It was not serfdom: the composer could seek to advance himself to a better place elsewhere, and might be granted leave to exhibit his gifts on tours. But it was a matter of strict and regular duties in a fairly humble rank.

2. The said Joseph Heyden [*sic*] shall be considered and treated as a member of the household. Therefore his Serene Highness is

graciously pleased to place confidence in his conducting himself as becomes an honourable official of a princely house. He must be temperate, not showing himself overbearing towards his musicians, but mild and lenient, straightforward and composed. It is especially to be observed that when the orchestra shall be summoned to perform before company, [he] and all the musicians shall appear in uniform, and the said Joseph Heyden shall take care that he and all the members of his orchestra follow the instructions given, and appear in white stockings, white linen, powdered, and with either a queue or a tie-wig . . .

5. The said Joseph Heyden shall appear daily in the antechamber before and after midday, and inquire whether his Highness is pleased to order a performance of the orchestra . . .

In such terms Haydn was engaged in 1761 as vice-*Kapellmeister* (deputy musical director) by Prince Paul Anton of the Esterházy family, one of the wealthiest families of the Hungarian nobility. Prince Paul Anton died in the following year, and his successor, Nicholas, combined ostentation (his new Esterháza palace was ranked by a traveller as second only to Versailles) with a genuine enthusiasm for music. The Esterházy estate lay chiefly in Hungary, but hardly 50 miles from Vienna, to which Haydn occasionally (not as often as he wanted) obtained permission to go. From Vienna the Empress Maria Theresa herself paid a festive visit to the Esterházy domain in 1773. To conduct opera, as well as concerts, fell within Haydn's domestic responsibility. Publication of his music, and personal report, spread his fame beyond the emperor's lands. Gifts, invitations and commissions came from Spain, England, France and Prussia. When Prince Nicholas died in 1790, and was succeeded by a prince who cared little for music, Haydn found himself in receipt of a pension and a salary but free to move. Immediately he transferred his residence into a friend's apartment in Vienna.

Within a few years he was persuaded to pay two highly successful and profitable visits to London (1791–2 and 1794–5) directing performances of 12 specially written new symphonies (nicknamed the 'Salomon' set, after the impresario who invited him). He returned to Vienna and died there in the midst of war, for in 1809 the Napoleonic forces of France were battling for Vienna. A special French guard of honour was placed round Haydn's house. Within, the dying composer played to his household the *Austrian hymn* – the anthem which (in emulation of 'God Save the King') he had composed twelve years before. After his death, a French military guard alternated with members of Vienna's militia to surround the bier. Mozart (the contrast is striking) had received a poor man's burial with a dozen other corpses.

In the comparative isolation of the Esterházy estate Haydn had been, as he put it, 'forced to become original'. Original he was, and knew it. His set of six so-called 'Russian' quartets (dedicated to the Grand Duke Paul of Russia, but in no way otherwise Russian) he declared to be written 'in an entirely new and unusual manner'. The novelty is in the closeness, or rigour, of the thematic working: the melodies are not merely melodies in themselves but material for subsequent splitting-up, transformation, and combination – in a word, development. The term 'development' is given to the middle stage of that tripartite structure called sonata form or first-movement form – rather inadequately, because it does not only occur in sonatas (or symphonies or string quartets, which are 'sonatas' for their media), nor only in first movements. But it *is* found in very nearly all the first movements of sonatas (and other such works) in the Viennese classical period. To attempt to understand the music of this period without reference to sonata form would be like omitting the importance of the sonnet from a discussion of Shakespeare or Milton.

The three instalments of the structure are: *exposition, development, recapitulation.* These conventional names conceal one essential point: the exposition presents a *duality* of material (starting off in the home key, moving to an opposite or complementary* key) whereas the recapitulation

---

*The term 'complementary', used by Donald Francis Tovey in his famous *Essays in Musical Analysis* (6 vols., Oxford University Press, 1935–9), seems to me the best term to denote 'the key to which a move-

emphasizes *unity* – re-using the exposition's material, but this time bringing into the home key what was in the other key before. Between these two the development 'plays with' or 'discusses' or 'argues about' the themes (or some of them), eventually moving to a point at which recapitulation seems inevitable. The tripartite scheme (exposition, development, recapitulation) is sometimes extended at the beginning or the end or both – by an *introduction* (which may be a slow introduction to a movement otherwise in faster tempo) and a final *coda* (anything occurring after the material originally heard in the exposition has been once recapitulated in its new key order).

Most composers of sonata-form movements, having presented their first big tune (the principal first subject) in the home key, present a contrasting tune (principal second subject) as soon as they have arrived at the complementary key. In the eventual recapitulation *both* tunes will be found in the home key. Haydn, however, generally proceeds otherwise: having arrived at his complementary key, he prefers to restate the *first* tune in that key, only later adding some new material. (Such a procedure, making one subject do duty in two roles, is sometimes called *monothematic*: not a good label, because other themes can still appear elsewhere.) Where the recapitulation of such a movement is reached, the emphasis on the home key cannot be made by transferring the principal second subject to it (because there was no principal second subject, as such). Instead Haydn may take some other (apparently subordinate) material which lay in the complementary key during the exposition, and invests *that* in the recapitulation with his new emphatic home-key feeling.

Almost any of Haydn's mature string quartets and symphonies will furnish an example. The quartet opus 77, No. 1 in G (1799) begins with slow, repeated phrases which, because they seemed to an older generation to say 'How d'ye

---

ment proceeds as its main intermediate goal before an eventual return to the opening key'. It will be used in these pages without further explanation.

do? how d'ye do?', have given the work its nickname, the 'Compliments' quartet (which must not prevent our speaking of complementary keys). In fact the complementary key, D major, is brought by a triplet figure. Now, instead of a new principal tune in that key, we meet the old one again ('How d'ye do?'), slightly varied, and in the new key. Only later (bar 39) comes the first new tune in the new key, and it is of a subordinate, less active feeling. Still in the new key, the triplets are transformed into great up-and-down arpeggios and the exposition ends in the complementary key with a pronounced dotted figure.

The whole exposition is marked to be repeated. There ensues the development, which for our present purpose we leave aside. Then the recapitulation begins (bar 128) as the exposition did, but this time the triplets, instead of moving to the complementary key, stick to the home key of G. As we are *not* in a new key there is no necessity to hear the main tune again here. Instead the great arpeggios confirm the home key. But we are not *quite* home. A coda (beginning at bar 168) brings back a further variant of the 'how d'ye do?' theme in G and (still in G) the dotted figure ends the movement.

All Haydn's mature string quartets and symphonies have four movements, and the above-described sonata form (or a near relation of it) may sometimes be found in as many as three of the movements – in this quartet, two (the first and the last). The exposition of such a sonata-form movement is always followed by the instruction to repeat it – except where, in some slow movements, Haydn writes out the repetition in full with melodic ornaments (players in Haydn's time would otherwise probably put in their own). Sometimes the remainder of the movement (development and recapitulation) is also marked with an instruction to repeat. Performances today often omit the repetition of the exposition, and nearly always omit the repetition of the remainder – a debatable liberty.*

* Even seasoned concert-goers would probably be surprised to learn that, in the finales of all his last three symphonies, Mozart specified that

We now proceed with our examination of this quartet. The slow movement comes second (in some quartets, it is third). Its key (different, as usual, from that of the first movement) is E flat. A memorable opening phrase is extended and developed to a prominent midway pause (bar 42) when the note C, low down on all the instruments, pivots the music into a new key. We soon arrive at a restatement of the opening, but now more richly harmonized, and the music proceeds to its calm end with many suggestions of the opening pages but no exact parallel.

A minuet movement follows, such as the Viennese composers chose almost always to include in their chamber music and symphonies. A well-known exception is Mozart's symphony No. 38 in D, the 'Prague' in three movements only. The minuet encloses a central section called a trio – so named because such a section used in former days to be scored as a trio, i.e. a threesome (see p. 151). Before the trio the first section is repeated, making the structure AABA or, as it might be put in verse form:

A  I shot an arrow into the air,
A  I shot an arrow into the air,
B  It fell to earth I know not where,
A  I shot an arrow into the air.

But a common Viennese form (as in this quartet) splits the first strain and repeats each half at a time:

Aa  I shot an arrow,
Aa  I shot an arrow,
Ab  Into the air,
Ab  Into the air,
B   It fell to earth I know not where,
A   I shot an arrow into the air.

Even this does not represent fully the interconnections of the

---

the second part (development plus recapitulation) should be repeated, as well as the exposition. Beethoven's string quartet in F, opus 59, No. 1 (1806) seems to prove the first example of a sonata-form exposition deliberately *not* repeated.

structure, because usually (as here) Aa ends in the complementary key, and the Ab turns out to be longer than the Aa, and to finish by incorporating a restatement of Aa, which changes course midway in order to end in the home key. Moreover, the B section may be similarly split and each half repeated. In his 'Russian' quartets, Haydn had already applied the terms '*scherzo*' or '*scherzando*' (joke, joking) to the minuet movements. Such movements retain the enclosed 'trio' section – as indeed do the 'scherzos' of later composers (including Chopin's for piano).

The final movement, when not in sonata form (as in the quartet we have been discussing), is generally a rondo – a French-derived form, as already noted. In, for example, the keyboard works of Rameau a rondeau consists of a number of recurrences of a principal tune (A), interspersed with different episodes in contrasting keys, thus: ABACA . . . (or longer). Haydn sometimes complicates this, giving varied versions (instead of exact repetitions) of the main tune, and allowing the episodes to seem like developments of the main tune. But he maintains the custom of presenting three or more appearances of that tune, always in the original key. Nearly always the rondo is associated with fast and gay music.*

In his mature string quartets (incidentally, the six quartets published as his opus 3 are not by him), Haydn promoted the second violin, viola and cello from a mere accompanying role. The slow movement of the 'Emperor' quartet in C (opus 76, No. 3, 1797) displays four variations on his own Emperor's Hymn in which each member of the quartet takes the tune in turn; some earlier quartets (three of the six of opus 20, 1772) have finales which are fugues – an assumption of equality between instruments.

In his symphonies, similarly, Haydn moves among his instruments with a great sense of freedom and a feeling for individual tone colour. These symphonies, like the quartets, exploit the sonata form (and its kindred), the minuet and

*For a further development of the rondo, see the discussion of a Mozart piano concerto (below, p. 193).

trio form, the rondo form, and, less frequently, the 'theme with variations' (i.e. a clear, song-like melody repeated with various changes but still remaining recognizable – as in the variations on the Emperor's Hymn, above). A particular feature of the late symphonies – present in 11 of the 12 he wrote for London (Nos. 93–104) – is the slow introduction to the opening (fast) movements. Superficially these introductions seem little more than a solemn call to attention, but analysis suggests that they contain in compressed form some of the basic musical ideas due to be expounded later. The tendency of such an introduction to wander chromatically from the home key emphasizes, by contrast, the strongly diatonic, straightforwardly tuneful, first subject of the Allegro that is to follow.

To take an example: the symphony No. 102 in B flat has such an introduction, followed by a sonata-form allegro, a slow movement near to sonata form (but with the exposition written out fully twice, differently scored each time), a minuet and trio, and a scampering rondo-finale, with some of those hesitations and not-quite-repetitions which make such a humorous effect in music – and which Beethoven was to exploit too. Typically the orchestra requires a pair each of flutes, oboes, bassoons, horns and trumpets; a pair of kettledrums; and strings, of which the double-basses always (unless otherwise indicated) reinforce the cello part an octave lower. The tiny, two-note phrases of the flute in the Minuet show a superb, craftsmanlike combination of thematic purpose and characteristic tone colour. The slow movement shows a bold use of trumpets and drums *outside* their usual context of loudness and festivity: here the trumpet is muted and the drums *muffled*, i.e. covered with a cloth. There are no clarinets, though elsewhere Haydn had begun (with symphony No. 99) to add a pair to the symphonic complement of instruments. There are no trombones (Beethoven was to bring them into the symphony), and none of the extra percussion which had been added for exceptional and purely picturesque reasons to symphony No. 100 in G – the 'Military' symphony. Such nicknames are given to a number of Haydn's

London symphonies. No. 94 in G is the 'Surprise' symphony, named from the sudden loud chord in the slow movement; No. 103 in E flat is the 'Drum-roll' symphony, opening thus. It is not clear why the last symphony of all should uniquely be called the 'London' symphony; and 'Miracle' turns out to be a misnomer for No. 96 in D. The miracle, i.e., that no one was injured when a heavy chandelier fell, actually occurred at the first performance not of No. 96, but of No. 102.

The success of the symphonies can be gathered not only from Haydn's own correspondence but from the London newspapers, which at this time published daily reviews of concerts (whereas criticism on the Continent was as yet confined to periodicals). Such treatment in the press reflects the way in which performers and composers were developing a new relationship to a paying public rather than to a patron. This new professional standing, as well as the social joy of being lionized, seems to have appealed to Haydn. He must have relished, too, the large orchestra which Salomon provided in London – about 40 at first (nearly twice as big as at Esterháza!) and about 60 towards the end. An even larger orchestra, with 40 violins and 10 double-basses, was boasted by the 'Concerts of the Olympian Lodge' in Paris, for which Haydn had written his 'Paris' symphonies (Nos. 82–7); but he had not attended their performance there.

The posthumous collected edition of Haydn lists 104 symphonies (there are a few errors in date order). With them we may place the work which Haydn simply called *concertante* when he composed it in London in 1792, and which contrasts a quartet of violin, cello, oboe and bassoon with the orchestra. This is now more methodically called a *sinfonia concertante* (approximately, concerto-ish symphony), like Mozart's for violin, viola and orchestra. (There are examples by J. C. Bach and other composers.) Of Haydn's concertos in the usual sense, for a single solo instrument, the most important are one for piano in D (1784) and two for cello. Of these two the one in D (1783) was formerly, but wrongly, attributed to Anton Kraft (1752–1820), a cellist and a pupil of Haydn; an earlier one in C did not come to light until the

1960s. One late work (1796) is a trumpet concerto, written for a newly invented trumpet with keys (the keys helping to provide the notes missing from the natural scale): players of the modern instrument with valves have welcomed this work.

Haydn's experience of hearing Handel performed by an assembly of several hundred singers and instrumentalists in Westminster Abbey seems to have been a stimulus to his composing *The Creation*. The German text, by Baron Gottfried van Swieten, was said to be translated from an English original (by one Lidley, otherwise unknown) and is based on Genesis and on Milton's *Paradise Lost*. Though first given in Vienna in 1798, *The Creation* was rapidly adopted by the English – and indeed belongs in spirit more to Protestant England, where Handel had grounded his oratorios on the English love of the Bible in the common tongue, than to Catholic Vienna with its Latin worship. The choral portions, setting the scene and then praising each successive act of creation, may be justly called Handelian both in their grandeur and in establishing a dramatic identity between the chorus and the listening audience.

There is a daring and deliberate naïvety in *The Creation* in the way that the orchestral music describes (*before* the bass soloist has vocally identified it!) each of various animals mentioned. The somewhat absurd diction to which English listeners are accustomed here – 'the flexible tiger', and so forth – is that of an early translator. The strange, slowly resolving discords of the opening *Representation of chaos* and the chords allotted to the divided violas, cellos and double-basses (violins silent!) at 'Be fruitful and multiply' are but two strokes of poetic mastery in this work. Somewhat of a sequel to *The Creation*, and with many similarities (even the passages descriptive of animals), is *The Seasons* (1801). This too had an English literary source – James Thomson's poem of the same name – which was again adapted (very freely) into German by van Swieten.

Of 12 surviving masses by Haydn no fewer than six are late works – that is, written in 1795 after he had ceased writing symphonies. They show symphonic characteristics in some of their structures as well as in their full orchestral accompaniment. The ninth mass, in D minor, is known as the *Nelson Mass* because it is supposed that a striking outburst of trumpets at the climax of the Benedictus represents Haydn's joy at hearing of Nelson's victory over the Napoleonic forces at the Battle of the Nile (1798). Haydn also wrote operas, some in Italian and some in German, which had considerable success at Esterháza; he wrote another one in Italian for London (though not produced there) on the well-used story of Orpheus – curiously called, in his version, *The Philosopher's Soul (L'anima del filosofo)*. But, as occasional modern revivals of his operas show, Haydn's talent in this field rivalled neither Gluck's nor Mozart's.

Haydn's success in England brought him commissions from three publishers to make voice and piano arrangements of Scottish, Welsh and Irish folksongs – a task he must have enjoyed, for he completed 445 of them, some long after returning to Vienna. Moreover, apart from such arrangements, he wrote 14 original songs with piano to English words. The publishers used the word 'canzonettas' and 'canzonets' for the first 12, which appeared in 1794–5, the years of his second visit to London. These include 'She never told her love', with words from *Twelfth Night*.

Haydn's were perhaps the first songs published in England to be printed on three staves (one for voice, two for keyboard). Previously, two staves sufficed: the upper stave held not only the voice part but (where space or vocal silence permitted) a few indications for the pianist's right hand. The change to three staves signified more than convenience: the accompaniment was now more precisely worked out by the composer, as the old conventions of the continuo vanished. The first *English* composer whose songs were so printed was probably Thomas Attwood (1765–1838), who met Haydn in London, had been a pupil of Mozart in Vienna and was afterwards to become organist of St Paul's Cathedral.

Mozart himself came to London in 1764 as a boy prodigy

of eight – when Daines Barrington, an English gentleman-scholar with an admirable bump of scepticism, doubted his age and sent to Salzburg for confirmation of the birth-date! Barrington was only one of many, from royalty down, who marvelled at the boy's skill in playing the harpsichord and organ, in improvisation, in formal composition and in memorizing. Paris, London, the Hague, Amsterdam, Zurich, and, nearer home, Munich, Vienna, Brno (now in Czecho-slovakia, then under direct Austrian rule): these were some of the cities to which the young boy was taken by his father, bumping over the long roads in stage coaches, before he was twelve. Soon afterwards, in Rome, Mozart went to a service in the Sistine Chapel, heard a famous nine-part *Miserere* by Gregorio Allegri (1582–1642), and thereupon wrote it down from memory, correcting only one or two passages on a second hearing.

Mozart's compositions of boyhood and early manhood do not give the impression of a miraculous maturity, as do the works which Schubert and Mendelssohn wrote at 17. Mozart's early years were, in the strict sense, formative. While appearing as a prodigy in London he had met Johann Christian Bach (see p. 150), the 'London Bach': the first three piano concertos 'composed' by Mozart (and dating from this period) are in fact arrangements of solo sonatas by J. C. Bach. In Italy, visiting Bologna, he studied with a great contrapuntist who was also a priest and mathematician, 'padre Martini' (Giovanni Battista Martini, 1705–84). He thoroughly absorbed the Italian manner, and in 1700 cries of 'Evviva il maestro! evviva il maestrino!' (Long live the master! Long live the little master!) greeted him at the successful performance of his opera *Mithridates, King of Pontus* at the Royal Ducal Theatre in Milan. He was destined to transform Italian opera, both its serious and comic types (at that time quite distinct); and to transform German opera too, partly by italianizing it. We may now set aside his juvenile works for the stage, and those he left unfinished; set aside also the pleasant, but musically slight, German one-act comedy, *The Impresario* (1786); and examine the seven major operas which took the stage in the last 11 years of Mozart's life . . . years which, as if the operas were not bounty enough, also harvested almost all the symphonies, concertos and chamber works by which he is best known.

Within the convention of Italian serious opera (the eighteenth-century *opera seria* which Alessandro Scarlatti had established and Handel had adorned) fall the first- and the last-performed of these seven. *Idomeneus, King of Crete* (*Idomeneo, re di Creta*) was produced at Munich in 1781; Mozart was at this time still in discontented servitude to the prince-archbishop of Salzburg, and the libretto of the opera was by Giambattista Varesco, the archbishop's chaplain. In 1791, when the Emperor Leopold II was crowned in Prague on assuming the additional dignity of King of Bohemia, the coronation festivities included the production of *The Clemency of Titus* (*La clemenza di Tito*). Here Mozart based his work on a libretto by Metastasio, the most favoured poet of opera seria – a text which had indeed been set several times by previous composers and was now modified for Mozart's use by Caterino Mazzolà, who held a court post in Dresden.

Mozart himself modified the musical and theatrical concept of opera seria, adding ballet in *Idomeneus*, giving a dramatic role to the chorus in both works, and making the arias move urgently forward instead of returning to the beginning (the older da-capo form). But he kept to the traditional use of castrato for the young heroic parts, and his music presents the traditional atmosphere of festive pomp, glorifying the benevolent despot (on the stage and in the audience). Recent revivals and recordings of these works have shown them to be by no means stiff corpses of music, though the replacement of the castrato brings special problems to stage presentation.

Italian serious opera having eliminated comic interludes altogether, the new Italian comic opera or opera buffa had grown to substance. Such a work as Cimarosa's *The Secret Marriage*, so warmly received by the emperor in Vienna (see p. 165), showed a complexity of musical ensemble to parallel the complexity of dramatic intrigue. The same parallel – seen most clearly in the long and complex finales to certain acts, with all characters on stage in a growing comic tension – is carried out by Mozart in his three great comic operas: *The Marriage of Figaro* (*Le nozze di Figaro*), produced in Vienna in 1786; *Don Giovanni*, Prague, 1787; and *Così fan tutte*, 1790. The gifted librettist of all three was Lorenzo da Ponte. *Don Giovanni* bears the Italian description of *dramma giocoso*, or comic drama, from which the unwary reader is tempted to suppose that this indicates a differentiation from comic opera in the usual sense, since *Don Giovanni* seems in certain aspects 'serious'. But this is quite erroneous, since 'dramma giocoso' was simply a common contemporary synonym for 'opera buffa'. The words actually occur on the first printed libretto of the purely comic and artificial *Così fan tutte* (So do all women) as well! Don Giovanni is the Italian form of Don Juan: Mozart's opera on the subject was originally entitled *The Rake Punished* (*Il dissoluto punito*), with 'or *Don Giovanni*' as its secondary title. The intention was perhaps to avoid confusion with another opera on the subject – *Don Giovanni Tenorio* by Giuseppe Gazzaniga (1743–1818), produced at Venice earlier in 1787, a work which seems to have been carefully studied by both Mozart and da Ponte.

The comic frame of Mozart's *Don Giovanni* is precisely established by the final sextet, in which, after the 'hero' has been dragged down to hell as a retribution for murder, the other characters point the moral. It is not an unflawed work, but a strangely powerful one: the intellectual inadequacy of the story is overridden by Mozart's genius for many-faceted musical characterization. Don Giovanni himself, who will not repent his licentiousness even at hell's gate; his outspoken servant, Leporello; the coldly outraged Donna Anna and the more passionate (yet ludicrously self-deceiving) Donna Elvira; the innocent (or not so innocent) peasant girl Zerlina and her honest lover Masetto – these are among the great characterizations of opera, even if Don Ottavio, Anna's suitor, is not. The dubious present-day practice is to perform *both* Ottavio's arias (though Mozart wrote them as alternatives on different occasions). The chorus has a tiny role in this opera, the orchestra a highly important one – with trombones (normally a church instrument) to suggest the supernatural, and with three dance tunes played simultaneously (including a waltz, the latest vogue) at Don Giovanni's party.

In a later scene Don Giovanni's private wind-band is heard playing well-known tunes of the day. (No problems of copyright in 1787!) The tunes come from three recent operas by Giuseppe Sarti (1729–1802), by Martín y Soler (see p. 173), and by Mozart himself, from *The Marriage of Figaro*. It is worth pausing to reflect that opera was then (and continued to be, at least up to Verdi's time) the prime source of hit tunes. A famous letter of Mozart's tells of his joy at hearing the tunes of *Figaro* sung and whistled by the folk of Prague (where it was given in 1786, a few months after the Vienna première). In *Figaro* the source of comic inspiration was the recent French play by Beaumarchais (1778), which itself requires song and dance. The play's ruthless exposure of aristocratic life, with sexual rivalry between master (Count) and servant (Figaro), without doubt appealed to what we know of Mozart's own egalitarian sentiments. Musically *Figaro* exemplifies the new handling of *action* in comic opera. An aria, a duet or an ensemble may now be not merely the response to, or the commentary on, an action or situation, but the frame for action itself. In the sextet of Act III Figaro has discovered that old Marcellina, to whom he owed money, is his long-lost mother, and Dr Bartolo his long-lost father; he embraces Marcellina, while his parents rejoice and while the Count and his lawyer (planning to outwit Figaro) are furious. Enter Susanna, Figaro's betrothed; she has borrowed money to repay his debt and now, misunderstanding Figaro's embracing of Marcellina, slaps his face – and has to have everything explained to her. The sextet has the grace and balance of a piece of chamber music, yet perfectly expresses not merely the situation but the changing sentiments of each character. Moreover the music is a close relation of sonata form, so that Susanna not merely enters the room, but enters the music as a second subject in the key of the dominant.

*Così fan tutte* is the most artificial of the three comedies, its six characters balancing each other like dancers, and the music exquisitely jewelled. The absurd story (two sisters claiming to be faithful to their absent lovers, but falling in love with the same men in disguise – or rather, each girl with the other's man) is made more absurd by the old stage convention of having the whole thing happen in a single day. The exaggerated protestations of the sisters are suitably exaggerated in the music, with slyly mocking glances at the conventions of opera seria.

German opera, before Mozart touched it, had been *Singspiel* (see p. 163) – homely 'plays with music'. The designation would still cover Mozart's *The Abduction from the Harem\** (*Die Entführung aus dem Serail*), with libretto by Gottlob Stephanie, produced in Vienna in 1782. In this story of captive Europeans benevolently released by a Turkish Pasha, the Pasha himself has a speaking role only. Some of the music is deliberately simple and catchy, some is deliberately exotic in an equally catchy way (in the 'Turkish' style then in vogue, with cymbals, bass drum and triangle). The final number is in the form of a *vaudeville* (a technical name for an ensemble in which different characters sing successive verses, with a common refrain) and points to the influence of French comic opera, already noted (p. 163). But the bigger and more florid arias inject the lofty, heroic note of Italian serious opera. Especially is this true of the heroine's aria of defiance ('Martern aller Arten': 'Torture me, but . . .') with its formidable difficulties for the singer and its elaborate orchestral introduction. *The Abduction from the Harem* boasts one of the great comic bass parts of opera (the Pasha's overseer, Osmin), but its mixing of styles is not altogether convincing. It was with *The Magic Flute* (*Die Zauberflöte*), given

* Also known in English as *The Abduction from the Seraglio*, as *The Seraglio*, and as *Il Seraglio*. This last is a legacy from Victorian times, when non-Italian operas were given in England in Italian, and is a pointless form of the title nowadays.

six months before his death, that Mozart achieved this con-
viction and established German opera.

As an allegory of good and bad, with a beneficent male
sun-symbol (Sarastro) and a malevolent Queen of Night,
who compete for the lives of earthly creatures, *The Magic
Flute* has been the subject of more interpretation than any
other opera – a task bedevilled by the fact that the libretto
itself, founded on earlier models, shows an apparent change
in the plot midway. Not that this makes Sarastro any less
noble when we see and hear him, Papageno any less funny,
the love of Tamino and Pamina any less heroic. Papageno is a
clown role, designated for Emanuel Schikaneder, the author
(or part-author) of the libretto, and manager of the original
performing company. He and Mozart were fellow-Free-
masons – a cult then associated with progressive views in
religion and politics. It is clear that Freemasonry was involved with the symbolism of the story, and that Mozart's
deepest musical insights were involved in the score. Two Men
in Armour, who indicate to the hero his coming trial by fire
and water, do so to the measured tread of a Lutheran chorale,
sung in octaves (tenor and bass); it must have been a strange,
alien sound in Catholic Vienna and perhaps derives from
Mozart's known admiration for Bach, who himself made use
of this chorale. Indeed Mozart uses a Bach-like 'chorale
prelude' technique in presenting this tune, in long-held notes
standing out amid a faster-moving contrapuntal web of
sound. The foreignness of this, in the context, serves to
emphasize the supernaturalness, or at least the special
solemnity, of the scene.

Mozart admired Bach, but it is not necessary to suppose
that an acquaintance with Bach's work taught Mozart
counterpoint. Counterpoint, the art of simultaneously combining melodies, was at this time part of any composer's
scholastic training (we have already noted Mozart's studies
with 'padre Martini') and considered to be an essential ingredient of church music and other works in a deliberately
severe or lofty style. We find it in the masses and other church
works which Mozart wrote as a young man in service at

Salzburg – and in the *Requiem* which, on his deathbed, he left unfinished in the hands of his pupil, Franz Xaver Süssmayr (1766–1803). We find him writing a fugue for two pianos, and contrapuntal music for a mechanical organ (of the rotating-barrel principle, similar to a musical box). Most remarkable is Mozart's combination in his late symphonies and other works of contrapuntal skill with the newer sonata-form construction. Here the merely galant is forgotten; simplicity is transformed into the weightiest of musical expression, both onward-moving and contrapuntally complex.

The outstanding example is the last symphonic movement Mozart ever wrote – the finale of the symphony No. 41 in C (nicknamed 'Jupiter'), composed with the two preceding symphonies within a space of scarcely over six weeks during the summer of 1788. This finale is sometimes said to be a fugue: it is not one, but it has the same kind of contrapuntal resourcefulness that a good fugue shows, and its four-note theme (CDFE) is an old tag or cliché of scholastic counterpoint. The impression that this movement conveys is of rich abundance of themes plus masterly economy and compression in their use. There is nothing quite like it in symphonic literature (it is, incidentally, the first symphony to place the main weight on the finale rather than the first movement) and a sentimentalist might say it *had* to be a swan-song.

The preceding symphony, No. 40 in G minor, shares key and mood with the greatest of those four string quintets (normal string quartet plus an extra viola) which comes from Mozart's mature years. The association of keys and moods is to be noted in many composers, but in none more strongly than in Mozart. It is thus no coincidence that the opera which most appealed to the coming romantic generation was *Don Giovanni* (basic key, D minor, as in the overture) and that the piano concerto which most appealed was also in D minor, K.466.* True, the use of this or that key is partly influenced by instrumental convenience. Three out of the four horn

* K. (for Köchel's Index) is the accepted way of numbering Mozart's works.

concertos are in E flat; both the clarinet quintet (clarinet and string quartet) and the clarinet concerto are in A. But that is not all: it is remarkable that the clarinet concerto and the clarinet quintet both begin with the falling pair notes E–C sharp, and even more remarkable that the same opening is shared by the piano concerto, K.488, in the same key.

The horn concertos are good-natured frolics; the five violin concertos are early (Salzburg) works, charming but slight; but the clarinet concerto is, with the clarinet quintet, the foundation of classical clarinet style. It is in fact Mozart's last concerto, and an epitome of his ripest musical language. It was incidentally written for a *basset-clarinet*, a normal 'clarinet in A' with an extension to provide lower notes: not the basset-horn, a lower instrument of the clarinet family also used by Mozart, for instance in the *Requiem*. The clarinet concerto is usually heard today in a slightly altered edition which equips it for the normal clarinet.

Mozart's 21 concertos for piano and orchestra (that is, excluding a concerto for two pianos and a concerto for three pianos, as well as seven early concertos arranged from existing works by J. C. Bach and others) span his whole creative career. Viewed from today, they stand as the earliest substantial body of piano concertos in the current repertory; historically they served also as the model for the concerto in its later developments.

Whereas most of Mozart's mature symphonies have four movements, the concerto retains the three-movement form of fast-slow-fast inherited from the baroque concertos of Vivaldi and J. S. Bach and the galant concertos of J. C. Bach. In their handling of themes (that is, in the way in which the themes seem to grow out of one another and to submit to interplay and development) the concertos seem symphonic. The modern listener might be pardoned for thinking the structure of a concerto rather like that of a symphony minus the minuet movement – a symphony into which the solo instrument is accommodated. The first movement would then be a kind of sonata-form movement, with the soloist contributing a solo display-passage (*cadenza*) towards the end.

But this symphonic analysis is deceptive. Mozart would have been surprised at it. Had he been writing the first movement of a symphony, he would have come to an emphatic close after the exposition and marked it by a double bar and the instruction to repeat. In a concerto he never does (nor do other composers). The form is conditioned by the fact that the soloist is the star, that the sound of the solo instrument will grip the listener's attention in such a way as to thrust the orchestra into the background. The very opening will normally call for a long, purely orchestral passage to prepare the way for the soloist's entry. (The king does not ride first in the procession, nor the prima donna sing the moment the curtain is raised.)

Thus Mozart, like his forerunners, constructs his movement on the basis of the orchestral ritornello – a passage which opens the movement (R1) and prepares for the soloist's entry; which will return in the complementary key (R2) when the soloist has pulled the music round to that key; and which will return again when the soloist has pulled the music back to the tonic. Let us see this process employed by Mozart in the already-mentioned piano concerto in A, K.488 (1786). R1 is rather long: 66 bars, about a fifth of the movement. It states *nearly* all the tunes which will be discussed, but never really leaves the home key. Now the first solo, S1: of comparable length (61 bars), it presents in new guise the material of R1 but pulls it to the dominant key, ending with a prominent trill. The orchestra breaks in (R2, bar 137) to greet us in that new key with material heard in the old, and to add an important new tune of its own (bar 143), also in the new key. This ritornello is very brief, a mere 11 bars drawn from R1 (not the very opening part); for now the solo takes command again (S2) with a development of the new tune, eventually turning the music back to the original key. Ritornello again (R3, bar 198), and again very brief (seven bars): the music is a repetition of the very opening, and in the original key. The piano enters and (S3) recapitulates not only the original material of R1 but also the new tune, all in the home key. The previous duality of keys and the previous separation of the new tune from the rest are triumphantly abolished. The piano's trill in the home key (compare the earlier-mentioned trill, in the *other* key) is a sign of arrival, of accomplishment – and the orchestra now rounds off the movement with one final ritornello (R4, bar 284). During this we reach a point of expectation in the harmony which is resolved by an extended cadence supplied by the soloist – that is, by a cadenza, for the two words are the same, and the English word was used for both functions in the eighteenth century.

Such an opening movement (almost invariably marked allegro) constitutes, in later composers as in Mozart, the concerto's most intellectual interplay of themes. The ensuing slow movement generally relies chiefly on the beauty of a song-like melody (in the present concerto this melody is in the familiar rocking or *siciliano* rhythm, 6/8), and is always in a contrasting key (here F sharp minor, the relative minor). The home key is naturally embraced again for the last movement – which is of merry character, is normally begun by the soloist alone, and is normally a rondo.

The simple rondo – ABACA, etc. – would not satisfy Mozart here: it would balance, but it would not provide enough of a positive onward drive. So here, as usual in his concerto finales, he employs a so-called sonata rondo (much used by Beethoven too), which allows the duality of key structure vital to Viennese classical works. The rondo material itself occurs four times (sometimes only part of it, but always recognizably and always in the home key: bars 1, 202, 313, 441); and the intermediate episodes are organized in a key relationship of a special kind. Between the first statement of the rondo theme and the second comes an episode, B, in the complementary keys of E (minor and major); between the second and third statement comes a further episode, C, in F sharp minor and D; after the third the B material returns, but now in the home key (again, minor and major). The relationship between this key treatment and that of sonata form will be noted.

In Mozart's career the work of the performer and the composer are intertwined. 'Today, Thursday 1 April' (ran an advertisement in a Vienna paper in 1784) 'Herr Kapellmeister Mozart will have the honour of holding a grand musical concert for his own benefit at the Imperial and Royal National Court Theatre. The pieces to be given in it are the following: 1. a grand symphony with trumpets and drums; 2. an aria, sung by Herr Adamberger; 3. Herr Mozart, Kapellmeister, will play an entirely new concerto on the fortepiano; 4. a quite new grand symphony; 5. an aria, sung by Mlle Cavalieri; 6. Herr Mozart, Kapellmeister, will play an entirely new grand quintet; 7. an aria, sung by Herr Marchesi, senior; 8. Herr Kapellmeister Mozart will improvise entirely alone on the fortepiano; 9. to conclude, a symphony. Apart from the three arias, everything is composed by Kapellmeister Mozart.'* ['Fortepiano' is an alternative word, at this period, for *pianoforte* – and in Polish and Russian is still the standard word for the standard instrument.]

In the previous month (March) Mozart played on four successive Thursdays at the house of the Russian Ambassador, Prince Golitsyn†; nine times at the house of Count Johann Esterházy (a fellow-Freemason of Mozart's); once at Count Karl Zichy's; and three times in a subscription series promoted by himself. Performances and lessons, not composition, earned his principal income. Some of his works were directly written for pupils – notably the piano concertos in E flat (K.449) and G (K.453) for Barbara Ployer (daughter of a Vienna official), with whom we also hear of him playing the

---

*According to Alfred Einstein's *Mozart, a Documentary Biography* (Cassell, 1965), on which the above quotation is based, the 'quite new' symphony was the 'Linz' (No. 36); Nos. 1 and 9 were perhaps the 'Haffner' Symphony (No. 35), given in two parts; the 'new' piano concerto must have been that in B flat (K.450) or in D (K.451); and the quintet was that for piano, oboe, clarinet, horn and bassoon, in E flat.

†I give the correct transliteration of this famous Russian name (another historic Prince Golitsyn appears in Mussorgsky's opera, *The Khovansky Affair*). The form 'Galitzin' was used in Vienna at the time and has been unthinkingly reproduced elsewhere.

sonata in D for two pianos, which has ever since remained such a favourite of sociable duettists.

He continued to play the violin too, though not on occasions of importance. In string quartets, for domestic pleasure, he preferred to play the viola. His two piano quartets and his ten mature string quartets (six of them, as we have seen, dedicated to Haydn) are marvellously idiomatic for the instruments. Church music he scarcely touched after leaving Salzburg (a mass in C minor, as well as the *Requiem*, is incomplete) and it seems reasonable to associate this abstention with his absorption in Freemasonry, hostile to the Church. The 'Masonic Funeral Music' for wind-band and two cantatas for male chorus and orchestra bear witness to this absorption. Dance music, marches and serenades Mozart composed naturally and for the occasion. 'Serenades', in the Vienna of this time, meant instrumental suites, normally for outdoor performance – many therefore scored for wind alone, like Mozart's pair of 1781 (in B flat, K.361, and E flat, K.375). But the serenade which the world has taken to its heart is that known by its German title, *Eine kleine Nachtmusik* (*A Little Night-Piece* or *Serenade*), for strings: the circumstances of its origin are unknown.

Beethoven, as a youth of 16, visited Vienna in 1787 and is supposed to have played for Mozart and perhaps to have had a few lessons from him; when he came for good, five years later, Mozart was dead. But one of Beethoven's patrons in Bonn, Count Waldstein (to whom the 'Waldstein' sonata for piano, Beethoven's opus 57, was to be dedicated) sent him forth with a famous and prophetic benediction: 'Receive the spirit of Mozart from the hands of Haydn.'

# 13

# Heroic Symphony

WITH Ludwig van Beethoven (1770–1827), history arrives at a new kind of composer: the composer who paces through the world like a prophet or hero. Nine symphonies, five piano concertos, 32 piano sonatas, and 17 string quartets are among the hero's labours. To no prince does he owe homage; princes are, on the contrary, privileged to ease his way. Compare the detailed duties laid on Haydn (see p. 174) with the terms of the contract by which an archduke and two princes combined in 1809 to pay Beethoven a yearly sum of 4,000 florins:

> The daily proofs which Herr Ludwig van Beethoven is giving of his extraordinary talents and genius, as musician and composer, awaken the desire that he surpass the great expectations which are justified by his past achievements. But as it has been demonstrated that only one who is as free from care as possible can devote himself to a single department of activity and create works which are exalted and which ennoble art, the undersigned have decided to place Herr Ludwig van Beethoven in a position where the necessaries of life shall not cause him embarrassment nor clog his powerful genius.

Beethoven's only obligation in return was to continue to live in Vienna, or in some other city under the Austrian emperor's rule, and not to absent himself except for good reason and with his patrons' consent. All three of his noble benefactors were younger than he. The Archduke Rudolph, then only 21, has perhaps enough reward in history's eyes in the nickname given to the most famous of Beethoven's trios for piano, violin and cello (the 'Archduke' trio, opus 97 in B flat), in the dedication of several other works, and in a sentence in one of Beethoven's letters to his publishers: 'There is nothing *smaller than our great folk* – but I make an exception of archdukes.'

These words have a gruff, Beethoven-like humour (we

recognize the same thing musically in such a movement as the finale of the Eighth symphony); but the composer's studied disdain for authority, his attitude of superiority to princes, publishers, and all others who might or might not stand in his way, was fundamental and serious. Goethe, 21 years his senior, described him in 1812 in a letter to Zelter (see p. 168):

I made Beethoven's acquaintance in Teplitz [now Teplice in Czechoslovakia]. His talent amazed me; unfortunately he is an utterly untamed personality, who is not altogether in the wrong in holding the world to be detestable, but surely does not make it any more enjoyable either for himself or others by his attitude. He is easily excused, on the other hand, and much to be pitied, as his hearing is leaving him, which, perhaps, mars the musical part of his nature less than the social. He is of a laconic nature and will become doubly so because of this lack.

Beethoven's deafness did not become total until the last three years of his life, but had long inhibited both his conversation and his ability to perform in public. He hardly ever appeared as a pianist after 1814 – the year from which we also hear of chaos when he attempted to conduct orchestral rehearsals. One hundred and thirty-eight 'conversation books' survive from Beethoven's last seven years, in which friends and acquaintances wrote down what they would have liked to say to him. But these notebooks are of far less value to our knowledge of Beethoven's own self than his letters and his musical sketchbooks (which enable us to see, to a degree unparalleled with any other major composer, how he hammered out his themes from their original inspiration and how he experimented in developing them). The letters are often explosive, abusive and petulant; it is clear that Beethoven demanded of others, especially of publishers and promoters, standards of rectitude and generous understanding well above his own. In 1815 the Philharmonic Society of London (now the Royal Philharmonic Society) paid Beethoven 75 guineas for what were to be three new overtures. Two of the three, on arrival, turned out to be five years old (*The Ruins of*

*Athens* and *King Stephen*) and the third (*Name-Day*) grievously disappointing to those London musicians who had rejoiced in the Fifth symphony.

The Philharmonic Society of London was an association of musicians, quite recently founded (1813); it was notable in its provision of regular orchestral concerts each season (only eight concerts at first), as distinct from the occasional single concert or short series promoted *ad hoc* by an impresario or by a musician for his own benefit. Vienna knew no such regular orchestral concerts (the Vienna Philharmonic concerts date only from 1842), and *ad hoc* promotions were the rule. When Beethoven's First symphony had its first performance in 1800, the composer himself had hired a Vienna theatre, engaged fellow-soloists and the orchestra of the city's Italian Opera, and put tickets on sale at his lodgings, as well as taking part in the concert. The programme announced that Beethoven would also play a piano concerto of his (it is not known whether No. 1 or No. 2) and would improvise at the piano; Beethoven's septet, a Mozart symphony and a vocal solo and duet from Haydn's *Creation* were also to be given. Note the mixed nature of the programme, including a chamber work – typical of the fashion of the time, not only in Vienna but in other countries too.

The type of piano in use during Beethoven's early years in Vienna was the 'Viennese' piano which Mozart had known, with a light touch (the keys needing to be depressed only about a quarter of an inch). The compass had by now been extended to five and a half octaves. In 1818 Beethoven was delighted to receive, as a gift from its English maker, a six-octave Broadwood with a heavier action and more able to produce that singing tone which we know he prized in piano-playing. Already a passage like that in the slow movement of the piano concerto No. 5 (1809) where the piano 'accompanies' the orchestral melody in high arpeggios in octaves, shows Beethoven's feeling for a new kind of piano-writing; and the huge climaxes and contrasts of his later piano sonatas, added to what we know of his own tempestuous playing, emphatically seem to require the most powerful available instrument. In these works he makes use of Broadwood's additional top notes.

If it was from Haydn and Mozart that Beethoven chiefly inherited his forms, we may seek elsewhere a precedent for that heroic, commanding, lofty manner which so clearly stamps Beethoven's music. It is to be remembered that, more than any other living composer, Beethoven admired Luigi Cherubini (1760–1842), who had left his native Italy to become the most powerful musical personality in Paris. Such of Cherubini's works as the opera *Medea* (1797) and the *Requiem Mass in C minor* (1817) show his combination of passionate, urgent phrases with a classical severity of style. The Gluck-like solemnity of certain hymnal passages in Beethoven perhaps comes through Cherubini and Mozart rather than from Gluck direct.

As for that strange (and now quite unknown) massive, simple choral music written to celebrate the French Revolution by such composers as Gossec (see p. 170) and Etienne Méhul (1763–1817), Beethoven presumably never heard or saw a note of it. Yet the French Revolution itself (1789) must be named as a further influence on his art. The triumphal march of the last movement of the Fifth symphony, the exultant crowd scene at the end of the Ninth – these are the legacy of 1789, as Mozart's *Marriage of Figaro* is the harbinger of it. *Fidelio*, Beethoven's only opera, belongs equally to that legacy. Its plot is a rewritten version of *Leonora, or Wedded Love*, a French opera by Pierre Gaveaux (1761–1825) which had been given in Paris in 1798. A historical incident during the Revolutionary Terror is said to have provided Gaveaux's librettist, J. N. Bouilly, with his story – in which a loyal and intrepid wife, by dressing as a boy, rescues her wrongly imprisoned husband.

Although, presumably to satisfy the Austrian political censorship, the scene of the opera had been transferred from France to Spain, and the villain made to incarnate only private vengeance and not political tyranny, Beethoven's music universalizes the plot. The prominence given to the undifferentiated mass of other prisoners, and the implication that Leonora is in some way the bringer of hope to all of them and not merely to her husband, gives the work a moral, oratorio-like atmosphere. *Leonora* (the German form is Leonore) was Beethoven's own intended title; *Fidelio*, which was preferred by the theatre authorities in Vienna, is the male name the heroine assumes in her disguise. Like Mozart in his German operas, Beethoven links his musical numbers not with recitative but with spoken dialogue. *Melodrama* in the technical sense (words spoken over music) is used in a famous scene where Leonora helps to dig what is intended to be her husband's grave.

Before the production of the opera in 1805, Beethoven had rejected his own first version of an overture (now known as *Leonora No. 1*). The production itself (with the *Leonora No. 2* overture) was a failure; and Beethoven's extensive revisions for a new production in 1806, in two-act instead of three-act form, included a new overture (*Leonora No. 3*). The public was appreciative but small, and Beethoven – who was being paid with a percentage of the box-office receipts, instead of by an outright fee as usual – accused the management of cheating him, demanded his score back, and withdrew the work after two performances. There was a further revision and a new production in 1814. For this (the version in which the opera is now known)* Beethoven wrote yet another overture, the tauter one which is now called the *Fidelio* overture: but *Leonora No. 3* has remained – with its off-stage trumpet call, as in the opera itself, and its marvellously exciting climax – a prime example in the concert hall of music *representing* a dramatic action but integrated in a thoroughly musical, indeed symphonic, way.

The year 1805 saw the first performance not only of *Fidelio*, but also of another work both revolutionary and

---

*There have been occasional modern productions of Beethoven's first (1805) version of the opera, and to distinguish this from the final version it has been called *Leonora*. But, as we have seen, *Leonora* was Beethoven's intended title throughout, *Fidelio* the title used in all versions by the Viennese theatre authorities.

French Revolutionary. We call Beethoven's symphony No. 3 the 'Eroica' without, perhaps, grasping the extraordinariness of the label. It is no nickname, but Beethoven's own title: *Sinfonia eroica* (heroic symphony). Not the *original* title, however. Beethoven's own manuscript of the work, sold after his death, bears the still legible inscription 'Composed on Bonaparte'. Legible, that is, although Beethoven tried to obliterate it. When the work was finished in 1804, news was received that Napoleon – hitherto First Consul of the French Republic – had taken to himself the title of emperor. For Beethoven it was a betrayal: 'Now he too will trample on all the rights of man and indulge only his ambition!' But for this, we might still know the work as 'the Napoleon symphony'. Instead the first edition of the work (1806) bears in Italian the subtitle: 'Heroic Symphony, to celebrate the memory of a great man.'

By what seems to be more than coincidence, the symphony is musically as new and extraordinary as the circumstances of its naming. It is sometimes counted as one of the two great milestones of the nineteenth century, Wagner's *Tristan and Isolde* (1865) being the other. The milestone once passed, music seems never to be the same again. The four-movement structure of the *Eroica* unprecedentedly spans more than 45 minutes. The opening allegro has that astonishing, impatiently 'wrong' entry of the horn just before the real re-entry of the first subject; the second movement is a funeral march, in which the apparently conventional insertion of a central, major-key section between two minor-key ones leads to an incredible intensification of feeling. After the relief of a scherzo, the finale presents a set of variations in which complicated fugal devices are turned to the creation of some epic hero's exultant dance.

A dance indeed: the music he had previously written for a ballet, *The Creatures of Prometheus* (1801) now gave Beethoven the theme for the variations in the finale of the *Eroica*. The legend is apt. In Goethe's poem (later to be set by Schubert and Wolf), Prometheus, in having learnt to fashion men from earth, has become a rival to almighty, jealous Zeus. Punished,

he remains defiant, alone, but loving the world of humanity –
the symbol of an artist, of a Beethoven:

> Here I sit, forming men
> In my own image,
> A race that will resemble me,
> Suffering, weeping,
> Enjoying, rejoicing
> And heedless of thee [Zeus],
> As I am!

Beethoven's music is conveniently divided into three
periods of his life. Up to about 1802, a little past his thirtieth
year, he seems to base his work on the forms given to him by
heritage and environment. There are surprises, of course –
for instance, the way the First symphony begins with a
chord not in its key. But an audience used to Haydn, Mozart,
and Salieri (see p. 173) would have found no upheavals of
structure, no disturbing strangeness of melody. Often there
seems a direct indebtedness to older models – as the temper of
Beethoven's piano concerto No. 3, in C minor (1800), recalls
that of Mozart's piano concerto in the same key. (Indeed C
minor seems to have for Beethoven precisely the meaning
that Mozart's work had lent to it.)

A new feeling enters Beethoven's music with his middle
period (approximately 1803–16): a new energy, a new boldness in structures. Here stand the *Eroica* and all the future
symphonies, save the Ninth; here the piano concertos Nos. 3,
4, and 5 (what Beethoven would have said of the English
nickname 'Emperor' for No. 5 can be guessed only too
well!) and the violin concerto; *Fidelio*; the overture and incidental music to Goethe's play *Egmont*, and the overture to
*Coriolanus* by H. J. von Collin (not by Shakespeare); the
three string quartets of opus 59, dedicated to Count
Razumovsky and named after him, and the two succeeding
string quartets (opus 74 and 95); such popular piano sonatas
as the 'Waldstein' (opus 53) and the 'Appassionata' (opus
57); and the last two violin sonatas in A (the 'Kreutzer',
opus 47) and in G (opus 96).

In the music of this period the drama inherent in the Viennese Classic forms – the feeling that the music presses onward through conflict to solution – is accentuated. In the Fifth symphony (completed in 1807) the scherzo, instead of formally ending, breaks down into drum taps, over which rises a mounting orchestral tension that breaks out into the conquering march of the finale. (In this finale the piccolo, double-bassoon, and trombones enter the traditionally restricted field of the symphony for the first time.) In the piano concerto No. 5, a similar join is made between the second and third (last) movements. The *Pastoral* symphony, No. 6, has five movements instead of four, the last three being linked in a representation of peasant merry-making, sudden rainstorm, and eventual serenity of atmosphere with shepherds' piping. Beethoven's well-known comment on this work, 'more the expression of feeling than painting', is a little too apologetic. Feeling, yes; but painting also, with calls of nightingale, quail and cuckoo as well as the lapping of the brook.

Beethoven's final period (from about 1816) is marked by intensely expressive, inward-turning music; by the exploitation of extremes of range and extreme contrasts of slow and fast, soft and loud; and by a technical preoccupation with variations and with fugue. The expressive powers of the piano, the string quartet, the orchestra, the voice (solo and choral) are pushed to what seemed to be their limit – not for the sake of beauty of sound but in exploration of expressive feeling. The enthronement of his old benefactor, the Archduke Rudolph, as Archbishop of Olmütz (now Olomouc in Czechoslovakia) prompted Beethoven to the composition of the mass in D (*Missa Solemnis*) – a work of huge proportions and rapt expression, making cruel and seemingly unvocal demands on the singers. Only part of it was ready for the actual ceremony in 1820, and Beethoven continued to work on it till 1823. Its length, its type of musical utterance, and its departures from the prescribed Catholic use of the text have made it more welcome in the concert hall than the church, and even in the concert hall it is difficult to perform satisfactorily.

At the same time Beethoven had been working on the creation of the work which was in two ways to burst the symphony's bonds. The Ninth symphony not merely lasts an unprecedented whole hour; it also introduces a chorus and four vocal soloists who – after three purely orchestral movements – sing a shortened version of Schiller's *Ode to Joy* (a political euphemism for 'Ode to Freedom'). Here military march, meditative hymn, florid solo vocalizing and exultant choral shout all have place. The Choral Symphony (as it is now called) is the last of Beethoven's line, and the first of that new line in which such composers as Liszt, Mahler, Busoni and Shostakovich have sought to fuse the disciplines of conventionally abstract forms with the concrete verbal meaning of a religious or otherwise ethical text.

No less remarkable than the setting of the ode is the manner in which it is introduced as the finale begins. First angry discord. Then the cellos and double-basses, alone, utter what seems to be a vocal recitative of pleading tone. The orchestra offers up reminiscences of all three previous movements, only to have the cellos and double-basses reject them. Then a serene melody in which the whole orchestra gradually joins. . . . Discordant anger again. Then this time the recitative is truly vocal – a bass soloist proclaiming: 'Oh, friends, not these sounds, but something more joyous.' And so the serene melody itself becomes vocal, a choral invocation to the 'daughter of Elysium', the divine Joy (or Freedom) herself.

The device of an instrumental recitative was a revival of an older practice; it is found in C. P. E. Bach (and Haydn too). Its revival here, however, exemplifies only one of the ways in which Beethoven gave a vocal character to some of the instrumental writing in his later music. Instrumental passages may unexpectedly bear vocal titles or directions – such words as 'recitative', 'arioso' (i.e. aria-like), and 'cavatina' (meaning, in an opera of this period, a short aria in a single tempo). A recitative and an *arioso dolente* (grieving) precede the fugue which is the finale of the piano sonata in A flat, opus 110 (1821), and the fugue is interrupted for a return of the *arioso*. 'Cavatina' is the heading given to a slow movement in the string quartet in B flat (opus 130), the second of those three late quartets (1824–6) which form an unprecedented cycle, unified by the presence of a single germinal theme.*

The order and the significance of these three quartets (not quite the last three, for opus 135 in F follows) are confused by the accident of publishing and by a major change to which Beethoven consented. In true sequence, the first is opus 132 in A minor (in five movements), then opus 130 in B flat (six movements), then opus 131 in C sharp minor (seven movements). The single, four-note theme which unifies the three occurs in various guises, some obscure. It becomes one of the subjects of the *double fugue* (that is, a fugue which treats two subjects) which Beethoven placed as the finale of the B flat quartet. But this fugue made such a long and such a difficult finale that Beethoven was persuaded by friends to withdraw it and substitute a newly written, easier movement. The omitted movement was published separately and is known as the Great Fugue (Grosse Fuge).

In some modern performances, with every justification, it has been restored to its original place in the B flat quartet. When so restored, its combination of impulsive energy with the most learned devices of counterpoint and with the most extreme dynamics and ranges of the instruments makes a drastic contrast with the two preceding (fourth and fifth) movements – a relaxed 'German dance' (i.e. waltz) of simple structure, and the emotionally intense 'Cavatina'. It is in this 'Cavatina' that Beethoven makes use of the direction 'anguished' (*beklemmt*). In all the last quartets – and here we mean all five, from opus 127 inclusive, plus the Great Fugue if counted separately – this quality of peculiar intensity is unmistakable.

This late-Beethoven quality is precisely what seems to have baffled the comprehension of even some well-qualified

---

*It is by analysis, not by any word of Beethoven's, that these three quartets have been identified by several commentators as a set or cycle. A dissenting voice is raised by the author of an impressive recent analysis: Joseph Kerman, *The Beethoven Quartets*, New York: Knopf, 1967.

musicians of the composer's time. Louis Spohr (1784–1851), a fellow-German though he was, believed that deafness had caused Beethoven to write in a style 'more and more eccentric, unconnected, and incomprehensible. . . . I freely confess that I have never been able to relish those last works of Beethoven. Yes! I must even reckon the much-admired Ninth symphony among them . . . Beethoven [showed himself] wanting in aesthetic feeling and a sense of the beautiful.' Yet Spohr was a widely cultivated, well-travelled musician. A distinguished violinist, he had also become one of the most celebrated of composers,* and was one of the first musicians (like Beethoven himself) to use the baton to conduct instead of leading with the violin bow or from the piano stool. The claim in his autobiography to have been the first to conduct with a baton at a London concert (in 1820) appears to be based on faulty memory, however; reports in London newspapers make no mention of the innovation until the 20-year-old Mendelssohn's visit as conductor in 1829.

Like Mendelssohn (see below, p. 225), Spohr was a composer for whom the classic ideals of grace and clarity meant more than Beethoven-like intensity. Similarly the once-celebrated pianist and composer Johann Nepomuk Hummel (1778–1837), a pupil of both Haydn and Mozart, cultivated forms and piano textures which proceed from Mozart himself, with the addition of new virtuosity and dazzle; Chopin (see below, p. 226) seems to have learnt from his works, as also from those of John Field (1782–1837) an English pianist-composer who settled in St Petersburg, toured Europe from there, and invented the name and form of the nocturne as a solo piano piece.

When not yet 20, John Field acted as a salesman and demonstrator for Muzio Clementi (1752–1832), an Italian composer whom Beethoven admired and who had settled in England and become an active partner in a London piano-

---

* A fame which extends to W. S. Gilbert's reference in *The Mikado* (1885): 'by Bach, interwoven with Spohr and Beethoven'. But no doubt Gilbert, having pre-empted Bach, had little remaining choice of one-syllabled composers.

manufacturing firm. England had at this time taken the lead in piano manufacture (we have noted Beethoven's liking for the Broadwood instrument), and the piano – either grand or square – had already become the ornament of gentility in England. Jane Austen's *Pride and Prejudice*, written in 1797 (though not published till 1813), tells us that great ladies had one instrument in the drawing-room and one for the house-keeper, whereas country lawyers and lesser clergymen did without. The invention (in England, in 1802) of the upright or cottage piano soon diffused the instrument throughout the lower-middle grades of society too. With the multiplication of pianos went a comparable increase in music for it, much of it as fleeting as today's pop, and usually fitted with a saleable title, often in fashionable French. Even Beethoven consented to label his sonata in E flat, opus 81a (1808) 'Sonate caractéristique: Les Adieux, L'Absence, et Le Retour' – in deference, apparently, to his publisher, who objected to a German title. Some other well-known Beethoven titles, e.g., 'Pastoral' for the sonata in D, opus 78 (1801), are publishers' nicknames.

Among the torch-bearers at Beethoven's funeral in Vienna was Franz Schubert (1797–1828), whose own short life had but 20 months to run. Living in Beethoven's Vienna, Schubert's individuality remained largely independent of Beethoven's influence. An exceptional and peculiar case of recall (deliberate or unconscious?) occurs in the finale of Schubert's Ninth symphony, where (bar 390) the great choral melody of the finale of Beethoven's own Ninth is unmistakably brought to mind. But Schubert's magnificent, hour-long symphony (which, like the two-movement No. 8 in B minor, the 'Unfinished', the composer was never to hear in performance), has a cogency rare in Schubert's large in-strumental works. Too often, lacking the tension and com-pression of Beethoven's, they tend to spread – to rely too much on repetition and too little on argument, or to rest simply on song-like beauty of melody. Thus it is with the symphonies before the 'Unfinished': of these Nos. 1–5 are youthful works (1813–16) and No. 7 was left by the composer only in sketch form. The simpler, lighter pieces aim less high and succeed: among them, the two *Overtures in Italian Style* (Schubert's tribute to Rossini, whose operas were beginning to capture Vienna along with other centres) and the enchanting entr'acte to the play, *Rosamond* (the German form is *Rosamunde*).

The most celebrated of Schubert's larger piano works is the *Fantasia in C* (1822), which quotes from his own song *The wanderer* – though the nickname of 'The Wanderer Fantasia' is not the composer's. Its transformation of themes foreshadows the method of Liszt who paid the work his own tribute in rearranging it for piano and orchestra. Schubert's other large-scale piano works include nine mature, completed sonatas – those numbered* as D.664 in A, D.784 in A minor, D.840 in C, D.945 in A minor, D.850 in D, D.894 in G, D.958 in C minor, D.959 in A, and D.960 in B flat. If, despite the advocacy of such pianists as Artur Schnabel and Svyatoslav Richter, these have not quite established themselves, the reason is perhaps again their structural *longueurs* – while the shorter pieces continue to delight, including the eight called *Impromptu*, the six called *Moment Musical*, and the waltzes. These shorter pieces represent the domestic Schubert, as does the *Trout Quintet* (1819) for the unusual combination of piano, violin, viola, cello and double-bass: here variations on Schubert's song *The Trout (Die Forelle)* form an extra movement inserted before the finale, making five movements in all.

Diverting as is the 'Trout' quintet, it was to be surpassed in cogency and richness by the string quartets in A minor (1824), D minor (1824), G (1826) and by the quartet movement of 1820, as also by the string quintet with two cellos (Schubert's last work – 1828). In the quartet in A minor, the slow movement is based on a familiar tune from the *Rosamond* entr'acte; in the Quartet in D minor, the slow movement takes as its basis Schubert's song *Death and the maiden*, which has therefore lent its name to the quartet as well. From 1824 also comes

* 'D.' in the numbering of Schubert's works stands for the authoritative list made by Otto Erich Deutsch and published in 1951.

the octet (clarinet, horn, basson, string quartet, double-bass).

Schubert hoped, in vain, to make a success of opera: *The Conspirators* (*Die Verschworenen*), never staged in his lifetime, is very occasionally heard today. He also wrote a fair amount of church music of the grand, orchestrally accompanied Viennese type, including an admired Mass in A flat, and (foreshadowing a large body of nineteenth-century choral music to vaguely ethical or uplifting texts) a superbly imagined setting of Goethe's *Song of the spirits over the water* (*Gesang der Geister über den Wassern*) for male voices with accompaniment of violas, cellos, and double-basses (1823). But in none of the large-dimensional vocal forms did Schubert's genius shine out with such bright, and such varied light as in the solo song. (The German word '*Lied*', plural '*Lieder*', has become accepted in the non-German world for the intense and highly artistic German song of this type, but in a sense it is a misnomer, being as generalized a word as 'song' itself.)

Schubert's 606 songs are an achievement unmatched in his day or since. He wrote 140 during the year 1815 alone. Gluck, Haydn, Mozart and Beethoven all left a few songs, and lesser composers like Reichardt and Zelter wrote many, but with Schubert there seems to come a new musical responsiveness to the text. Such responsiveness wells forth not merely in the vocal line but in the piano accompaniment, often a marvellous fusion between pictorial imitation and a purely musical idea. We may instance the many and varied representations of the running brooklet in his *Fair Maid of the Mill* cycle (*Die Schöne Müllerin*) of 1823, or the melancholy droning of the barrel-organ in *The Organ-Grinder*, the last song of his other cycle, *The Winter Journey* (*Die Winterreise*). The so-called 'Swan Song' set, published posthumously, is not a cycle but a miscellany.

One of the most famous of these pictorial-musical fusions is the triplets of the galloping horse in *The Erl-King* (*Erlkönig*). This, on the poetic image of Death as ghostly pursuer, is one of Schubert's 1815 songs, and one of his 71 solo settings of Goethe; even earlier, when he was but seventeen, he set

*Gretchen at the spinning-wheel* (*Gretchen am Spinnrade*) from Goethe's *Faust*. The flowering of German lyric and romantic poetry – from Goethe (1749–1832) to Heine (1797–1856) – inspired Schubert. Yet it was a less distinguished writer, Wilhelm Müller, who was the poet of his two great cycles; poetry that carries *less* richness of meaning sometimes gains more from music. His songs were welcomed at musical evenings organized by prosperous middle-class Viennese, the composer accompanying while his friends sang.

A Schubert song may be of a simple, verse-repeating kind (that is, the identical music is repeated for each successive stanza of the text), like a folksong – as in *Wandering* (*Das Wandern*), the cheerful song which opens *The Fair Maid of the Mill*. Such songs are often called *strophic*, the term 'strophe' here meaning a stanza of verse. At the other extreme is the song in which the melody has no repetitions at all, the 'on-running'* song. A famous example is *The phantom double* (*Der Doppelgänger*), to a text by Heine in which the speaker sees an anguished figure outside a house and recognizes that it is himself. In this song, one of Schubert's last, no two bars in the singer's line are identical. Yet there is a compelling unity about the song, not merely through the repetition and variation of a sequence of four chords in the accompaniment, but through the pattern of the vocal melody itself: an eight-bar strain, a second eight-bar strain which is a variation of the first, a contrasting strain (fundamentally 16 bars, but ex-tended to 18), and a final strain which recalls the first but which is 'distorted' by emotional harmonies and extended to 14 bars.

Some of Schubert's most characteristic, and most telling, songs are those which take a mid-stand between these two extremes – that is, with certain sections which give literal repetition of melody, while other sections are new episodes, or variations of what went before. In this middle category

* Or 'developing' song. Such terms are attempted equivalents to the German analytical term '*durchkomponiert*' ('through-composed', if that were English). I should be grateful for a more elegant, yet lucid, substitute.

belong, in their different ways, the second song of *The Fair Maid of the Mill* (*Whither?* or *Wohin?*) and the justly admired *Resting-place* (*Aufenthalt*, poem by Ludwig Rellstab).

There is perhaps but one contemporary of Schubert's who deserves to be mentioned with him as a composer of German songs: Carl Loewe (1796–1869). Some have preferred his *Erl-King*, written when Schubert's was yet unpublished, to Schubert's own. Such a setting of a poetic narrative, as distinct from a poem of 'first-person feeling', is called a ballad (a different sense from that which we have encountered in ballad opera; see p. 162).* Another famous ballad of Loewe's is *Edward* – the Scottish folk-poem of that name, in German – and his other settings include 24 to translations of texts by Byron, whom he favoured more than any other poet except Goethe.

The fascination exerted on composers by Byron, and also by Scott, may take by surprise anyone mindful only of their present reputations. To Donizetti's *Lucia di Lammermoor* (after Scott's *The Bride of Lammermoor*), we must add Verdi's early operas *The Two Foscari* and *The Corsair* (Byron); likewise Berlioz's *Harold in Italy* (Byron) and his *Rob Roy* and *Waverley* overtures (Scott), Bizet's opera *The Fair Maid of Perth* (Scott), Schumann's incidental stage music to *Manfred*, and Tchaikovsky's *Manfred Symphony* (Byron). The admiration given to these two writers was prompted alike by the delicacy of their lyrics and by their epic boldness of theme. Schubert was too early for Byron, but in 1825 he set three lyrics from Scott's *The Lady of the Lake*. One is the well-known *Ave Maria* – not, incidentally to the liturgical prayer of that name; Scott's title was simply *Ellen's song*.

Were there no English song-writers to catch, at this time, the inspiration of this flow of English lyric verse? Thomas Attwood (see above, p. 184) interpreted this *Ellen's song* of Scott's before Schubert did, in a fine setting that deserves a

---

* Different too from the Victorian ballad, i.e. a sentimental drawing-room song. The 'narrative' sense of the term is, however, present in various operatic examples including 'Senta's Ballad' in Wagner's *The Flying Dutchman* and Dame Hannah's 'Ballad' in Sullivan's *Ruddigore*.

modern reprint.* Later Edward Loder (1813–65) set Longfellow's English translation of *Wohin?* (the second of the poems of *The Fair Maid of the Mill*) : whether or not he knew Schubert's, his own is a little masterpiece. But the combination of genius and circumstances which came together in Schubert and Vienna was not to be found in England – where, indeed, the suffocation of Loder by the cruder sentimental taste of the Victorian ballad (as in his own *The diver*) is painfully clear. The successors in song to Schubert were those who shared his native tongue – Schumann, Brahms and Wolf.

* The music of this song is quoted in my essay on English Song in *A History of Song*, ed. Denis Stevens, Hutchinson, 1960.

## 14

# The Romantic Impulse

WITH its mysterious chords for four kettledrums and its frenzied shrieks on the clarinet, Berlioz's 'Fantastic' symphony is different in kind, as well as in length, from a symphony by Mozart. The secret messages that peep through Schumann's *Carnaval** have no counterpart even in the most rich and strange passages of one of Beethoven's late piano sonatas. The scene in the Wolf's Glen from Weber's *Der Freischütz*, when the whole of nature is upheaved during a black-magic ceremony, is a world away from the orderly miracles of Gluck's *Orpheus*. At the hands of Chopin and Liszt, the piano shimmers, cascades and thunders. Mendelssohn, in the overture to *A Midsummer Night's Dream*, 'brought the fairies into the orchestra and fixed them there' (a famous comment by Sir George Grove, a great Victorian who first edited the famous many-volumed *Dictionary of Music and Musicians* which still bears his name).

We recognize here the phenomenon of the romantic composer. Similarly we speak of the romantic orchestra, newly enlarged, newly expressive – and newly codified by Berlioz in his *Treatise on Modern Instrumentation and Orchestration* (1844), still the most famous work of its kind; and of the romantic interpreter, passionate and possessed – a Paganini, of whom profitable legends circulated that his inspiration came from the devil. If there is one central idea among so many different manifestations, it is of the musician as the vehicle for *feeling*, rather than as the expert in construction. The musician becomes a kind of priest or prophet, making explicit the messages of contemplation and dream, of creation itself.

The moment of rapture was described by Wordsworth: the moment when

* The French (not German) title is deliberate on the composer's part: see p. 229.

> we are laid asleep
> In body, and become a living soul:
> While with an eye made quiet by the power
> Of harmony, and the deep power of joy,
> We see into the life of things.

Wordsworth found it relevant to specify the place of his inspiration in the title of his poem ('Lines written a few miles above Tintern Abbey', 13 July 1798). Mendelssohn in 1829 travelled by train, coach and boat to the Hebrides . . . and 'the following came into my mind there' he wrote in a letter shortly after, jotting down what we now know as the principal theme of the *Hebrides* overture. Romantic music often takes its inspiration from a scene, an event, a poetic idea. Works for which the composers did *not* supply a picturesque or similar non-musical title often acquired one by nickname – Chopin's so-called *Raindrop* prelude (opus 28, No. 15 in D flat) and *Winter Wind* study (opus 25, No. 11 in A minor) for instance. In the case of Liszt's orchestral work, *The Preludes*, we even find the composer himself deciding on a title with an outside reference (a poem by Lamartine, not really related to the music at all) *after* the piece had been composed. The frequency with which Shakespeare was drawn on for romantic musical subjects, and the general homage paid by composers to Shakespeare in the nineteenth century (after almost total indifference in the eighteenth) is no accident. The romantic artist was attracted not only by the character of Shakespeare's heroes and heroines, but by the free construction of his plays (as opposed to the classically unified, formal French drama of Racine and Voltaire). The international vogue of Scott and Byron has already been noted – Scott with his historical narrative and exotic Caledonian locations; Byron, who proclaimed freedom as well as adventure and who died (1824) in support of Greek national rebellion.

What then does 'romantic' mean? Little significance is to be found in early musical uses of the term 'romance' – a heading for the slow movement of Mozart's piano concerto in D minor; the title of two short works by Beethoven for violin and orchestra. But from about 1820 romanticism in music becomes the counterpart to literary romanticism. Distrustful of traditional forms, it devises new ones to accommodate new and particular sentiments. It exalts active heroism – but contemplation too. It recognizes the tormented mind, even the mind of superstition and madness. It calls on sympathy for humanity and awe in the presence of nature. It cultivates the tale of high adventure and of devoted love: the *tale* is important, for here is not only a link with the 'romance' of medieval authors but a hint of the special place now won by *song* – that is, the solo song, often to a narrative text. One meaning of *romance* in French (now obsolete) and in Russian (still current) is simply a song of a personal, expressive type.

Romanticism in music may borrow romantic literary subjects (for an opera, for the newly developing art of ballet, for a choral cantata or a song) and may also devise a musical idiom which itself suggests romantic pathos. Certain musical symbols become current. The horn-calls sounding through the dark forest – Tennyson's 'horns of Elf-land, faintly blowing', or hunters' calls, or danger-signals for warriors or lovers – are heard in Weber's *Oberon* (1826) and Schubert's Ninth symphony (1828); in Berlioz's *The Trojans* and Wagner's *Tristan and Isolde* . . . and on through Bruckner and Mahler to Schoenberg's *Songs of Gurra*. The diminished seventh becomes the 'anxious' or 'spooky' chord, and the tremolo of strings (mimicking a trembling of the body) indicates suspense or terror.

The tale, the narrative in music, is cultivated much, and in various forms. It is at the basis of Chopin's *Ballades*,* of Liszt's symphonic poems, and of songs such as those which Schumann entitles *Romances and Ballads*. Of these the most famous is *The Two Grenadiers*, in which Heine's poem imagines Napoleon's soldiers rising from the dead at the emperor's call. (Schumann's resurrection signal is the

---

*Despite the insistence of modern writers that these works of Chopin's were *not* a direct interpretation of poems by his compatriot, Adam Mickiewicz (1798–1855), 'ballade' here still implies narrative, even if an imaginary one.

*Marseillaise*.) This poem was also set by the young Wagner. Perhaps the most celebrated of all Heine's lyrics, *The Lorelei* (about the siren of the Rhine), achieved a folksong-like popularity in a simple setting by Friedrich Silcher (1789–1860) and was later set by Liszt as well.

But the inspiration given by Heine (1797–1856) to the musical romantics was not merely as a writer of verse. A prose tale of his directed Wagner's imagination to *The Flying Dutchman*. He was also a critic, employing a mordant wit in writing about the musical scene in Paris for a German newspaper. He was, says the historian of criticism,[*] 'the first to write about music and musicians not as an expert but as a journalist'. Romanticism in music and in literature fed on each other. Already the German novelist E. T. A. Hoffmann (1776–1822) had reinterpreted Mozart's *Don Giovanni* in a romantic spirit and had himself composed, as an amateur, several operas: he was himself to become the hero of Offenbach's *The Tales of Hoffmann* (see below, p. 251).

A number of composers ably expressed their artistic creeds in literary form. Schumann, at the beginning and end of his activities as a music critic, discovered both Chopin and Brahms. Though Schumann's and Berlioz's critical essays and notices have become famous and have often been reprinted, it is less often remembered that Weber also wrote criticism (and an unfinished novel). Among the works he praised was E. T. A. Hoffmann's *Undine* (1816), of which the fairy-tale plot – and some musical characteristics – prefigure the operas Weber himself was to write. Spohr wrote an entertaining (not wholly reliable) autobiography, already referred to (p. 207). Liszt wrote critically on Chopin, Field, Wagner and many others, and specifically proposed that composers should equip themselves to become critics. Wagner was a prolific autobiographer, pamphleteer, and essayist for more than 40 years.

Pursuing an ideal of freedom in music – a freedom from supposedly fixed classical forms – the romantic composer was generally also on the radical left, in social and political

[*] Max Graf, *Composer and Critic*, Chapman & Hall, 1947.

matters. The physical involvement of Wagner in the German revolutionary movement of 1849 (see below, p. 234) is an extreme case of a general tendency to be against the establishment – of courts and Church. Verdi, whose operatic plots had led to clashes with the Austrian censor at Venice (over *Rigoletto*) and with the Bourbon censor at Naples (over *A Masked Ball*) felt it his duty in 1861 to become a member of the parliament of the new, liberal Italy.

The political passion of nationalism, active at this period, overlaps the romantic movement in date and spirit, but is not to be identified with it. Verdi and Wagner, both born in 1813, will be dealt with in the next chapter, where the special role of opera in musical nationalism is noted. The remainder of the present chapter treats of certain composers born rather earlier, in whom the romantic impulse is seen variously to ebb and flow, to triumph or to be resisted. In chronological order of birth (which will be followed) they are Weber, Rossini, Berlioz, Mendelssohn, Chopin, Schumann and Liszt.

Carl Maria von Weber (1786–1826), north German by birth, died prematurely in London, less than two months after the first performance of his *Oberon* there (1826) – the sole example, until Stravinsky turned to *The Rake's Progress*, of an original English opera by a major composer whose native tongue was not English. *Oberon* had been commissioned for Covent Garden after the international success won by *Der Freischütz* (1821): that title, literally 'the freeshooter', can be approximately rendered as 'the marksman with the magic bullets'. To both these works Weber gave the description 'a romantic opera', perhaps with particular allusion to the supernatural elements in their plots. Commerce with the devil has objective human consequences in *Der Freischütz*; and in *Oberon* the fairy king transports the hero bodily and by magic from scene to scene. Between these two works came *Euryanthe*, 'a heroic-romantic' opera, without supernatural elements but with a pseudo-medieval plot even less credible in human and theatrical terms.

*Oberon* and *Euryanthe* both furnish classic examples of bad, botched librettos crippling the music's power; and even *Der Freischütz* is now theatrically little more than a funny, folksy German tale. Yet the shapeliness of melody, the urgent rhythms, and the strong contrasts of mood which characterize these operas are striking features of their overtures – all based on tunes of the operas. That to *Der Freischütz*, in particular, lets the music speak in a remarkably individual way, thanks to the new, romantic orchestration. Little wonder that Berlioz in his treatise on that subject drew attention to the agitated string passage, the threatening horn-call, and the way the solo clarinet pierces the tremolo of strings with a phrase which begins, 'fortissimo', on a top G: 'Does it not depict the lonely maiden, the forester's fair betrothed, who, raising her eyes to heaven, mingles her tender lament with the noise of the dark woods agitated by the storm? Oh, Weber!'*

*Der Freischütz* and *Oberon* follow conventional German use and employ spoken dialogue; *Euryanthe*, with recitatives, is exceptional. But all three make a point of recurring themes in the orchestra to suggest recurrent ideas, characters, or presences. Here is the foreshadowing of Wagner's technique of leading-motives. Indeed in such a relatively early opera of Wagner's as *Lohengrin* (1850) the analyst spots *fewer* separate leading-motives than in *Euryanthe*. Weber's accomplishment here depends on his being (just as Wagner was) a master orchestrator. Nothing could be more simple – so simple indeed that it has since become a cliché of atmospheric music – than the evocation of a sinister atmosphere in the overture to *Der Freischütz* by three repeated low notes on pizzicato double-basses and kettledrums, against the conventional 'horror' chord of the diminished seventh. But how unmistakable is its effect! And, when we later discover that it accompanies the successive appearances on stage of the Devil (in this opera called Zamiel – a speaking role), how effective again!

---

* It is a pity to have to puncture Berlioz's eloquence by saying 'No, it does no such thing'. It depicts not the heroine but the hero, who, on the stage, is to sing the phrase of the clarinet.

Weber's other works include two concertos for clarinet, plus one clarinet *concertino* (little concerto) which, perhaps uniquely for its period, begins in one key (C minor) and ends in another (E flat).* Even less often heard are his two piano concertos and the *Concert Piece* (*Konzertstück*) for piano and orchestra, a title which perhaps arises from a reluctance to give the name 'concerto' to a work in four movements, rather than the usual three. A number of songs, 13 of them with guitar accompaniment, and a miscellany of piano solos and piano duets were evidently intended chiefly for the amateur and the domestic circle. The best-known of these piano pieces, the *Invitation to the Dance*, was orchestrated by Berlioz.

The difference in attitude between Weber and his long-lived contemporary, Gioacchino Rossini (1792–1868) was seized on by the French novelist, Stendhal, in his witty and justly famous *Life of Rossini* (1824). As he pointed out, the storm in *Der Freischütz* represents the upheaval of nature, the horror in trafficking with the devil, the tragic event in store for the hero: the storm in Rossini's *Cinderella* (1817) is simply a storm, an event useful because it allows the Prince's coach to break down, but not in the least cosmic, and, as Stendhal puts it, 'quite innocent of Teutonic implications'. Musically Rossini's storm (we may say the same about the storm in *The Barber of Seville*, dating from the previous year) is suitably loud and agitated, but regular and indeed repetitious. Certainly Rossini was in his day widely considered a noisy composer, yet his construction is one of almost excessive formality – both in the disposition of numbers within a score, and in the piling of four-bar phrase on four-bar phrase. There is nothing of wild sublimity, of sudden fancy, in him; almost nothing of romanticism, save in occasionally borrowing a romantic story or location here and there.

In composing his comic operas (on which his reputation mainly rests) he follows operatic procedures of a previous generation (Cimarosa's). He adapts them, however, to a more popular audience, with trombones and bass drum and

*See p. 274 for a late-nineteenth-century development of progressive tonality.

with those long gradual crescendo sections over a fast and steady beat – the so-called Rossini crescendo. He also exhibits a thoroughly eighteenth-century willingness to borrow from one work to another: one of the heroine's main tunes from *Cinderella* was originally given to the tenor in *The Barber of Seville* (but is usually cut in present-day performances of the latter). His comic types are stock: minx-ish heroine, noble tenor hero, comic elderly bass, stupid servants. Rossini's genius lies in the endless resource with which he invents, varies and embellishes the music of these various types, and in the speed with which a situation evolves on stage by means of masterly use of duet and ensemble.

Sometimes resource fails and routine sets in; at certain points Rossini could fall back (as a letter-writer does in ' I am, Sir, your obedient servant') on routine. Hence those stock cadences which Berlioz quotes for parody's sake in *Benvenuto Cellini*. Yet without such routine, who could have written, as Rossini did, two dozen operas by the time he was 26? – at a time, be it remembered, when effective copyright did not exist and it was by commissions for *new* works that an operatic composer survived.

The soprano voice had not at this time reached its later dominance on the opera stage, nor had the contralto settled into its later heavy, motherly type. Both *The Barber* and *Cinderella* have coloratura mezzo-soprano or contralto heroines. Of such a type, too, is the heroine of *The Italian Girl in Algiers* (1813), another sparkling work; likewise *The Turk in Italy* (1814), a not quite successful sequel, and *The Touchstone* (*La pietra del paragone*), of early date (1812) and clumsy dramatic shape.

Though a large number of operas by Rossini have been considerably revived since the Second World War, it is *The Barber of Seville**\* that remains the favourite. Beaumarchais's

---

\* An earlier (and successful) opera on *The Barber of Seville*, by Paisiello, was mentioned on p. 165. Beaumarchais's third play, *The Guilty Mother*, was eventually turned into a French opera (1966) by Darius Milhaud; an alternative modern sequel, in sardonic vein, is *Figaro Sues for Divorce* (1963) by the German composer Giselher Klebe (b. 1925).

play of the same name, from which it comes, is the first of three connected plays of which *The Marriage of Figaro* is the second. Almaviva and Figaro, suitor and go-between in the earlier play, have in the second play become married philanderer and his personal servant. In Rossini's hands Figaro as the ubiquitous barber and master of intrigue ('Figaro here, Figaro there') attains a peculiar reality which has made him a proverbial figure in the way that few operatic characters are. There are two further magnificent comic delineations in Bartolo (the heroine's jealous guardian) and Basilio (the priest, music-master, and gossip). But the pre-eminence of this work is no less secured by the way that comic intrigue is matched by musical invention. Uttering the same phrase in turn, all the characters urge Basilio with insincere solicitude to depart – in music that mocks operatic formality at the same time as mocking the empty compliments of conversation.

Italian comic opera was not Rossini's sole preoccupation. The work that first made him famous was *Tancred* (the Italian form is Tancredi) in 1813: the role of the hero, a warrior of the Crusades, is given to a mezzo-soprano, a successor to the rapidly vanishing castrato voice. *Othello* (after Shakespeare) took the stage in 1816, *Moses in Egypt* in 1818, *The Lady of the Lake* (after Scott) in 1819, *Semiramis* (after Voltaire) in 1823 – all 'serious' works, now surviving only by their names, their overtures, and an isolated aria or two. In such works, though not in his comic operas, Rossini dispensed with traditional Italian dry recitative, accompanied only by harpsichord and cello, in favour of fully written-out, orchestrally accompanied recitative – in what had been the French, not the Italian, fashion.

Later Rossini himself embraced and enlarged French opera: settling in Paris from 1824, he proceeded to write a delicious and delicate French comic opera in *Count Ory* (1828) and, with *William Tell* (1829), to inaugurate the long, brilliant, historically based, patriotic, pageant-like spectacle which we now know as French grand opera. (The end, a slow and spacious hymn to liberty instead of the expected peremptory rejoicing, is a rare touch in Rossini of romantic sublimity

– like a Wordsworthian landscape.) The most successful practitioner of this form turned out to be another non-Frenchman, the German-born Giacomo Meyerbeer (see p. 250).

Perhaps deliberately refusing to emulate such works, Rossini wrote no operas in the 39 years of his life which remained after *William Tell*. His mass (a concert-setting nearly two hours in length, ironically entitled *Little Solemn Mass*) and a few piano pieces and songs are almost his only musical legacy of those last years. Among his visitors in Paris was the young Arthur Sullivan (1842–1900), who was not slow to profit from Italian comic opera, particularly its complex intermediate finale. And did the young Gilbert, when he came to prepare the topsy-turvy plot of *The Pirates of Penzance*, ever learn from his collaborator that Rossini had been born in leap year on 29 February?

That Hector Berlioz (1803–69) was unsympathetic to the formulas of Italian opera and to most of Rossini's works is typical of his approach to art. Berlioz is Rossini's opposite, a true romantic, one who prizes sublime irregularities and singularities, and whose gods are Gluck and Beethoven, Virgil and Shakespeare. For Berlioz the artist is a being possessed by divine fire; artistic laziness is therefore a kind of blasphemy, and life and art are inseparable. In a letter of 1859 Berlioz complained to a friend of Rossini's 'ranting, buffooning and joking – sometimes stupid joking': he is referring to personal demeanour, but one may suppose that an artistic criticism is implied too. It would be tempting to identify Rossini with Italian exuberance, Berlioz with French sensibility – save that Berlioz has never won much of a following among his own countrymen.

He is commonly thought of, and not unjustly, as a cultivator of the colossal. His *Fantastic Symphony* (1830), characteristically bearing the quasi-autobiographical subtitle 'Episodes in the Life of an Artist', goes outside conventional symphonic limitations in calling for two tubas, a high clarinet in E flat, English horn, deep-sounding bells, and four kettledrum players who evoke distant thunder by unprecedented soft chords for four drums. His *Requiem* (1837) increases the demand to 10 drummers playing 16 drums, and four groups of brass instruments in different corners of the building. Later came a *Te Deum* using 900 singers and instrumentalists, 'performed today with the most magnificent exactitude', wrote the composer to a friend in 1855. 'It was colossal, Babylonian, Nineveh-ian. . . . My God, why weren't you there? I assure you, it's a formidable work: the "Judex" surpasses all the enormities I have been guilty of before.' Four years before he had been in London and had heard 6,500 'charity children' sing in their annual festival service in St Paul's Cathedral. He was moved to tears: 'Nature reasserted its right to be weak, and I had to make use of my music copy, as Agamemnon did of his toga, to veil my face. . . . A great nation, which possesses the instinct of great things! The soul of Shakespeare lives in it!'

Berlioz's opera *The Trojans* is gigantic in its epic, Virgilian theme as well as in its dimensions. The whole of Berlioz is here – which means some passages of extreme delicacy, as well as of mighty force. The desperate yet triumphant self-immolation of the Trojan virgins, the widely known *Royal hunt and storm* exemplify its imaginative power. Unusually long, it is sometimes given as two operas on two evenings: *The Capture of Troy* followed by *The Trojans at Carthage*. (The second of these was first given in Paris in 1863, the first never in Berlioz's lifetime.) After *The Trojans* Berlioz composed *Beatrice and Benedick* (1862) which requires the speaking of Shakespeare's lines. His first opera of all had been *Benvenuto Cellini* (1838), a work full of fire but flawed in story, proportion, and detail – or so it seemed till 1965, when a reconstructed 'original' score was found at Covent Garden to make more theatrical and musical sense than the reduced version which Berlioz was later induced to publish. The popular *Roman Carnival* overture was drawn by Berlioz from this work. *The Damnation of Faust* (1846) is a concert work for soloists, chorus and orchestra, but has sometimes been theatrically staged; *Romeo and Juliet* (1839), called a 'dramatic symphony, with choruses' (it has also contralto and tenor soloists) was intended – as the instructions on the score make clear – for a spatial, though not scenic, performance.

Aeneas, Cellini, Faust, Romeo . . . such are some of the heroes whom Berlioz chose to depict in music. Another was Byron's Childe Harold: Berlioz's *Harold in Italy* (1834), the most famous work ever written for solo viola and orchestra, was commissioned by Paganini but apparently never played by him. The concert overtures *Waverley* (*c.* 1827) and *Rob Roy* (1832) refer to Scott; *The Corsair* (1855) to Fenimore Cooper's *The Red Rover* (not Byron's *The Corsair*). The song-cycle *Summer Nights* testifies (especially in its orchestrally accompanied version, mostly dating from 1856) to a delicacy, and a skill as miniaturist, which might not be suspected from the colossal Berlioz. Delicacy and detail also characterize much of the oratorio *The Childhood of Christ* (1854).

Berlioz remains an island of music. The individuality of his style is founded on melodies of irregular length and harmonic progressions often wrong by the textbook: as in Gluck, as in Mussorgsky, one may admit that there *is* a lack of schooling here, but that a strange, compulsive individual logic is often enough to replace it. Formally the *Fantastic Symphony*, with its single theme representing 'the beloved' and appearing in altered form in various movements, leads directly to Liszt's symphonic poems.

Mendelssohn too (properly Felix Mendelssohn Bartholdy, 1809–47) lent non-musical associations to his orchestral works. Like the *Hebrides* overture, the 'Scotch' symphony (symphony No. 3, completed 1842) was born of the composer's visit to Scotland in 1829. The 'Italian' symphony, though finished earlier (1833) was begun later and so is numbered 4. The symphony No. 5 (1830, but later revised) is the 'Reformation' symphony, quoting the (Catholic) *Dresden Amen* in the first movement and Luther's *A stronghold sure* (see p. 64) in the last. But none of these works tells a story or displaces formal balance for a pictorial effect. Even the overture to *A Midsummer Night's Dream*, admittedly representative of the characters of the play, keeps all within a formal frame: the musical hee-haw of Bottom (in his ass's

head) is like an impishness of Haydn's rather than a
grotesquerie of Berlioz's.

Mendelssohn is, if the paradox be permitted, the classic
among the romantic composers. In the 'Italian' symphony
the third movement is conspicuous for its regular balance and
symmetries (on classic minuet-and-trio lines), though with
romantic horn-calls incorporated. The modest orchestra
(double wind, but no trombones) is also characteristic;
Mendelssohn's cunning orchestration gives the illusion of
four-note horn-calls with two horns, two bassoons. The
violin concerto (1844), bold in bringing in the soloist without
a conventional first section for orchestra, is more romantic
in the songful tune of the slow movement and in the
recitative-like bridge between slow movement and quick
finale.

Mendelssohn was a highly skilled pianist, organist, conductor (one of the first, in the modern sense) and a musician
of some historical vision: his revival of Bach's *St Matthew
Passion* (Berlin, 1829) amounted to a rediscovery of a buried
work. As a composer, he began with comet-like brilliance: to
have achieved the *Midsummer Night's Dream* overture at 17
was perhaps the most prodigious feat of youth in the entire
history of musical composition. Seventeen years later he went
back to compose the incidental music to the play itself.
Mendelssohn's famous Wedding March comes from this
(and has no connection with church whatever). His grace of
style won an extraordinary domestic popularity for the *Songs
without Words* for piano – six books, 36 pieces, composed
1830–45: most of the popular titles, e.g. *The bees' wedding*,
are not the composer's own. He successfully updated the
ideas of Handelian oratorio in his own *St Paul* (Düsseldorf,
1836) and *Elijah* (Birmingham, 1846). The easy or comfort-
able qualities of his melodic and harmonic style have proved
less to the taste of posterity than to that of his own generation.

Many of the piano works of Frédéric Chopin (1810–49;
original Polish form, Fryderyk Franciszek Chopin) similarly
have the effect of songs without words. This songful quality
resides in a concentrated, powerful, well-curved melody and

short 'lines' like those of a verse stanza, and also in the composer's preference for forms where repetition, alternation, and variation are more important than development. The nocturne – a form popularized by Chopin, though pioneered by John Field (p. 207) – is almost always founded on straightforward ABA form (with the second 'A' freely varied), like a da-capo operatic aria. The well-known waltzes and polonaises and the much less well-known mazurkas (there are at least 55) preserve the easily appreciable formal qualities, as well as the rhythms, of the dance. The musical nationalism implied here will be discussed in the next chapter.

'Scherzo', which in Beethoven denotes a movement in a larger work, is for Chopin an independent piece in (basically) quick 3/4 time. The original connotation of humour has quite gone, but the relation to the minuet's basic ABA form remains. Chopin wrote four scherzos and four ballades – the latter having a less regular form and corresponding, as we have seen (p. 216), to imaginary narratives. With studies, preludes, two mature sonatas (the Funeral March was the first part of the B flat minor sonata to be written), and two concertos (numbered in the wrong order), Chopin gave almost his whole creative life to the piano as a solo instrument. A cello and piano sonata and 19 Polish songs are less often remembered.

An excellent pianist himself, he extended the pianist's technique, not least in the imaginative use of the sustaining pedal to produce special harmonic effects. He employs complicated simultaneous rhythms, wide leaps, rapid reiterations – and slow, singing lines too. Compare the melody of one of Chopin's most popular nocturnes, in E flat (opus 9, No. 2) with 'Casta diva' from *Norma* by Bellini, or some other contemporary Italian operatic air in slow time. In the opening of this same nocturne may be also noted that pathos in harmony (the second beat has a diminished-seventh chord) which sounds so characteristically romantic; but elsewhere Chopin's harmony has a fiercer sparkle about it and is historically audacious and far-reaching. Liszt and Wagner begin here.

Chopin belonged to the new music of his time, and it was brilliantly perceptive of a critic to declare 'Hats off, gentlemen, a genius!' as early as 1831 – in the presence of a very early work, Chopin's Variations for piano and orchestra on a theme (the duet, 'La ci darem la mano') from Mozart's *Don Giovanni*. The critic was himself a composer, born in the same year as Chopin: Robert Schumann (1810–56), whose writings proclaim him the foe of routine, the defender of such new talents as that of Berlioz. His criticisms, which introduce anecdote and imaginary characters, seem to reflect that same romanticism which is evident in Schumann's piano pieces, his songs and even such apparently abstract works as his symphonies.

Schumann's love-songs are *his* love-songs – so many of them from 1840, the year when marriage crowned his courtship of Clara Wieck (who, as 'Madame Clara Schumann', was later to be an internationally celebrated interpreter of her husband's piano music). The songs speak of romantic adoration. Birds, the spring, an old lute, the fancies of dreams and the mysterious transformations of night – the poets' romantic symbols prompt Schumann to delicately imaginative interplay of voice and keyboard. The keyboard is sometimes indeed the inner voice or the mind of the music. The seventh and last song of the cycle *Woman's love and life* (*Frauenliebe und -Leben*) tells how a blissful love ended with the husband's death. As the singer ceases, the piano immediately glides into the *first* song of the cycle. . . . The dawn of love is thus remembered, and the remembrance is conveyed by the piano alone.

Schumann's chosen poet in this cycle was Adalbert von Chamisso (1781–1838); but a greater poet, Heine, provided the verses for another famous cycle, *Poet's Love* (*Dichterliebe*) and other settings. This new quality for the instrument is but one of the ways in which Schumann is prophetic of Hugo Wolf (1860–1903). In three of his songs (and in four part songs) Schumann set words by Eduard Mörike (1804–75), whom Wolf was to cultivate so notably; and Schumann similarly anticipated the fancy of Gustav Mahler (1860–1911) and

Richard Strauss (1864–1949) in setting two poems from *Des Knaben Wunderhorn* (*The Youth's Magic Horn*), a collection of re-worked German folk poetry which had been published in 1806–8 by Achim von Arnim (1781–1831) and Clemens Brentano (1778–1842).

Schumann's best-known piano works are as personal as his songs. The *Carnaval* of 1834–5 – for which the *Papillons* (Butterflies) of 1832 seems in retrospect like a kind of pre-liminary study – may be taken as an example. The French language pays tribute to fashionable gallantry. The work is subtitled (also in French) 'pretty scenes on four notes', the notes corresponding to the letters A, S, C, and H – which calls for further explanation. 'S' means 'Es' (German form of E flat) while H stands for what we call B. These letters are the only 'musical' ones in Schumann's own name, as well as making up the place-name Asch, which is where his friend Ernestine von Fricken came from.

The four notes enter recognizably into most (not all) of 20 short pieces, and are also printed between two of the pieces in non-playing form under the heading 'Sphinxes'. The titles of the pieces introduce us to Eusebius and Florestan, members of the imaginary League of David whom Schumann created to give battle against the philistines of anti-art. (The members of the league are also to be encountered in Schumann's critical writing.) Another of the pieces is headed (and represents) *Chopin*; yet another is *Chiarina*, Italian diminutive for Clara, i.e., Clara Wieck. A *March of the League of David against the Philistines* concludes the carnival in high spirits. This is only one of many works by Schumann in which there are private references; indeed it seems likely that he employed actual ciphers (with letter-to-note correspond-ences) to an extent unguessed-at till recently.

*Carnaval* displays Schumann as a romantic – in its not purely musical 'programme', its short and non-developing numbers, and the intimacy of its private meanings. Yet its composer was to be more and more attracted to a severe and lofty style. Again four musical letters of the alphabet in-spired him: those of the name of Bach (B and H are the

German equivalent of our B flat and B natural.) The six fugues (1845) on the name BACH, for organ (or for piano with pedal-keyboard attached) display Schumann's own prodigious skill in the art of counterpoint. There are other works which similarly show Schumann's admiration for Bach, though his provision of piano accompaniments to Bach's unaccompanied works for solo violin and solo cello seems now a misplaced labour.

Schumann's four symphonies (all falling within the period 1841–51) apply a consciously traditional symphonic technique – based chiefly on Beethoven and Schubert – to the handling of romantic, often song-like melodies. Those who value severity of control above this buoyant romantic element prefer the four symphonies of Schumann's protégé, Brahms. Less controversy surrounds Schumann's piano concerto (1846), light in tone yet most cleverly worked out, with a marvellously eloquent solo part. A modest output of chamber music includes a much-liked piano quintet (1842).

That Mendelssohn and Schumann should have cultivated the 'baroque' Bach (though that is not a label they would have used) is not as odd as it may seem. The romantic vision was conscious of history and admiring of its monuments. Bach was, moreover, a German possession: 'Would it not be a timely and useful undertaking', Schumann wrote, 'if the German nation decided to publish a complete collection and edition of all the works of Bach?' The English revival of Bach, though gaining from the early initiative of the organist and composer Samuel Wesley (see p. 138) reached its peak in the wake of German example, when – by the mid nineteenth century – English non-operatic musicians had predominantly shifted to a German allegiance. The first London performance of the *St Matthew Passion* took place in 1854 under the (German-trained) composer William Sterndale Bennett (1816–75), pupil of Mendelssohn and friend of Schumann; the (London) Bach Choir was founded in 1875 under the conductorship of the German-born Otto Goldschmidt (1829–1907), husband of the 'Swedish nightingale', Jenny Lind (1820–87) – who typically had given up operatic stardom for the 'higher' service of oratorio and the like.

Schumann himself thought that choral-orchestral music was the loftiest form of composition. Moreover Bach seemed to offer an ideal of religious expression in music to composers who still hoped to stir their listeners with religious or loftily ethical texts. Composers who were freethinkers, such as Berlioz, Verdi, Brahms and Sir Hubert Parry in England), did not advertise the fact. The case of Liszt is of signal interest here, and we need not assume that the 'Abbé' Liszt (as he called himself after taking minor orders in the Catholic Church) is a less genuine article than the 'Don Juan' Liszt. Liszt represents not only romanticism but also a new nationalist inspiration in music. Grounded in the political nationalism stirred by Napoleon, this inspiration was to run its vital current through Europe for over a century.

An unsurpassed virtuoso of the piano, Franz Liszt (1811–86) wrote over 400 solo works for the instrument. (Franz is the German form of the Hungarian 'Ferenc'.) The *Studies in Transcendental Execution* (1851) provide astonishments of piano technique, paralleling Paganini's exploitation of the violin; the *Hungarian Rhapsodies* evoke the dashing Hungarian-gipsy style, sometimes suggesting the cimbalom (Hungarian dulcimer). Ravel's impressionism is foreshadowed in *The Fountains of the Villa d'Este* (1877). Following Beethoven, Liszt gave choral endings to his two symphonies (*Dante Symphony* and *Faust Symphony*, both first heard in 1857). He established the symphonic poem, an orchestral narrative in which a musical theme stands for a person or idea: *Mazeppa* (1851) alludes to the Cossack hero of Victor Hugo's poem. Precursor of Wagner's innovative harmonies, and a champion (as pianist, conductor and writer) of diverse talents from Berlioz to Grieg, Liszt has a historic importance not to be guessed at from the small proportion of his work surviving in the current repertory.

# 15

# The Verdi–Wagner Era

OPERA was a more popular medium in the nineteenth century than it is today. Even those who never entered an opera house might hear the latest operatic hits played by military bands, street organs, and café orchestras. Gathered round the household piano, singers would essay such morsels as 'Even bravest heart' from Gounod's *Faust*, or the favourite tenor aria from Flotow's *Martha*. Quadrilles and other dances were arranged (with piano accompaniment) from the favourite tunes of this or that opera. Operatic scores were available in special form for the domestic pianist – that is, with the vocal melody incorporated in the keyboard part, so that no singer was required.

Outside their theatrical engagements, opera stars appeared at concerts, mingling arias with popular ballads. Such stars, sopranos especially, aroused frenzies of enthusiasm almost comparable with today's stars of pop. The great American showman, P. T. Barnum, having already exhibited 'General' Tom Thumb, the midget, brought Jenny Lind to the United States in 1850 as the greatest conceivable attraction in what would now be called show business. The allure attaching to Jenny Lind and to the Italian, Adelina Patti (1843–1919), represents the phenomenon of prima-donna-dom at its height.

The travelling virtuoso pianist was expected to play a brilliant fantasy on operatic themes (Liszt wrote more than 50). The Wedding Chorus from Wagner's *Lohengrin* became the familiar 'Here comes the bride' of the English marriage ceremony, coupled in use with Mendelssohn's equally theatrical piece from *A Midsummer Night's Dream*. Operatic selections, sometimes sung by celebrated singers, were a regular component of English music-hall and the American vaudeville – mixed light entertainments which reached their peak of organization and social importance in the last decades of the century.

Odd though it now seems, what was then modern opera circulated more easily than what we now consider the symphonic classics. Orchestral concerts remained somewhat sparse and specialized until the second half of the century, and even in *their* programmes a heavy reliance was placed on operatic overtures, ballet music and vocal excerpts. The theatre was a more widespread form of public entertainment; and the operatic theatre, like its spoken counterpart, kept constantly in touch with current excitements and social themes. To a consciously nationalist composer – a Smetana, a Rimsky-Korsakov – opera gave the opportunity not only of appealing by fictional example to current political passion, but also of using a nationalist type of musical expression, particularly in rustic scenes and dances. Verdi, within an already secure Italian tradition, stood in less need of picturesqueness and peasantry, yet does not disdain the popular Italian touch in song and march.

Verdi's plots too have many topical references indicating his own sympathy with political liberalism and nationalism. In Naples in 1858, where *A Masked Ball* was about to receive its first performance, the crowd shouted 'Viva Verdi!' in the knowledge that the letters of the composer's name stood for *V*ittorio *E*mmanuele, *Re d'I*talia – Victor Emmanuel, King of Italy, the liberal sovereign who they hoped would replace the alien and tyrannical Bourbon dynasty. It was an identification of causes, not just an acrostic. (And indeed the Bourbon dynasty was overthrown in 1860, Victor Emmanuel being crowned as 'King of Italy' in the following year.) Like the Bourbon rule in the south and the Austrian rule over the northern part of Italy, the maintenance by the papacy of a harsh secular rule in the central region (the 'papal states') was obnoxious to liberals, and the liberal cause was necessarily anticlerical. In such a context it would not be thought accidental that the priesthood is the villainous element of both *Don Carlos* and *Aida*.

Wagner's work has equally clear political affiliations. At a time when German nationalism was passing from a liberal impatience with petty tyranny to a more aggressive exaltation of Prussian power, Wagner glorified German history and legend. In 1849, when he had just begun to write the libretto of *The Ring*, Wagner's known liberal opinions led the police to suspect him of complicity in the unsuccessful uprising in Dresden which had sought liberal reform in Saxony. A warrant was issued for his arrest as a 'politically dangerous person' and he fled to Paris, then to Zurich. Nearly 20 years later *The Mastersingers* proclaimed 'holy German art' as the supreme reconciling force between the best of tradition and the best of novelty. That was in 1868, just after the newly powerful Prussia under Bismarck (the 'Iron Chancellor') had inflicted on Austria an unprecedented military defeat; in 1871 she was to do likewise to France. It is understandable, if perhaps unfair, that the flaxen-haired, helmeted, breast-plated warrior-maiden of *The Ring* should have remained (right up to the Second World War) a political cartoonist's stereotype for German political ambition.

Giuseppe Verdi (1813–1901) and Richard Wagner (1813–83) dominate the operatic history of their time, Wagner adding to his specifically operatic achievement an enormously influential innovation in harmony, orchestration and theatrical practice. I shall discuss these two, and their respective Italian and German forerunners, in some detail, and then proceed to their contemporaries.

As Verdi was growing to manhood, leadership in Italian opera had passed from Rossini (who, as noted on p. 223, wrote no more for the stage after *William Tell*, 1829) to Gaetano Donizetti (1797–1848) and Vincenzo Bellini (1801–35). From literature they borrowed fashionably romantic subjects, but there is no romantic wildness (of Berlioz's or Weber's kind) in their music. They may spice their music with an occasional chord of emotional stress, but the melodies are all marked by formality and a certain superficial charm, just as elegance and poise are the main qualities required of its vocal performers. The heroine of Donizetti's

*Lucia di Lammermoor* (1835), may inhabit a gloomy castle in Sir Walter Scott's savage northern land, and may indeed murder her husband and go mad – but the symmetrical, gently curving melodies which insane Lucy sings are remarkably similar to those which serve other, sane heroines. The Italian expression *bel canto*, literally just 'beautiful singing', is often applied to the vocal art demanded in such works, where the singer displays an almost instrumental virtuosity of technique and never lets the emotional colouring of the words distort the essential purity of the line and beauty of tone.

The two main accomplishments of such singing, an intense and beautifully shaded slow delivery and a brilliant, accurate, fast delivery, are brought out in the chief formal construction used in such operas. This construction may be called the compound *scena* – a slow aria (*cavatina*) followed by a fast one (*cabaletta*), each introduced by its own recitative, the second recitative serving to change the mood from the slow aria (meditative) to the fast one (resolute). The whole *scena* (we use this Italian word, pronounced *shayna*, rather than its ambiguous English equivalent, 'scene') is commonly in a single basic key and focuses on a single character – or two characters. Other characters may join, conversation-like, in the recitative, and may also reinforce the end of the cabaletta (sometimes the end of the cavatina too). Lucy's mad scene (slow aria beginning 'Ardon gl'incensi', fast aria beginning 'Spargi d'amaro pianto') is exactly in this form, and is further typical in that slow and fast arias each have two stanzas to the same music, or the same with variations. But the transition between the two arias is unusually long and expressive.

Inherent in such dual construction is a psychological push (slow meditation yielding to vigorous resolution), which is also to be seen elsewhere in these operas, notably in similarly compound finales. This dynamism contrasts absolutely with the static, back-to-the-beginning quality of the da-capo aria favoured in the previous century. These dynamic constructions were not original to Donizetti's period; they had been developed earlier, mainly in comic opera. But they are now harnessed to the new kind of serious opera (or, to use a word sometimes found on the Italian title-pages, 'semi-serious'), in which the characters and situations are deployed to suggest pathos rather than grandeur.

Conversely, this note of pathos is now also cultivated in comic opera, where the comedy usually stops well short of farce and the love is genuine. It is in a *comic* opera of Donizetti's, *The Love Potion* (*L'elisir d'amore*), 1832, that we find one of the most famous of plaintive tenor love-lyrics, 'Una furtiva lagrima' (A furtive tear) with its superbly imagined bassoon *obbligato*. When for once Donizetti did go into farce, he excluded love altogether – in *Upstage and Downstage*,* about operatic squabbles, in which the role of a young female singer's interfering mother is played by a baritone.

Apart from *The Love Potion*, Donizetti's best-known comic operas are *The Daughter of the Regiment* (1840) and *Don Pasquale* (1843). The former, written in French for the Paris stage, has spoken dialogue in place of Italian recitative, following the fashion of French *opéra comique*. France's own contemporary practitioners of this genre are now barely remembered, save for Daniel Auber (1782–1871) and his *Fra Diavolo* (1830).

Rossini had already made an opera of *Othello* (1816) and now Bellini further exhibited the current passion for Shakespeare in *The Capulets and the Montagues* (1830). Here a curiosity survives. As if harking after the vocal postures of by-gone, baroque serious opera, Bellini makes Romeo a mezzo-soprano (successor, evidently, to the no longer available castrato). But in his later works he dropped the practice and cultivated, as other composers were to do, the soprano–tenor–baritone or soprano–mezzo-soprano–tenor 'triangle'. The semi-serious *The Sleepwalker* (*La sonnambula*, 1831) was

---

*This is the title under which the piece was first heard in English, translated by the present writer (B.B.C., 1969). The original Italian title, *Le convenienze e inconvenienze teatrali*, involves a double meaning of 'con-venience' and 'prerogatives'. The work was originally (1827) in one act, later extended by the composer to two.

followed later in the same year by *Norma* with its 'wild', northern Druid setting and its famous, long-spun soprano invocation to the moon-goddess, 'Casta diva'. (In this opera the third member of the triangle, Norma's rival Adalgisa, is designated a second soprano – though it is usually sung by a mezzo-soprano today.) In these works, as in *The Puritans* (1835), all the singing including the recitative is accompanied by the orchestra; the old dry recitative (accompanied by harpsichord or piano) has disappeared.

This change to a fully orchestral accompaniment was not merely a technical musical matter. A more homogeneous texture tends to suggest a greater continuity in the drama which is displayed on-stage. To Verdi this continuity was a consideration of the greatest importance. His operas show a perpetual search to create a forward-moving, realistic drama with as little 'standstill' as possible. Here he shows the influence of the contemporary French realistic play. Two of the works which did most to establish him internationally, *Rigoletto* (1851) and *La Traviata* (1853), are based on such plays, respectively Hugo's *The King Takes his Pleasures* and the younger Dumas's *The Lady of the Camellias*.

Verdi himself dated his career from *Nabucco* (short for Nabucodonosor, i.e. the biblical Nebuchadnezzar), produced in 1842. At a time when leading Italian liberals could not with safety remain in the autocratically ruled parts of their own country, 'exile' might be a word of political heroism: and sympathetic audiences could hardly fail to respond to the patriotic ardour of the chorus of Israelites exiled in Babylon. A similar response was aroused by the chorus of exiled Scottish noblemen in Verdi's *Macbeth* (1847). A political message was no less explicit in *Rigoletto*, in which the hunchbacked jester hero denounces the 'vile race of courtiers' after the abduction of his daughter. The Austrian censor at first flatly refused permission to have *Rigoletto* staged, yielding only after modifications were made to the text. Later *A Masked Ball* (1859) similarly collided with censorship: in this opera the historic assassination of a king at a masked ball (Gustav III of Sweden in 1792) was thought too dangerous for public exhibition and had to be replaced by an improbable slaying of a New England colonial governor. The Swedish setting is often restored in modern productions.

*Rigoletto* may be said to be realistic not only in the sense of being honest (the court's true corruption shown beneath its outward finery) but in its music. As confrontation and conversation are more frequent in real life than soliloquy, so here the solo display aria is subordinated to duets and ensembles. The rakish Duke's famous song on women's fickleness ('La donna è mobile') is not a display-piece but, so to speak, the Duke's favourite tune – that is, it might well be a song even if the rest of the drama were spoken. Later, at the height of dramatic tension, it serves to convey that the Duke, believed the victim of a hired assassin, is still alive. The well-known quartet is not four simultaneous soliloquies (as the sextet from *Lucia di Lammermoor* is six simultaneous soliloquies) but two simultaneous conversations.

A similar desire to bring the dramatic action of opera nearer to the crowded emotions of real life is *La Traviata* (The title is a term sentimentally bestowed by the courtesan-heroine on herself – not 'a wicked woman' but 'a woman who has strayed'.) There is extreme contrast between the glittering wealth of the Parisian party-scene and the poverty of the apartment where the heroine dies; and, within that apartment, no less a contrast between her own frail utterances and the rude carnival song of merry-makers outside in the street. Verdi's skill is to combine this truth with the purely musical, melodic appeal of the traditional Italian scena form described above – fundamentally, slow aria followed by fast, each introduced by recitative (but, with Verdi, slow aria and fast are not necessarily in the same key).

So in *La Traviata* the heroine's slow 'Ah, fors' è lui' (wondering if true love has come at last) is followed by 'Sempre libera' (resolving to banish such thoughts in a life of gaiety and freedom). Here Verdi injects a further constructive device, to be justified as representing dramatic truth. A main element in the slow section (beginning 'Ah,

quell'amor') is her recollection of the words and tune previously addressed to her by her suitor; and at the end of the
faster section, his voice joins in, not merely to support her but
to remind her (he is outside, having left the house) of that
melody and those sentiments.

Later, as she is on her death-bed and reads a letter from her
lover, this same theme of his returns – in the orchestra. Verdi
here admits the power of such 'reminiscences' both vocal and
orchestral; yet in *Il Trovatore* (1853) – the other corner-stone
of the *Rigoletto* and *Traviata* period – he does not use them.
The somewhat sprawling drama of *The Force of Destiny* (1862)
is given an element of unity in the recurrence of two purely
orchestral motives heard in the overture, one of them like the
hammer-blows of fate and the other a typical anxiety or
agitation theme. Yet Verdi never lets musical recurrence
become, as in Wagner, a principal and constant procedure.
In Verdi's later works, however, the orchestra speaks more –
that is, it utters arresting melodic phrases of its own in introductions or accompaniments to the voices – and the voices
themselves shift away from older recitative (in free rhythm,
approximating to speech rhythm) to a kind of measured
declamation which dovetails with the utterance of the
orchestra. Memorable examples of this vocal-orchestral language of Verdi's (using recitative, measured declamation,
and 'speaking' figures in the orchestra) are to be found in the
scene between King Philip V and the Grand Inquisitor of
Spain in *Don Carlos* (composed to a French text, 1867) and the
denunciation of the villain in the revised version (1881) of
*Simon Boccanegra* (end of Act I).

In his vocal requirements Verdi shifts the emphasis away
from agility and refinement (the old bel-canto accomplishment) towards weighty and passionate expression. As early as
1847 we find him rejecting a singer for the role of Lady
Macbeth because she sings too beautifully and 'Lady
Macbeth should not sing at all' (a comic exaggeration, of
course). He relegates the coloratura display to minor
characters like the page (soprano) in *A Masked Ball* and the
*vivandière* or camp-follower (mezzo-soprano) in *Don Carlos*.

His tenor heroes launch massive high notes over a weighty, pounding orchestra and make scarcely any use of their lower ones. The principal baritone parts (the Count of Luna in *Il Trovatore*, the Marquis of Posa in *Don Carlos*, etc.) are similarly concentrated on their highest and most forceful notes, in such an individual manner that 'the Verdi baritone' is now almost a technical classification of a type of singer.

Verdi maintained the traditions of separate-number opera up to *Aida* (1871). Commissioned to celebrate the opening of the Suez Canal, and with a story located in ancient Egypt, *Aida* includes processions, rituals and dances which bear witness to the inflation of the opera by the French-style requirements of the Cairo Opera House. But Verdi confines his picture-postcard, oriental touch to dancers and priestesses. The main characters speak without accent – or rather with that forceful accent of Verdi's own which was soon to stamp the *Requiem* (1874). This large-scale concert work, in which off-stage trumpets signal the day of judgement in a theatrical (and Berlioz-like) way, is one of the composer's few non-operatic works. The string quartet dates from 1873, the so-called *Four Sacred Pieces* (not really a set: one for chorus, three for chorus and orchestra) from the 1890s.

A more compressed harmonic language and a departure from traditional expansive melody mark Verdi's last two operas *Othello* (1887) and *Falstaff* (1893). The librettos were skilfully turned from Shakespeare's *Othello* and *The Merry Wives of Windsor* by Arrigo Boito (1842–1918), who had already revised the libretto of *Simon Boccanegra* for Verdi and was himself the composer of the opera *Mephistopheles* (1868) and other works. The hero of *Othello* has not as much as a single aria, and only one regular duet in firm-rhythmed metrical lines (the oath duet with Iago); for the rest, his character is displayed almost entirely by command or conversation. Iago has a little more of solo prominence – his brief Creed of Evil, his brief feigned account of Cassio's dream ('Era la notte'), and his drinking song (almost overwhelmed, rather than supported, by the chorus). To Desdemona, at least, the Willow Song and Ave Maria give something of an old-fashioned *scena,* but now with a newly elliptical harmony: a single plaintive D natural on the clarinet is succeeded by hushed orchestral chords of F sharp before Desdemona gasps forth the anguished high A sharp of her last good-bye to Emilia. *Falstaff,* with much recurrence of themes for the illustration of intrigue or comedy, has no larger quota of solo set-pieces for its principal characters. Ensemble is all, and the comedy ends with a fugue to the Italian equivalent of 'All the world's a jest'.

In Germany the 17 years between Weber's death and Wagner's first mature work (*The Flying Dutchman,* 1843) saw two lasting contributions by Albert Lortzing (1801–51) to the country's repertory: *Tsar and Carpenter* (1837) and *The Poacher* (*Der Wildschütz,* 1842), lightly tuneful comedies in the old German spoken-dialogue tradition. They failed, however, to win the international acclaim which came to *Martha* (1847) by Friedrich von Flotow (1812–83) – work in a not dissimilar musical mould, but pathetic as well as comic, with the English heroine going fashionably mad, a condition from which she is rescued by hearing 'The last rose of summer'.

By this time Wagner had started on his operatic self-apprenticeship, fashioning Shakespeare's *Measure for Measure* into *The Ban on Love* (*Das Liebesverbot,* 1836) and turning a recent English novel by Bulwer Lytton into *Rienzi, the Last of the Tribunes* (1842). *The Flying Dutchman,* his first success, significantly concerns itself with the notion of redemption through woman's love which Wagner henceforth found so dramatically fertile. In *The Flying Dutchman* the redemption idea takes the form of a recurring musical theme associated with the heroine, with another recurring theme to represent the storm-tossed, accursed Dutchman himself. The overture does not merely quote these (and other) themes, but does so in the manner of a symphonic poem, almost telling the story. Yet Wagner was here still writing old opera: that is, a work with each act divided into separate numbers and having more or less regular tunes. The Spinning Chorus would not be out of place in *Martha,* and Senta tells the story of her longed-for hero in a traditional ballad of three successive stanzas with chorus.

The redemption idea is again found in *Tannhäuser* (1845) and *Lohengrin* (1850), both on specifically German historical subjects. Here again is the old opera with its separate numbers, its tunes, its formal pageantry of procession, song contest, court ceremony. As distinct from what Wagner was later to contrive, ' the voice is still the statue and the orchestra the pedestal' (Ernest Newman). Yet already the orchestra's part becomes more meaningful in itself, actually seeking to interpret the text or actions, or to differentiate the characters in musical gestures like those of a symphonic poem. Recitative is now 'almost fully-clothed song' (Newman). Wagner had achieved in these works a highly individual, and superbly articulated, form of opera: a balance between word, note, gesture and scene, and a relation between the short phrase and a whole evening's music, which is given only to the greatest masters of the operatic theatre.

Yet it was *after* this, in 1865, that Wagner produced *Tristan and Isolde*, the work which not only demonstrates his new ideas of *music-drama* but which exposes a new harmonic idiom (partly developed from Liszt) – an idiom so influential that Romantic music is sometimes classified as pre- and post-Wagner, meaning pre- and post-*Tristan*. Here redemption yields to the dramatic acceptance of death as love's consummation: the name of Love-Death (*Liebestod*) is given, though it was not Wagner's term, to the ecstatic expiring of Isolde over her lover's body. Chromatic harmony expressive of yearning and torment attains an unprecedented force here.

Then in the four works which constitute *The Ring* (The Rhinegold; The Valkyrie; Siegfried; The Twilight of the Gods)* Wagner vastly enlarged the range and suppleness of

---

*The full title is *The Ring of the Nibelung* (not 'Nibelungs': it refers only to Alberich, who forswears love, snatches the gold, and forges the ring). The celestial warrior-maidens are usually called in English by the Norse-mythological form with an English plural: *The Valkyrie* (title of the work), *The Ride of the Valkyries* (German *Die Walküre, Walkürenritt*).

the orchestra, calling into existence the bass trumpet and the 'Wagner tubas' (tenor and bass instruments which bridge the gap between horn and true tuba tone) – and incidentally demanding six harps and, for Mime's underground smithy, 18 'anvils'. Unprecedentedly, there were 114 musicians in the orchestra when the first complete performance of *The Ring* was given in 1876 at Bayreuth, where Wagner had persuaded King Ludwig II of Bavaria to build him a festival theatre to his specifications.

The revolutionary theatrical architecture at Bayreuth (an indoor amphitheatre where every seat faces the stage, and where conductor and orchestra are submerged from view) achieved its triumph with *Parsifal*, Wagner's Christian legend (1882) where something very like the rite of Communion is seen on the stage. Here is not only the composer as priest or seer, but the composer's auditorium as temple. Wagner was his own stage director and also established our modern custom of completely darkening the theatre (with the result that librettos could not, as formerly, be read during performances) and of excluding late-comers. The astonishing thing is the consistency, the all-embracing quality, of Wagner's revolution. The works need that kind of theatre: the long-range interplay of themes (stretching in *The Ring* over four nights) demands the new instrumentation; the length of individual acts (up to two hours) is wholly consistent with the slow deployment of themes and the slow (yet not necessarily monotonous) general pace. That long, depths-of-the-Rhine chord which unfolds from a primeval bass at the beginning of *The Ring* is never afterwards belied.

Like other composers of his age, Wagner took to literature. His *Opera and Drama* (1851) represents both his historical view and his own plans for what he called music-drama as distinct from opera. The latter term had gathered associations with too many inartistic abuses (as he considered them), such as the routine *rum-ti-tum* accompaniments and meaningless word repetition notorious in Rossini and other Italians. Such music, he believed, betrayed its true purpose of expressing the drama: it misused the drama for indulgent musical self-display. On the other hand, Beethoven had produced symphonic music which did express a dramatic life of its own, articulated by thematic development. Let the theatre now be given similar music – but 'music fertilized by poetry'. In such music, expressing the stage action *as the composer conceives it* (not merely in how the moment is viewed by one of the characters themselves), musical development will take the form of the deployment of *representative themes* associated with ideas of the drama. These *representative themes*, capable of ever-new transformations and juxtapositions, are otherwise called leading-motives.*

Wagner's previous work had incorporated leading-motives (such as those for the Dutchman and his female 'redeemer') but only partially, without disturbing the division into 'numbers' or the primacy of the voice. Now leading-motives took over a pervasive role; division into 'numbers' was dropped; melody became endless instead of regular, and the voice became a strand of the total web of musical argument, and not always the most powerful strand. Wagner's music-dramas were thus planned to be symphonic, and it is true that extracts from them (even with voice parts removed) can be quite satisfactorily played by an orchestra alone. But Wagner's forms are not in fact as rigorous in development as the word 'symphonic' usually implies, and his practice is less consistent than his theory. The sailor's song in *Tristan and Isolde*, Siegfried's forging song in *Siegfried* and the chorusing of Hagen's warriors in *The Twilight of the Gods* are operatic – that is, they constitute independent vocal melodies; likewise the dance of the Flower Maidens in *Parsifal*. In *The Mastersingers* (1868), where Wagner forsook tragic symbolism for human comedy, opera (regular tunes) and music-drama (symphonic interplay of themes) meet happily in mid-territory.

It must be added that, the theoretical distinction between music-drama and opera once made, Wagner's later as well as his earlier works are still called operas for theatrical convience and will be so here.

*The German is *Leitmotiv*, singular; *Leitmotive*, plural.

Wagner was his own librettist. The part of *The Ring* which he first conceived was what eventually became its finale (*The Twilight of the Gods*), from which he worked backward to what became the three earlier operas of the cycle. An active political revolutionary when he wrote the literary texts, Wagner doubtless saw them as in some sense a political allegory. Bernard Shaw expounded such an allegory brilliantly in *The Perfect Wagnerite* (1898) – Wotan, ruler of the gods, as the representative of State power, the Nibelung or dwarf Alberich as unintelligent capitalist accumulation, the *Tarnhelm* (a helmet which changes its wearer's form at will) as a top hat which

makes a man invisible as a shareholder, and changes him into various shapes, such as a pious Christian, a subscriber to hospitals, a benefactor of the poor, a model husband and father, a shrewd, practical, independent Englishman, and what not, when he is really a pitiful parasite on the commonwealth, consuming a great deal and producing nothing, feeling nothing, knowing nothing, believing nothing, and doing nothing except what all the rest do, and that only because he is afraid not to do it, or at least pretend to do it.

Shaw's analysis is in no way diminished by the preference of more modern writers to refer the mythology of *The Ring* to the psychology of our interior life.

Wagner's use of leading-motives in *The Ring* is strikingly varied. The heavy descending scale in the brass is first of all visually associated with Wotan's spear, but the spear itself represents the sanctity of contract or oath, so the theme may be heard when oath or contract is involved even without reference to Wotan – as in the plighting of blood-brotherhood between the guileless Siegfried and the duped Gunther in *The Twilight of the Gods*. The musical flickering which in *The Rhinegold* accompanies the entrance of Loge, god of fire, is related to the 'Magic Fire Music' with which Wotan lays his beloved, erring daughter, Brünnhilde, to sleep amid a protective circle of fire at the end of *The Valkyrie*. Very often the significance and identity of recurring themes is emphasized by the recurrence of a characteristic instrumental colour and even of a certain key. The sound of the sword motive (the sword by which the human hero Siegfried is to effect his conquests) rings out first of all in C major on a solo trumpet when it is conceived as a thought in the mind of Wotan near the end of *The Rhinegold*, and it is still in C major and still on the trumpet when (in *The Valkyrie*) the real sword is pulled out of a tree's stem, with heroic strength, by the weaponless Siegmund.

Wagner made no list of his leading-motives: that was left for his commentators, who may (depending on the subdivisions) enumerate well over a hundred for *The Ring*. The musical interrelation of the motives is sometimes dramatically explicable, sometimes not: it seems odd that in the transition from scene 1 to scene 2 of *The Rhinegold* the theme of the ring itself slips so unresistingly into the theme of Valhalla, the newly built abode of the gods. But as I have said above, Wagner's practice does not always match his theory. Shaw long ago pointed out how inconsistent it is that Brünnhilde should announce her triumphant self-immolation at the end of *The Twilight of the Gods* to a melody originally associated (in *The Valkyrie*) with Sieglinde's joy that she is pregnant with Siegfried-to-be. Even one of the doughtiest defenders of Wagner's psychic symbolism, Robert Donington,* has to resort to claiming that Brünnhilde is comparably 'pregnant with the future of the psyche'.

That some of the best of the younger German composers should enlist under Wagner's banner was natural. But Peter Cornelius (1824–74) wrote his comic opera *The Barber of Baghdad* (1858) before *Tristan* – and, though richly chromatic in harmony and richly full in orchestration, it is not otherwise Wagnerian. Engelbert Humperdinck (1854–1921), who lived through the full Wagnerian explosion, harnessed a Wagner-like interplay of themes and a Wagnerian solidity of orchestral sound to the simplicity of nursery-type tunes in *Hansel and Gretel* (1883): its charm, backed by prodigious musical craftsmanship, is perennial. There were other com-

* In *Wagner's 'Ring' and its Symbols*, Faber, 1963.

posers, now forgotten (some French as well as German) who
deliberately tried to follow Wagner in the choice of epic-
legendary stories as well as in his musical techniques.
But his most remarkable influence was on those composers
who resisted his dogmas of ' music-drama' as such, yet
allowed the interplay of themes to enrich their dramatic
structures.

For example, consider the use of short, pregnantly expressive themes, and the relationship of voice and orchestra,
in one of the most celebrated scenes of Russian opera:
Tatyana's Letter Scene in Tchaikovsky's *Eugene Onegin*. Not
only the scene itself, but its musical relation to the rest of the
opera would be inconceivable without Wagner, for all
Tchaikovsky's declared distaste for him. *Eugene Onegin* (1879)
and *The Queen of Spades* (1890), respectively based on a
Pushkin poem and a Pushkin short novel, are the major
operas of Pyotr Ilyich Tchaikovsky (1840–93),\* they show a
profound Russianness of melodic style maintaining its contact with the western European romanticism of Schumann
and Liszt – and of Bizet, whose *Carmen* Tchaikovsky had seen
in Paris. As a ballet composer, Tchaikovsky had a more direct
French example – particularly *Giselle* (1841) by Adolphe
Adam (1803–56), and *Coppélia* (1870) and *Sylvia* (1876) by
Léo Delibes (1836–91). Emulating them, and surpassing
them in melodic and harmonic richness and mastery of the
orchestral paintbox, Tchaikovsky completed those full-
evening works which, brimming over with melodic invention and a mastery of the orchestra, are the corner-stones
of Imperial Russian ballet: *The Sleeping Beauty* (1890), *The
Nutcracker* (1892), and *Swan Lake* (1895). The Dance of the
Sugar Plum Fairy from *The Nutcracker* takes the newly invented celesta into an unforgettable partnership with the
bass clarinet.

In turning to Pushkin (1799–1837) Tchaikovsky had been
anticipated by the 'father of Russian opera' (so recognized,
though not the first practitioner): Mikhail Ivanovich Glinka

---

\*The non-theatrical work of Tchaikovsky, and of some other com-
posers mentioned in this chapter, is discussed in the next chapter.

(1804–57). Glinka's *Ruslan and Lyudmila* (1842) was not only the first of the many operas by Russian composers inspired by Pushkin, but was also prophetic in its use of near-eastern dance music for picturesque purpose. Glinka had previously composed the patriotic work *A Life for the Tsar* (originally intended to be called *Ivan Susanin* and now known in Soviet Russia by that name). Produced in 1836 in St Petersburg, at that time the capital, it still forms the annual opening of the season at the Bolshoi Theatre, Moscow.

In the face of Tchaikovsky's achievement, in face of the unmistakably individual savour of all his best-known music, it may seem odd to assert that Modest* Mussorgsky (1839–81) was a more original genius: let us say a more radical one. Virtually self-taught, he developed a harmonic language whose discords and unconventional transitions are more acceptable to the twentieth than the nineteenth century. It was in order to make the melody and harmony smoother and more 'correct' – as well as to provide a new and glossier orchestration – that his friend Rimsky-Korsakov issued after Mussorgsky's death a revised version of *Boris Godunov* which is still impertinently substituted for the tougher-sounding original.

*Boris Godunov*, a chronicle of the historic Tsar who was a contemporary of Queen Elizabeth I, exists in two authentic versions – that of 1869 and a longer version (with the added 'Polish act', bringing in a love episode) of 1874. Like the Pushkin play on which it is based, it is episodic rather than continuous in character. A tragic grandeur is achieved both by the guilt-ridden Boris himself and by the Russian people – represented both in chorus and by the Dostoyevsky-like figure of the Simpleton, whose lament for Russia closes the work (in its original version). Russian folktunes are deliberately quoted: the prayer of the people at Boris's Coronation is, coincidentally, the same tune as Beethoven quoted in his string quartet opus 59, No. 1, as a tribute to its dedicatee, Count Razumovsky. Apart from folktunes, the

* English writers generally give him the French 'e' (Modeste) presumably to avoid complimenting him.

rhythms and inflections of Russian speech are reproduced in the characteristic, and often irregular, rhythms and melodies. The dependence on speech and the willingness to use ' wrong' discord for expressive purpose is even more apparent in Mussorgsky's song-cycle *Songs and Dances of Death* (1875–7). Similarly, Mussorgsky applied a defiantly unorthodox piano technique in his *Pictures at an Exhibition* (1874), which is now better known in Ravel's orchestration.

It is to be noted that, of Mussorgsky's other operas, *The Khovansky Affair* (Khovanshchina) was never completed by the composer in orchestral score; someone else's orchestration *has* to be used – better Shostakovich's, which keeps the original harmonies, than Rimsky-Korsakov's revision. *The Fair at Sorochints*, on a tale of the Ukraine by Gogol, is likewise performable only in one of the completions made by various hands.

The sole opera of Alexander Borodin (1833–87) is the loose, episodic, yet richly laden *Prince Igor*, containing the famous *Polovtsian Dances*, and displaying a not uncommon Russian bias towards baritone and bass voices. With the orchestration completed by Rimsky-Korsakov and Glazunov, it was posthumously staged in 1890. Nikolay Rimsky-Korsakov himself (1844–1908) seems most likely to be remembered by *The Golden Cockerel* – also posthumously staged (1909), in this case because of earlier opposition by the censorship to its political satire. The same composer's *Sadko* (from which comes *The flight of the bumble-bee*) and *The Tale of Tsar Saltan*, respectively produced in 1898 and 1900, are distinguished for the ingratiating melody and invigorating rhythms so evident in the composer's symphonic poem, *Scheherazade\** (1888) on the famous story from the *Arabian Nights*.

Liberal political sentiments, which are evident in such Russian nineteenth-century writers as Gogol and Tolstoy, and which at least achieved the abolition of serfdom in 1861, were expressed by Russian composers too. Glinka is said to

*The German spelling of the Persian name is generally used for this work and was so (in Russian letters) by the composer.

have replied, when someone complained that *A Life for the Tsar* was fit only for coachmen, 'Why not, since the men are so much better than their masters?' But, since Russia was a conservative, dominant European power, this is not the music of nationalist protest – rather of national rediscovery. Its best products became a national possession, and still are: Borodin's handling of the ancient epic sources of *Prince Igor* is referred to with tragic and topical irony in Alexander Solzhenitsyn's Soviet novel, *The First Circle*.

A different political background belongs to the operas of what is now Czechoslovakia, then under Austrian imperial rule. In a cautious response to the revolutionary upheavals which had shaken its domains in 1848–9, Austria permitted the Czechs (for the first time since the early seventeenth century) to develop indigenous cultural institutions. On the establishment at last of a Czech-speaking theatre in Prague, back came Bedřich Smetana (1824–84) from his self-imposed exile in Sweden and gave the Czechs their lasting national opera *The Bartered Bride* (1866), with its rustic subject, its folk-inspired songs and dances, and its comic good humour: its vitality and tunefulness made it the pre-eminent example of a people's opera of this kind. The heroic opera *Dalibor* (1868) is almost as notable an exhibit of the composer's gifts.

Antonín Dvořák (1841–1904) was also a persistent composer of operas, undergoing (like Smetana himself in his later works) the influence of Wagner: the opera known as *Rusalka* has had some international success (it should really be *The Water-Nymph*: 'Rusalka' is not a proper name). But it is not a success to match that of his orchestral and chamber music.

In France the operas of Berlioz (see p. 224) were disregarded. Prevailing taste favoured the grandiose – and sometimes genuinely grand – works of Giacomo Meyerbeer (1791–1864). *The Huguenots* (1836) retained enough international popularity to be chosen to open the rebuilt Covent Garden Opera House more than 20 years later, in 1858 – in Italian, for from 1847 to 1892 Covent Garden was the 'Royal Italian Opera'. But *The Huguenots*, like *The Prophet* (1849) and others of his works, now survives as a curiosity only: the true originalities of Meyerbeer's style were seized on, and incorporated into something more lasting, by Verdi. *The Jewess* (1835) by Jacques Fromental Halévy (1799–1862) is another work of Meyerbeer's type. Jacques Offenbach (1819–80), a German-Jewish immigrant like Meyerbeer, caught the taste of Paris – which almost meant the' taste of Europe – with his frivolous operettas, among them *Orpheus in the Underworld* (1858), *The Lovely Helen\** (1864) and *La Vie Parisienne* (1866). Offenbach's one 'serious' opera – but fantastic, not realistic – is *The Tales of Hoffmann*, left unfinished and posthumously produced in 1881.

The operettas produced more progeny than *Hoffmann* did – not only in France, but in setting a successful example for the two men who were to become the leading operetta composers of Vienna and London. Johann Strauss the younger (1825–99) created *The Bat* (Die Fledermaus) in 1874 and *The Gipsy Baron* in 1885, and Arthur Sullivan (1842–1900) began his run of successful collaborations with W. S. Gilbert with *Trial by Jury* in 1875 – successes that lasted up to *The Gondoliers* in 1889. The survival of Gilbert and Sullivan as middlebrow entertainment would seem to owe much to the *tone* of these works – a light irony which avoids such oversentimentality as has presumably killed off the earlier, once-popular English serious opera. The soprano aria, 'I dreamed I dwelt in marble halls', stands like a phantom reminder of *The Bohemian Girl* (1843), by Michael William Balfe (1808–70), and other such works.

While Offenbach was amusing Paris with operettas by the dozen, one man and one work virtually established a new kind of French serious opera – serious, but not pompous, sensuously lyrical rather than grand. The one work was *Faust* (1859), the composer Charles François Gounod (1818–93). Its style permitted occasional coloratura, but kept mainly to a simple and direct matching of one syllable to one note; it permitted a recall (in the character's mind) of

---

\* It is odd that *La Belle Hélène* should customarily retain French form in English use when *Orpheus* and others of Offenbach's classical figures do not.

a tune, but without Wagnerian heaviness. The ballet scene – the infernal revels witnessed by Faust, under the guidance of Mephistopheles – seems a mere imposition dictated by custom; the ballet is perhaps less of an imposition, more warranted by the drama, in Gounod's *Romeo and Juliet* (1867). The fame of the composer prompted the oratorio-hungry English to commission *The Redemption* (1882) – one of the works in which the English public sought a successor to Mendelssohn's *Elijah* (see p. 226).

The new taste in French opera, with melodies of the simple yet sensuous type already referred to, was also catered for by Ambroise Thomas (1811–96) with *Mignon* (1866); by Camille Saint-Saëns (1835–1921) with *Samson and Delilah* (1877); and by Jules Massenet (1842–1912) with *Manon* (1884) and *Werther* (1892). Exotic subjects, allowing a picturesque evocation of oriental music, were widely favoured in the second half of the century, showing in works as dissimilar as Verdi's *Aida* and Borodin's *Prince Igor*: from France came *Lakmé* (1883) by Delibes, with its Indian setting, and *The Pearl Fishers* (1863) of Bizet, set in Ceylon. But Georges Bizet (1838–75) left his chief memorial in *Carmen*, produced in 1875, a few months before his death.

The first performance of *Carmen* and the first production of the complete *Ring* took place within 18 months of each other. It is tempting to regard the styles of Wagner and Bizet as antithetical – as did the German philosopher Friedrich Nietzsche (1844–1900) when, turning from his first adoration of Wagner, he set up Bizet's 'Mediterranean' clarity as a preferable ideal. Wagner tried to make something symphonic of the opera; he certainly made the orchestra eloquent in the theatre as never before, and almost the whole of subsequent operatic history to about 1950 can be viewed as an extension or rejection of his achievement and aims. *Carmen*, by contrast, sticks remarkably to the form of older song-and-dance opera.

Yet the swiftness of Bizet's dramatic movement within that form, and the new realism of its story, were themselves highly influential. It is a realism that goes further than Verdi's in avoiding romantic poses: compare the death of Gilda in

*Rigoletto*, with exquisite, long-drawn-out music and a conventionally pious reference to the angels in heaven, with the swift, mute, and brutal death of Bizet's heroine. Bizet's lesson was taken to heart by Italian composers in such works as *Cavalleria rusticana* (see p. 277). Carmen herself remains one of the few operatic characters to have entered the òrdinary literate frame of reference of the non-musical public. She is as Bizet and his librettists made her. Her later incarnations – including the staged and filmed musical, *Carmen Jones* (1943), and the unspeakably orchestrated *Carmen* ballet (1967) by the Soviet composer Rodion Shchedrin (see p. 324) – are tributes in their way to the creation of 1875.

# 16

# Symphony, Sonata, Song

THE symphony and the sonata, forms of classical balance and elegance in the time of Haydn and Mozart, were not driven out by the surge of romanticism: they were transformed. The symphony characteristically became longer, louder, more ponderous, more highly coloured in instrumentation. In the period 1850–1914 the symphony was perhaps the most important form of western European music – except for the opera in Italy. The symphony could fuse in Tchaikovsky's hands with the symphonic poem; in Mahler's it could embrace the cantata and the solo song. Liszt (see p. 231) had already pointed in that direction. Even Brahms, who clung to tradition in the structure and orchestration of the symphony and in preserving it as absolute music (non-vocal, non-illustrative), nevertheless gave the symphony a feeling of increased density or weight. He likewise saddled his second piano concerto with the four-movement symphonic form, a symphonic length, and an appropriate gravity: even the traditionally placed cadenza has disappeared.

By this time the symphony orchestra had achieved in essentials what we recognize today as its characteristic sound. In the brass section the invention of the valve (varying the length of the tube) had revolutionized the horn and trumpet, which were previously restricted to the gapped notes of the harmonic series, like a bugle. Halévy in his opera *The Jewess*, produced in 1835 (see p. 251), seems to have been the first to write for valved horn and valved trumpet in the orchestra: Schumann and Wagner followed. (The cornet had emerged a little earlier, so that Berlioz's *Fantastic Symphony* of 1830 displays two cornets skipping about enterprisingly while the unvalved trumpets are still confined to a few basic notes.) The modern flute and clarinet, each with a system of finger-keys associated with the German inventor Theobald Boehm

(1794–1881) date from the 1840s. As to numbers, a full orchestra of from 80 to 100 was not uncommonly seen at major concerts in Europe's leading musical cities in the mid-nineteenth century.

Moreover the symphony orchestra achieved a new stability as an institution providing regular concerts under the patronage of an enlightened middle class. The Vienna Philharmonic Orchestra (or rather its differently named ancestor) dates from 1842, the Boston Symphony Orchestra from 1881, the Amsterdam Concertgebouw (Concert hall) Orchestra from 1883. In Manchester, in 1857, Charles Hallé founded the orchestra which still bears his name. Two years previously, Wagner and Berlioz had been employed as rival conductors in London by the Philharmonic Society (today the Royal Philharmonic Society) and the short-lived New Philharmonic Society. In the same year, August Manns, directing the concerts at the Crystal Palace on the outskirts of London, proceeded to fashion the first really popular series (huge audience, cheap price) to be firmly devoted to 'serious' music in England. In the programmes of such orchestral enterprises the symphony was recognized as the high or ultimate form, and the concept of a stable symphonic repertory was developed.

The piano itself in this period became a quasi-orchestral thunderer, or the source of a quasi-orchestral palette. We speak here not of the ubiquitous domestic upright, but of the 'concert grand' – iron-framed and more powerful in tone from the 1850s. The great pianist-conductor Hans von Bülow (1830–94) in his edition of Beethoven's piano sonatas even felt impelled to add directions like *quasi corno* ('like a horn'). Piano recitals would include transcriptions of overtures or other short orchestral pieces, as well as variations and fantasias on operatic airs and national songs. The very concept of a recital, in the sense of a one-man performance without the assistance of other artists, was still somewhat new. The term 'recital' itself, in the current sense, seems to have been first used of an appearance by Liszt in London in 1840. Newly promoted to his sole throne, the pianist had to be the purveyor not only of his instrument's special repertory, but of music in general.

Yet even here a special dignity was attached to the name 'sonata' as a classic type, subordinating display to careful, serious thematic construction. In 1839 the label '*fantasia quasi sonata*' ('like a sonata') had been given by Liszt to his piano work, *After Reading Dante*; in 1853 he compressed the normal multiple-movement form into his uniquely formed, one-movement sonata in B minor, about half an hour in length. Schumann and Brahms kept the term for a more conventional 'classic' form. Not only the piano sonata but also the duet sonata was cultivated – most often for violin and piano, as in Brahms's three examples and Franck's one.

The string quartet (fundamentally, as we have noted, a sonata for its instruments) remained a favoured 'classic' form even with romantic composers – among them Wolf, Borodin, Tchaikovsky, Smetana and Verdi. Joseph Joachim (1831–1907) was the first great violinist to be also the leader of his own regular string quartet. He gave early performances of works not only by his friend Brahms but by Dvořák too – Dvořák, whose trios and quartets yield the prime example of the fusion of classic forms with newer, romantic, nationalist inspiration.

The major portion of published piano music and published chamber music was suitable, and easy enough, for amateurs to play on their domestic instruments. In 1827 the pianist-composer Ignaz Moscheles (1794–1870) had noted how the mammas of London begged him to teach their daughters 'something with a pretty tune in it, brilliant but not difficult'. (A particularly sociable form, with obvious opportunities for gallantry and even courtship, was the piano duet.) Likewise with song: amateurs could not only essay the easier extracts from opera and operetta, but were specially catered for in 'drawing-room songs'* by composers of various nationalities. Among such composers was the virtually untrained American Stephen Foster (1826–64), who wrote the words as well as the music of *Old folks at home*, of *Oh, Susanna* and other songs

---

* '. . . ballads amatory
And declamatory.' – W. S. GILBERT, *Princess Ida*, 1884.

which were popularized at first in black-faced minstrel shows and then attained a quite unexpected international circulation and longevity. In England a late-Victorian album of assorted songs might juxtapose Schubert's *To Music* and the most banal-seeming Victorian ballad.

Such mixed items were not separately categorized: the term 'art song' (today often used to distinguish the 'serious' composer's song from the products of folk music or commercial entertainment) was unknown. But a few composers, notably Hugo Wolf and Debussy, were to take the art of song into more subtle and refined regions, with new harmonies and non-symmetrical periods. Such songs belong to professional music-making – not embracing both professional concert and domestic informality, as did the songs of Schubert and Brahms, Gounod and Massenet, Sullivan and Stanford.

In the following pages we consider singly the leading composers of song and of orchestral, chamber and solo instrumental works, noting how far they found the old, 'classic' forms compatible with that more emotional feeling which is the most obvious characteristic of the music of the period. We begin with the composers of Germany and Austria (notably Brahms, Bruckner, Mahler, Wolf and Richard Strauss); then those of France, Bohemia and Russia (the only other three countries whose contributions reached leading international importance in this period), finally noting developments elsewhere.

If the term 'conservative' is used of Johannes Brahms (1833–87), its meaning is that he resisted the romantic fashion of associating instrumental works with non-musical (programmatic) content, and that he also resisted the romantic expansion of the orchestral palette. His large forms are deliberately traditional. Yet in his use of cross-rhythm, in harmony, and in the cut of individual phrases and the peculiarly dense texture to be found alike in his orchestral and in his piano music, Brahms is an innovator and an individualist. (In 1933 Schoenberg was to hail him, in an essay, as 'Brahms the Progressive'). No composer's music is more strongly finger-printed.

His four symphonies (1876, 1877, 1883, 1885) were preceded in 1873 by the orchestral work which Brahms entitled *Variations on a Theme of Haydn* (he also scored it for two pianos). Since the theme (St Anthony's Chorale) is now considered not to be by Haydn but borrowed by him, the title *St Anthony Variations* is now preferred for Brahms's work. To Weber or to Schubert (as to Mozart) 'variations' had first of all implied an entertaining elaboration of a melody. But in this work Brahms transforms the melody and the harmony drastically (that is, beyond the point of immediate, pleasurable recognition) and, in the final section, adopts the more intellectual procedure of the repeated ground bass of baroque times (see p. 132). Such a weighty effect is characteristic of Brahms, and is paralleled in the final movement of the Fourth symphony, in which an eight-bar theme is varied in ground-bass fashion. Brahms's two piano concertos (1858, 1881) both seem heavy, even clumsy in sound when set beside other piano and orchestral works of their day; their appeal is in their massiveness and in structural tensions rather than in sensuousness and virtuoso skills, the hitherto normal concerto qualities. A little more concession is made in the violin concerto, first performed by Joachim in 1879, with its Hungarian-dance finale. The double concerto for violin and cello of 1887, less often performed, nevertheless remains the unique example of such a concerto in the current repertory.

The presence among Brahms's piano works of titles like *intermezzo, ballade, romance,* and *rhapsody* implies only a remote kinship with the brilliant, ingratiating, sometimes capricious pieces written under those names by more romantically-inclined composers. In these works Brahms sometimes shows a certain gruff humour, but rarely shows charm (except in the rippling syncopations of the *Intermezzo* in C major, opus 119, No. 3). They are distinguished in form rather than in spirit from the composer's three piano sonatas and the several sets of variations (notably those on a theme of Paganini, and on a theme of Handel). Brahms notably combined the piano with strings in a piano quintet, three piano quartets, three piano trios, two other trios (one with violin and horn, one with clarinet and cello), three violin sonatas and two cello sonatas; the clarinet is also used, with a fine appreciation of its lyrical powers, in two sonatas with piano and in a quintet with strings. A deliberately lighter, drawing-room side of Brahms is seen in the waltzes and Hungarian dances for piano duet and the two sets of *Love-Song Waltzes* for four voices with a piano duet.

Brahms's songs range wide: from simple folksong arrangements (*The Sandman*) and original songs with melodies quite in the direct, folksong style (*The Fruitless Serenade*, as we may translate *Vergebliches Ständchen*) to the long, dignified, declamatory strains of the *Four Serious Songs* on biblical texts. These last provide a direct link with Brahms's best-known choral work, the *German Requiem* (1869), with a non-liturgical text selected from Luther's translation of the Bible. Shorter choral works with orchestra include the so-called *Alto Rhapsody* (with contralto solo and male chorus) and the *Nenia* (Latin for dirge; the German form is *Nänie*): the two works have texts by Goethe and by Schiller respectively. Brahms also wrote partsongs and other works for smaller choral groups (male, female, mixed-voice) in more intimate settings with piano or without accompaniment – music less sentimental, and probably more worth reviving, than most composers provided for such contexts.

Where the origins of Brahms were north German and Protestant, those of Anton Bruckner (1824–96) were Austrian and Catholic. A major part of his work consists of settings of Catholic liturgical texts, mostly for actual use in the service – including two festival masses with full orchestra (in D minor and F minor, first performed in 1864 and 1872 respectively, both afterwards revised). Save for a string quintet and some pieces for his own instrument, the organ, his instrumental work is almost entirely concentrated on his nine numbered symphonies, composed from 1865 onwards. (There exist two further symphonies, known as the 'Study' symphony and 'No. 0', discarded by the composer.) Of the nine, various versions exist, partly because of Bruckner's own revisions and partly because of unauthorized editorial handling by others.

The Ninth is unfinished, having only three movements instead of the planned four.

All his other symphonies have four full movements; all are purely orchestral and non-programmatic. To this extent Bruckner is as much of a traditionalist as Brahms. But the Bruckner symphonies are, on average, longer (No. 7 and No. 8 last about 70 and about 80 minutes respectively); their melodies tend to be more complete and song-like, often with long, sectional repetitions; their harmony (in the later works especially) is more chromatic, more complex; the orchestration of Nos. 7, 8 and 9 includes four Wagner tubas (see p. 243). The individual finger-prints of Bruckner, as distinctive as those of Brahms, are quite different (easier to hear, of course, than to describe) and Bruckner's evocation of marches and of the Austrian *Ländler* or country waltz-tune goes back to Schubert and forward to Mahler. Contrast, cumulation and climax are achieved by Bruckner in a more physical way (with full use of the dimensions of volume and orchestral colour) than Brahms deems proper.

Only after 1950 did Bruckner win full international esteem – thanks to a public that knows Mahler as a kind of symphonic son of Bruckner (and even Shostakovich as a son of Mahler). Gustav Mahler (1860–1911), Bohemian-Jewish in origin, lived in Vienna and became conductor of the Court Opera there. As a composer he took the complexity of late-Bruckner harmony and used it to express the agonies of a newer, more modern generation – Freud's generation. 'Naïve' tunes are exposed in distorted, grotesque shapes, sometimes in a strained, unexpected instrumental colour. (Who but Mahler would turn out a minor-key version of *Frère Jacques* as a funeral march for a solo muted double-bass – in the symphony No. 1, 1888?) Against such agonies, the composer counterposes the ringing affirmations of mystical faith, uttered in religious texts and reinforced by trumpets, organ, choirs, in hallelujahs of diatonic chords. He yearns, if not for the unreasoning comfort of religion, then for the unreasoned comfort of childhood. After three purely orchestral movements of his symphony No. 4 (1900), a soprano rises to utter a

child's description of heaven with all kinds of goodies to eat:
'St Martha must be the cook!' The deliberate primitiveness
of the harmony at this point is the perfect musical expression
of the sophisticated longing for a return to the mother's
breast.

His symphonies No. 2 (the *Resurrection Symphony*), No. 3,
and No. 8 (the Symphony of a Thousand) are choral, lasting
respectively 100, 90 and 90 minutes. Two distinct parts form
No. 8, first a setting of the ancient Catholic hymn 'Veni,
creator spiritus' (Come, creator-spirit) and then of the end of
Part II of Goethe's *Faust*, with its expressions of mystic
ecstasy and its invocation of the Female Principle ('Eternal
Womanhood leads us onwards'). Not only seven solo
singers, a boys' choir and two mixed choirs are demanded,
but a huge orchestra and a brass group set apart. The
symphony here reaches out for the colossal in more than one
sense. After this work (1907) Mahler completed a purely
orchestral Ninth symphony (1909) and left an almost completed Tenth of which Deryck Cooke's completion was first
performed in 1960.

Before his death Mahler was able to complete (though he
never heard) *The Song of the Earth*, which he also called a
symphony. An hour long, it is a setting for tenor, contralto
(or baritone) and orchestra of six German translations of
ancient Chinese poems. *The Song of the Earth* is a farewell to
beauty: the words 'ever, ever' are repeated as the music dies
away. It is best considered not as a symphony but as the
climax of Mahler's treatment of solo song, in which he had
already used an orchestra in preference to a piano accompaniment in order to add to descriptive effect (animal
sounds, military fanfares) as well as to heighten the emotional
colouring. About 1886, after having already written *The
Songs of a Wayfarer* (*Lieder eines fahrenden Gesellen*), he had discovered the collection of old German folk-poetry called *The
Youth's Magic Horn* (see p. 229). Ten orchestrally accompanied songs, completed about 1896, were the result, plus two
more (*Reveille* and *The Drummer Boy*) later. Another set, the
*Songs on the Death of Children* (*Kindertotenlieder*), was completed

in 1904. Often the orchestral writing shows a chamber-musical handling of the instruments – 'each part standing out like a line in an engraving', as Cooke puts it.

Hugo Wolf (1860–1903) had been a fellow-student of Mahler in Vienna, and shared with him an admiration for Wagner and Bruckner. He became an aggressively partisan (pro-Bruckner, anti-Brahms) music critic and a composer whose work was concentrated almost entirely in song. He wrote more than 350 songs for voice with piano accompaniment (in a few cases, with orchestral accompaniment as an alternative). A great number are grouped by their literary sources – songs to poems by Mörike (1889), by Goethe (1890), poems of a *Spanish Song-Book* (in German translation, 1891), and of an *Italian Song-Book* (similarly, 1892 and 1896). These are not song-cycles in the close-knit or narrative sense, but collections from which the singer may choose at will. The harmony is freely chromatic, sometimes in Wagnerian style, but the chief model in sensitivity of word-setting, and in the musical equality of the piano with the voice, is Schumann.

In Wolf the words seem to determine the character of melody and harmony, with many a cunning subtlety of expression; but this does not exclude the possibility of a traditional regularity in metre or indeed of melody. Such a song as *The forsaken maiden* (*Das verlassene Mägdlein*, No. 7 of the Mörike set) shows just such regularity, yet also the subtlest variety in near repetition, the utmost freedom of harmony, and an exactness of mood painting which even matches in music the suggestion of cock-crow in the opening words.

Song was also important, though not so dominant, in the career of Richard Strauss (1864–1949). His so-called *Four Last Songs* (1948), with orchestra, have become well known as an example of his late, mellowed style; but most of his songs date from 1900 or before and often show a rich, impulsive vein of romantic feeling. *Morning* (*Morgen*) and *Dream through the twilight* (*Traum durch die Dämmerung*) are examples. The wide-sweeping melodies of Strauss's songs, and their often enriched diatonic harmony, are not part of a special song style; they are related to Strauss's more distinguished fields of activity, the symphonic poem and the opera. And these two are themselves interrelated. As Strauss's output of illustrative orchestral works tailed off towards the conjugal-auto-biographical *Symphonia domestica* (1902–3) and the *Alpine Symphony* (1911–15), so his concentration on opera increased. His operas (see p. 278) afforded him not only a larger time-scale, but also a more concrete, verbalized, objective link with the three-dimensional world.

The best-known of Strauss's orchestral pieces are *Don Juan*, 1888; *Death and Transfiguration*, 1889; *Till Eulen-spiegel's Merry Tricks*, 1895; *Thus Spake Zarathustra*, 1896; *Don Quixote*, 1897; *A Hero's Life*, 1898. Berlioz may be reckoned the godfather of such works. Their story-telling character is evident in the grotesque nature of some of the themes, in some frankly imitative effects (the rattle to denote a street disturbance, the drum-roll of an execution, both in *Till Eulenspiegel*), and in the sudden, dramatic juxtaposition of musical ideas. But Strauss is careful to maintain a purely musical control over his formal schemes: he goes so far as to label *Till Eulenspiegel* a rondo and *Don Quixote* variations. The orchestration of such works displays Strauss's pre-dilection (again Berlioz-like) for enlarging the orchestra beyond convention: *Till Eulenspiegel* allows for four extra horns *ad lib.* and three extra trumpets *ad lib.* (a total of eight and six); *Don Quixote* requires six horns and a tenor tuba (as well as bass tuba), not to mention a wind-machine.

Richard Strauss thus placed himself firmly on the side of what was called the new music (as represented by Berlioz, Liszt and Wagner, leaning to pictorial expression and to an expanded orchestra) as against the classical conservatism of Brahms. Turning now to Russian composers, we find them similarly inclined – profiting from the orchestral palette of Berlioz and from the plastic or 'gesture-like' music of Liszt. Perhaps on the inspiration of Schumann, they married the long, multiple-movement form of the symphony with that song-like, fresh-seeming type of melody so characteristic of romanticism. The most important Russian composers of symphonies are Alexander Borodin (1833–87), who completed two, and Pyotr Tchaikovsky (1840–93), whose six numbered symphonies do not include his *Manfred Symphony*. Two symphonies by Mily Balakirev (1837–1910) are also not to be forgotten.

Borodin's No. 2 – with its languorous slow-movement melody, its insistent and unusual rhythms, its strange harmonic implications (in the opening theme), and its colourful orchestration – comes from the same musical world as his opera *Prince Igor* (see p. 249). Its sustained transition from third movement to finale, with an unexpected transformation of harmony, is characteristic of the romantics' wish to unify the symphony: such a wish leads Tchaikovsky to use a recurring motto theme in his Fourth and Fifth symphonies.

These two and the Sixth symphony (the *Pathetic*) best represent that characteristic, individual accent of Tchaikovsky's within a long, massively powerful four-movement form. Power – that is, an emphasis on dynamics and attack – is of the essence of this accent. Observe the way that horns and bassoons open the Fourth symphony fortissimo and are joined by trombones, then by tuba, just before that shattering change-of-key entry by trumpets and high woodwind. Observe the opposite extreme, equally characteristic: the exhausted fading-out of the Sixth symphony on bassoons and lower strings, pianissimo – the first symphony ever to end other than with a positive gesture. The novel pizzicato movement in the Fourth symphony, the waltz (in place of scherzo) in the Fifth, the unprecedented 5/4 time for the whole third movement of the Sixth symphony . . . these, even when they have ceased to be arresting in their sheer novelty, retain their purely artistic effectiveness within a convincing total symphonic plan.

Although Tchaikovsky was not a member of the group of St Petersburg musicians who regarded Balakirev as their mentor, it was Balakirev who suggested to Tchaikovsky the composition of his *Romeo and Juliet* and virtually supervised the process. (Tchaikovsky later revised the work to form the present definitive edition, 1881.) This and *Francesca da Rimini*, composed in 1876 and inspired not only by Dante's poem but by the illustrations of the nineteenth-century French artist, Gustave Doré, are Tchaikovsky's most successful illustrative works. Of his three piano concertos No. 1 in B flat minor (1874, later revised) has achieved its success despite the unique structural oddity of starting with a whole large section to which no reference is ever made again. His single violin concerto dates from 1878, his *Variations on a Rococo Theme* for cello and orchestra from two years earlier. These variations exemplify Tchaikovsky's homage to the vanished elegance of the eighteenth-century rococo ideal (see p. 137) as he conceived it. It is a homage paid also in some other works, notably a 'pastoral' inserted into the opera *The Queen of Spades*.

That Nikolay Rimsky-Korsakov (1844–1908) composed three symphonies is scarcely remembered: his best-known works are the *Spanish Caprice* of 1887, with its exotic colours and insistent rhythms, and the *Scheherazade* (already alluded to, p. 249) of the following year. It was also Rimsky-Korsakov who arranged that extract from Mussorgsky's *The Fair at Sorochints*, which is usually known as *Night on the Bare Mountain*. Borodin's sole descriptive orchestral work, and a distinguished one, is *In Central Asia* (1880): the commonly encountered western title 'In the Steppes of Central Asia' is not authentic. Borodin's two string quartets are the sole examples of Russian chamber music (until Shostakovich) which have earned their regular place in the repertory.

The symphonic, solo and chamber music of what is now Czechoslovakia is dominated by the two figures whose work in opera has already been noted (p. 250). Bedřich Smetana (1824–84), admiring Liszt, turned the symphonic poem to his own individual expression. In his cycle of six symphonic poems entitled *My Country* (1874–9), the most famous is the second, *Vltava* (the name of the river which flows through Prague, called by Germans the Moldau). His piano music is notable, and includes a number of works in Czech folk style, especially polkas. Nearly all his music is illustrative or has some external reference: even the string quartet, hitherto the most abstract of forms, acquired autobiographical significance in 1876 with Smetana's No. 1 in E minor, entitled *From My Life* (with a polka in the second movement to express youthful exuberance, and with the fourth movement interrupted by a high-pitched note expressing the onset of his deafness). A second string quartet is apparently also autobiographical, though less explicit.

Antonín Dvořák likewise enriched chamber music – if not by autobiography, at least by the admixture of Czech folk elements, used both melodically and in new structural ideas. The polka is heard, and likewise the *scočná* (a reel) and the *furiant* (a quick dance which normally changes its rhythm, though Dvořák sometimes uses the term differently). The string sextet of 1878 and the string quartet in E flat (opus 51) of the following year introduce, under the title of *dumka* (lament), a characteristic form of alternated and contrasted sections, grave and gay. The so-called 'Dumky' trio (*dumky* being the plural form) for violin, cello and piano of 1891 consists entirely of six thematically independent dumka movements in different keys. The string quartet in F (opus 96; the so-called 'American' quartet) was composed in 1893 during the composer's visit to the United States and apparently makes some use of Negro melodies.

The most famous examples of such transatlantic borrowing by Dvořák comes in his last symphony *From the New World*, 1893: the resemblance of one tune to 'Swing low, sweet chariot' has often been remarked. This symphony's name (it is not merely a nickname, but appears on the printed score) is probably responsible for its becoming the most popular of the five symphonies brought out during the lifetime; but today a knowledgeable consensus might prefer the symphonies in D minor (No. 7) and in G (No. 8).* These works have their own

---

*Because of the fairly recent publication of four earlier Dvořák symphonies (plus the discovery that the old numbering of the familiar five was chronologically wrong), the whole series has now been renumbered from 1 to 9. The above-mentioned D minor and G major, Nos. 7 and 8, were formerly known as Nos. 2 and 4; the *New World*, No. 9, was formerly No. 5.

native (that is, Czech) accents, and also (as in the slow movement of No. 8) a daringly direct evocation of bird-calls. This contact with nature's music is a characteristic of romanticism, a characteristic of Dvořák himself, and a forecast of his great Slavonic follower, Janáček (see p. 294).

Dvořák's other works include the concert overture *Carnival* (1891), its companion pieces *Amid Nature* and *Othello*; a cello concerto (1896) which is more often played than any other for the instrument, a violin concerto, a set of symphonic variations (perhaps inspired by the *St Anthony Variations* of his friend and champion Brahms), and an enchanting *Scherzo capriccioso* – an orchestral symphonic scherzo in isolation. The two sets of *Slavonic Dances*, orchestrated by the composer from his original piano duets, are original compositions in folk style, not arrangements: they include Serbian and Ukrainian as well as Dvořák's own native dances. The Slavonic idiom was warmly welcomed as picturesque, by German-speaking (and English-speaking) audiences, but a certain difficulty arose from Dvořák's natural propensity to choose Czech texts for his songs. His set of *Biblical Songs* was composed in Czech, but with an altered musical line for the German text: it is a pity that the standard English version follows the (inferior) German line. To appeal to a wider audience, however, Dvořák set his *Gipsy Melodies* originally in German: from these seven songs comes the ever-popular *Songs My Mother Taught Me*.

A Czech composer of marked originality, Zdeněk Fibich (1850–1900) wrote not only five operas and three symphonies but a number of works for speaking voices and orchestra or piano – *melodramas* in the technical sense, for both theatre and concert hall. Josef Suk (1874–1935), who became Dvořák's son-in-law, was both violinist and composer, and his works include a fantasy for violin and orchestra as well as the *Asrael* Symphony and the ten piano pieces, *Things Lived and Dreamed*.

In France a rapid transformation overtook orchestral and other instrumental music between 1869, when Berlioz died, and 1894, when Debussy's *The Afternoon of a Faun* was unveiled at a Paris concert. Composers active and influential in the intervening period include Charles Gounod (1818–93); César Franck (1822–90); Edouard Lalo (1823–92); Camille Saint-Saëns (1835–1921); Leo Delibes (1836–91); Georges Bizet (1838–75); Emanuel Chabrier (1841–93); Jules Massenet (1842–1912); Gabriel Fauré (1845–1924); Ernest Chausson (1855–99); and Vincent d'Indy (1851–1931). Gounod, Delibes, Bizet and Massenet did their most important work for the theatre (see pp. 251–2). But the others were responsible for the distinctive French development of the symphonic poem, the symphony, the concerto and the substantial forms of chamber music. Eventually Debussy transformed the prevailing musical atmosphere from a rhetorical, explicit romanticism to the more shaded and reticent tones of impressionism, in songs and piano works no less than with the orchestra.

Born in Belgium of a German mother, Franck has what some would call an un-French quality: his music chiefly appeals through its emotional intensity rather than through elegance and grace. He discovered (at the same time as Liszt) the principle of transformation of themes – a process of melodic, harmonic and rhythmic alteration which may change the emotional character of a theme yet preserves its aurally recognizable identity. The method is exemplified at its happiest, in conjunction with the typical chromaticism of Franck's melody, in the *Symphonic Variations* of 1885 for piano and orchestra. His symphony, with a not quite similar process of links between the three movements, followed (1888). His best-known other works are likewise products of his last ten years – the piano quintet and string quartet; the sonata for violin and piano, with its canon finale; and the symphonic poems, *The Jinns* and *The Accursed Huntsman*.

A distinguished organist, Franck wrote with distinction for his instrument – festive pieces as well as more learned works which, doubtless in homage to Bach, revive some deliberately archaic forms and usages. The three *Chorales* for organ, 1890 (the French form, like the German, is *Choral*), are not hymn-tunes, as might be supposed, but sets of variations. Similarly his piano music includes a *Prelude, Chorale and Fugue* (1884). Saint-Saëns, likewise a celebrated organist, brought the instrument into his third (and last) symphony in C minor, which also employs a piano duet. Partly under Liszt's influence, Saint-Saëns attempted to infuse into the symphony and the piano concerto (he wrote five) a new feeling of concentrated connection. History has ironically immortalized him chiefly by two small and humorous works, the *Danse macabre* of 1874 (the earliest well-known orchestral work to employ the xylophone) and the *Carnival of Animals* for two pianos and orchestra (1886), which he intended for private performance only.

Mention of such works illumines the particular success of French composers in writing music of a deliberately light, diverting sort – without symphonic or similar pretensions, but without crudity. Here a pictorial touch was often applied, as in Saint-Saëns's *Algerian Suite* (1880) and the class of Spanish–French works by Lalo, Chabrier and others. This exotic quality, and specifically the exploitation of Spanish musical features, persists up to Debussy (*Iberia* for orchestra; *La Puerta del vino* and other piano preludes) and Ravel (*Spanish Rhapsody, Bolero*).

As opposed to such consciously extroverted composition, Franck's more inward and abstract type of music was continued by his pupil, Ernest Chausson. His works include a symphony, a famous *Poem* for violin and orchestra, a piano quartet, and an unusually designated 'concerto' (for piano and violin with string quartet accompaniment). As a song-composer, Chausson shares importance with Fauré and with Henri Duparc (1848–1933), an amateur who published 14 songs and little else, being incapacitated by a nervous illness. With harmonies which seem to glide into one another, with smooth melodies and rippling piano accompaniments, Fauré and Duparc achieve a song style which might almost be Debussy's starting point. Duparc's *Invitation to the Journey*, to a famous poem by Baudelaire, has a couplet which is almost a key to Debussy's world:

> Nothing is found there but order and beauty,
> Sensuous pleasure, calm, and love's desire.

Claude-Achille Debussy (1862–1918) set both Baudelaire and Verlaine, French poets who handled verse in a particularly musical way. Other poets chosen by him for song setting include Stéphane Mallarmé, who wrote the original poem of *The Afternoon of a Faun* and whose deep-layered, somewhat obscure verse was later to become a treasure-trove for Pierre Boulez. Two of Verlaine's poems which curiously bear English titles, *Green* and *Spleen*, were among the six songs which Debussy originally designated (in 1888) simply as 'ariettes' or 'little airs', changed on later republication to *Ariettes oubliées* (forgotten). In Debussy's songs the verse is unemphatically mirrored in the music, as if the composer were extending the poet's own musical values.

The subtle, evanescent, unemphatic quality of Debussy's work – chords fading into one another, a thematic idea quickly appearing and quickly disappearing – furnishes in part the reason for the label 'impressionist', so often attached to his music. Where contemporary painters such as Monet (with whom the word 'impressionism' is apparently first associated) and Renoir seem to paint the moment rather than the object, points of light rather than outlines, Debussy's musical presentation sometimes seems similarly prismatic. Debussy disowned and disliked the label, but it seems (from his letters to his publisher, Durand) that he disliked its application to painting too – so if we accept it in the one sense, we may do so in the other! Debussy's impressionism was itself frequently of a declared pictorial basis, taking a sound-image (wind, bells, a serenade with a guitar) or a movement image (sea, clouds) for its inspiration.

For such effects Debussy found an apt medium in the piano with its unique capabilities for blurred or blended sound (capabilities increased by the invention of the middle or *sostenuto* pedal in 1874). Debussy's preludes (12 published in 1910, 12 more in 1913) yield many examples. The titles, such as *Sounds and Perfumes Turn in the Evening Air*, often deliberately suggest a quality of languor or subtly apprehended pleasures.

These titles are notably placed in the text at the end of the pieces, not the beginning – the impression first, the words after! Among other well-known sets of piano solos by Debussy are his *Suite bergamasque*, *Etchings* (Estampes), and *Children's Corner* (including *The Golliwog's Cakewalk*). The early suite simply called *For the Piano*, and the late set of 12 studies, are abstract and formal in a way which detaches them from the better-known, impressionistic pieces.

As orchestral composer Debussy takes his revolutionary stance as early as 1894 with the brief, deceptively quiet *Afternoon of a Faun*. It is really (as the title states) a prelude to Mallarmé's poem. The first phrase pivots not between a given note and its perfect fifth or octave, as do so many expository phrases of classical and romantic music, but between two notes separated by the unusual interval of a diminished fifth: indeed the opening harmony sets up a deliberately blurred effect, suggesting no key at all. The first key that is eventually suggested (D major) turns out *not* to be the key of the piece (E major). No classical form is followed, and unity seems to come less through recapitulation (though this element is present) than through immediate repetition or quasi-repetition of short phrases. In the delicate orchestration Debussy reserves for the end three bell-like strokes on the tiny tuned cymbals (ancient cymbals) supported by harmonics on the harp.

Of Debussy's larger orchestral works, naturally embracing a wider emotional range, the best known are the three *Nocturnes*, of which the last, *Sirens*, has a wordless female chorus; *The Sea* ('three symphonic sketches'); and *Iberia* (impressions of Spain – likewise in three movements). These works were first performed respectively in 1900 (first two of the *Nocturnes* only), 1905 and 1910. *Iberia* itself was meant as a component part of a larger threesome, the other limbs being the *Gigues* (orchestrated by his disciple, André Caplet) and the *Spring Rounds*. These two late works have recently won a respect formerly denied to them, along with the composer's three late sonatas – for cello and piano, for flute, viola and harp and for violin and piano. His other well-known chamber work, a string quartet, is, however, an early composition (1893) which attains happy results despite a structure more characteristic of Franck (a single main theme metamorphosed in the different movements) than of later Debussy.

Among Debussy's French contemporaries Paul Dukas (1854–1935) is now hardly remembered except for that masterpiece of humorously illustrative orchestral music, *The Sorcerer's Apprentice* (1897). Ravel, whose compositions and influence continued much later, is more appropriately considered in the next chapter (p. 281).

In Britain Hubert Parry (1848–1918) and Charles Villiers Stanford (1852–1924) had pushed their countrymen towards the serious ideals of Brahms. But their contribution, parochially described as 'the English renaissance', made no international mark, nor lasted long in Britain itself except in the backwaters of church music. A stronger growth is manifest in Edward Elgar (1857–1934) and Frederick Delius (1862–1934, of German descent). Delius is to some extent an impressionist, like Debussy – but showing his gifts best, not in his songs or piano pieces, but in his orchestral and choral works. A common ancestor for Delius and Debussy is perhaps unexpectedly to be found in the Norwegian composer, Grieg (see below), whose music contains sliding chord formations and other harmonic unorthodoxies. It is well known that Grieg first brought to Delius's notice the Norwegian folk melody enshrined in *On Hearing the First Cuckoo in Spring* (1913); less well known that Grieg's own prior piano arrangement (1896) already sounds like Delius.

Delius's gift lay pre-eminently in such miniatures as this, with their tender feeling and superbly colouristic orchestration. A rather longer piece, equally successful, is *Brigg Fair* (1907), a series of orchestral variations on an English folksong which had been discovered by the Australian, Percy Grainger (1882–1961). In his own work Grainger's harmonic and formal unorthodoxies have much vigour, not so much persuasiveness – except in small, light orchestral works (such as the jolly *Handel in the Strand*) and in songs and folksong arrangements.

Edward Elgar (1857–1934), virtually self-taught as a composer, has his Continental affinity not with Debussy but with the more brashly extrovert Richard Strauss. A characteristically heroic vein, expressed through a virtuoso command of the resources of the orchestra, runs through the 'Enigma Variations' (1898),* the two symphonies (1908, 1911), the violin concerto (1910) and the 'symphonic study', *Falstaff* (1913) – a series to which the cello concerto (1919) is a kind of subdued epilogue. The power of emotional expression, plus a Wagner-like technique of thematic recurrence, enabled Elgar to revivify English oratorio with *The Dream of Gerontius* (1900). The Introduction and Allegro for string quartet and double string orchestra (1905) is one of the earliest and most notable explorations of exclusively string sonorities by twentieth-century composers; the violin concerto has been in the repertory of many major violinists since Fritz Kreisler (1875–1962), to whom it was dedicated.

The Scandinavian countries, which in literature join the European mainstream with Hans Andersen (Danish, 1805–75) and Henrik Ibsen (Norwegian, 1828–1906), make a similar arrival in music with the advent of Edvard Grieg (1843–1907). Grieg's music for the original production of Ibsen's *Peer Gynt* (1876) shows the composer's characteristic vein of simple joy or strongly pathetic melancholy. The inspiration of his native Norwegian folk music, not swamped by his German training, led him to an idiom which is often fresh and individual in both melody and harmony. If his songs, piano pieces and chamber music have now lapsed in favour, his piano concerto (1868) still takes a place in the succession to the concertos of Schumann and of Liszt – who personally welcomed Grieg's concerto and much encouraged its composer.

Grieg wrote no other concerto, and no symphony. It was

---

* The actual title is simply *Variations on an Original Theme*. The word 'enigma' over the opening bars does not refer to the puzzle of identifying the subjects of the variations among Elgar's friends, but to the hidden relationship of the theme with some other tune, which has been tentatively identified as *Auld lang syne*.

left to two other Nordic composers to attempt a classic series of symphonies. Carl Nielsen (1865–1931) and Jean Sibelius (1865–1957) are held in patriotic honour in their respective Denmark and Finland, though they (like Elgar) seem to forge an accepted national style from their own minds, and do not seek any enrichment from folk music. Both composers developed their symphonic ideas continuously over a long span of years. In Sibelius's case musical nationalism has a link (like earlier nationalisms) with political protest: it was only in 1917, under the stress of the First World War, that Finland won its independence of Russia, fulfilling the aspirations which Sibelius's *Finlandia* had seemed to express in 1900.

Sibelius's First symphony was composed in 1898–9, his last (Seventh) in 1924. A certain Tchaikovskian romanticism in the first two symphonies is later submerged. Bleak textures and tough harmonies mark the fourth, and the Seventh has a remarkable formal compression and tautness: it is in one movement only. The ancient Finnish epic poem, the Kalevala (brought into modern printed form only in the mid nineteenth century) gave inspiration to a number of Sibelius's works including four orchestral *Legends* of which *The Swan of Tuonela* (1893) is the third: the spare, dark-coloured scoring and the cast of melody are alike characteristic.

In 1891–2 Nielsen composed his symphony No. 1, apparently the first symphony ever to begin in one key and end in another (so-called progressive tonality; see also p. 220). His six symphonies show a Brahms-like quality of close thematic argument – and yet, on the other hand, a bold and even wilful individualism which erupts into an improvised cadenza for side-drum in the Fifth symphony (1920–22). This is a superb gesture, entirely solved (i.e. put into a musical relationship with the whole) – which cannot so easily be said for the grotesqueness in the Sixth symphony (1924–5) or the clarinet concerto (1928). Nielsen's (and Sibelius's) classical moderation in orchestral resources should be noted, in contrast with Mahler's gigantic embrace. Nielsen's extreme is to demand a (wordless) soprano and baritone in his *Sinfonia espansiva* (No. 3) of 1911 – and even here he allows their optional replacement by clarinet and trombone.

Such composers as these are only composers. But one composer of the period stands also as pianist, conductor, librettist, teacher, and theoretician – recalling those musicians of an earlier generation (Berlioz, Schumann, Liszt) who manifested an artistic commitment in a great number of ways. This late figure is that of Ferruccio Busoni (1866–1927), born of a German mother and Italian father. His major works include a five-movement piano concerto (1903–4) with choral finale, and a strikingly original operatic treatment of the Faust legend (*Dr Faust*; incomplete, finished by his pupil Philipp Jarnach and first performed 1925). In some of his music ideas seem still grappling with form, and he has remained an honoured rather than an accepted composer.

# 17

# Twentieth-century Ferment

WHEN Debussy died in March 1918, Paris was being inter-mittently shelled by German long-range guns. The 1914-18 war, and the Soviet Revolution of 1917 in Russia, are often said to mark the end of one period and the beginning of another in the arts. But, though war and revolution may facilitate the acceptance of artistic change, it is clear that the great challenges of twentieth-century music had been made earlier.

At the Promenade Concerts in London in September 1912, Sir Henry Wood conducted the first performance of the *Five Orchestral Pieces* by Schoenberg: music in no key, major or minor. The listener, said *The Times*, 'was like a dweller in Flatland straining his mind to understand the ways of that mysterious occupant of three dimensions, Man'. In May 1913, in Paris, Pierre Monteux conducted the first per-formance by the Diaghilev ballet of Stravinsky's *The Rite of Spring*: 'The cult of the false note', said the critic of *Le Temps*, 'has never been practised with such zeal and persistence as in this score.'

These two composers, the Vienna-born Arnold Schoen-berg (1874-1951) and the Russian expatriate, Igor Stravinsky (1882-1971), are now seen to be, with Debussy, the main agents of musical change in the three decades beginning about 1905. In this chapter we first of all consider four older masters whose work straddles, as it were, the previous period and this more modern one: Puccini, Richard Strauss, Rakhmaninov and Ravel. We then turn to Schoenberg and Stravinsky in some detail, and finally to five notable continuators of musical nationalism: Falla, Bartók, Vaughan Williams, Janáček, Bloch. Others contemporary with these will be grouped in this survey round their com-patriots, but the new phenomenon of Soviet nationalism (and the modern political control of music) will await the next chapter, which concentrates on the 1930s and 40s.

Giacomo Puccini (1858–1924) was the last Italian composer to concentrate almost entirely on opera and to achieve an enduring international success in so doing. In *La Bohème* (1896 – the title means Bohemian Life), he succeeded in placing memorable, well-characterized song melodies within a seamless texture. In the last act the lovers' recall of earlier days together allows the music to proceed – for minutes on end – almost entirely by quotation of previous material, sometimes through the voices and sometimes through the orchestra. Italian opera had, so to speak, learned its lesson from Wagner without losing its own Italian directness and regular song-quality.

The equally popular *Tosca* (1900) and *Madam Butterfly* (1904) followed. In the latter Puccini adopted a far-eastern touch of melody, harmony, even of orchestration – borrowing some actual Japanese tunes and, for the wedding ceremony, Japanese-style gongs. He was to indulge in similar musical orientalism in *Turandot* – his last (unfinished) opera, set in ancient China. Since such orientalism is incongruously suggested even in *The Girl of the Golden West* (1910) it becomes clear that for Puccini it was more than an exotic device: it was a search for the vocabulary of a new style. In pursuit of such a style Puccini also learnt from Debussy and from Stravinsky, as is evident from both *Turandot* and *The Cloak* (*Il tabarro*, the first work in Puccini's triptych of short operas, produced in 1919).

*Turandot* lacked its completion when the composer died: the final pages as performed today were supplied (after the composer's sketches) by Franco Alfano (1876–1954). The only other Italian operas of the period which maintain a firm place in the repertory are the accidentally twinned *Cavalleria rusticana* (*The Rustic Code of Honour*) by Pietro Mascagni (1863–1945) and *Pagliacci* (Clowns) by Ruggero Leoncavallo (1858–1919) – two one-act pieces originally given in 1890 and 1892 respectively. These two works, with a certain emphasis on violence and low life, represent an operatic tendency sometimes called *verismo* – which in Italian, simply means realism in the sense applied in literature to Balzac or Zola, with the connotation of true-life stories, which do not gloss over the sordid and violent. Other Italian opera composers included Umberto Giordano (1864–1948) whose *André Chenier* (1896) is a fictional story woven round a historical poet at the time of the French Revolution, and curiously anticipates the plot of *Tosca*; and Ermanno Wolf-Ferrari (1876–1948).

Wolf-Ferrari, an Italian whose father was German, departed from the prevailing addiction to violent tragedy and wrote *The School for Fathers* (*I quattro rusteghi*, literally 'The four boors') and *The Secret of Susanna*, produced respectively in 1906 and 1909. These are comedies, the one on a large and the other on a small scale, and they are conspicuous for that formality and ironic observation which comedy allows. After the operatic preoccupation with heavy tragedy in the second half of the nineteenth century this is almost a new aesthetic ideal (or a reversion to a Mozartian one). Something of the same shift in operatic aim is to be found in the evolving career of Richard Strauss.

Having won success as a writer of symphonic poems and other illustrative pieces (see p. 262), Strauss intermittently continued working in this vein up to the *Alpine Symphony* of 1915, by which time he had already made a further mark with three of the most successful operas of the twentieth century. *Salome*, an almost word-for-word setting (in German) of the play which Oscar Wilde wrote in French, was produced in 1905. Lasting almost two hours without an interval, it proceeds by a Wagner-like use of characteristic motives, but in an idiom screwed to a greater dissonance than Wagner's. (The succession of unrelated chords which underlie Herod's final words 'Kill that woman!' may well be contrasted with the final utterance in any Wagner work.) The story of Salome's lust after John the Baptist was intended to be shocking, and (in proper operatic fashion) the musical means were accurately tailored to the desired psychological effect. *Elektra* (1909) was equally in one long act, equally shocking in psychological aim, and (except in the inappropriately comic waltz of Elektra's triumph) equally harsh in musical effect.

The work of fashioning Sophocles' *Elektra* into an operatic libretto had been accomplished for Richard Strauss by the distinguished playwright Hugo von Hofmannsthal, who now provided the libretto of *Der Rosenkavalier* (*The Knight of the Rose*). This is an amorous comedy, but with the intended effect of being shocking too: after an orchestral prelude evidently depicting a tempestuous night of love, the curtain rises to show the bed, the (married) Princess, and her young lover, Oktavian. The latter role is sung by a woman (mezzo-soprano) – a conscious reversion to the convention immortalized in the character of another amorous page, Cherubino, in Mozart's *Marriage of Figaro*. The action of *Der Rosenkavalier* being itself set in the eighteenth century, Strauss was able to make other musical references to the period, particularly in a certain graciousness and elegance of melody (and in an entire Italian aria given to an Italian singer commending himself to the Princess – or, as she is called, the Marschallin, i.e. Field-Marshal's wife). There is also a deliberate anachronism: the score is pervaded by waltz-tunes reminiscent of Strauss's unrelated namesake. The opera's final trio (scored, unusually, for two sopranos and a mezzo-soprano) is recognized as a peak of Strauss's art.

'Back to Mozart' was evidently a call with a genuine appeal to Strauss from this period on: an appeal to which he responded primarily in terms of gracious melody (made piquant by his own new chromatic harmonies), clarity of texture, and lightness of scoring. There was scope enough for this in Hofmannsthal's and Strauss's next operatic collaboration, *Ariadne on Naxos*, originally designed to follow a condensed version of Molière's play *Le Bourgeois Gentilhomme*, and first performed thus in 1912. Four years later a second version of the opera was unveiled, which replaces the play by a musical prologue (introducing the figure of the Composer, again a young man played by a female singer!): this version, despite the oddity by which the Composer (the most interesting character) disappears half-way through the evening, is a revelation of the composer's gift for writing a diversity of styles. Strauss's later operas (which include *Arabella*, 1933) have achieved less currency. But it is possible that two at least would succeed in English-speaking countries, given the essential condition of performance in the audience's language: *The Woman without a Shadow*, vast and allegorical (1919; another collaboration with Hofmannsthal) and the composer's last-completed opera, *Capriccio*, intimate and conversational (1942).

Operas apart, Strauss's nostalgia for the eighteenth century may be variously seen in such late works as the concerto for oboe and small orchestra (1946), and the two sonatinas for wind-band (1943 and 1944–5; published posthumously as 'Symphonies for Wind'). The first of the sonatinas is dedicated 'to the spirit of the divine Mozart at the end of a life filled with gratitude'.

Western writers on music are prone to depreciate Sergey Rakhmaninov* (1873–1943) for alleged obviousness and monotony. The admiration shown by the musical public, however (especially in Britain, America, and his native Russia), has been remarkably persistent and perhaps speaks for itself. Rakhmaninov's piano concerto No. 2, performed with the composer as soloist in 1901, made it clear that the romantic-heroic piano concerto of Tchaikovsky could be born again, in music of a Slav melancholy very like Tchaikovsky's own. The dazzling technique required of the soloist is always subjected to the composer's highly individual expression. Of similar power are the first piano concerto (1890–91; revised 1917), the third (1909) and the *Rhapsody on a Theme of Paganini*, also for piano and orchestra, 1934; a fourth concerto (1927) is less successful on similar terms, and indeed exemplifies the general failure of Rakhmaninov's gift in later life, the *Paganini* piece being an exception. He belongs primarily to the pre-1918 period, from which also come all his songs (more than 50, holding an important place in

---

*This is the spelling consistent with the modern transliteration of Russian names. The older and more common styling for the composer is Serge Rachmaninoff.

Russian song) and all his many works for piano solo and piano duet.

Rakhmaninov's elder contemporary, Alexander Glazunov (1865-1936), similarly, wrote most of his music by 1906 – including eight symphonies and, more famous, the symphonic poem *Stenka Razin* (1884) and the ballet *Raymonda* (1896). Anton Arensky (1861-1906) is best known for his four suites for two pianos and for his piano trio. A more complex figure, Alexander Skryabin (1872-1915),* began by writing piano pieces in a style related to Chopin's but by 1908 had evolved a harmonic idiom in which key tends to disappear. His symphonic poem, *Prometheus, or the Poem of Fire*, demands a 'keyboard of light' to project colours in a way related to the music, but no such instrument had been evolved by the first performance (Moscow, 1911). He further aspired to a synthesis of artistic and religious experience. His new 'scientific' system of harmony has a theoretical interest; but in their actual sound, full of chromatic yearning, such orchestral works as *Prometheus* or the *Poem of Ecstasy*, 1908, liable today to suggest a curious cousinship to the later descriptive orchestral works of Richard Strauss – whom Skryabin detestd.

Maurice Ravel (1875-1937) shares with his compatriot, Debussy, a certain type of emotional approach (summed up in the word 'impressionism'), a fondness for exotic musical expression, an affinity for the piano and the use of certain chord formations. On the other hand, each has his own characteristics, both of scope and of style. A brilliant, virtuoso type of writing for the piano is frequent in Ravel, rare in Debussy: significantly, Debussy wrote no piano concertos, Ravel two (both dated 1931, one of them for left hand alone). Ravel's orchestration is similarly more glittering. Yet, curiously, some of his most successful orchestral works appeared first of all in versions for the piano – including the *Pavan for a Dead Infanta*, the *Alborada del gracioso* (a Spanish title meaning clown's morning song), the *Valses nobles et sentimentales* (categories he borrowed from Schubert), and the

*Also Scriabin, Skriabin, etc.; accent on the 'a'.

*Mother Goose* suite (originally for piano duet). Emotionally Ravel ranges from the warm, voluptuous romanticism of the ballet *Daphnis and Chloe* (produced in 1912) and the Introduction and Allegro for seven instruments (1905–6) to a cool brilliance and a deliberate return to classical proportions in the *Sonatina* for piano (1905) and in *The Tomb of Couperin* (six movements for piano, 1917, four of which he later orchestrated). This sense of 'tomb' (French *tombeau*) revives what we have seen (p. 135) to be a seventeenth-century usage.

An older tradition of more abstract symphonic writing was meanwhile renewed in France by Albert Roussel (1869–1937) with four symphonies and an orchestral suite; he was also able to absorb themes and practices of Indian music in his opera-ballet, *Padmâvati*. His contemporary, Charles Koechlin (1867–1950) wrote music of a powerfully individual style with a wide variety of technical devices. Four of his symphonic poems are based on Kipling's *The Jungle Book*.

A more radical stance was taken by Erik Satie (1866–1925), whose *Socrates* (a 'symphonic drama', 1918), for four sopranos and chamber orchestra, has no emotional expression but only a transparent poise and gravity. More celebrated are his piano works with jesting titles like *Three Pear-shaped Pieces*. Elsewhere the composer was not above telling the pianist to play 'like a nightingale with toothache'. Such things were meant to burst the balloon of romantic feeling, to shock conventional notions of the beautiful. It was an outlook that appealed to the influential writer, Jean Cocteau, who in 1917 collaborated with Satie and Picasso in a ballet for Diaghilev, *Parade*. Cocteau (1891–1963) and the impresario Sergey Diaghilev (1872–1929) set the predominant tone of music-making in Paris for a decade after the 1914–18 war. It was in Paris that Diaghilev's Russian ballet company decided to stay, rather than return to Russia after the Soviet revolution. Even before the war Diaghilev had produced three ballets in Paris which were to establish the fame of that long-lived, Protean genius, Igor Stravinsky.

Of these ballets *The Firebird* (1910) and *Petrushka* (1911) proclaimed their composer a pupil of Rimsky-Korsakov, as he was. They are colourful, picturesque, rhythmically exciting, harmonically piquant. (What became known as the Petrushka chord is a simultaneous combination of C major and F sharp major). *The Rite of Spring*, as indicated at the beginning of this chapter, had an altogether different effect. It displays a barbaric force, violent rhythms, orchestral sounds chosen for their extreme or uncouth character. (A deliberate harshness of this kind was a quality evidently appealing at this time: compare Bartók's *Allegro barbaro* of 1911; *Mars* in Holst's *The Planets*, composed 1914; Prokofiev's *Scythian Suite*, 1916.) But Stravinsky, instead of continuing in the bombshell vein, shifted his direction. In subsequent works his music began to abjure excitement, massiveness, and warmth, and became decorative, intimate and cool. Of his *Symphonies for Wind Instruments*, first performed in 1921 and dedicated to Debussy's memory, he wrote: 'This music was not meant to please nor to excite passions. . . . It is an austere ceremony . . .'

The octet for wind instruments, two years later, definitely established this cool style in its purely musical aspect. Already in *The Soldier's Tale* (1918) Stravinsky had found a cool stylization of musical drama: the use of a narrator, mimes, and a *visible* instrumental ensemble is the opposite of operatic illusion. In 1927 he again declined to be traditionally operatic in his *Oedipus Rex*: Jean Cocteau's text, in French, had been translated into Latin precisely to make it emotionally remote from the listener, and the action, disdaining an operatic quasi-realism, was to be similarly frozen. In 1928 the composer who had demanded quadruple woodwind and eight horns for the huge orchestra of *The Rite of Spring* was content merely with a small monochrome orchestra of strings only for his new ballet, *Apollo Musagetes* (Apollo, Leader of the Muses).

This cool style as displayed in the octet or *Apollo Musagetes* – placing a premium on elegance and clarity, employing modest forces, and using certain types of musical phrase which recall the eighteenth century – is often given the name 'neo-classicism'. (This tends to mean, however, a supposed kinship with the Bach of the baroque era rather than with the classical Haydn and Mozart.) Stravinsky sometimes similarly reverted to an archaic form of titles: his 'concerto' of 1938 is simply a concerted piece for chamber orchestra (without solo instruments) and, just as Bach's *Brandenburg Concertos* bear the name of *their* dedicatee, is known as the 'Dumbarton Oaks Concerto' from the estate of the American patron who commissioned it.

Compared to the exuberance of romantic composers' settings of religious texts Stravinsky's *Symphony of Psalms* (in Latin, 1930) is deliberately austere: chorus without soloists, orchestra without violins or violas. But already Stravinsky showed himself able to adopt, and adopt with mastery, any one of several different musical outlooks. In the ballet *The Fairy's Kiss* (1928) he honoured Tchaikovsky not only by the use of the older composer's themes but in lyrical expression; and in 1940 he surprisingly composed a four-movement symphony in C which adopts the traditional style of symphonic development and more than once suggests Beethoven.

In later years, as we shall see (p. 316), Stravinsky shifted yet again, to embrace the aesthetic concepts of Webern and the 12-note method of composition, which dispenses with tonality. But all his music in the period so far discussed *has* tonality, either simply or in bitonal (two-key) constructions. Indeed 'neo-classicism' implies a clear assertion of key. There is thus a clear contrast between Stravinsky and Arnold Schoenberg (1874–1951) who from about 1908 evolved a key-less music (normally called *atonal*) and from about 1923 established within atonal music a new ordering of notes known as 12-note technique and described below.

The first works of Schoenberg's maturity, however, show him simply as a late romantic composer, a little younger than Mahler and Richard Strauss. The romantic urge to narrative expression led him to the string sextet, *Transfigured Night* (1899) – perhaps the first work of chamber music to borrow the narrative device of the single-movement symphonic poem. With its yearning expression and rich harmony, it ironically remains (after all the controversy of the composer's later career) perhaps Schoenberg's best known work, performed either in its original medium or in its later (1917) version for string orchestra. By 1901 he had completed, except for its concluding chorus, the gigantic *Songs of Gurra* (Gurrelieder), a huge composition on a love-and-death theme for multiple choirs, vocal soloists, narrator, and outsize orchestra including iron chains. By the time he came to finish this work (1911) he had already turned to writing his new, totally different atonal music. The shift away from key into new, unanchored music seems linked with the exploration of strange, irrational, dream-like mental states. The resultant art admits shapes and progressions previously considered ugly or unresolved; there are essentially no forbidden chords in atonal music. Such works may be called expressionist like the paintings of Kandinsky (with whom Schoenberg, himself a painter, was associated). Schoenberg's Vienna was also the city of Freud, with his new uncovering of the unconscious and irrational.

A prime manifestation of the new style is *Pierrot Lunaire*, 'three times seven' songs for voice and five instrumentalists. The 'singer', instead of hitting specified notes precisely, passes *through* them in a kind of chant (speech-song, German *Sprechgesang*). The atmosphere is nightmarish (*lunaire*, moonstruck); the melody and harmony are so chosen as *not* to suggest the recognized scales and chords of tradition. A similarly nightmarish atmosphere, and a similar method of musical construction, is found in Schoenberg's one-woman opera, *Expectation* (*Erwartung*) – completed 1909, though not staged till 1924. The *Five Orchestral Pieces* (see the opening of this chapter) are likewise atonal. One of the pieces in particular displays the *melody made out of separate notes of different instrumental tone-colours* (German *Klangfarbmelodie*, literally 'sound-colour melody') which was to be so influential on Webern and others.

If we do not hear traditional scales and chords in this music, then what *do* we hear? What relates the notes together? Where is the sense of logic of this music? The logic lies, it would seem, partly in an oblique reference to those very scales and chords which, being absent, are constantly being suggested. Thus this music seems most convincingly associated with neurotic or otherwise abnormal states and, over a pretty long period (60 years), has still not established itself with ordinary music-lovers as a normal vocabulary of discourse. The same must be said of Schoenberg's attempt (single-handed, though one or two others tried independently) to establish a new form of discipline within atonal music: a discipline which would replace the lost discipline of key. He called his new order a 'method of composing with twelve notes which are related only to one another'. Its earliest manifestations are to be found in his *Five Piano Pieces*, the *Serenade* for seven instruments and baritone and the *Suite for Piano*, all completed in 1923.

Music so composed is often called 12-note music – a somewhat absurd abbreviation, because *all* western music for centuries has been able to draw freely on all the 12 notes (as represented by the seven white and five black keys in each octave on the piano).* Schoenberg's innovation was in using all 12 on a basis of theoretical equality, none achieving more prominence than any other. For each piece a chosen *row* or *series* presents all the 12 notes in a certain order, no note being included twice. Although the order may be varied by mathematical processes (for instance, the notes may simply be played in reverse order), it is present in some form throughout. The row, or a part of it, may assert its presence either melodically – let us say, by the succession of the three notes C, C sharp, G, in whatever rhythm the composer pleases – or harmonically, by the sounding of those notes as a simultaneous chord.

Moreover, *any* C or G sharp will do (that is, high or low, in any octave). It is possible to conceive of a serial system of pitches where this freedom is not allowed, that is, where one

---

*The American usage is 'tone' instead of 'note' – 'all twelve tones in the octave', '12-tone music'. British usage more logically reserves 'tone' for an interval (equal to two semitones) not a pitch. In British usage therefore '12-tone music' is wrong.

C and a higher C would not count as the same in a series, but as different values. It is possible even to conceive of a series being applied to other musical matters than pitch: say, a series of six gradations of loudness, mathematically permutable. Such ideas were in fact to be put into practice after the Second World War (p. 322, 332). But till then 'Schoenberg' and 'serialism' became virtually identified, and 'serial music' and 'a serialist composer' are usually found to refer to his method, or something like it.

Mathematics rules the behaviour of the series: it does not rule the piece. For one thing it is the free and undirected composer who decides how long a note will continue to sound once it is struck (even after others have been struck in their turn); for another, as soon as the series has been exposed in any one shape, the composer is free to choose its next shape (transposing it, permuting it, etc.). In this way two occurrences of the same note may happen to come quite close together – somewhere near the end of the first exposure of the row, and somewhere near the beginning of the second, different exposure. So one note may become (temporarily) more prominent than the rest. Since a genuine, and very large, element of composer's choice is present, objections to the system being 'mechanical' 'or like a straitjacket' cannot stand. But, for the same reason, dogmatic assertions on the system's behalf are out of place. The analytic 'explanation' which occupies 90 per cent of literature on 12-note music, and which consists simply of showing the derivation of all parts of the work from the composer's chosen row, is no argument for the music itself, any more than would be a triumphant proof that Bach used the major and minor keys.

Schoenberg, having arrived at his method after he had already taken the step from tonal into atonal (keyless) music, carried over into his new method a rigorous theoretical avoidance of key – an avoidance therefore of note combinations and chord progressions which might suggest key. The revolutionary nature of that decision needs no underlining. Yet in the matter of structural form Schoenberg remained a traditionalist and a Viennese. In such works as the wind quintet (1924) the third and fourth string quartets (1926, 1936), the violin concerto (1936) and the piano concerto (1942) we find the traditional Viennese instrumental forms (sonata, concerto, etc.) – or rather, these forms in a special compressed presentation in which all literal restatement is avoided and a principle which Schoenberg called *continuous variation* used instead. The 12-note row was applied both in small and large compositions. Even the huge dimension of a three-act opera, *Moses and Aaron*, was planned on the basis of permutations of a single row (and, of course, on the avoidance of key); but for musical or psychological reasons Schoenberg was unable to complete it, and performances (the first was in 1954, in concert form at Hamburg) have had to omit or fabricate the missing final act.

In some of his late works Schoenberg wrote tonally: the *Theme and Variations*, 1943, for symphonic band or for orchestra, has a key-signature of G minor. In such works he was of course not writing according to his 12-note method. But his pupil Alban Berg (1885–1935) combined the two practices. That is, he characteristically chose rows which, in part, positively suggest (instead of deliberately avoiding) a major or minor chord. The most famous example is the row of the violin concerto (1935), where notes 1, 2, 3 of the row form a chord of G minor, overlapping with a chord of D major (notes 3, 4, 5). Moreover this is announced in a particularly clear way by the solo instrument (not at its very first entry but at its first big entry). Similar suggestions of tonality are conveyed by the note-rows of Berg's *Lyric Suite* for string quartet (1925–6) and the opera *Lulu* (the orchestration of which was not quite completed by the time of the composer's death). Certain movements and sections of the *Lyric Suite* are not 12-note; the opera is completely so.

Berg's earlier opera, *Wozzeck*, however, was composed before the 12-note method had been evolved by Schoenberg; dating from 1921, it is in free atonal style. Yet even here Berg characteristically does not embrace pure atonality but constantly suggests that a major or minor key is round the corner: and in one famous orchestral interlude (just after the death of the tragic, simple-minded soldier of the title) he plunges into an explicit D minor. Matters of tonality and atonality apart, both operas are important for their use of apparently strict instrumental forms (a sonata movement, a fugue, variations, etc.) in harness with dramatic action. The so-called *Lulu Symphony*, incidentally, is the composer's own five-movement orchestral suite (with solo soprano) drawn from the opera.

Berg had begun his composing career, as had Schoenberg, with music in the late-romantic style. What are now known as the *Seven Early Songs* date originally from 1905–8 and spring from the same impulse as Mahler's or Wolf's. Even in his later work Berg retains this Viennese romantic feeling and the all-important *dimensions* of composition (lengths of phrases, lengths of whole movements) which go with Viennese tradition. The revolution worked by Schoenberg's other famous disciple, Anton von Webern (1883–1945), was precisely in establishing new dimensions, the dimensions of a miniature world: the fourth of his *Five Pieces for Orchestra* (1913) takes 19 seconds to play. Schoenberg, Berg and Webern were all born in Vienna and are sometimes referred to as the second Viennese school (Haydn, Mozart, and Beethoven constituting the great figures of the first).

The brevity of Webern's pieces goes with an extreme concentration on the expressive quality of each note: often the texture is extremely sparse (only two or three notes heard at a time) and often a particular instrument will contribute merely a single note to a melody, the next note being supplied by another instrument. This happens, for instance, in No. 4 of the *Five Pieces* already referred to: the instruments used, with the utmost refinement and delicacy, consist solely of clarinet, trumpet, trombone, mandolin, celesta, harp, kettledrum, violin and viola. Such works of Webern's were atonal, following Schoenberg's approach of that period; similarly Webern later followed Schoenberg's 12-note method but with his own refinement and concentration of form. The string trio (1927) lasts a mere nine and a half minutes. The eight minute, two-movement symphony (1928) has four solo strings instead of a normal string section. The quartet for clarinet, tenor saxophone, violin and piano (1930) is in only two movements, the first only 41 bars long (though with two sections repeated).

In such works there is much use of involved, imitative counterpoint of a kind which is largely hidden from the ear and seems to function as a composer's discipline (as in much medieval music). This concentration in sound, this intricacy in musical construction, has made many disciples for Webern after his death: among them Stravinsky (from the early 1950s). But meanwhile by no means all German and Austrian music went the way of Schoenberg. By an impressive number of substantial compositions, and by theoretical treatises, Paul Hindemith (1895–1963) reasserted the structural power of the key system. We return in the next chapter to this German musician, apparently so shocking in his outlook when he began to be known, but fundamentally a German traditionalist.

The German tradition, like the French and Italian, is so strong in European musical history that its proponents are not felt as nationalist, i.e., as nationalist protesters, in the way that composers of the surrounding countries seem often to present themselves. We have already observed the creative force reached by such protesting nationalism in the previous century – with Liszt, Smetana, Dvořák, the Russians, and Grieg. In Spain the impetus came later, especially from the composer and musicologist Felipe Pedrell (1841–1922) who brought the light of publication to some of his country's old musical treasures. Among younger men directly encouraged by Pedrell were Isaac Albéniz (1860–1909), whose *Iberia* for piano of 1906–9 is the first important manifestation of a twentieth-century Spanish style; Enrique Granados, whose *Goyescas* (i.e., Goya-like works) for piano were first performed in 1914, and were the partial source of his opera, *Goyescas*, 1916; and Manuel de Falla (1876–1946).

All these composers make use of Spanish dance rhythms, the characteristic intervals of Spanish melody, and the sonorities suggested by the guitar, just as nineteenth-century

French composers like Chabrier, Lalo and Bizet had done for effect. But they do so in a more intense way, and often with a hint of Debussy-like impressionism (broken or suggested phrases) in place of easy-going romantic melody. Falla's 'nationalist' works include the opera *Brief Life* (*La vida breve*), 1913, and *Master Peter's Puppet Show*, 1919; the ballets *Love, the Magician* and *The Three-Cornered Hat* of 1915 and 1919; and *Nights in the Gardens of Spain* for piano and orchestra (1909–15). His *Homage for the Tomb of Debussy* is one of the first major works (1920) written in modern times for solo guitar – specifically, for Andrés Segovia (b. 1893), whose revival of the instrument may itself be considered part of twentieth-century Spanish musical nationalism. Falla's harpsichord concerto of 1926 (with accompaniment of only five instruments) is likewise a tribute to a great revivalist, the harpsichordist Wanda Landowska (1877–1959). Its chamber-music dimensions, regular rhythms and rather brittle style locate it among the neo-classical (back-to-Bach) pieces which Stravinsky, Hindemith and others were also writing at this period.

In Hungary musical nationalism as revived by Béla Bartók (1881–1945) and Zoltán Kodály (1882–1967) was, like Liszt's, an assertion against German and academic musical conventions. (Their compatriot Ernst von Dohnányi, 1877–1960, was more prepared to accept German, and specifically Brahmsian, models.) Political nationalism forms the background here: Hungary declared its independence from Austria in 1918, and a national celebration in 1923 (for the fiftieth anniversary of the union of the two cities, Buda and Pest) prompted both Kodály's *Psalmus hungaricus* for tenor, chorus and orchestra and Bartók's *Dance Suite* for orchestra. Both composers were ardent collectors of folk music and used it in their work. Kodály's compositions include the opera *Háry János* (1926) and the popular orchestral suite from it; the *Peacock Variations* (1938–9, on a Hungarian folksong) for orchestra; a remarkable sonata for unaccompanied cello (1915); and many fine choral pieces (original and folksong arrangements). As a composer of music for amateurs and young people, and a practical musical educator, he is of first importance.

Bartók's musical outlook, however, was more radical. With Kodály he had succeeded in identifying a new (or rather, very old) kind of Hungarian folk music – belonging to the indigenous peoples, not the travelling gipsies (from whose music Liszt had mainly derived what the world called Hungarian style). This true Hungarian music – and the neighbouring Romanian and Slovakian music, which Kodály was also drawn to investigate – had peculiarities of melody and rhythm which were to fertilize Bartók's own compositions. Sometimes he directly quoted folk music, sometimes explicitly varied it; sometimes he seemed simply to use its harsh intensity as a protest against romantic smoothness and opulence – as in the *Allegro barbaro* (1911), already referred to (p. 283). Himself a concert pianist, Bartók 'comes of age' in this work (to borrow a phrase from his American biographer, Halsey Stevens).

Wishing *not* to harmonize folktunes in a way that would suggest an earlier romantic style, Bartók used new chords suggested by the tunes themselves, or harnessed the bitonal procedures which were also being explored in other contexts by Stravinsky and by the French composer Darius Milhaud (see pp. 284 and 296). The combination of technical modernity with the melodic and rhythmic novelty of folksong is at the root of Bartók's own mature style. Works which also show his interest in new sonorities (often hard, or barbarous, like his harmonies) include the *Music for Strings, Percussion and Celesta* (1937) and the *Sonata for Two Pianos and Percussion* (1937; also transcribed as a concerto for two pianos and orchestra). Certain late works are more relaxed, less tough in feeling, notably the second violin concerto (1938), the third piano concerto (1945), and the concerto for orchestra (1943; compare Stravinsky's use of the word, p. 284). The opera *Bluebeard's Castle* is an early untypical, impressionist work (staged 1918, but composed 1911). The six string quartets, their dates ranging from 1910 to 1939, form a conspectus of his whole developing musical style and, in the opinion of many, rank as the most substantial contribution to the medium since Beethoven's. In these works Bartók writes, on occasion, the freest and harshest of harmonies – but never, one feels, loses sight of tonality (or rather of tonality plus the modes of folk music) as an ultimate harbour.

Bitonality, which was felt by Bartók to be a new and liberating technique, sometimes in conjunction with folk melody, had a similar function for the English composer, Ralph Vaughan Williams (1872–1958): a function best seen in such works as *A Pastoral Symphony* of 1922 (which incorporates a wordless high voice) and *Flos campi* (Latin for the flower of the field; the allusion is to the Song of Solomon) of three years later, scored for viola, small orchestra and wordless chorus. Vaughan Williams started off his output of nine symphonies with what is really a choral cantata (the *Sea Symphony*), first performed in 1910; in the same year he brought out his *Fantasia on a Theme of Tallis* for string quartet and two string orchestras – which, with its remarkably controlled though apparently rhapsodic impulse, and its splendid sonorities, has remained internationally its composer's best-known work.

Like Bartók a collector of folksongs, and a believer in their value as material for new composition, Vaughan Williams wrote two deliberately folkish operas, *Hugh the Drover* (not produced till 1924, but apparently composed 1911–14) and *Sir John in Love* (on Shakespeare's *The Merry Wives of Windsor*), produced in 1929. Greater concentration and greater dramatic impact is felt in the one-act *Riders to the Sea*, a setting (with biting, bitonal harmonies) of J. M. Synge's Irish play (composed 1926–7; produced 1937). Like Kodály, Vaughan Williams wrote much good music for amateurs and young people; he also wrote, in *Linden Lea* (about 1900), one of the last really popular English songs by a highbrow composer (he would have hated the term).

Closely associated in his life with Vaughan Williams, Gustav Holst (1874–1934) was prepared for more radical departures. The one-act opera *Sāvitri* (composed 1908, performed eight years later), one of several works based on

Hindu writings, opens not with an overture nor with any instrumental sound but with one solitary, unaccompanied voice, off-stage, in an ambiguous tonality; as in the sliding, clashing chords of the choral *Hymn of Jesus* (1917) the effect is unique and audacious. After completing *The Planets* (hour-long, superbly orchestrated) in 1916, Holst never communicated so well again in the more restrained language he thereafter sought to use. *The Planets* remains his memorial: the barbarism of its opening movement, *Mars*, now reveals its kinship to the spirit which at this time animated Bartók, Prokofiev, and Stravinsky.

The musical nationalism of Leoš Janáček led him to derive the rhythms and inflexions of his vocal melody from those of his native Czech speech – as Mussorgsky had done with Russian (see p. 248). Responsive to Russian as well as to Czech literature, Janáček based his operas *Katya Kabanova* (1921) and *From a House of the Dead* (posthumously staged, 1930) respectively on the Russian writers Ostrovsky and Dostoyevsky. His first operatic success was *Jenůfa* (1904) and his late works include a *Glagolitic Mass* (1927), the title referring to an obsolete Slavonic alphabet. His freely discordant idiom is conveyed in fiercely individual orchestration.

Ernest Bloch (1880–1959), Swiss by birth and American by adopted nationality, occupies a special position as an exponent of Jewish nationalism – not in the political or Zionist sense, but in his affixing of specifically Jewish titles to many of his works and in borrowing inflexions from Jewish traditional (religious) melody. *Shelomo* (Hebrew for Solomon), a rhapsodic work for cello and orchestra, dating from 1916, has been conspicuously successful. So has *Baal Shem* for violin and piano, 1923, also arranged for violin and orchestra: the Hebrew title, literally 'master of the name', refers to the sect of Hassidism. The *Sacred Service* of 1930–33 is a weakly spread-out work, though as a curiosity it has achieved repeated concert performances: ironically it is *not* suitable for most synagogues, since it has orchestral accompaniment, and traditional Jewish worship excludes all instruments, even the organ, from the Sabbath service.

# 18

# Jazz Invasion, Political Intervention

*The Golliwog's Cakewalk* was just an isolated and charming novelty when Debussy introduced its frivolous rhythm into his set of piano pieces, *Children's Corner* (1906–8). But it proved the vanguard of an invasion. The rhythms, melodies, and characteristic tone colours of Negro-derived jazz (or, as it is now more appropriately called, Afro-American music) provided European musicians with a challenge and a new source of exotic local colour. They also gave a partial inspiration to non-Negro American composers, who now, for the first time, achieved international recognition as a national group.

Afro-American music, whether in its purer unlettered origins or in its sophisticated Broadway forms, was a people's art, not unreasonably described as urban folk music. Contact with it was, for a conservatory-educated musician, the crossing of a social as well as a musical line. Afro-American became a universal entertainment music, progressively driving out the old light music which (in the hands of an Offenbach, a Johann Strauss, a Sullivan) had maintained a continuum with the 'serious' music of the day. The arrival of Afro-American altered the social functioning as well as the technical language of music; and in that sense it may be linked with another part-musical, part-social phenomenon which rose to formidable influence in the 1930s and 1940s. This was the drive of totalitarian governments to control musical composition, performances and education – particularly in Germany, and later Austria, under the Nazis (1933–45) and in the Soviet Union under Stalin (1927–53).

In continuing the story of musical developments to about the middle of the twentieth century, we shall note different reactions in different countries to these new phenomena. But it is a matter of preliminary interest that this was not the *first* introduction of the Afro-American musical idiom into

'European' music. In 1845 the (White) American pianist-composer Louis Moreau Gottschalk (1829–69), who studied in Europe and enjoyed the acquaintance of both Chopin and Berlioz, composed a dance piece for piano called *La Bamboula* in the authentic cakewalk rhythm which he had learned in his Louisiana boyhood. He performed it, but it sired no European progeny; and indeed Gottschalk's importance as a pioneer in his own country's music has only lately been recognized.

In Debussy's day, with Negro entertainers now performing in Paris, the impetus came again – this time propitiously. The cakewalk rhythm had already become an essential ingredient in the popular American piano style known from the 1890s as ragtime – to be celebrated in 1911 by Irving Berlin (b. 1888) with *Alexander's Ragtime Band*. The percussive piano style of ragtime plus its characteristic syncopations were seized on by Stravinsky in his *Ragtime for Eleven Instruments* of 1918 and his *Piano Rag Music* a year later.

This was the time when Stravinsky was attracted by various exotic sounds: the cimbalom, or Hungarian dulcimer, appeared not only in the *Ragtime for Eleven Instruments* but in *The Soldier's Tale*. Moreover, the jumping rhythms of Afro-American derivation were no doubt a useful contribution to Stravinsky's aesthetic, which valued a lively, propulsive melodic line and avoided pathos of a German romantic kind. Cocteau too (see above, p. 282) hailed a cabaret singer's jazz accompaniment as 'a cataclysm of sound'. The young French composer Darius Milhaud (b. 1892), coming to London, heard an American band at the Hammersmith Palais de Danse, and noted 'the saxophone breaking in, squeezing out the juice of dreams'. Going to New York, he discovered Harlem: 'The music I heard was absolutely different from anything I had ever heard before, and was a revelation. Against the beat of the drums the melodic lines criss-crossed in a breathless pattern of broken and twisted rhythms . . .' Milhaud's ballet, *The Creation of the World*, produced in Paris in 1923, uses a chamber orchestra of 17 with many allusions to jazz in rhythm and melody: it is one of the most enduring encounters of the two musical cultures.

Even before this Milhaud had visited Brazil and written a fantasy-medley for small orchestra on a selection of Brazilian popular tunes, borrowing this title from one of them: *The Ox on the Roof*. Enthusiastically fitted with a scenario by Cocteau, it was given a staged, danced form in Paris in 1920 (with the subtitle *The Nothing Doing Bar*). Meanwhile Milhaud, who was to show himself exceptionally prolific in a long career, had begun to develop in other directions. His music to Aeschylus's tragedy *The Libation-Bearers* (in French, *Les Choëphores*) was given in concert form in Paris in 1919. By the following year he had written five string quartets, a series which was to culminate in quartets Nos. 14 and 15 (1948–9) which can be played separately or together. Milhaud's music persistently exploits polytonality (simultaneous use of more than one key) and he was one of the first composers to develop this technical enrichment. His early successes were not matched in his later works – including, as we have seen (p. 221) an opera on Beaumarchais's sequel to *The Marriage of Figaro*.

The traditional symphony must have seemed to a French composer at this time an obsolete and unattractively grandiose form. Milhaud wrote five 'little symphonies' for various chamber-music combinations (short and quite without traditional symphonic weight) but did not begin to write full-orchestral symphonies until he arrived in the United States in 1940, a refugee from war-torn Europe. Another prominent figure of the Parisian musical world, Arthur Honegger (1892–1955), similarly avoided the symphony until prompted to his first by an American commission: the performance was in Boston in 1931. A shorter, non-symphonic, deliberately brutal-sounding orchestral piece had made his name seven years before – *Pacific 231*, the representation of a railway engine. Two major works of his inhabit that half-world between opera and oratorio to which Stravinsky's *Oedipus Rex* also belongs: *King David* and *Joan of Arc at the Stake* (with a speaking role for Joan), first performed in 1921 and 1937 respectively. In these works Honegger looked back to classical oratorio, with its dramatic identification between the people (chorus) and the people (audience).

At the hands of Francis Poulenc (1899–1963) there emerged a cool and classical piano style and a style of chamber music which is more akin to the elegant eighteenth-century divertimento than to the inward-searching quartets of a Beethoven or Brahms. Among the best-known examples are Poulenc's *Perpetual Motion* (*Mouvements perpetuels*, 1919) for piano, and his sextet for piano and wind (1930–32). His songs, some in a humorous vein not unlike Chabrier's, are also notable: he was long the pianist-partner of the celebrated French baritone, Pierre Bernac (b. 1899). It apparently needed the experience of the Second World War to stir from him the satirical (yet earnestly moral) comic opera *The Breasts of Tiresias*, first performed 1947, and his opera on the heroism of the religious life, *Dialogues of the Carmelites* (1957).

Milhaud, Honegger and Poulenc were grouped by a French critic in 1920 with three other composers under the name 'The Six': a journalistic sally which has somewhat unfortunately persisted. Of the other composers Georges Auric (b. 1899) has won a minor fame; Louis Durey (b. 1888) and Germaine Tailleferre (b. 1892) hardly that. A more important compatriot, sharing something of Poulenc's lightness of style, was Jacques Ibert (1890–1962).

The aesthetic ideas associated with Cocteau and Stravinsky penetrated easily enough to Britain, partly through the success there of the Paris-based Diaghilev ballet. Diaghilev not only commissioned works from Poulenc, Milhaud, and Auric, but did the same for a 20-year-old Englishman: Constant Lambert's *Romeo and Juliet* was duly produced in Monte Carlo in 1926. Lambert (1905–51) was to achieve greater success in 1929, when he embraced the rhythmical displacements of jazz, borrowed its percussion outfit and its muted trumpets, and produced *The Rio Grande* – an astonishingly assured setting for chorus, orchestra and piano solo of a poem by Sacheverell Sitwell. His other compositions, including a piano concerto with chamber orchestra (1931), brought him less fame than his work as musical director of what became the Sadler's Wells Ballet (now the Royal Ballet).

A set of poems by Sacheverell Sitwell's sister, Edith, spoken through a megaphone by a concealed reciter, to the accompaniment of flute, clarinet, saxophone, trumpet, cello and percussion – this marked the emergence in 1923 of the young William Walton (b. 1902). The work was *Façade*, later used in an orchestrated form for ballet.* The saxophone was one tribute to jazz; another was the popular style which invaded some of the numbers. The rhythmic displacements of jazz similarly inspired Walton's *Portsmouth Point* overture and were even to turn up in the triumphant final section of his oratorio, *Belshazzar's Feast* (1931) – for which the words were written by yet another Sitwell, brother Osbert. Walton wedded a modern musical language to a traditional romantic impetus in such works as the viola concerto, 1928–9, the symphony No. 1, 1932–5, and the violin concerto (1939). He was to maintain much the same approach to orchestral music after the war with his cello concerto (1956), symphony No. 2 (1960), and *Variations on a Theme of Hindemith* (1962). That the dedications of these two concertos should be accepted by such international virtuosi as Jascha Heifetz (b. 1901) and Gregor Piatigorsky (b. 1903) was testimony enough to Walton's status in the concert hall. His ventures into opera are mentioned on p. 320.

The modern symphonist most respected in Britain at this period was Sibelius, whose examples seem to have helped sustain a British devotion to the form. Vaughan Williams (see p. 293) wrote nine symphonies; Sir Arnold Bax (1883–1953) seven, though he was more successful with illustrative

---

*The number of poems in the spoken version was originally 16, increased shortly to 26, reduced in what is now called the definitive version (1942) to 21. The 10 numbers selected for the ballet, and the 11 which comprised two concert orchestral suites, are not all to be found in the definitive 21.

orchestral music such as *The Garden of Fand* (1916). Edmund Rubbra (b. 1901) has also written eight; Sir Arthur Bliss (b. 1891) a *Colour Symphony* (1922) as well as a big, romantic piano concerto (1939). John Ireland (1879–1962) wrote no symphony and was chiefly admired for a piano concerto, piano solos and songs. But today all these and many lesser composers, resting on the examples of Elgar or Delius (or both, like Bax), turning to Sibelius or to the Elizabethan past (or both, like Rubbra), seem to form a curiously insular chapter in British musical history.

If in France it was the ballet, in Germany it was the opera which enabled young composers to express a social as well as a musical protest and to use jazz (or rather the entertainment music which Europe derived from it) in so doing. There was a reaction from the all-embracing doctrines of Wagner, from the notion of the sublimity of art. In Leipzig the young and militant Ernst Krenek (born in Austria, 1900) launched his jazz-influenced opera about a Negro violinist, *Johnny Strikes Up* in 1926; three years later Paul Hindemith's opera *News of the Day* exhibited to its Berlin audience an aria sung in a bath. Kurt Weill in collaboration with the playwright Bertolt Brecht brought out *The Threepenny Opera* (1928) and *The Rise and Fall of the City of Mahagonny* (revised version 1930), savagely satirizing capitalist morality.

Weill (1900–1950) showed not only ingenuity but genuine creative feeling in his use of the rhythms, melodies and square construction of popular song. Hindemith (1895–1963) did more: in opera and ballet, in symphonies and chamber music, in sonatas for almost every instrument, in songs and choral works, he attempted a whole renewal of the aesthetic of music, reinforced by formidable treatises and other writing. Tonality, which had been eroded from various directions, was to him still valid and indeed extendable. In an enormous output a few works have tended to stand out: the operas *Cardillac* (1926; revised version 1952) and *Mathis the Painter* (1938); the symphony based on parts of the latter opera (and performed earlier, 1934); the song-cycle *The Life of Mary*, to words by Rilke (1923, revised 1948); the set of piano studies, *Ludus tonalis* (Latin for the play of notes); the sonatas for viola (Hindemith's own instrument) and for other instruments. A certain dryness of personal expression accounts for his rather restricted success with the general musical audience.

The advent of the Nazis (National Socialists) to power in Germany in 1933 brought an attack on composers of radically new music (held to be decadent 'cultural Bolshevism'); on composers who persisted in political opposition; and on composers of Jewish birth or descent (excluded, as indeed were Jewish conductors and performers, from normal professional life). The same persecution was put into effect in Austria when Nazi Germany annexed it in 1938. The result was the departure of Schoenberg, Hindemith, Krenek, Weill and many executants – among them the conductor Bruno Walter (1876–1962) and the pianist Artur Schnabel (1882–1951) – an emigration which chiefly benefited the United States. Webern's activity was muted. The ageing Strauss accommodated himself to Nazi rule. Two younger composers whose development in Germany was not impeded were Werner Egk (b. 1901), who followed an opera on *Peer Gynt* (1938) with one on Gogol's *The Government Inspector* (1957), and Carl Orff (b. 1895).

Ironically, a work of Orff's composed and first performed in Nazi Germany (1937) has become since the war perhaps the best-known of new choral works. It is *Carmina burana*, a setting of medieval German and Latin songs of pleasure (goliard verse: see p. 19). Supposedly designed for some kind of mimed or danced visual presentation, it has more usually been given as a concert work. It is built on the use of massive blocks of sound (largely percussive), insistent, repetitive rhythms, and deliberately plain harmonies – evidence of a radical, questioning, creative mind which was later to win Orff a double international fame as an exponent of musical education for children (and the sponsor of special instruments for this) and as a radical re-thinker of the problems of opera (p. 321).

In Italy, with Puccini's death (1924), opera ceased to

occupy undisputed primacy. Ottorino Respighi (1879–1936) had begun to find fame for his series of brilliantly coloured, orchestral pictures – more in the extrovert manner of a Rimsky-Korsakov or a Richard Strauss than with the reticence of a Debussy. One of these works is pictorial even in name, the *Botticelli Triptych* of 1927; before this came *The Fountains of Rome* and *The Pines of Rome*, first performed in 1917 and 1924. The latter score includes a snatch of nightingale's song on a gramophone record: a literal (some would say, a self-defeating) realism even outdoing the wind-machine and thunder machine of Richard Strauss's *Alpine Symphony* (1915).

Other Italian composers turned as decisively from such grandiloquence as from operatic emotionalism, choosing instead (as had Stravinsky and certain French composers) a neo-classical path. But the Italian pioneer of this path, Alfredo Casella (1883–1947), rejected the label: 'We are in the presence of a total reaction against immediate and superficial sentiments, in place of which we are trying to substitute the return to the contemplated feelings of the great classics. Therefore not "neo-classicism" improperly so-called by certain critics, but a true and right return to the pure classicism of our ancestors.' In such works as the *Partita* for piano and orchestra (1925), the *Concerto romano* for organ and orchestra (1926) and the *Serenata* for five instruments (1927) he established this lucid, balanced, consciously anti-romantic style. Something of the same attitude can be seen in the more prolific Gian Francesco Malipiero (b. 1882) whose works include 11 symphonies and eight string quartets.

Equally characteristic of the new Italian outlook is Malipiero's approach to the stage. Among his operas the one-act *Seven Songs* (1920) is as totally opposed to Puccini's dramatic conceptions as an opera can be. Each of the 'songs' (which follow one another in seven anecdotal scenes) displays a character, but does not show what happens to the character, which may indeed be conveyed by gesture and orchestra alone without vocal intervention. Ildebrando

Pizzetti (b. 1880) similarly retreats from Puccini's emotional style, manifesting a scrupulous respect for inner expression and for the word which led him to put T. S. Eliot's *Murder in the Cathedral* into operatic form (1958). His earlier operas include a biblical *Deborah and Jael* (1922).

Malipiero and Pizzetti both made important new editions of some of Italy's musical classics – gestures consonant with the artistic nationalism encouraged under Mussolini's dictatorship (from 1925). Though Italian Fascism exercised far less artistic distortion than the German variety, the alliance with Nazi Germany brought an official antisemitism which drove the composer Mario Castelnuovo-Tedesco (1895–1968) into exile. Luigi Dallapiccola (b. 1904) was, one might almost say, driven into an inner exile: his adherence to Schoenberg's 12-note principles ('decadent' in Fascist ideology) plus his marriage to a Jewess laid him under a constraint from which he was to emerge only in the 1950s as the leading Italian composer of his generation.

His affinity is less to Schoenberg himself than to Berg: that is, he combines 12-note (serial) procedures with a feeling of key. His best-known work is the opera *The Prisoner* (*Il prigioniero*), first staged in 1950, in which a music of intense expression is harnessed to a text of clearly implied political commitment: the same is true of a related cantata, the *Songs of Prison* (*Canti di prigionia*) of 1938–41. Notable among his other works are some songs with chamber-music accompaniment on ancient Greek poetry in Italian translation.

Dallapiccola's most eminent Italian contemporary is Goffredo Petrassi (b. 1904), whose works include opera, ballet, five 'concertos for orchestra', and a much-admired choral and orchestral setting of classic Italian verse by Leopardi: the *Chorus of the Dead* (*Coro de' morti*) which has some affinity with Stravinsky's *Symphony of Psalms*.

In the Soviet Union Marxist doctrine suggested that, since art historically *is* determined by economic circumstances and the class struggle in particular, therefore art *ought* in the first socialist State to express the aims of the proletariat as supposedly realized in that State. The practical implications of such thought were set out, well before Russia's 1917 revolution, by Lenin: 'Literature must become Party literature. Down with unpartisan *littérateurs*! Down with the supermen of literature! Literature must become a part of the general cause of the proletariat, "a small cog and a small screw" in the social-democratic mechanism.' (*Party Organization and Party Literature*, 1905.)

In the early years of the Soviet Union there was a certain willingness to link 'progressive' (i.e. Soviet) politics with 'progressive' (i.e. technically advanced) international composition; Berg's *Wozzeck* was staged in Leningrad in 1927, only two years after the Berlin première. Associations of Soviet musicians were allowed to differ in public controversy. But in 1932 the State established the monolithic Union of Soviet Composers (today still the supremely authoritative body), and Communist Party intervention became direct and all-powerful. Of foreign works only those judged free of radical, modern tendencies were admitted to Soviet programmes, and Soviet composers themselves were kept tightly reined. In 1936 the Party's daily newspaper, *Pravda*, condemned Shostakovich's opera, *Lady Macbeth of Mtsensk*, as 'a leftist mess instead of human music' in which the composer 'rushes into the jungles of musical confusion, at times reaching complete cacophony'.

The opera, first given in Leningrad in 1934,* had already won some success abroad – which for *Pravda* only made matters worse: it 'tickles the perverted taste of bourgeois audiences with its fidgeting, screaming, neurasthenic music'. The young Dmitry Shostakovich (b. 1906) was already in the world's eyes the leading Soviet composer: his symphony No. 1, performed in 1926 before he was 20, was to remain one of the most widely known symphonic works of our time. In criticizing (which meant, in effect, banning) the opera, the Party asserted its naked power. Accepting that assertion, Shostakovich headed his Fifth symphony (1937) 'a Soviet

---

*On the occasion of its Moscow production later in the same year it was given the title *Katerina Izmailova*, (after the heroine) retained by the composer in his revision of 1963.

artist's reply to just criticism'. The international success of that symphony, and indeed of many of his later works, cautions us against imputing hypocrisy here. Shostakovich has now written 14 symphonies, 11 string quartets and a celebrated piano quintet (1940), and is recognized as one of the few to have revitalized these classical forms. His strong liking for shock-effects and grotesqueness has been sufficiently absorbed within a style which retains (or rather develops) a traditional use of key and a traditional, late-romantic type of melody.

Success was not to spare him another major condemnation by the Party in 1948 for alleged formalism (broadly, an exaltation of form at the expense of content or feeling) in his Eighth and Ninth symphonies and other works. This condemnation, which embraced other Soviet composers too and marked the height of the artistic dictatorship by the politician A. A. Zhdanov, was followed by another recantation on Shostakovich's part. He survived the episode and went on composing in much the same vein: notable is the cello concerto which he wrote in 1959 for Mstislav Rostropovich (b. 1927), one of the great performers of our day. Later, with a relaxation of the political atmosphere, Shostakovich had the satisfaction of seeing both the Eighth and Ninth symphonies performed and recorded by leading Soviet orchestras and conductors. But in 1965 the symphony No. 13, a vocal setting of words by the poet Yevtushenko, apparently brought official (though milder) disfavour again. No. 14 (also vocal, and dedicated to Britten) was first performed at the Aldeburgh Festival in 1970.

The temporary surge of pro-Soviet feeling in Britain, America and elsewhere in the Second World War served to introduce two other composers. Dmitry Kabalevsky (b. 1904) has written four symphonies and three piano concertos; Aram Khachaturian (b. 1903) made a piquant borrowing from his native Armenian music in the slow movement of his piano concerto (1936), and his *Sabre Dance* from the ballet *Gayaneh* (1942) became one of the best-known pieces in the light classical or semi-pop repertory the world over. That *no*

younger composer from the Soviet Union has won an international reputation since the Second World War may be
taken to indicate the inhibition of genuine creativity there.
Official circles, at least until the 1960s, would not countenance 12-note music or other radical ideas at all.*

The fullest, most dramatic and most bitterly ironic interplay between the Soviet and the western forms of musical
life arose in the career of Sergey Prokofiev (1891–1953).
Early works such as the *Sarcasms* and *Fugitive Visions* for piano
and the piano concerto No. 1 had established his individuality
before the 1917 Soviet revolution, and in 1918 he conducted
in Petrograd (shortly to become Leningrad) the first performance of his witty, Haydnesque *Classical Symphony*. He
then chose to live outside Russia, writing the ballet *The
Buffoon* for Diaghilev in Paris (1920) and conducting the
première of *Love for Three Oranges* (the opera from which
comes a famous March) in Chicago in 1921. Such works are
anti-romantic both in explicit sentiment and in a harmonic
style which constantly cheats expectation – sometimes
humorously. As already noted, the *Scythian Suite* (completed
1915 and intended for ballet), displays a deliberate barbaric
frenzy like that of Stravinsky's *Rite of Spring* – a work which
Prokofiev must have known.

Even when living abroad, Prokofiev had continued to
make occasional visits to Russia. In 1933 he began to extend
these visits, then soon adopted Russian residence again.
Whatever the reasons that prompted his return (dissatis-
faction with his status in the West, or a desire to belong
again?), he was well aware that the decision would mean
some modification of his modernism. The music to the film
*Lieutenant Kije* (1934), the violin concerto No. 2 (1935), the
'symphonic tale for children' *Peter and the Wolf* (1936) and
the ballet *Romeo and Juliet* (first staged at Brno, Czechoslovakia, in 1938) display examples of the new, more

* I had the experience, in visiting Moscow and meeting official musical
spokesmen in 1960, of hearing everything from Schoenberg to Boulez
dismissed as avant-gardism and thus irrelevant to the Soviet composer
and his audiences. But see page 340.

approachable style. The war brought from him not a direct, almost pictorial evocation like Shostakovich's Seventh (Leningrad) symphony, but the concise and powerful Fifth symphony (1944) and the prodigious yet problematic opera on Tolstoy's *War and Peace* (abbreviated concert performance, Moscow, 1944). In 1947 he completed what was to be the last of his piano sonatas (No. 9).

Then in 1948 the Zhdanov condemnations struck at him too. A time-serving composer, Tikhon Khrennikov (b. 1913), installed as general secretary of the Union of Soviet Composers, launched the official attack on Prokofiev for alleged formalistic tendencies in certain works from both before and after his return to Russia – *War and Peace*, incredibly, included. Prokofiev 'apologized' and promised to do better (it is tempting to detect irony in some of the phrases of his letter to Khrennikov). It was not enough. His last opera *The Tale of a Real Man* was prevented from reaching the stage in 1948 and did so only posthumously in 1960. Only in 1958, five years after his death (and Stalin's), were the Soviet condemnations of 1948 officially declared 'incorrect'.

In some other countries of what is loosely called Eastern Europe (though Prague lies *west* of Vienna), politics made the Second World War a sharp dividing-line in musical activities. The leading Polish composer, Karol Szymanowski (1882–1937), absorbed the influence of French impressionism without losing an addiction to certain national traits: he wrote 20 mazurkas for piano, and his ballet *Harnasie* (composed 1926, staged 1935) is based on the life and music of the Tatra mountain-dwellers. *The Fountain of Arethusa* for violin and piano (1915) is his most celebrated instrumental piece. Immediately after the war, under Soviet influence, national musical idioms and traditional forms such as the symphony and strongly committed music was naturally at a premium in Poland: but whatever the pressures, a clearly individual voice spoke up the person of Witold Lutosławski (b. 1913). After his *Mourning Music* of 1958 (in memory of Bartók) he built a substantial bridge between what might be called the Bartók style and later West-European radicalism. Some orchestral improvisation is required in his *Venetian Games* (Venice, 1961), in the French song-cycle *Woven Words* (*Paroles tissées*, Aldeburgh, 1965) and in the Cello Concerto (London, 1970). The relaxation of restrictions in Poland's cultural climate in the mid 1950s had evidently proved congenial to him – as also to Krzystof Penderecki, 20 years his junior, who will be seen in the next chapter to have effected a similar bridge.

In Czechoslovakia, as in other advanced European countries, the interwar years presented the most diverse trends side by side: Jaromir Weinberger (1896–1967) looking back to Smetana while writing his popular opera *Švanda the Bagpiper* (1927), Alois Haba (b. 1893) boldly experimenting with music in quarter-tones (i.e. intervals half that of the semitone, the conventionally smallest interval) – even composing an opera, *The Mother* (1931) in that idiom. The strongest musical personality among Czechoslovak composers was that of Bohuslav Martinů (1890–1959): his works, in a forceful vein not disdaining the traditional means of expression, include six symphonies, a double concerto for two string orchestras with piano and kettledrums, and several operas – notably *Comedy on the Bridge* (radio, 1937), *Julietta* (1938) and *The Greek Passion* (after Kazantzakis' novel, *Christ Recrucified*; concert performance, 1961). Since the Second World War such operatic composers as Eugen Suchón (b. 1909) and Jan Cikker (b. 1911) have also become known: Suchón's *The Whirlpool* was first given in 1949, Cikker's *Resurrection* (after Tolstoy) in 1962. Few other names have travelled, and of some 50 gramophone records by the Czech Philharmonic and Prague Symphony Orchestras available to the British public in late 1971, none included a single item by any native composer junior to Martinů.

In Hungary a continuity with the past was assured after the war by the position of honour awarded to Kodály (see p. 291) right up to his death in 1967. Kodály's pupil, Paul Kadosa (b. 1903), and Ferenc Farkas (b. 1905) were among the representatives of the next, still traditionally inclined, generation. The Romanian violinist, conductor, and composer Gheorge Enescu (1881–1955), settling in Paris and adopting a French spelling, Georges Enesco, brought his country's folk idiom in a refined concert form to the attention of western Europe and America – in three orchestral *Romanian Rhapsodies* and other works. The most widely known piece of Romanian music, however, is presumably the *Hora Staccato* by Gheorge Dinicu (1865–1930) in its transcription as a violin showpiece by Jascha Heifetz.

An isolated figure, barely recognized in his lifetime, the Greek composer Nikos Skalkottas (1904–49), now has a considerable and well-qualified following. A pupil of Schoenberg and a developer of his serial idiom, Skalkottas left at his death a large, unexplored output including 50 chamber works and a 30-minute symphony in one movement, intended as the overture to an opera, *The Return of Ulysses*. In his isolation from national trends Skalkottas suggests a parallel with Fartein Valen of Norway (1887–1952), whose music – in an atonal style of his own, having some affinity with Schoenberg's – won recognition only from his last years. A violin concerto (1940) and a symphonic poem, *The Marine Cemetery* (1934), have become known.

In general musical life in Scandinavia (with few big cities) has tended to a somewhat localized flavour. The Norwegian, Geirr Tveitt (b. 1908) has even written a concerto for his country's ancient folk instrument, the Hardanger fiddle. In Denmark Vagn Holmboe (b. 1909) seems to have synthesized the influences of Carl Nielsen and Bartók: he has written ten string quartets and a number of concertos for various solo instruments. Prominent in Sweden was Karl-Birger Blomdahl (1916–68), whose opera *Aniara* (1959), set in a space-ship, was widely reported; but a more important figure is probably Blomdahl's teacher, Hilding Rosenberg (b. 1892), composer of five symphonies (one with chorus, called *The Revelation of St John*) and other works in an individualized yet firmly traditional style.

Rosenberg was among the many composers who found a forum at the annual festival of the International Society for Contemporary Music, which played an important part in the diffusion of new music between the wars. The first president (1922–38) was the English musicologist, Edward J. Dent (1876–1957). The festivals (held in different countries by turns) were perhaps particularly important for composers from countries which had generally been regarded as not holding first musical importance. So it was that a qualified and critical audience met the music of, for example, the Dutch composers Willem Pijper (1894–1947) and Henk Badings (b. 1907) and the Swiss, Willy Burkhard (1900–1955) and Frank Martin (b. 1890). Martin's chief fame, however, was to come after the Second World War with his *Little Sinfonia Concertante* (*Petite symphonie concertante*) for harp, harpsichord, piano and double string orchestra, 1946. The presence of Aaron Copland's *El Salón Mexico* in the 1938 festival (in London) was also significant: it was in the period between the wars that American music, internally revitalized, began to assert itself internationally.

The new vitality came from the composers' recognition of America's own folk sources, both Afro-American and those which sprang from European (particularly British) folk music as imported by early settlers. This turning inward, as it were, contrasted with the attitude of those late nineteenth-century American composers such as Edward MacDowell (1861–1900) whose success had sprung from a simulation of European manners. MacDowell indeed seems European even in pieces headed with titles redolent of American history or landscape – *A.D. 1620*, for instance. In addition to such pianistic miniatures as this (Grieg often in the background), MacDowell also composed two piano concertos. His music has faded from view, like that of Horatio Parker (1863–1919), composer of the once well-known American oratorio *Hora novissima*.

The new American music was French-nurtured. It was first of all the work of men like Walter Piston (b. 1894), Virgil Thomson (b. 1896) and Aaron Copland (b. 1900). But apart from them and from Paris stood one lone, older figure now recognized as a pioneer: Charles Ives (1874–1954). Working unprompted, uncommercially, and in virtual isolation, he

used polytonality, polyrhythm, quarter-tones, barless notation and free improvisation within a notated piece – in
music which is full of overt American references and which
was nearly all composed before 1920, yet little recognized for
another 25 years. His works include four symphonies, songs
(114 privately printed, 1922) and the huge, programmatic,
extremely difficult sonata No. 2 for piano, subtitled 'Concord,
Mass., 1840–60' with four movements – Emerson, Haw-
thorne, The Alcotts and Thoreau. *The Unanswered Question*
(see p. 335) demands spatially separated performers. Such
music did not immediately influence younger composers:
their formative years passed in ignorance of it. But when they
had matured, it enabled them to claim a long-lost father.

MacDowell, Parker and other composers had studied in
Germany. Immediately after the First World War a German
orientation was obviously less attractive. Going instead to
Paris, Piston, Thomson and Copland all came under the
famous French teacher Nadia Boulanger (b. 1887), learning
clarity, sensibility and economy as an aesthetic (that of the
neo-classical Stravinsky, it might be said). Thomson further-
more found himself responsive to the deliberately simplified,
anti-romantic, mini-tensioned outlook of Satie: the maxim
'Never banality, but as many commonplaces as possible'
might apply equally to Satie's 'symphonic drama' *Socrates*
(see p. 282) and Thomson's opera *Four Saints in Three Acts*
(1934) with text by Gertrude Stein: it has four acts and a
great number of saints. Piston, much more concerned with
musical argument in the traditional sense, expressed himself
in an authoritative series of eight symphonies and other,
mainly abstract, works. Copland was to become the all-
American composer to an even greater degree, in a wide
range of idioms – with a prodigious extra activity as conductor and champion of other American music besides his
own.

Of these three Piston makes little use of native American
musical material – but there is a deliberate and witty sense of
musical quotation in one of his best-known works, *The Incredible Flutist* (1938; intended for ballet). Thomson's music,

however, often breathes American hymn-tunes (there is even a *Symphony on a Hymn-Tune*, 1928 – actually on *two* such tunes); and Copland is equally happy in evoking urbanized jazz (piano concerto, 1927), cowboy tunes (the ballet, *Billy the Kid*, 1939), or popular Latin-American style (*El Salón Mexico* – the name of a Mexico City dance hall – 1937), or the religious songs of the Shaker sect (the ballet, *Appalachian Spring*, 1944). No less remarkable is the range of Copland's idiom when he is *not* writing Americana – from the hard, percussive strength of the piano variations (1930) through the almost romantic warmth of the Third symphony (1946) to the *Connotations* for orchestra (in the 12-note technique) of 1962.

Not all his compatriots were as Americanist* as Copland. For Roger Sessions (b. 1896) there was the inspiration first of Bloch and then of Schoenberg: Sessions' works (a piano concerto, a violin concerto and five symphonies among them) tend to a tough, dense texture and have won more professional admiration than public following. There are American references, to be sure, in the music of William Schuman (b. 1910): but his main achievement is perhaps in his eight (purely abstract) symphonies, and when he begins his *American Festival Overture* with a representation of a street-cry he is careful to point out that 'the development of this bit of "folk-material" is along purely musical lines'. European late-romantic idioms continued to make an appeal to Samuel Barber (b. 1910), noted for two symphonies, an *Adagio for Strings* (drawn from a string quartet) and the opera *Vanessa* (New York, 1958).

It is also true, conversely, that some of the most Americanist composers of the 1930s have exerted a much diminished appeal in the 1970s (like Bax and Ireland among British composers): among these is Roy Harris (b. 1898), the composer of nine symphonies including a *Folk-Song Symphony* for chorus and orchestra. Yet the finding of America's own music provided, even for those who refrained

---

* I borrow the term from Gilbert Chase's compendious and classic book, *America's Music*, McGraw-Hill, second edition, 1966.

from embracing it, a point of magnetic opposition, an invitation to public dialogue. Something of the same dialogue can be seen continuing in the music of the 1950s: in the work of an Americanist like Leonard Bernstein (of whom more in the next chapter) as contrasted with, say, a 'European' like Elliott Carter. Born in 1908, but making his reputation a good deal later than Barber or Schuman, Carter writes post-Schoenbergian music with the dense, uncompromising texture of a Sessions. His two string quartets and his double concerto of 1961 (for harpsichord, piano, and two chamber orchestras) have been particularly admired.

Back in the 1930s, when composers such as Copland and Harris were reaching out to draw the vernacular idiom into the established forms and modes of serious music, one man successfully crossed the frontier in the other direction, raising the vernacular idiom itself to the dignity of a true and fully conscious art. He was George Gershwin (1898–1937), whose *Rhapsody in Blue* for piano and jazz orchestra (Paul Whiteman's) in 1924 proved the forerunner of the no less remarkable piano concerto (1925), *An American in Paris* (1928) and the opera *Porgy and Bess* of 1935 (not only jazzy but also quoting Negro folk material direct). Gershwin had begun as a popular song composer: at the age of 19 he had written *Swanee*, with a sale of over two million gramophone records, and continued to compose for musicals and their film equivalents. Gifted and sophisticated as some other song-composers of similar Broadway and Hollywood careers have been – notably Jerome Kern (1885–1945) and Cole Porter (1892–1964) – they never achieved Gershwin's breadth.

In discussing American musical life between the wars two more composers remain to be mentioned: both oddities, both pioneers, both propagandists. Neither the French-born Edgar Varèse (1883–1965), who settled in the United States in 1915, nor Henry Cowell (1897–1966) lived the physically and musically secluded life of a Charles Ives. Beginning conventionally, Cowell progressed in more than 1,000 works to an aggressive modernism: he developed the keyboard *cluster* of adjacent notes (played, if need be, with the forearm) and was co-inventor of a mechanism called the rhythmicon for the precise reproduction of complex pre-determined rhythms. Eight *Hymns and Fuguing Tunes* (founded on original music by the American primitive, William Billings, 1746–1800), not to mention 19 symphonies, were among his orchestral works. Varèse is remarkable for an extension of the sound-spectrum, particularly in the exploitation of percussion: his *Ionization* of 1931 is a work lasting about six minutes, solely for percussion instruments of indefinite pitch and two sirens. Luckily he survived till the electronic (post-1945) age, when his position as a pioneer could be historically recognized and respectfully saluted: his *Electronic Poem* was composed for the Brussels Exhibition of 1958 and spatially distributed there over 400 loudspeakers.

The pavilion at that exhibition had been designed by a young Greek architect who was also a musician – Yannis Xenakis. Subsequently, for the Montreal Exhibition (1967), Xenakis provided music which a computer had helped him to compose. This is a phenomenon of our present era, to which the last two chapters of this book must now be devoted. Meanwhile, America must not be quitted without mention of the flowering of composition in Latin America between the two World Wars. Often the spur was deliberately nationalistic – as in the series of vocal and instrumental works called *Bachianas Brasileiras* with which Heitor Villa-Lobos (1887–1959) sought to combine Bach-like counterpoint with the musical riches of his native Brazil.

# 19

## Continuation

ELECTRONIC resources have decisively changed both the sound and the diffusion of music. Classics and new works alike reach a greater, more differentiated public through radio, records, and tape (and, increasingly, television) than through the act of attending the concert or theatrical performance. Composers who reached maturity in the 1950s often found their musical imagination working in a radically new context. Was it any longer necessary to compose for a performer or a performance? Is there a fixed boundary between humanly produced and electronically produced notes, between notes and noise, between noise and what we call silence?

We consider these new worlds in our next and final chapter. But older composers (meaning here those active before the Second World War as well as after it) were on the whole naturally reluctant to abandon the disciplines and boundaries of their established musical worlds. In electronic sound they rightly saw an implicit threat not merely to the hierarchy of notes but to the relationship of performer, composer and listener. This chapter examines the work of these continuators, with a special note on attempts to revivify that most conservative and institutionalized musical type, the opera. Although certain of these older composers were receptive to newer technical possibilities (Gerhard, Krenek and Blacher have all made use of taped sound as an element in live performance), the historical interest of their work lies precisely in its link with the period when these technical resources did not exist.

For such composers, 12-note music tends not to be a combative issue. They may follow Schoenberg himself in combining serial principles with music of a traditionally emotional kind on traditionally large scales; or they may follow Webern (as Stravinsky did) in wedding a strict serial technique to very short forms and sparse, spiky textures. They may employ a 12-note row for a special purpose in otherwise tonal music (Walton, theme of the second movement of the sonata for violin and piano, 1949; Britten, cumulative theme in the opera *The Turn of the Screw*, 1953). In such ways serial technique is recognized as (at least) an available procedure, and the position of Schoenberg, Berg and Webern as a second Viennese school (see p. 289) is accepted as a valid phenomenon of twentieth-century music.

Stravinsky's is the most remarkable example of musical longevity in our time. We have already noted (p. 284) his astonishing many-sidedness – how the neo-classic, back-to-Bach 'Dumbarton Oaks' concerto of 1938 was followed at two years' distance by the almost Beethoven-like symphony in C – and, we may now add, by another symphony (1945), confusingly titled not by a key but as *Symphony in Three Movements*. In 1946 he brought out, for Woody Herman's band, an *Ebony Concerto* (the allusion is to the clarinet, which has a solo role) in a style which made a deliberate rapprochement with jazz. In 1951 he developed a back-to-Mozart and back-to-Bellini stylization in his opera *The Rake's Progress*, with English libretto by W. H. Auden and Chester Kallmann – a stylization which goes so far as to reproduce the *Don Giovanni* type of epilogue, the characters stepping out of their frame to moralize humorously in the direction of the audience.

It is tempting to describe all these works of Stravinsky's as encounters of the fully twentieth-century musician with earlier musical styles. Never has there been such a historically minded composer. The austere mass (1948), for boys' and men's voices and ten wind instruments, is a similar encounter – with Gregorian chant, with fifteenth-century music, perhaps also with Byzantine chant (the music of the eastern-European Orthodox churches). In the light of this capacity for absorption the apparently revolutionary step taken by Stravinsky in the early 1950s becomes less astonishing. This was the adoption of serial technique – more particularly, of Webern's form of that technique, in association with brevity of span and closely wrought canons. Webern, as we have seen (p. 289), was a disciple of Schoenberg, a composer with whose aesthetic outlook Stravinsky had seemed to have nothing in common. Their antipathy seemed to be mutual: Schoenberg, in his *Three Satires* for mixed chorus (1925), had actually made fun of the other as 'Modernsky', whose 'genuine false hair' makes him think he looks exactly like Papa Bach. Stravinsky reached Webern not via Schoenberg but perhaps via medieval music: mathematical ingenuity, even to achieve results apparently hidden from the ear, is prized both by the fifteenth-century composer of motets and by the modern serialist.

In a number of works, notably the *Cantata* (1952) on old English texts, for soprano, tenor, female chorus and instrumental quintet, Stravinsky began to apply serial technique while still remaining within tonality. By serialism in this sense is understood the constructive method of treating a theme of a few notes either in its original state, or upside-down, or backwards, or upside-down and backwards. Then Stravinsky added to this the complete equality of all the 12 notes – though whether the title of Stravinsky's *first* 12-note work should go to the *Canticum sacrum* of 1955 or the *Threni* of 1957–8 is a matter of definition. The *Canticum sacrum ad honorem sancti Marci nominis* (Sacred Canticle in honour of St Mark), scored for tenor and baritone, mixed chorus, and an orchestra which excludes violins and cellos, begins with a sung dedication to the city of Venice and its patron saint. The *Threni, id est Lamentationes Jeremiae prophetae* (Lamentations of Jeremiah) is for six solo singers and a larger chorus and orchestra. Both these works, with Latin words, represent Stravinsky's increasing preoccupation with religious texts, which he treats in an emphatic but austere manner – an austerity which has its precedent, a quarter of a century before, in the *Symphony of Psalms*. The *Requiem Canticles* (1966), in small, Webern-like dimensions, shows the same preoccupation.

The physical presence in wartime America of Stravinsky and Schoenberg, Bartók and Hindemith, along with many other refugee musicians from Europe, may have helped to turn American composers away from overt nationalism towards the musical heritage of Europe (the vanished, Nazi-overridden Europe!). As we have seen, even Copland's music became a good deal less American in feeling after the war. With Copland, Sessions and Piston now in the position of elder statesmen, the European line of tough, argumentative music continued in the hands of such younger American composers as Ross Lee Finney (b. 1906) and Elliott Carter (see p. 313). All these cultivated mainly the sonata, symphony, concerto and other traditional abstract forms. In opera the only American of this generation to succeed resoundingly has been Gian-Carlo Menotti, born in Italy in 1911 but based in America since student days. His admitted stance as an 'entertainer' (in the way that Puccini was) has led to critical underestimation of his best work, notably *Amelia Goes to the Ball* (1937) and *The Telephone* (1947), both neat social comedies in the spirit of Wolf-Ferrari (p. 278); *The Medium*, produced in 1946 (and later filmed with the composer as director), a psychologically subtle horror story; *Amahl and the Night Visitors* (1951), a Christmas story, originally for television; and – not an opera at all, but a series of madrigals with a staged action mimed and danced – *The Unicorn, the Gorgon, and the Manticore* (1956). The prodigiously gifted composer-pianist-conductor Leonard Bernstein (b. 1918) gave the American musical a new seriousness in *West Side Story* (1957), but it had no sequel. The pure song-writing gift of Richard Rodgers (b. 1902) proved more renewable – such sentimental vehicles as *The Sound of Music* (1959).

In Britain, after Vaughan Williams and Walton (pp. 293, 299), decisive leadership was taken by Benjamin Britten (b. 1913). His *Variations on a Theme of Frank Bridge*, for orchestra, had won him international notice in 1937; wartime brought such works as the orchestral *Sinfonia da Requiem* (1940) and the *Serenade* for tenor, horn and strings (1943); and the success of his opera *Peter Grimes* in 1945 led to a succession of further dramatic works. In retrospect *Peter Grimes*, *Billy Budd* (1951) and *Gloriana* (1953) will perhaps be seen as late examples of a dying form, the big heroic opera;

the chamber operas, notably *The Rape of Lucretia* (1946), *Albert Herring* (1947) and *The Turn of the Screw* (1953) are notable mainly for the new solo-instrumental sound palette masterfully used. (*A Midsummer Night's Dream*, 1961, preserves something of its chamber-orchestral delicacy even in the later version for full orchestra.) *Owen Wingrave* (1971) was retreading of old ground, disguised as a new television opera. More radical, alike as music and as a new effort to find a meaningful social context for operatic composition, are the three 'parables for church performance', *Curlew River*, *The Burning Fiery Furnace*, and *The Prodigal Son* (respectively 1964, 1966 and 1968): all are for male (including boys') voices only, the Madwoman in *Curlew River* being a tenor.

The break from the opera house meant a new assertion of musical drama, an independence from a fundamentally nineteenth-century, grand-opera, theatrical presentation. As if to signalize this liberation, Britten in his church parables not merely let his orchestra (of less than a dozen) participate physically in the entries and exits of the drama, but also adopted a musical style involving oriental heterophony (the staggered treatment of melody) which is as different from the traditional delivery of his previous stage works as can be imagined. We must not here forget the precedent of *Noye's Fludde* (1958) for (mainly) child participants, which is also designed for church and uses the voices of the congregation in a masterly quotation of traditional hymns.

Britten's friendship with the Soviet cellist Mstislav Rostropovich (b. 1927) has added to his works a cello symphony (cello and orchestra), first given in Moscow in 1964; a sonata for cello and piano (1960) and two suites for unaccompanied cello (1964, 1967) in the rather tougher style the composer has recently adopted in instrumental writing. But he remains pre-eminently a vocal composer, with songs not only in English but in French, German, Italian and in Pushkin's Russian, and with choral works which range from the modest anthem to the ebullient *Spring Symphony* of 1949 and the large-scaled *War Requiem* of 1962 with solo parts intended for Peter Pears (Britten's leading vocal interpreter for some 30 years), Dietrich Fischer-Dieskau, and Galina Vishnevskaya. The *War Requiem* boldly confronts the church's traditional Latin requiem text with anti-war poems by Wilfred Owen (1893–1918).

British composers older than Britten followed him into opera: notably Walton and Michael Tippett (b. 1905). Walton's attempts were formula-filling (*Troilus and Cressida*, 1954; *The Bear*, 1967, not even rescued by Paul Dehn's exceptionally neat libretto on the Chekhov tale). Tippett's first two operas – *The Midsummer Marriage*, 1955; *King Priam*, 1962 – were more individually arresting in dramatic scheme and musical content, but hampered by the composer's own foggily philosophical librettos. Undaunted, he engaged the same librettist for his next opera, *The Knot Garden* (1970), with an equally crippling result. Tippett's fame appears to rest more securely on his wartime oratorio, *A Child of Our Time*, first given in 1944 (with its highly effective use of Negro spirituals to parallel the chorales of Bach as a 'people's' commentary), on his concerto for double string orchestra (1939), his three string quartets (1935, 1942, 1946), and the *Variations on a Theme of Corelli* for string orchestra (1953). Less heroic in temper, perhaps more refined in execution, were the works of Lennox Berkeley (b. 1903) and Alan Rawsthorne (1905–71). Both composed notably for the piano, though Berkeley's gift is nowhere better shown than in the *Four Poems of St Teresa* (1947) for contralto and string orchestra.

In Germany older composers found themselves after the war free to take up again the modernism banned by the Nazis, in particular Schoenberg's 12-note method and its developments. Two leading figures did so: Karl Amadeus Hartmann (1905–63), composer of eight symphonies, and Wolfgang Fortner (b. 1907), known for the opera *Blood Wedding* (1957, after Lorca's play), a *Fantasy on the notes B–A–C–H*\* for two

---

\* H in German represents our note B; German B is our B flat. The use of names as note-formulas in this way dates back at least to J. S. Bach himself; by repeating the musical notes in order through the alphabet, equivalents may be devised even for non-musical letters, as in Ravel's *Minuet on the Name H-A-Y-D-N*, for piano, 1909. See also p. 229.

clarinets, nine solo instruments and orchestra (1950) and a wide variety of other works. But in a sense the most original of this generation of German composers is the most (superficially) reactionary: Carl Orff, already alluded to (p. 301). Having simplified harmony and rhythm to a primitive basis, in order to establish tune and chordal sonority once again, he effected a similar purge of operatic complexities in the cause of dramatic force.

Orff's *Antigone* (1949) is not an opera *based* on Sophocles' tragedy; it is simply a setting of the poet Hölderlin's German version of the play. This version is followed, word for word and line by line, mainly in strictly rhythmic recitative or in metrical choruses, with a multiple-percussion accompaniment. It more closely resembles a work from the birth-era of opera, the early 1600s, than any opera written since. (By no coincidence Orff has also edited Monteverdi's stage works for modern performance.) Of a similar type, though perhaps less convincing, is Orff's *Oedipus the King* (again on Hölderlin's version of Sophocles; 1959). In 1968 Orff attempted, not to every critic's taste, the experiment of a *Prometheus* which set Aeschylus in the original Greek.

By contrast, Orff's *The Moon* (*Der Mond*) and *The Clever Girl* (*Die Kluge*), produced in 1939 and 1943 respectively, are simply humorous fables with catchy, ballad-like songs – a medium of stage expression which in its way is as powerful an opposition to traditionally complex opera as is the neo-Monteverdi style of the tragic Greek settings.

We turn to France and to the composer who more than any other bridges the gap between the new music of the 1930s and the new music of the 1950s and beyond: Olivier Messiaen. Born in 1908, Messiaen has written much for organ (he is himself a distinguished organist), for piano, for solo and choral voices and for orchestra. He proclaims a Catholic devotion: 'My preferences are for music that glistens, that is refined and even voluptuous (but definitely not sensual!) . . . a music that expresses the end of time, ubiquity, the blessed saints, the divine and supernatural mysteries.' Apart from the impressionism of Debussy, he has found inspiration in birdsong and exotic (particularly Indian) music. His *Turangalîla Symphony* (1948), lasting approximately 75 minutes, and scored for piano and very large orchestra, is in 10 movements of which three are specifically labelled *turangalîla* (apparently a Sanskrit equivalent for lovesong). In *The Awakening of the Birds* (1953) for piano and orchestra he claimed that the score contained *nothing but* the authentically reproduced calls of 38 birds, named in five languages on a prefatory page. His earlier works include *Harawi* (1945), a 'song of love and death' – a work in 12 numbers for dramatic soprano and piano, set to his own words, and making use of Peruvian folk music.

The use of birdsong was not in order to arouse pastoral pathos; the use of folksong was not in order to write folksy music. These sources gave Messiaen new melodic and rhythmic figurations. In the first movement of his *Quartet for the End of Time* (1940, for violin, clarinet, cello and piano) a 17-unit rhythmic figure is present in continuous repetition against a chain of 29 chords also in continuous repetition – the two sequences (rhythm units and chord units) coinciding at different points each time, just like the simultaneous, unequal patterns of rhythm and of melody in the fourteenth-century isorhythmic motet (see p. 37).

With a musical mind of such inclinations, it was the middle-aged Messiaen and not the young Boulez who in 1949 wrote the piece which prefigured the application of serial method not merely to pitches of notes but to durations of notes and other constituents. This piece (the second of *Four Studies in Rhythm*, for piano) was called *Mode of Time-Values and Intensities*, an oddly incomplete title. Messiaen had already written pieces in specially devised scale-type formations, which he called *modes*; in effect the mode restricts the piece to a set of preselected notes. In this case the mode consisted of 36 selected notes, from E flat nearly two octaves above the treble stave, down to C sharp an octave and a half below the bass. But the new feature is that each of these notes has always the same time value whenever it occurs ranging from a 32nd-note (♪) for that top E flat, through ♪ and advancing by 32nd-note increments to a dotted whole-note ($\circ\cdot$) for the low C sharp. Moreover each note is always paired with the same kind of attack, selected from 12 (staccato, sforzando, etc.) and always the same indication of intensity (loudness), one of seven such indications from *ppp* to *fff*.

The piece is not serial in Schoenberg's sense – that is, the succession of notes does not go right through a 12-note pattern – but it marks a new stage in bringing not only rhythmical elements under a mathematical scheme but expressive elements as well. It will be noted, however, that a difficulty arises in performance. Different pitches are absolutely disjunct. But differences of duration, loudness and types of attack cannot always be so clearly communicated – a formidable obstacle to the adoption of this kind of music.

The *total serialist* works that followed are subject to the same practical objection. In these works, produced in the mid 1950s, the composers sought to apply mathematical control to duration, attack and loudness – as well as to pitch, not in Messiaen's manner but serially in Schoenberg's sense, i.e. in non-repeated order. Such composition exercised the minds not only of younger composers (such as Nono, Berio, and Boulez, to be considered in the next chapter) but of some older ones too – notably Fortner (p. 320) in his cantata *The Creation* (1955) and Krenek (p. 300) in his *Six Measurements* (Sechs Vermessene, 1958) for piano solo. But there was a fairly rapid retreat from such super-mathematical construction, partly because the type of music which resulted (violently contrasted and fragmentary, lacking melody and rhythm in the older sense) could well have been arrived at from spontaneous choice, if not by random means.

Krenek has, however, remained adventurous in other directions. In 1970, at the age of 70, he responded to a commission from the Hamburg State Opera with *This Comes from That* (*Das kommt davon*), an opera during which Mozart's *Così fan tutte* is heard on radio as part of the stage action and integrated into his own score. The willingness to see a continuing life in the old theatrical forms of opera and ballet, and in the older musical structures (sonata, symphony, concerto and the like) is possibly sufficient to denote a continuator as distinct from a revolutionary; or, to use another terminology, a traditionalist from one of the vanguard (of which the fashionable French 'avant-garde' is a superfluous equivalent). These are *not*, let it be emphasized, judgements of value: the new in technique, which is possibly only apparently or superficially new, may not be the most lasting in worth. Just as the conservative Bach is now so much more honoured than the modish Telemann, so the 1960s may be in posterity's view remembered more for Shostakovich than for Stockhausen.

Mention of Shostakovich (see p. 304) underlines the isolation of Soviet composers, apparently confined for ideological reasons to an extreme conservative position in which 12-note music is regarded as tainted, key as essential and thematic discussion still the normal process of larger structures – all in the name of optimistic, purposive, socially acceptable music. Some departures from this were to be manifest in the 1960s (see p. 340). Yet perhaps in no other country could a composer born as late as 1932, Rodion Shchedrin, have achieved celebrity with such traditionally inclined works as his piano concerto (1954), his ballet *The Little Hump-backed Horse* (1960) and his re-treatment of Bizet's *Carmen* (as a ballet). Adherence to this Communist ethic apparently sustains a few notable older non-Russian composers in their adherence to a conservative formal and harmonic style – Paul Dessau (b. 1894) in East Germany, Alan Bush (b. 1900) in England, Elie Siegmeister (b. 1909) in America.

In the next chapter we consider composers whose music shows a radically modern stance – partly under the spur of new electronic devices, partly in a general rejection of closed artistic forms, parallel to a rejection which is also to be seen in the developments in visual art. But the development of electronics has by no means arrested the centuries-long expansion of the range and tone palette of conventional instruments. Forgotten instruments have been revived, and others transplanted into western music from exotic cultures. The mandolin, a picturesque element in Mahler's *Song of the Earth* (1908), already legitimized as a chamber-music instrument in Schoenberg's *Serenade* (1923), expands its role in Boulez's *Fold upon Fold* (*Pli selon pli*, first performed in 1960). The apparently obsolete alto trombone was called back into use by Stravinsky in *The Flood* (a 'musical play', 1962, on the English medieval literary sources) and by Britten in *The Burning Fiery Furnace* (see p. 319). Schoenberg's Spanish (English-resident) pupil, Roberto Gerhard (1879–1970), found a place for the accordion in his *Nonet* (1956–7) and his *Concerto for Eight*, 1962.

A revolution has overtaken the piano. Its capacity has been newly explored, especially for its resources in the single note, the resonating string, and the cluster (adjacent notes). It is the distinction between 'playing a keyboard' in the older fashion and 'using the piano as a sound-source' – to quote a leading pianist-interpreter of the new music, John Tilbury (b. 1936). He traces this new technique back to the demands made by Webern's *Variations*, opus 27 (1926), though it did not become widely exploited until the 1950s. The 'prepared piano' introduced in the late 1940s by the American composer John Cage goes further: the strings are muted or modified at various points by bits of wood, rubber, metal, glass, etc. (Virgil Thomson described the typical sound of the prepared piano as 'a ping, qualified by a thud'.) Cage and others occasionally ask the performer to lean over and pluck the strings directly.

In the 1960s woodwind players began to be asked for 'freak' high notes, and even for the freakish simultaneous sounding of more than one note. In Harrison Birtwistle's *Interludes for a Tragedy* (four pieces for solo clarinet, 1969, with a tape-recorded background), ultra-high notes are balanced by a downward extension of range as well, since the composer specifies the so-called basset clarinet, the original instrument of Mozart's clarinet concerto (see p. 192). In his *Sequence V* Luciano Berio similarly asked in 1966 for chords and other unheard-of effects on the trombone.

In a work called *Eonta* ('Beings', 1964) Xenakis sent two trumpeters and three trombonists to blow their instruments over an open grand piano, arousing the resonance of the strings. In *The Raft of the Frigate 'Medusa'* (1968), Hans Werner Henze demands among his orchestra the electric guitar, electric bass guitar and electric organ of pop groups; and also three metal plates, five different gongs, an Indian wooden drum, 17 other types of percussion, and two sizes of ophicleide (a lower-pitched brass instrument which fell into disuse in the mid nineteenth century).

Cage, Xenakis, Berio, Henze and Birtwistle – to name them in order of birth – are representative figures of the newer musical scene. Or post-musical? It is now necessary to raise the question of who the composer is and what he is doing.

# 20

# On and Off the Frontier

PERSPECTIVE inevitably magnifies what is nearest to us, and every age tends to think its own crisis a major one. But, even allowing for the distortions of viewpoint, it does appear that 'new music' has undergone a radical change since the early 1950s. In the previous 200 years or so, despite the explosive force of a Beethoven, a Wagner, a Stravinsky, a Schoenberg, the ideas of a musical composition and a musical performance remained much the same, and so did the basic forms and processes of music. A Haydn symphony and a Vaughan Williams symphony, an opera by Cimarosa and one by Prokofiev, have something in common in their artistically conceived shape, and in the type of social organization involved in their presentation to the intended public. But there is no such link between these and certain typical works of Cage, Stockhausen, or Boulez.

These three composers have been among the most prominent of the musical vanguard (which, as we have remarked, is necessarily a provisional term). Some features of the new music entail further developments in a direction which had been already apparent: music continues to seem more and more like a series of exclamations rather than like discourse, and extremes of spiky, harsh sonorities are more and more cultivated. But the special, and new, characteristics of this latest music rest on the acceptance of: (1) electronics, (2) new relationships between composer and performer, (3) new spatial relationships in performance and (4) new fluidity of the boundary between what is art and what is not.

Electronic modification or generation of sound, however, goes back several decades. In 1929 the *theremin* was commercially marketed in America: a short, perpendicular rod emitting a sound which varied in pitch according as the operator's hand was brought nearer to or farther from it. In the previous year the *martenot* had been publicly heard in

Paris – similarly using electronically generated sound, but (in one form) having a keyboard capable of inflections smaller than a semitone. Among the works in which it is used is Messiaen's *Turangalîla Symphony* (see p. 322). In the 1930s the so-called electric guitar (i.e. with electric amplification, shortly entailing structural modification of the actual instrument) came into general use in dance-bands and, later, in pop-groups and the like. From the same period dates the electronic organ, in which electronic generation of sound replaces the vibration of air in pipes – the most successful type proving to be the Hammond Organ (1935). The player of such an electronic organ selects his tone colour from a range of combinations determined by the maker's specifications, and other effects (e.g. vibrato and echo) may also be at his disposal.

Electronic organs work on the long-recognized knowledge that what we regard as characteristic tone colour (of an oboe, a violin, Miss X's soprano voice or Miss Y's) is the special combination of pure tones in the harmonic series.* Such pure tones can be demonstrated in the laboratory but were never considered as directly available to the composer until, shortly after the Second World War, magnetically sensitized tape displaced wax as the customary initial medium for gramophone recording. Unlike a wax disc, tape could be cut, spliced, reversed, accelerated or decelerated at will, bringing a controlled transformation or distortion of the original sound. The sound of, say, a flute, could be recorded on tape; then that tape could be played at half speed (therefore an octave lower) and, if desired, backwards; and *that* sound-impression recorded on a second tape . . . and so on *ad infinitum*. Sound which, though 'natural' in origin, was processed in the electronics laboratory became the material of the so-called concrete music produced by Pierre Boulez (b. 1925) and other young musicians and engineers in the studios of the French radio in the years round 1949.

* See the article 'Harmonic series' in my *A New Dictionary of Music*, Penguin Books, 1968.

But why use a natural source at all? Why not start with electronically generated pure tones and the other originations of the laboratory? Assemble the sound components on tapes, mix and combine these in further cumulative instalments of tape-recording . . . and eventually the composition itself emerges on tape, fixed and final and in the form of sound, not of marks on paper. Such compositions were commonly given the simple name 'electronic music' (though 'tape-synthesized electronic music' would have been better). This electronic music was developed principally in the Cologne radio workshops and studios from 1951, and its practitioners soon appropriated concrete music as well. *The Song of the Three Holy Children* (*Gesang der Jünglinge*, using the Apocryphal text) by Karlheinz Stockhausen, dating from 1955–6, is an example of concrete combined with electronically originated sound.

Stockhausen, born in 1928 in Cologne, became in 1956 the first composer to have an electronic work (No. 2 of *Electronic Studies*) published in score – or rather in diagram, since it presents the technician with the timed instructions for assembling the work, pitch being specified in Hertz (cycles per second) and volume in decibels. But there is no need for such a pseudo-score, nor can there be any performance (in the sense of interpretation) of such a work. Tape-synthesized electronic music thus became the first music in history to eliminate the performer and to be subject to no interpretation.*

In this way taped electronic music seemingly liberated the

---

* It is none the less instructive, particularly for those brought up on the traditional identification of the note heard with the note written, to study an electronic piece in aural and visual form simultaneously. A short work, *345*, by Tristram Cary (b. 1925), perhaps the major British composer of electronic music, has appeared in an admirably suitable package (stereo recording, colour-printed score, composer's spoken introduction) from Galliard Ltd (U.K.) and Galaxy Music Corporation (U.S.). It is to be noted, however, that this score is specifically prepared for the listener and uses certain symbols of traditional music notation: it is not a complete diagram of instructions for a technician, as is the Stockhausen example.

composer both from the limits of conventional notation and from his previous dependence on the availability and responsiveness of the performer. But was it really a deliverance? Composers soon showed themselves reluctant to give up the uniqueness of the performing *occasion*. Some called for the combination of electronically taped sounds and live performance on the concert platform. In 1961 the American composer Milton Babbitt (b. 1916), a defender of a rigorously mathematical approach to composition, produced *Vision and Prayer*, to a text by Dylan Thomas, for soprano solo and tape-synthesized electronic music. The same combination of tape with live performers might even be demanded in the opera house – as in Blomdahl's Swedish space-fiction opera *Aniara* (1959) or Blacher's *Incidents at an Emergency Landing* (1966), described by the composer not as an opera but as 'a report for electronic devices, instruments and singers'.

There is another way (besides human intervention) of making electronic music unique to an occasion, i.e. to a performance. The chosen sounds and formulas may be fed to a computer along with the possibility of combining them in several different solutions. The computer may then be instructed to choose one such solution, thus yielding a performance of what is then called a computer-composed work – though it might be more accurate to ascribe to the computer only the final stages of composition. A *Partita for Unattended Computer* by the English composer Peter Zinovieff (b. 1933) was included in a London concert in January 1968, with the note that 'there has been no actual rehearsal of this piece, for the simple reason that each realization [by the computer working on its programme] will be essentially different'.

From the mid 1960s, however, composers of the vanguard have inclined to another method of combining electronic resources with the immediacy and uniqueness of performance – the method known as live electronics. The sounds made by conventional instrumental and/or vocal performers, instead of reaching the audience directly, are fed, on the spot, through an electronic process of amplification and distortion, as specified by the composer. The ultimate decision on what is heard rests with fingers on a potentiometer (volume control). Thus Stockhausen's *Microphony I* (1964) requires two performers to beat, scratch and otherwise excite a giant gong, while two others explore the surface with directional microphones, the result being processed by two more 'performers' each adjusting a filter and a potentiometer.

Stockhausen has particularly associated the technical control by live electronics with the creation of a special occasion and atmosphere in a not purely musical sense. A work of which the German title, *Stimmung*, means both atmosphere and tuning is an example: what is basically a single chord, though with interruptions and shifts, is sung into microphones by six unaccompanied singers for 75 minutes, to words of intendedly magic or ritual significance. 'Time has stopped,' the composer wrote of this work (1968), adding that it should be 'a speedy aircraft making for the Cosmos and the divine'.

Live electronics received a further stimulus in the late 1960s with the availability of the instant electronic synthesizer – a portable apparatus by which the composer could select the electronic components of whatever sound he wanted and 'play' it immediately to an audience without pre-recording on tape. The Moog Synthesizer (named after its American inventor, Robert Moog) is the best-known type; the (British) VCS-3 is another, of more modest capabilities. Such a synthesizer may be fitted with a keyboard and can then play tunes (but only one note at once); but this is, except perhaps in the pop world, the least part of its musical value. Its essential is that it allows the deployment of an infinite choice of electronic sound (noises and random patterns as well as exactly controlled musical notes) in real time – i.e. in the time of a live performance.

The operator of a Moog can do much that an ordinary performer cannot – for instance, he can programme a lengthy sequence of varying sound-events and have it infinitely repeated. But the old performing skills of resource and dexterity are also involved, so the word 'performance' is not inappropriate, and the linear relationship of composer–

performer–listener is preserved. It is the earlier tape-synthesized electronic music as described above which, by eliminating the performer, makes the composer's relationship with
the listener a new one. In 1969 the American composer
Eric Salzman (b. 1933) produced a quasi-dramatic work on
gramophone record, *The Nude Paper Sermon,* and claimed that
this was not a recording *of* the work: it *was* the work, existing
in multiple copies (the records) but in no other form.

The acceptance of electronics thus opens to the composer
the possibility of handling noise (i.e. sounds which do not fall
in the realm of notes) in a fully controlled, composer's
manner. But some of the most advanced in other directions
(Boulez, Berio) have firmly asserted the primacy of notes, and
have seemingly shifted away from electronic manipulation;
and their processes of composition are processes *with notes,*
not unconnected with quite traditional methods of composing.
We have observed above (p. 323) the exploration by certain
older composers in the mid 1950s (Messiaen, Krenek,
Fortner) of a *multi-serial* or *total-serial* technique, applying
serial order not only to pitch, as in Schoenberg, but to
rhythm, attack, volume, etc.* Such schemes also exercised
the minds of a number of younger modernists – Boulez in his
*Structures I* for two pianos (1954), Berio in his *Nones* for orchestra (1954), the Belgian Henri Pousseur (b. 1929) with
his *Symphonies for Fifteen Instruments* (1955), and the Italian
Luigi Nono (b. 1924) in his *Variants* (1957) for solo violin
with strings and woodwind.

But, as we have seen, there was a fairly rapid retreat from
such mathematical determinism, and composers who had
hitherto practised multi-serialization now embraced a
totally free system of construction instead – a system which
is non-serialist but is more usually called (since this indicates
the manner of its evolution) post-serialist. Among the monuments of this style are Boulez's cantata for contralto and six
instrumentalists, *The Hammer without a Master* (the French
title, *Le Marteau sans maître,* is a virtual pun), and his *Fold upon*

* These variable constituents (pitch, loudness, etc.), when forming a
set order, are sometimes referred to as *parameters* of the music.

*Fold* (*Pli selon pli*) for voice and orchestra of 58 players. First given in 1955 and in 1960, they respectively use poetry by René Char and by Stéphane Mallarmé: the latter is in fact styled a 'portrait of Mallarmé'.

Such music is impressionistic in its presentation of sound, non-logical in its handling of words, prodigal or eclectic in its choice of resources. The *Marteau*'s six instrumentalists play alto flute, xylorimba (i.e. a xylophone lower in pitch than standard), vibraphone, 'percussion' (i.e. other speci-fied, non-pitched percussion instruments), guitar, and viola. This instrumentation may be contrasted with the much more traditional instrumentation of a comparable work of four decades before, Schoenberg's *Pierrot Lunaire*: piano, flute/ piccolo, clarinet/bass clarinet, violin/viola, cello.

Boulez is also among those composers of the vanguard who in certain works and within certain limits have renounced the total supremacy of the composer and allowed the per-former to make decisions about what notes, or what order of notes, is to be performed. Sometimes the performer's freedom of action is fairly narrowly circumscribed: Berio, in his *Tempi concertati* for flute and chamber ensemble (1959), en-closes certain notes in rectangles indicating that they are to be played in whatever order the performer decides. In the same work the percussionist is at one point told to strike all his instruments in quickest succession in any order he pleases.

Alternatively the area of indifference may be that of *large-scale* order. In the second movement of Boulez's *Third piano sonata* (1961) we find a printed sequence of four sections with the following instruction:

A beginning may be made with any one section, the three others then following. The section entitled *Commentary* has two possible placings: for any given performance, one or the other is to be chosen. In two sections, *Parenthesis* and *Commentary*, will be found certain compulsory and certain optional structures (passages) – the former printed in normal type, the latter in smaller type within parentheses, and each of these may be played or not played independently of the others.

What is more, the whole movement (or 'formant', as it is

called) under certain circumstances changes its place among the four other movements of the sonata. In *Fold upon Fold* there are also options to be exercised by the performers (but controlled by the conductor, who is required to direct ambidextrously). Stockhausen's *Cycle* (*Zyklus*) for percussion alone (1960) stipulates that the performer should begin anywhere, then proceed straight through the work (back through the beginning if necessary) and 'finish with the first stroke of the page you started with'.

Boulez himself attempted an explicit verbal justification of such processes: 'What we must do from now on, following the examples of Joyce and Mallarmé, is to stop regarding the [musical] work as a simple trajectory, traced between a point of departure and a point of arrival . . .' Instead there should be 'works destined to be renewed at each performance'. Something similar was suggested by Stockhausen apropos his *Carré* [French for square] for four orchestras, four choruses, four conductors, and four sides of a room (first performed in Hamburg, 1960):

> The work is composed in *moment-form*: each moment, in itself static or in process, is a personal, central fact that is to exist for its own sake. The musical events do not have a precise course from a determined beginning to an inevitable end; a moment is not only the consequent of the preceding and the cause of the succeeding; the concentration on 'now', on each 'now', on the contrary, is incised, so to speak, vertically through a horizontal notion of time ending at that negation of time that I call eternity: an Eternity that does not begin at the end of Time, but in each moment must be attained.

In several other ways *Carré* deliberately negates the traditional idea of a piece of music. Its creation involved an assistant composer, Cornelius Cardew (see also p. 343). The instructions given to the conductors and performers allowed a large measure of choice; and, as part of this instruction, a special form of notation was devised (as indeed has been the case with many works of the vanguard). It may be remarked that such music, having many different possibilities of realization, is at the opposite extreme from tape-synthesized electronic music, which is fixed in advance at the moment the composition is completed. But *both* types are specifically mid twentieth century, to be distinguished from the conventional earlier practice in which the interpreter guides the performance in pursuit of an idea which is conceived as belonging to the uniquely written score.

In these vanguard works the range of choice may be very large. The French composer, André Boucourechliev (b. 1925), in his *Archipelago IV* for piano puts his note forms and instructions on a large sheet from which the performer has 'an infinite choice' (the composer's words) of order and duration. In such cases the work can properly be described, from the composer's point of view at least, as being indeterminate. But only misleadingly can it be described as *aleatory* (dependent on chance). It replaces a decision of the composer by the decision of the performer, who will no doubt think carefully in advance of what he will do: what the listener hears therefore is not dependent on chance at all. Aleatory music proper implies the importation of random factors, and would more clearly be called random music: we deal with it later (p. 342).

But there is another variable which modern composers have increasingly brought under their own control, instead of regarding it as an outside factor, and that is *space*. Only occasionally in previous musical history have composers apparently calculated musical effects as *not* coming from a single, unified sound-source. The three simultaneous, different-rhythmed orchestras in Mozart's *Don Giovanni* and the four distanced groups of extra brass in Berlioz's *Requiem* are two notable exceptions. Our century has gone further. In *The Unanswered Question* (composed 1906, not published till 1941) Charles Ives called for a trumpet solo, a woodwind group and a string group, spatially separate, the strings having no fixed rhythmical coordination with the rest. The Canadian composer, Henry Brant (b. 1913), has concerned himself particularly with spatial effect: his *Voyage Four* (first performed in 1964) was conceived for an orchestra distributed in two back balconies and two (opposite) side balconies, on a stage, on the main floor and under the main floor. Stockhausen's four-walled *Carré* has already been referred to.

In 1965 the Swedish composer Lars Johan Werle (b. 1926) presented in Stockholm his opera *Dreaming of Thérèse*. The dramatic action takes place on a central platform; the audience surrounds it in a circle; and the orchestra in an outer circle surrounds the audience, the members of the orchestra being also required to change their positions during performance. The same year saw the production at Cologne of the opera *The Soldiers* by Bernd Alois Zimmermann (1918–70) which was designed for simultaneous performance on 12 small stages surrounding an audience on swivel chairs – conditions impossible to realize in performance in a conventional theatre. More common (and more practical) than attempts to redimension the opera house have been newly theatrical treatments of the concert platform and the concert experience. A famous example of spatial movement for an individual concert performer is in Berio's *Circles* for solo voice, harp, and percussion (1960), where the singer moves between three positions on the platform.

Spatial movement of that kind, i.e. *seen* movement, makes a theatre out of the concert hall. (The normal concert has strong elements of visual ritual in which the audience also performs, but it is not, in the ordinary sense of the word, theatrical.) The performance given in such works by Berio's chosen soprano interpreter, Cathy Berberian (b. 1925), is certainly in the nature of theatre. (Among the most distinguished of the interpreters of the new music, Berberian is also the composer of a highly inventive, unaccompanied vocal montage of comic-strip noises: *Stripsody*, 1968.) Berio's *Sequence V* for trombone, already mentioned (p. 325), is also explicity visual in its directions to the performer. ('He strikes the poses of a variety showman about to sing an old favourite . . .') One of the two trombonists for whom this piece of Berio's was designed, the American Stuart Dempster, has also performed *One Man* (1967) by Ben Johnston (b. 1926), in which he is required to play various percussion instruments by movement of his legs and feet.

In another attempt to make theatre out of a concert, the Argentinian composer Mauricio Kagel (b. 1931) published in 1967 his *Match* for two cellists and percussionist, who must all speak as well as play. Part of the instructions to the percussionist run:

> With trembling right hand, very slowly raise the castanets and follow them with your eyes (the left hand resting on the table) . . . When the castanets are raised to breast height, do not lift them further, but continually shake them, and suddenly stand up (avoid making a noise with the chair). Still standing up, lift the castanets further up to the left shoulder and follow with your eyes. (Do not turn the body.) . . .

With certain younger British composers the interest in spatial music appears more explicit as a wish to renew musical drama without the expense (and the social deadwood) of traditional opera and ballet. Some of these dramatic works exhibit a curious archaism of symbols, an openness to mumbo-jumbo, mysticism, medievalism and antique-collecting. Peter Maxwell Davies (b. 1934) incorporated foxtrots, musical-boxes, Victorian hymns and the tinkling of Roman Catholic ritual bells into a kind of one-man ballet (the dancer playing the piano too, and sharing the platform with a non-dancing cellist) called *Vesalii icones* (1969), a work which purports to refer not only to the anatomical images which illustrated Vesalius's anatomical treatise of 1543, but also to the Stations of the Cross in Christian myth. Another work by Davies (p. 87) refers back to a keyboard piece by the sixteenth-century composer John Bull.

Harrison Birtwistle (b. 1934), whose characteristic idiom is tougher in sound, employed a partly mimed, partly concert presentation of a dramatic idea in *The Visions of Francesco Petrarca* (1966). Then, at the 1968 Aldeburgh Festival, he launched a kind of ritual, non-human opera, *Punch and Judy*: never before, at any rate under cover of the British musical establishment, had the full stylistic vocabulary of the post-serialist revolution been exposed in a fully-staged, fully sung work. Alexander Goehr (b. 1932) in *Naboth's Vineyard* (1968) had the action mimed while the singers remained static – a leaf out of the Stravinsky of the 1920s, even to the employment of Latin, as in *Oedipus Rex*. But Goehr was also willing to come to terms with opera in its traditional form (*Arden Must Die*, Hamburg, 1967).

If we may risk the construction of a spectrum, then Davies and Birtwistle are radicals, and so too is the younger composer (and pianist) Roger Smalley (b. 1943); Goehr's position is more in the centre – like that of Richard Rodney Bennett (b. 1936), Nicholas Maw (b. 1935), and Gordon Crosse (b. 1937), all of whom have written not only operas of more or less traditional dramatic kind, but symphonies, concertos, string quartets or other works which bear a recognizable relationship to older forms and melodic types, whether Schoenberg's or Britten's. If Malcolm Williamson (Australian, b. 1931) seems operatically more skilled than any (especially in *The Violins of Saint-Jacques*, 1966), it is perhaps precisely because opera is a past form, and Williamson has fewer inhibitions about attaching himself to past styles – even past light-music styles, notably those of Richard Rodgers and of Latin-American dance.

By contrast, a Continental composer such as Pousseur, who had won a reputation in electronic music, total serialism (p. 332), and other advanced techniques, apparently felt that he could not come to opera straight. In *Your Faust* (Milan, 1969) he presented a work in which the theatrical audience is invited to intervene and decide the hero's course of action – a decision for which the composer has provided different musical consequences. But there has been no evidence that the basic opera-house situation could be breached by such gestures, as the traditional concert situation has been.

A German composer who won international success in opera, but who appears to have abandoned the form precisely because of its institutional legacy, is Hans Werner Henze (b. 1926). His operas include *Boulevard Solitude* (1952), *The Prince of Homburg* (1960) and *The Young Lord* (1965) in German, and *Elegy for Young Lovers* and *The Bassarids* in English (1961, 1966 – both with texts by W. H. Auden and Chester Kallman, who had been Stravinsky's librettists for

*The Rake's Progress*). His other works, including two piano concertos and six symphonies, show his evolution from Schoenbergian 12-note technique to a somewhat freer style – but always more inclined to curving, lyrical melody than to what we have called exclamatory music. In 1968 he revitalized the oratorio form (directing his audience to topical politics instead of fossilized religion) with *The Raft of the Frigate 'Medusa'*, dramatizing the struggle of the oppressed: an extraordinarily large, extraordinarily constituted orchestra (see p. 326) is used, with voices not only narrating and impersonating in the audience's vernacular but quoting from Dante's *Divine Comedy* in Italian. The result is a double-planed effect like that in Britten's *War Requiem* (see p. 320).

The chief nurseries of the new music in Western Europe have been the state radio corporations; in the United States, the universities. As we have seen, it was the Paris radio station which provided the facilities for the development of concrete music from 1948, and the Cologne radio which nurtured German electronic music. The first performances of Stockhausen's *Carré* and of Henze's *Medusa* (above, pp. 326 and 334) were typically sponsored by the North German Radio (Hamburg) – only such an organization being capable, in the currently prevailing economics of concert-giving, of rehearsing and presenting such a complex new work. In Britain the appointment of William Glock to head the music division of the B.B.C. in 1959 revolutionized not only the B.B.C.'s own programmes but the quantity and kind of new music in British musical life. The radio corporations have often also provided composers with employment as producers and the like. In the United States no such situation exists, since the tiny public-service sector of radio finds its musical fare almost entirely in the broadcasting of commercial gramophone records; but, as if in compensation, American universities have provided composers with positions as teachers (or as 'composer-in-residence') and have often also provided electronic workshops and facilities for live, public performance.

With the partial easing of the Communist artistic straitjacket from the late 1950s, it became clear that the new international language had spread to Eastern Europe as well. From Poland Krzystof Penderecki (b. 1933) offered an orchestral *Threnody for the Victims of Hiroshima* (1960), with various extreme instrumental effects (the violins having 'an *arpeggio* on four strings behind the bridge', etc.); he then brought out a *St Luke Passion* (1967), and other works which seemed to aim at a reconciliation of modern style with traditional choral technique – and perhaps at reclaiming a traditionalist public still responsive to a Catholic devotional text. Penderecki's works also include an opera, *The Devils of Loudun*, first given by the Hamburg State Opera in 1969. A similar contact with traditional choral usage may be seen in the *Requiem* (1963–5), by the expatriate Hungarian, György Ligeti (b. 1923): scored for soprano and mezzo-soprano solos, two mixed choruses and orchestra, the *Requiem* combines the traditional (Verdian) explosion at the *Dies irae* with the composer's own characteristic dense note-clusters (bunches of adjacent notes). Such density is also characteristic of Ligeti's *Atmospheres* (1961) for orchestra, in which 56 stringed instruments are, on occasion, each provided with individual parts.

From the mid 1960s a few younger Soviet Russian composers also began to exhibit works in Western vanguard idioms, sometimes in specially devised new notations. Among these are Edison Denisov (b. 1929), Alfred Shnitke (b. 1932) and Valentin Silvestrov (b. 1937).

Ligeti, with the Swede, Bengt Hambraeus (b. 1928), is one of the few such modernists to write for the organ: his *Volumina* (1961–2) again exploits clusters, but in a new and specifically organ-like way. Clusters are also typically used by the Australian, Peter Sculthorpe (b. 1929). Among other post-serial modernist composers have emerged a Korean, Isang Yun (b. 1917), and several Japanese, including Toru Takemitsu (b. 1930). These Far Eastern composers have not disdained an oriental heritage, musical and literary; and it is now possible to see also that the vogue for serialist, then post-serialist, music has by no means obliterated historic national dispositions and preferences in the West itself. Boulez's

Frenchness shows in an affinity with Debussy, partly through their common French literary heritage. Berio's predilection for the voice may be said to be typically Italian. Not only employing the natural or electronically distorted solo voice in many works, he also enlisted the Swingle Singers (previously celebrated for near-pop vocalizations of Bach) for his long, five-movement symphony (*Sinfonia*, 1969). Here he made a verbal and musical collage from many sources, in particular using the scherzo of Mahler's Second symphony almost in the way that Renaissance composers 'parodied' the works of others (see p. 73). Another Italian composer with a vocal bias is Luigi Nono, already mentioned (p. 332): his works include a vocal-orchestral setting of anti-fascist texts, *The Suspended Song* (*Il canto sospeso*), 1955–6, and an opera, *Intolerance* (1961).

Yannis Xenakis (b. 1922), of Greek parentage although born in Romania, favours Greek abstract terms (sometimes in his own compound forms) for his titles – among them *Nomos Alpha* ('nomos'=law) for solo cello, 1955–6; *Metastaseis* (i.e. after-standstill), an eight-minute piece (1953–4) for an orchestra of 61 solo players. The latter work, with its simultaneous combination of individually different *glissandi* (upward or downward continuous sliding of pitch) exhibits the thick sound of adjacent notes in clusters – an effect particularly associated with this composer (as also with Ligeti, mentioned above). This simultaneous multi-sliding effect creates (in the composer's own words) 'sound spaces in continuous evolution, comparable to ruled surfaces and volumes'. For working out the individual notes of a big sound space Xenakis has in certain cases employed a computer: he uses the mathematical term '*stochastic*' and the initial letters S T (e.g. in his S T/48, for 48 players, 1959–62) to indicate such working-out of individual notes as components of a large sound event. (The computer thus serves to speed up the detailed mapping-out of the composer's idea: it does not, as in the cases referred to on p. 330, exercise a determining say on what the listener hears.)

Xenakis has also (perhaps naturally, as an engineer and

architect by upbringing) been keenly interested in new spatial arrangements for music. His *Terretektorh* of 1966 (roughly, 'construction by action'), is for 88 players scattered among the audience; his *Strategy* (1962), is 'a game for two orchestras': two conductors oppose each other according to prescribed tactics of sound, each communicating his decisions where necessary to his players by holding up big letter-cards from A to U. One conductor is the winner.

Some of the foregoing manifestations may appear bizarre and some are intended to appear so. But none invoke random, unthought-of events. Even where the composer allows a large measure of decision to the performer, he is (as we saw on pp. 333–5) only shifting responsibility, not saying 'no one is responsible'. But this is implied in certain typical products of John Cage (b. 1912: see also p. 325), the American who has more than anyone else put forward the *irrational phenomenon*, and the *operations of chance*, as a substitute for what was previously thought to require determination by creative choice.

Thus in Cage's *Imaginary Landscape no. 4* (1951) for 12 radio sets, two 'players' manipulate each set – one tuning to the specified wavelength, one regulating the volume. The 'score' determines the gradation from loud to soft and the ratio of sound to silence, but which radio stations are broadcasting the stipulated wavelengths is determined by what city the 'performance' takes place in, and what is to be heard from those stations varies uniquely with each 'performance'. What is more, the composer in choosing his specifications of volume and silences did not do so rationally or by inspiration but by the operation of a Chinese game of chance corresponding to western dice-throwing. The Latin word '*alea*', dice, gives rise to the adjective '*aleatory*', which exactly describes this operation. (The form '*aleatoric*' is illiterate.) *Random music* would be an alternative term.

Cage has since gone further in abjuring what Hindemith in his famous textbook (1937–9) called the *craft* of musical composition, and in blurring the distinction between a musical and non-musical event. In 1954 he published *4′33″* which consists of a silence for that period (never, as he would point out, a complete silence in our human environment); the performer is solely instructed to convey the idea of three movements (time divisions) within the period stated, but without any note being sounded. Cage's celebrated interpreter, the American pianist David Tudor (b. 1926), performs this piece by *closing* the keyboard lid at the beginning of each section and opening it at the end. The orchestral part of Cage's *Concert for Piano and Orchestra* (1958) may be realized by any number of players, including none, on any number of instruments, playing any number of the total pages provided, including none. What Cage has set down is not the directions for realizing a certain sound-sequence of his own imagining, but the prescription for minimum and/or maximum limits for a certain kind of social event.

A New York group close to Cage, though considerably younger – Earle Brown (b. 1926), Morton Feldman (b. 1926) and Christian Wolff (b. 1934) – has similarly become known for works which are prescriptions of limits of action. Another American, La Monte Young (b. 1935), published, as one of his *Compositions 1960*, the following:

*to be held for
a long time*

The duration of this work in a New York performance (by string trio) in 1961 was 45 minutes.

An English follower of Stockhausen and Cage, Cornelius Cardew (b. 1936), published in 1962 his *Octet 61*, 'not necessarily for piano', to be played 'for any length of time': it consists of 61 instructions only partly in musical notation, but 'free use may be made of notes apart from those provided'. Cardew's *Schoolroom Compositions* (1968), though called by the composer an opera book, is a compendium of activities to be performed simultaneously in various media: some material provided (including that for the chorus) uses musical notation, but some does not. The prompting came perhaps from Cage's own, similarly diverse *Theatre Piece* (1960), plus Cage's own remark: 'Music is an over-simplification of the situation we actually are in . . . It is one part of theatre.'

The composer, instead of fulfilling a part in a prescribed social situation (a church, an opera house) may now be the architect of a situation that is new and unique. The American composer Pauline Oliveros (b. 1932) has an all-join-in piece involving concentric marching circles round an accordionist who plays the single note A. Violinists are required who do not need to know how to play the violin, plus four conductors, and any number of other people vocalizing the note A. The duration is not fixed. The piece is called A O K, and O K is indeed what A is.

No one who has participated with about a hundred others in this work could say that the resulting activity is humanly unproductive. Nor could anyone but a composer have designed it, even though no notated music is necessary for its realization. If we decide to deny it the name 'composition', it should be because it does not invite the aesthetic response, but only the social pleasure of participation: it is a group-therapy exercise, or a parody of one. Because of its frankly jokey nature, such a piece will not be misunderstood. There is much more danger that a false solemnity, and an attempt at an aesthetic response, will attend other action patterns of a less transparent nature. Rather than that, it might be appropriate if Cage's 4'33" (for pianist) provoked a consequent or simultaneous noisy 4'34" (for audience).

Such are some excursions on the most perilous frontier of all, that which hitherto seemed to divide irrevocably the musical from the non-musical event. It is a mistake to suppose that a musician inclined to such gestures must have thoroughly shaken off his connection with the historical mainstream. The commission to write a film score or a church anthem may quite reasonably engage such a composer in traditional problems. Cardew, whom we have already observed leaving the boundaries of music altogether, published in 1963 an exactly notated, totally musical and readily practical four-part vocal setting of William Blake, *Ah Thel*.

Among those who take their chief musical pleasure in the

Bach-to-Rakhmaninov period, the most extreme products of today's composers often arouse not only dislike but the feeling that they are being duped with non-music. Precisely similar is the reaction of a traditional art-lover when confronted with a canvas completely of black but for two dabs of white, or a length of commercial metal tubing displayed on a pedestal as some artist's 'found object'. The reaction is not only understandable but justified. It may indeed be non-music, or non-art in the traditional aesthetic sense. But *most* of the new music appears perhaps shocking only in the sense that *Tristan and Isolde* or *The Rite of Spring* once were – works which are now seen in context. The context in which Boulez and Birtwistle may seem normal is, of necessity, only now being worked out.

I have in these pages equated the term 'music' with one main tradition of music, on the whole co-terminous with that of western christendom. Such a field, too narrow for any consideration of the physical sciences today, is also too narrow here. Modern audiences have shown a readiness to listen not merely to music which borrows from Far Eastern culture – as Britten borrowed heterophony or staggered melody in *Curlew River* (p. 319) – but also to listen to oriental music itself, mainly from the Indian subcontinent, but also Japanese, Persian, and others. Ravi Shankar (b. 1920) became the first internationally celebrated player and composer of music for the *sitar* (the classic Indian plucked-string melody instrument: his performances attracted both classical and pop audiences, and incidentally made familiar the sound and technique of the finger-played small drums (*tabla*), used as an accompaniment.

Pop itself, rather than being a foothill of classical music – as the light music of previous generations had been – emerged in the 1950s as a distinct musical phenomenon of its own, able to absorb folk, classical, jazz, exotic and other elements on the basis of the persistent Afro-American beat. Jazz in its original (and now historical) sense had been a performer's music and an essentially live, spontaneous music. The gramophone record served only as a means of diffusion (as with classical music). The great thing was to have been right there in New Orleans or Chicago when 'King' Oliver (1885–1938) played the trumpet or 'Jelly Roll' Morton (1885–1941) the piano: the record is a lucky or unlucky attempt to capture the sort of experience that happened. But pop inhabits the electronic age. While the possessor of a record by the great blues-singer Bessie Smith (?1898–1937) may lament that he never heard Bessie Smith, the possessor of a Beatles record *has* heard the Beatles. Their *Sergeant Pepper's Lonely Hearts Club Band* (1967) took six months and several hundred hours in the studio to produce: their personal appearances at concerts were only secondary occasions at which there was no possibility of reproducing the balanced, precise, electronically layered, authentic sound of the record.

Certain qualifications must be admitted here. The personal, show-business magnetism of certain pop artists is not to be denied – especially that of the soloists deriving from older blues traditions, such as Elvis Presley (b. 1937) or Jimi Hendrix (1948–70). But especially with groups the essential contact is via the disc. What climbs the charts is not a performance: it is a disc – a multiple, as might be said in the modern critical language of visual art. Eric Salzman's claims on behalf of *The Nude Paper Sermon* (p. 332) do no more than follow what is accepted without question in the pop world. The sight on television of the pop-group miming to its own record, because the recorded sound simply cannot be reproduced in the real time of a performance before a studio audience, is significantly familiar.

Pop is the musical facet of a whole cultural phenomenon involving dress, dance, social protest, the preference for marijuana over alcohol, and a particular age group. The basis of this music is the voice (from falsetto to hoarse shout, from deliberate meaninglessness to near-satire), the percussion outfit, and guitars (including bass guitar, often preferred to the more blurred sound of the plucked double-bass). In concert, the pop sound, though live, is still electronically conditioned, since high-powered amplification is used to distort the sound and stun the ear.

Despite (or perhaps because of) the enormous sales of pop records, despite the largest audiences (over 150,000) ever assembled for any form of live entertainment, the resistance shown to pop by the traditionally trained serious musician or music critic has been very strong. Just as the supposed non-music of Cage won its first acceptance not among musicians but among dancers and their public, so pop has found its expositors among poets, novelists and others – willing to discriminate, to sift the genuinely creative from the admittedly overwhelming preponderance of mike-fodder. Such an expositor may write under the heading 'Pop' in a culture-conscious Sunday paper, while the hallowed heading of 'Music' is reserved for the classically oriented music critic. When certain middle-aged authorities from the classical side did discover pop in the mid 1960s, it took the characteristic form of a canonization of the Beatles, a clean-looking quartet with some songs not too far from music-hall models (*Lovely Rita, When I'm Sixty-four*). The exploders of harsher sounds, the purveyors of the more extravagant, irrational-seeming patterns were less easily given house-room.

Yet it is between this far-out pop and the vanguard of the straight world that a creative musical intercouse is likely to take effect. Indeed it seems already to have begun. Roger Smalley's *Beat Music* (1971) for orchestra and electric instruments acknowledged a debt to 'certain pieces of rock music, notably *Viola Lee Blues* (Grateful Dead) and *Sister Ray* (Velvet Underground)'. Cornelius Cardew has performed his work in pop circles and has apparenJly influenced the Pink Floyd, while *The Whale*, a 'dramatic cantata' by John Tavener (b. 1944), though first performed in 1968 at a London concert along with a work by Richard Strauss, appeared on record under the Beatles' own label, Apple. There are comparable interactions in the United States. The adherents of fairly experimental pop are more likely than Beethoven-addicts to respond to electronics, random music, freakish piano, and the other resources of the post-serialist vanguard – and much less likely to be outraged at the idea of a performance actively involving the audience, or a performance that started before the audience arrived.

Pop is indeed one of those factors which seem to make the possibilities of musical experience richer than ever before. Composers command ever-widening resources, music-lovers have instant history in recorded form and a great diversity of types of encounter. Some 300 years ago the functional music of ritual, work, dance and worship yielded in importance to the specific musical occasion; now the musical occasion is ubiquitous, wherever there is a record-player or radio, a juke-box or a commercial background music installation. It is a situation of both peril and promise. It would seem equally short-sighted to assume that Beethoven will have the same place in this situation as before and that pop is mud, or that Beethoven will have no place and pop is salvation.

All styles are the styles of now. In 1968 Stanley Kubrick, director of the film *2001 : A Space Odyssey*, brought in Johann Strauss's *Blue Danube* waltz to accompany the whirling of a spaceship through the cosmos, and employed the modern cluster patterns of Ligeti's *Atmospheres* for the strangeness of personal inter-world encounters – the point being that the recognized Strauss as well as the unrecognized Ligeti allows a quite specific and telling use of music. Two years later, though it might have been 35 years before, the film *Waterloo* could still use a score (by Nino Rota, b. 1911) linked to the romantic musical aesthetic of Schumann or Liszt – a score in which the Marseillaise and other national songs were transformed (but still in identifiable form) to reinforce the spectacle of military and national triumphs and reverses. In 1971 the music to Fellini's film *Clowns* (again by Nino Rota) included Wagner's *Ride of the Valkyries* – in a distorted, circus-band scoring – as a comic accompaniment to a staged female wrestling-match.

It is all music. It is all ours. It is all history seen and heard through the only working eye and ear, the eye and ear of the present.

# Index

All names of composers and other historical persons mentioned are indexed. Individual works are not indexed except those of a collective or anonymous nature. Subjects are indexed to show the first or most important references: the word *passim* is used to indicate a multiplicity of subsequent references throughout the book.